The Merchant of Prato

The Merchant of Prato

Francesco di Marco Datini · 1335–1410

---

by IRIS ORIGO

Foreword by Barbara Tuchman

NONPAREIL BOOKS
David R. Godine
Publisher · Boston

This is a *Nonpareil Book* published in 1986 by
DAVID R. GODINE, *Publisher*
Post Office Box 450
Jaffrey, New Hampshire 03452
www.godine.com

Library of Congress Cataloging-in-Publication Data
Origo, Iris, 1902–
The merchant of Prato, Francesco di Marco Datini, 1335–1410.
(Nonpareil books ; #41)
Reprint. Originally published: New York, Knopf, 1957.
Inludes index.
1. Datini, Francesco, 1335–1410. 2. Merchants—Italy—Biography.
I. Title. II. series: Nonpareil Books ; #41.
HF3584.6.D37075 1986 380.1'092'4 [B]86-4715
ISBN 0–87923–596–9

SECOND PRINTING 2002
Printed in Canada

FOREWORD

By

Barbara Tuchman

HY IS THIS BOOK ONE OF THE GREAT WORKS OF historical writing of the twentieth century? As a restoration of living, breathing, everyday life to a long-gone figure from a long-gone age, it is the historian's miracle no less than that accomplished for Lazarus, though not this time by miraculous powers but by the unparalleled skill and artistry of the author in weaving the multiple threads of an original contemporary archive into a compelling narrative. Through her intimate understanding and patient examination of and beautiful selection from 150,000 letters, 500 account books and ledgers and other documents in the medieval papers of Francesco di Marco Datini, a hard-driving merchant or businessman of the fourteenth century, Iris Origo has fulfilled the motto attributed to Michelet once engraved over the doorway of the National Archives of France, *Reddimus Vitam Mortuis*, "We give back life to the dead." No one else I can think of has done it better—or as well, with the possible exception of my other favorite, the recreation by Cecil Woodham Smith in her book *The Reason Why* of the unforgettable, incredible Lord Cardigan, who led the Charge of the Light Brigade.

The great biographies or studies of a notable character transmitted

V

to posterity—Plutarch's or Boswell's or the Gospels of the New Testament or Saint Simon's Louis Quatorze—have been written by familiars who knew their subjects when alive, or who lived in approximately the same period and surroundings. Even Lord Cardigan was less than one hundred years distant from the world of Mrs. Woodham Smith, whereas Marchesa Origo, although she shares the same language and has long lived in Tuscany, the same region as her subject, had to bridge a gap of 650 years. Her success in resurrecting not only a personality whom we can recognize as we might a brother-in-law or a local town lawyer, but also his times, his town, his marriage, his household, his country home, his friends and associates—and, rather painfully, his business dealings—makes a work of extraordinary interest with that quality to grip and take hold of a reader that makes a book everlasting.

How Francesco Datini, coming from small beginnings as the son of a poor taverner, drove his way through the risks and opportunities and profits of medieval trade and international banking to become a rich and prominent figure in the region of Florence, and in the bustling papal capital of Avignon, makes the story the Marchesa has to tell an equivalent of the modern success story of a self-made millionaire. Accompanying the success is the cost in vexation and anxieties that wrecked Francesco's peace of mind and took the heart out of his marriage. It is a story told from the inside of Italian business and labor relations, the soil-bed of modern capitalism, through the eyewitness reports and values of the people engaged, so that we come away feeling we know them as individuals, and share their endless struggle between the spoils of this world and the judgment of the next. Through them we discover how that struggle wrought the change in Datini's lifetime that transformed the medieval world into the early modern.

Without fictionalizing or intrusive comment, Marchesa Origo lets the development happen under the reader's eyes, drawing always on the letters from Datini's anxious friends who see him losing his soul for the sake of material gain; on his incessant instructions to business employees, associates, servants, and, not least, to his wife;

and finally on his financial accounts, which reveal so much, as they do for every era of history, of the actuality of time and place. She shapes all this into a history of the period, with the reader feeling not that he is being instructed but rather as if he were seeing a vivid film unfold before his eyes.

He sees sailing ships manned by crossbowmen for defense against corsairs, and the oared galleys that were the workhorses of sea traffic. He sees pack-trains of mules plodding over the Appenines, voracious bands of *condottiere* plundering farms and villages, money-changers doing business at their tables in the marketplace, magistrates and doctors wearing the hooded scarlet cloaks reserved for them making their dignified rounds, cripples and beggars sharing the streets with the retinues of princes, and does not miss the omnipresent clergy, from rusty black priests to fat prelates and red-hatted cardinals. He sees peasant women in the *contado* who grease and wash the imported raw wool, spin it at their distaffs, dye it blue and crimson and black, bending over the tasks that extend the process for finished product over six months and longer. He sees wide-spread buyers and sellers in Alexandria, Barcelona, Lisbon, and Arles exchange the painted panels, linens, and needlework made by Italian artisans.

History, a British critic, Arthur Marwick, has well said, "is finished product, not raw material." It is the baked cake, not the ingredients. What Iris Origo has done with superb skill is to present a finished product fashioned entirely from authentic raw material of real life, taken from the remarkable archive that was Datini's gift to posterity.

During his lifetime, with an unusual concern for records, Datini collected all his letters and business documents, ordering the managers of all his branches to do likewise. Preserved in cupboards of his house in Prato, they remained for four hundred years undisturbed by intruders, except for a few nibbling mice: a unique private collection of medieval business, with account books, insurance policies, bills of exchange, deeds of partnership, and—what is very rare in such records—a body of domestic correspondence between husband and wife, owed to the circumstance that Francesco and Margherita lived apart, the wife keeping house in Prato while her compulsive husband looked after his business in Florence or Pisa. As a result, we have the personal report of a troubled medieval marriage, supplemented by the running comments in the private letters of friends and relatives that illumine the character of the immoderate Francesco.

Marchesa Origo uses the archive as it comes, writing her book in the innocent 1950s, a generation before the birth of that mongrel form called "faction" or "the new journalism." She has spared us the peculiar deviant of depicting her protagonist (as has been the fate of Aaron Burr and Stanford White, among others) as behaving in terms that the author, out of his own experience of quite another time and place, happens to think appropriate. Human nature and conduct, it is true, change little in reaction to historical events and pressures, yet the circumstances and motivations that determined the actions of, for example, Burr and White (not to mention those of Emma Goldman, who, though a most unlikely associate of the Stanford White circle, is pulled into E. L. Doctorow's *Ragtime*, for no reason that I can suppose other than that she is contemporaneous) are not the motivations that govern the lives of Mr. Vidal or Mr. Doctorow generations later. I do not deny fellow writers the faculty of sympathetic imagination—as long as it avoids anachronism—but I do not see the point of their imposing the psychology and habits of their own times upon real persons who lived real lives in an age that the novelists who selected them as subjects never knew. It is an affront, it seems to me, to the grave. Should not the dead too enjoy the right of privacy? As a disciple of the authentic, I am all the more an admirer of Origo, knowing that her readers may be happily confident that everything we learn about the Merchant of Prato and his affairs was actual and took place in real life.

Absorbing the flavor of this actuality from the correspondence in the Datini archive, we feel ourselves almost participants in the medieval business society of Tuscany and its region. Tuscan merchants traded across the medieval world from the Levant in the East to London in the West. They imported raw wool from England and North Africa, armor and steel blades from Spain, saffron from Majorca, spices from the East, dyes from the Black Sea, finished cloth from Flanders. They monopolized the luxury trade, primarily in cloth—especially the cloth of gold and sumptuous fabrics and furs demanded by the papal court—as well as in wheat, wood, cheese, vegetables, horses, hides and leather harnesses, silk curtains and sewing thread, and in the precious chalices and reliquaries and goblets of the goldsmiths' art. Their trade merged easily into international banking and moneychanging. Their letters, written in Latin, French, English, and Flemish as well as in Italian, even some in Arabic and Hebrew, exhibit their reach.

Determined to grasp the last florin from this rich coil of business, Francesco opened retail shops in Avignon, Pisa, and Florence and entered the export trade, selling fine enamels and other fashionable items overland to France. Soon he established branches of his business and even companies with different sets of partners in Pisa, Genoa, Lucca, and further abroad in Catalonia, Arles, London, and Bruges. Above all he imported wool from England and Flanders, Spain and North Africa for his workshops in Prato, a center of the wool industry, where the finished cloth was fabricated for foreign markets. Given pirates and storms, shipwrecks and lost cargoes at sea, brigands on land and outbreaks of plague, the deficiencies of his agents and partners not immediately under his control, and the fact that he trusted nobody—not partners or agents or ship captains or managers or workmen—all his transactions plunged Francesco into a miasma of worries and apprehension. His bulging prosperity dragged behind it matching worries, so that when he was past sixty he wrote to his wife the miserable admission: "Destiny has ordained that from the day of my birth I should never know a whole happy day."

The trouble was that, apart from his character, Francesco was caught in a crux between a faith-centered world that was waning and a money-cum-power–centered world that was developing with greater disposable force than it had ever had before.

ix

FOREWORD

The crunch can be heard almost audibly in the letters of the extraordinary Datini archive that Marchesa Origo has plumbed: "Give thanks to God, for you already have enough. Crave not for all, crave not for all," wrote Francesco's hometown friend Niccolozzo di Naldo, trying to persuade him to leave his business concerns long enough to come home to see his old and sickly foster-mother, who "thinks she will never see you more." But Francesco, for all his promises and good intentions, could not tear himself loose from his ledgers and business correspondence, which he insisted on writing all himself, sometimes, as he once recorded, spending two days working at it without rest. "I am not feeling very well today," he wrote at the age of over sixty, "on account of all the writing I have done in these two days, without sleeping either by night or by day, and in these two days eating but one loaf." When his business letters were done, ever the compulsive correspondent, he would write long letters to his wife and friends.

Even his closest friend, the notary Ser Lapo Mazzei, the most appealing character in this book, could not move him. When Ser Lapo used all his influence in a suit to relieve Francesco of certain enforced loans imposed by Florence and won his case, he urged his friend not always to complain of his own injuries but to "Incline your thoughts rather towards the men whose bed has been taken from under them who suffer from cold or have to give up buying wine and, in the name of God's charity, weep for them rather than for yourself." "In Christ's name," warned another friend, Giovanni Dominici, "beware of rising too high: that snare has caught some very big birds." Even his business partners joined in the chorus. "Let me remember and beseech you," wrote a friend, "clutch not at every bird that flies. . . . Be content with what God has given you, and strive to keep it." And, in another letter: "In good faith, Francesco, a man must think of earning money, but also of taking pleasure with his friends. But you think each man is like unto you." And Ser Lapo begged him increasingly not to take "these enterprises of yours with so great an avidity, desire, solicitude and anguish. It is not good. A wise man should learn moderation for, as in a house where the maid rules the mistress, so the house of the soul where will rules reason is displeasing to God."

Francesco listened and grew uneasy when he found that in one Lent he had heard "only six sermons," "a fine thing for one of my standing!" He promised that "at no price will I go on leading the life I have led . . . at least I will wind up what I am doing and lead a better life." But when a new ship came in or a new loan was to be written, the resolution was forgotten, and the grasping merchant was at the helm again.

The domestic tale that emerges from the correspondence is invaluable, revealing conditions of marriage, household habits, furnishings and utensils, meals, clothing, cooking methods and recipes, medications and treatment of illness. In the matter of doctors we hear Petrarch, a notable contemporary, expressing a certain disesteem. When ill of a fever he was visited by physicians who

> ordained that at midnight I would be dead; and the night had already begun. . . . They said that the only remedy by which I might prolong my life would be to draw some little cords tightly around me, to keep me from sleep, and thus I might perchance live to see the dawn. . . . Their orders were not carried out, for I have always besought my friends and bidden my servants to do naught of what physicians have commanded, but if indeed something must be done, to do just the opposite. Wherefore I spent the whole night in a deep sweet sleep. . . . I, who was like to die at midnight, was discovered by the physicians, when they came back on the morrow, writing.

Here is Origo's deft enrichment, born of wide and intimate familiarity with the sources—in this case Petrarch's letters—that enables her to extract precisely the appropriate comment or anecdote to illustrate the matter at hand.

The Marchesa's interest is especially caught up in the puzzling problem of Datini's marriage. From hints in the letters and references in his private notebook, she discovers him to be a philanderer, and in one of her few resorts to theorizing supposes a case for him which I have the temerity to doubt. The abiding sorrow of the Datini marriage was childlessness, which was naturally ascribed to a failing of the wife since Francesco believed he had previously fathered a child on a servant girl, although we do not know how he could be sure it was his. In any event, what he wanted from marriage was heirs to whom he could leave his riches, "in love and delight." All sorts of advice and remedies were offered to the infertile couple whose constantly renewed disappointment explains the strain and exasperation revealed in the letters. After opening a branch in Pisa, Francesco spent most of the year there or in Florence looking after his business interests, and when Margherita came to join him, it was he who went away back to Pisa or Prato. Margherita could not resign herself to these absences, and Francesco himself deplored them yet continued the divided residence. "Since Margherita could not give him a child," writes the author, "he turned to other women who could." This is where my doubts begin to prick. If what Francesco wanted was to raise a respectable *famiglia* with heirs for his fortune, the fathering of a few bastards on a household slave or servant girl or woman seduced from the countryside would not have satisfied the condition. I think Francesco was merely that character not unknown to Italy, or the United States for that matter: a chaser. I hope Marchesa Origo, who knows Francesco's personality as well as the customs of his locality far better than this writer, will not feel offended by my small venture in contradiction. It is offered unofficially, so to speak, not in a capacity as historian of terrain that is entirely hers.

An aspect of the historian's business of which Marchesa Origo is a master is the portrayal through her choice of visual detail of the manner of life of a given place and period. Women writers on the whole do this better than men because they are accustomed to coping with the small matters of getting through a day, while men like to think of their concerns as large, philosophical, and generalized, like that now dated couple who divided responsibilities on a plan giving small decisions to the wife—such as the choice of house to buy, allocation of expenses in the budget, where to spend the summer vacation, what school the children should attend—while the husband decided the larger questions such as shall we admit Red China to the U.N. History used to be conceived and written on the husband scale, but in recent decades has turned to the social history of more intimate things. If history's business is to understand past behavior, it is now less concerned with "Red China" than with what people eat and drink and how they furnish their homes and spend their Sundays.

A gleaming example of the new history, chosen from the protagonist's words rather than the author's, is Francesco's instructions to his wife on the care of their home and provisioning:

> . . . Tomorrow morn send back the branches of dried raisins and the bread, by Nanni of S. Chiara. And send the barrel of vinegar. . . . Remember to wash the mule's feet with hot water, down to her hoofs, and have her well fed and cared for. And have my hose made and then soled by Meo . . . And give some of the millet that is left with you to the nag, and see that it is well mashed . . . And speed the sale of the two barrels of wine in Belli's house; and empty all the other vats in the cellar, the ones with white wine, that have already been opened. . . . [Send 50 oranges ("in such a manner that they are not spoiled"), 25 loaves, 2 barrels of oil ("for the monks of 'gli Agnoli'"), and a bushel of grain. . . .] And remember to do all you have to do, and look well to the barrels, and feed the beasts well; and every evening shut the door well and look to the light, and see to it that I shall not have to scold. . . .

The home scene too is enriched by evidence from outside, taken from a sermon by the greatest popular preacher of the time, San Bernardino, who tells what is expected of a good housewife. She looks to the granary to keep it free of insects, to the oil jars to determine what must be thrown away if rancid, "she sells the bran, and with the profits she gets the linen out of pawn. She looks to the wine barrels, if any are broken or leaking. She watches over the whole house," and the kitchen garden, the stables, the mill are all in her province.

It is no accident that these remarkable passages, for me the most vivid in the book, deal with the life of women and tell us more about their sphere, the domestic scene, with an item like getting the linen out of pawn than a whole volume by Braudel or his lesser followers.

Plague, the black cloud that hung over the era, penetrated the lives of the Datinis and their neighbors, driving Francesco and Margherita in flight to Bologna and blighting the family of their friend Ser Lapo.

> "I have seen two of my children," Lapo wrote, "die in my arms in a few hours. God knows how great my hopes were for the eldest, who was already my companion, and a father, with me, to the others. And how well he had got on in Ardingo's firm! . . . and God knows that, for many yeas, he never failed to say his daily prayers, at morn and even on his knees in his room, so that often I pitied him, in the cold or heat. And God knows, and saw, his demeanour when he died: what counsels he gave, and how he said he was called to judgement, and was ready to obey. . . . And in the same hour Antonia was sick to death, and in the same bed with her the second boy, who died beside her. Imagine how my heart broke, as I heard the little ones weeping, and their mother not strong, and hearkened to the words of the eldest. Think of it; three dead! . . ."

In his grieving letter we tremble with the pity of that awful hour of the Middle Ages.

In 1410, Francesco's approach to death marked the change, hastened by the Black Death, toward the modern mood of reliance on man's will in place of total dependence on God's. Francesco could not believe the end was near. Unlike most men, the author writes, who, "before their last hour has come, have already shaken off . . . the dust of their worldly cares," Francesco "could not take in that his masterful will was now powerless: he resigned himself to death as little as he had to life." Yet under the powerful urging of his friends to make his peace with God, he bequeathed his property to a foundation for the "perpetual use" of the poor of Prato, to be administered, significantly, not by the Church but by a Council appointed by the Commune together with his own executors, including his wife, to whom he left a small annual income so long as she remained "a widow and chaste" and a "suitable" house with "two furnished beds" for herself and her maid, as well as other household goods and the use of a plot of land. In 1955, when the Marchesa was writing her book, the foundation for the poor, called the *Casa Pia del Ceppo dei poveri di Francesco di Marco* was still in operation, distributing income at the rate of 700,000 lire a year.

Francesco had found at last the heirs for the fortune he had so strenuously gained at the risk of his soul, and by the gift of alms he had saved his soul as well. Half medieval, half modern, he expressed his modernism in concern for the keeping of records and care for their preservation. Using the unique legacy of this archive with incomparable knowledge and sympathy, Marchesa Origo has illumined a historic period and raised, for the obsessive unquiet figure who was Francesco di Marco Datini, a permanent memorial.

—Barbara W. Tuchman

INTRODUCTION

"L'historien ressemble à l'ogre de la fable. Là où il flaire la chair humaine, il sait que là est son gibier."

—BLOCH, *Métier d'historien*

N THE SQUARE OF THE BUSY LITTLE CITY OF PRATO, beneath the faded brick walls of the Palazzo Comunale in which he sat as a councillor, stands the statue of a merchant. Clothed in the round biretta and sweeping robes of the fourteenth century, he holds in his hand a sheaf of bills of exchange. This is the man to whom Prato owes the foundation of her riches: Francesco di Marco Datini.

The story of the rise of his trading-houses in Avignon, Prato and Florence, in Pisa and Genoa, in Spain and Majorca, is as remarkable as the success-story of a modern millionaire, and quite as fully recorded. His fellow citizens to this day pride themselves on it and dwell, above all, on the charity which bequeathed to the poor of Prato not only his whole fortune of 70,-000 gold florins, but the very house in which he lived, and in it, his greatest gift to posterity, his papers. During his lifetime he himself collected every letter and business document he received, telling the managers of all his branches to do the same, and in his will he left instructions for all these papers to be collected and preserved in his own house in Prato.

These instructions were carried out somewhat carelessly, for

xvii

although there is a record in 1560 that Francesco di Marco's ledgers and papers had been carefully put away in cupboards in his own house, they were found three hundred years later in sacks in a dusty recess under the stairs. But in the long run this neglect may not prove to have been entirely unfortunate. *"Bene qui latuit, bene vixit."* A few of these pages were nibbled by mice or worms; but at least thieves and fools remained unaware of their existence—and when in 1870 some learned citizens of Prato brought them to light, an astonishing number still remained: some 150,000 letters, over 500 account-books and ledgers, 300 deeds of partnership (some of the other small companies connected with his own), 400 insurance policies, and several thousand bills of lading, letters of advice, bills of exchange, and cheques. Thus has been preserved, in the very house of the man whose life-work it represented, an invaluable and indeed, in its fullness and homogeneity, a unique record of medieval trade.

The picture of commercial activity which these letters present is very remarkable. When Datini returned to Italy from Avignon in 1382, his branch in that city (entrusted to two Tuscan partners) continued to be as active as before; and he at once opened a central house in Prato, as well as branches in Florence, Pisa, and Genoa, in Barcelona and Valencia, and finally in Majorca and Ibiza, all managed by his own partners or *fattori* on the spot but controlled by his own untiring pen. Between these *fondachi* sailed the ships which carried his wares: lead and alum and pilgrims' robes from Roumania, slaves and spices from the Black Sea, English wool from London and Southampton and African or Spanish wool from Majorca and Spain, salt from Ibiza, silk from Venice, leather from Córdoba and Tunis, wheat from Sardinia and Sicily, oranges and dates and bark and wine from Catalonia. . . . Small wonder that Francesco's fellow citizens gaped as the great bales came pouring in, and whispered that he was "the greatest merchant who ever came out of Prato!"

Some of the business documents in these archives have already formed the subject of special monographs; others (especially those concerning deeds of partnership, bills of exchange, bills of lading, insurance policies, and other contracts) have been fully studied and described in Professor Bensa's full-length study of Datini and his trade. And—owing to the research and enterprise of Professor Federigo Melis—an exhibition opened in May 1955, in the Palazzo Pretorio of Prato, the *Mostra dell' Archivio Datini*, enabled the general public to see for the first time not only a selection of these papers, but much additional material: portraits of some of Datini's contemporaries and pictures of the setting in which they lived, maps showing his main trading-routes by land and sea, pictures of the places from which his merchandise came, and—in a room given up to the cloth industry of Prato—charts and account-books and letters showing the whole complicated organization of a medieval cloth manufacturer, from the first purchase of the imported wool in Majorca, Catalonia, or the Cotswolds, through all the stages of spinning, weaving, dyeing, and finishing, until the cloth was sent abroad again for sale.

All these studies, however, have dealt only with Datini's trade. Except for the delightful letters written to him by his friend and notary Ser Lapo Mazzei, which were published by Cesare Guasti in 1880, his private correspondence has remained almost untouched—in particular, the letters he exchanged with his wife, his partners, and his *fattori*. It is from these letters that most of the information in this book is derived—although indeed even now these sources are far from being exhausted, or even fully tapped. This book is merely an attempt to draw, from this vast and miscellaneous material, a picture (even if fragmentary and incomplete) of the daily life of the time, and a portrait of the merchant himself, of his wife, his friends, and his underlings.

The flavour of these letters is completely consistent: in the vision of life they present, only two things have any importance —religion and trade. On the first page of Datini's great ledgers stood the words: "In the name of God and of profit," and these were the only goals to which these merchants aspired: profit in this world or in the next, as if the whole of life were one vast counting-house—and at its end, the final Day of Accounting. Many of the chief events of the time have found their way into these papers—but the peep-hole through which they are observed is always the merchant's, on the look-out for a good deal. A new Pope's election—a truce with the Duke of Milan, an approaching famine, a treaty between Christians and Turks, a royal wedding—are all merely grist to his unresting mill.

It is, however, with the private papers in this collection that this study is chiefly concerned: Datini's personal account-books and note-books, and the forty folders containing his voluminous correspondence. Here, if any were still needed, is a refutation of the belief that the merchant of the *trecento* was not ready with his pen. "I am not feeling very well today," wrote Francesco at the age of over sixty, "on account of all the writing I have done in these two days, without sleeping either by night or by day, and in these two days eating but one loaf." When his business letters to his *fondachi* were finished, he would take up his pen again and write his long personal letters: to Ser Lapo Mazzei about the wine he was bottling, and the partridges they would eat together next week, and Fra Giovanni Dominici's sermon in Santa Liberata; to his partner in Florence about the picture he needed for his bedroom, and a new scarlet biretta, "dyed in England"; to his agent in Genoa about buying a strong little slave-girl; to the one in Venice about sending him a piece of brocade for his wife's gown, and a couple of peacocks (but how were they fed? and how many hens were needed for each cock?)—and, above all, at least twice a week, to his rebellious and singularly outspoken young wife.

The most remarkable thing about this domestic correspondence (for over a hundred of Margherita's letters are here, too) is not that it should have been preserved, but that it should have been written at all. Public and official documents of this period, as well as records of business transactions, are abundant; but private letters, containing the small change of everyday life, the details of domestic intercourse, are rare. In particular, we possess remarkably few letters between husbands and wives, for they were seldom parted. Sometimes, indeed, a husband was abroad for long years at the Crusades, or trading in foreign ports, but in such cases letters home were necessarily few, and often very slow to reach their destination. But in this correspondence we have a wife who lived in Prato, looking after her husband's house, and a husband who lived (during the years of this exchange) no further off than Florence or Pisa; and their letters, together with the washing, which was done in Prato, and the fowls, eggs, and vegetables, which were sent from the farm to Florence or Pisa, went up and down on mule-back once or even twice a week. Thus this correspondence possesses an immediacy and contains a fulness of detail which we associate rather with letters of the eighteenth and nineteenth centuries. Francesco sends his wife minute instructions as to every detail of the household management; and Margherita, in reply, accounts for all she has done, or offers much sound advice. Moreover, a great many things which, if the couple had lived together, would no doubt merely have been *said* in moments of exasperation were thus put down on paper.

These papers thus provide a singularly genuine picture of married life in the fourteenth century. They hold a double interest: as a record of facts and as a study of character. The information they provide about the everyday life of a Tuscan merchant and his family is so detailed that we almost feel as if we had been to stay in the solid square brick house which Francesco built to show off his riches on his return from Avignon, and which he guarded so jealously that in his absence he would not even allow the front door to be opened until his wife was up and about. We learn what clothes Francesco and Margherita wore and how much they paid for them, what they ate and drank, what servants and slaves they kept and how unsatisfactory they were, what Francesco spent respectively on his illegitimate daughter's dowry, on buying a horse, on marrying off a pregnant maid-servant, and on foods, gifts, and alms; how he went on a pilgrimage to Signa; how he dosed himself in sickness; how he fled with his whole family to Bologna, to escape the plague. But, above all, we learn a great deal about Francesco and Monna Margherita themselves. What emerges from these unliterary, unpolished, unromantic, self-repetitive letters is the portrait of a man and a woman, so clearly outlined that we could hardly fail to recognize them if we met them in the streets of Prato today.

It is interesting to compare the picture of married life that emerges from these letters with the one shown in the "Advice to his young wife" of a French husband of almost precisely the same period and of similar standing, the *Ménagier de Paris*. The *Ménagier* was more gentle in tone than Francesco; but we must remember that his letters were intended for publication, and Francesco's were not. Moreover, Monna Margherita's replies—although she was nearly twenty-five years younger than her husband, who was over forty when he married her—are not always patient or submissive. She could disagree with Francesco's decisions and criticize his behaviour with a shrewdness and plainness of speech which he took with surprising meekness. "What you say," he wrote to her on one occasion, "is as true as the Lord's Prayer."

Francesco's own character is very sharply etched. It is impossible to imagine a more completely Tuscan figure. Intensely individualistic, he owed his success entirely to his own personal enterprise, to an audacity always tempered at just the right moment by shrewdness and mistrust of his neighbour. A hard business-man, he gathered his golden florins wherever he could find them: he traded in armour, wool, metals, and wheat; he made cloth and bought slaves; he opened (though this laid him open to the accusation of being a usurer) a bank. But he also never failed to conform to the conventions of pious practice: he neglected no fast-days, assigned a due proportion of his profits to alms and charity, built chapels and adorned churches. Self-indulgent during his prosperous years in Avignon—"keeping women and living on partridges," and begetting several little bastards—he was also capable, in the pursuit of his business, of a life as industrious and exacting as a monk's.

His life was not a serene one. "Destiny has ordained," he wrote to his wife at the age of over sixty, "that from the day of my birth I should never know a whole happy day." The canker which ate all joy away, both in youth and in old age, and which is revealed by almost every line of this correspondence, was anxiety. It is this, perhaps, that makes Datini seem so akin to us, so much the precursor of business-men of our own time. He was an astute and successful merchant; but he was, above all, an uneasy man. Each of his *fondachi* was a constant source of anxiety: he mistrusted his partners, his managers, and the captains whose ships carried his merchandise; and he went in constant fear, too, of all the misfortunes that might overtake these ships —shipwreck, piracy, overloading, or an outbreak of plague among the crew. And when his great fortune was made at last, fresh anxieties sprang up; he worried about his investments, his taxes, and his fines. He trusted his bailiffs and servants at home no better than those abroad. He lived in daily apprehension, according to Mazzei, of being defrauded, "even of the shoe-buckle of the wench who serves your slave."

And with old age came the last and worst anxiety: overwhelming fear of what would happen to him in a future life. Pilgrimages and periods of fasting, gifts of pictures to churches and of lands to convents, and, finally, the bestowal of all his great fortune to charitable works—none of these sufficed to dispel the haunting sense of guilt that darkened his last years—a gnawing anguish, a perpetual *maninconia*.[1]

[1] It is quite plain from the context that this word, which is constantly to be found in both Francesco's and Margherita's letters, is not used in the modern sense of "melancholy," but rather to mean distress and anxiety—*Angst*.

Other figures, too, emerge as we go on reading. There are the rapacious poor relations, Margherita's family, perpetually hoping for crumbs from the rich man's table, perpetually dissatisfied when they fall, "for Francesco is able to do more than this." "You have demeaned yourself in such a fashion," wrote Margherita to her brother after one of his begging letters, "that you have sealed my mouth for ever in Francesco's presence." Yet so strong was the convention of the family tie that when this same brother (the family black sheep) died, Francesco felt obliged to spend no less than 259 gold florins on mourning cloaks for the whole family. There are Francesco's partners and friends, among them the cheerful shrewd Florentine, Domenico di Cambio, whose chief quarrel with Francesco was that his riches did not make him happy. "I vow I get more pleasure in a day from my handful of *soldi*, than you in a whole year." And there is the wise, kindly family friend Ser Lapo Mazzei—the personification of the Tuscan virtues of piety and moderation—quietly counselling prudence and charity; proud of his friend's riches, but with no desire to share them; glad to enjoy with him a fat partridge or a glass of red Carmignano, but accepting no richer gifts; and gently striving, as the years passed, to loosen his friend's hold from the things he must soon leave behind him. His relationship with Francesco is the most pleasing note in the whole correspondence: it provides the spectacle of a disinterested friendship.

Ser Lapo's letters are a real contribution to literature—lively, gentle, wise, and written in the purest Tuscan of the *trecento*—but only a few more have now been added to those already published. Francesco's and Margherita's have much less literary value. They are chiefly marred by a fault common to many medieval letters: the cumbersome repetitiveness of writers who cannot quite believe that a written instruction is really as effective as a spoken one. We must remember, too, that during the early part of her marriage Margherita herself could neither read nor write; she dictated even her letters to her husband, and his were read aloud to her. Both of them seem to have felt that if a thing was worth saying once, it was worth repeating; and, in addition, we know that Francesco requested his instructions to be read aloud to his wife, not once but over and over again, to make sure that she had fully mastered them! It is for this reason that whole letters have very seldom been quoted here; the second paragraph is often only a repetition of the first.

On the other hand, the letters also have the *merits* of the spoken word: directness, raciness, and a complete lack of affectation. The language is the Tuscan of Boccaccio and Sacchetti— but broader, more colloquial, less polished.

A great deal of the liveliness of the letters is derived from their colloquialisms, their proverbs, and their popular aphorisms. *"Non son villana perch'in contado stia, ma gl'è villano chi fa la villania,"* [2] Margherita quoted to her city relations. *"Chi si leva a tempo,"* writes Niccolò dell'Ammannato, *"fa buona giornata e si può riposare all'albergo."* [3] And *"Non vorrei che isteste chostà tanto,"* writes Domenico di Cambio when the plague is raging, *"per richogliere i chiovi [chiodi] che voi vi lasciate i ferri."* [4] *"Ha più corta la fede, che la lepre la coda!"* [5] he exclaims about a mutual friend. And Lapo Mazzei, of a man he does not expect to see again: *"Arrivederci, come le volpi, in pellicceria!"* [6]

Sometimes these aphorisms have a strongly moralistic turn. *"Chi ogni ingiuria vorrà vendicare, o d'alto stato cade, o non vi sale."* [7] And sometimes, too—and this also is very Tuscan—the writers use a device imitated from the sermons of such expert preachers as San Bernardino or Fra Giovanni Dominici: they interrupt whatever they are saying to make use of a story or an

[2] "I'm not a boor because I am a countrywoman: the boor is the man who does a boorish deed."

[3] "The early riser makes a good profit, and can lie down at night in an inn."

[4] "I would not have you stay there so long, picking up nails, that you lose the shoe."

[5] "His faith is shorter than a hare's tail."

[6] "Au revoir, as the foxes say at the furrier's" (i.e., in another life).

[7] "The man who seeks revenge for every injury will either fall from high estate, or never reach it."

assempro (parable). "You are like the countryman who went to an apothecary . . ." or "You put me in mind of the tale of . . ."

"You seem to me," wrote Francesco to a greedy factor, "like a priest who says: 'If only I had a poor little church of my own, where I could find a living, and every morning say my Mass, I would ask nothing more of God, and would be the happiest man in the world'; and then when he has got the church, he cannot rest until he has become Pope, and then the spiritual power will not suffice without the temporal. . . ."

Sometimes, too, a completely prosaic business letter ends with a story—which suggests that, when books were scarce, it was not unusual for friends to copy out for each other any tale that had taken their fancy. "I will tell you the story of the man who set out to seek the wrath of God. . . ."

Above all, we are made aware in these letters of how frequently—in a period in which men read few books, but read them often—the maxims in these works became part of common speech. Seneca, the *Letters* of St. Jerome, Boethius, Dante, Jacopone da Todi, the *Fioretti*—these were Francesco's reading —and he was also familiar with many quotations from the Bible, heard over and over again (for he was a great sermon-goer) from the lips of popular preachers. These tags Francesco repeated in his letters without quotation mark or comment, perhaps even—so accustomed was he to hearing them—without being aware that they were not his own. He uses, in speaking of his old age, Dante's phrase *"calar le vele e raccoglier le sarte"* (or was it a phrase already then in common use, which Dante had absorbed? For Francesco adds: *"e morir in porto"*).[8] He speaks of "rendering unto Cæsar the things that are Cæsar's." And after having heard a Lenten sermon, he sits down in the evening and writes to his wife: "I have founded my house upon sand, and my wall is falling. I have placed greater hopes in the men of this world than in God, and the world has repaid me." Here, plainly,

[8] "Dip the sails and gather in the ropes." (*Inferno*, XXVII, 81.)

is both the content and the phrasing of the sermon he has just heard.

The chief value of these letters—apart from their contribution to the history of trade—is as an echo and a mirror. The society which they reflect is the world of Boccaccio and Sacchetti: a small, busy, earthy society. It is a world neither sophisticated nor subtle: its members like jokes that are broad and simple, food that is heavy and heavily spiced, gowns of rich velvet and fur covering coarse, scanty linen. It is, in spite of violence, greed and social injustice, a curiously innocent world—in the sense that, like the cruel practical jokes of children or a peasant's violence, it is lacking in guile. It is an urban society which has not yet lost the tang of country air, in which orchards and gardens hold almost as much place as houses within the city walls, and a great preacher does not hesitate to hold the crowd's attention by imitating the croaking of a frog or the crowing of a cock. A world in which men have put on city clothing, but still retain in their minds a countryman's shrewdness, suspiciousness, and stark realism.

But this is not the whole picture. For this is also a society in transition, in which the corporative organization of the guilds has given place to the control of a few great entrepreneurs, and the rule of the Commune has been taken over by a handful of rich merchants and bankers. In this world of contrasting trends, in which a Franciscan cult of poverty is to be found side by side with a rapacious struggle for wealth, we may see, on the one hand, a small enclosed society of craftsmen and shopkeepers, still wholly preoccupied with local interests, and on the other, a handful of men whose market-place is the whole of Europe, and whose ambition and enterprise are as wide as their field of action. Here most men are still ordering their lives according to the precepts of the Church and the statutes of the guilds, but a few are already merely using these rules as a screen behind which to form their own audacious schemes. The unquestioning orthodoxy of the Middle Ages is giving place to the sceptical, inquiring mind of the Renaissance, and among the pioneers of the new order are the men who perforce have had to depend upon their own enterprise, adaptability, and shrewdness, to achieve their ends: the merchants.

Francesco Datini belongs to one of these trends, his friend Lapo Mazzei to the other. It is not possible—or necessary—to claim that either of them was a great man. Ser Lapo was a shrewd notary, a true Christian, and a charming writer; Francesco a self-made, ambitious man—a taverner's son who, without help or backing, had become a rich and influential merchant. But it is precisely because no greater claim than this can be made for them that the record of their daily lives has a peculiar value. Great men—leaders, geniuses, saints—are poor mirrors, because they rise too far above the common level. It is the smaller men, who belong most completely to the climate of their times, who can tell us most.

Between them, Datini and Mazzei reflect very faithfully the two dominant trends of their time. Ser Lapo was held by the older tradition: his life was shaped by local custom, rooted in piety and moderation. Francesco—though he did not fully possess the wide vision or fine taste of some of the merchants of the Renaissance—stood upon the threshold of the new age. In his moral values he still belonged to Ser Lapo's world—unquestioningly accepting not only the rulings of the Church (even when he disobeyed them) but the iron law of custom. Even the "change of heart" of his later years, with its final act of contrition, was as much within a familiar convention as the grasping ruthlessness of his prime—seeming, both to himself and to his friends, as natural in old age as the hardening of a man's arteries. In youth a man was ruled by his senses; in his prime by Mammon; in old age he turned to God. But in his business dealings Francesco was already a man of the new world: he belonged to it by his spirit of enterprise, his commercial methods, his international connections—and his own intense individualism.

To some extent this last trait may have been due not only to Datini's own temperament, but to an accident of circumstance. "The medieval man," as Professor Rodolico has said, "was esteemed in so far as he formed part of an aristocratic clan, a guild, or a party; in the Renaissance, he was assessed by what he had made of himself." The power of all the great merchant-companies had been built up by the united efforts of a compact clan: the very structure of their companies rested upon this basis. But Datini had no family with whom to share his labours or his profits. His father, a humble taverner, had been carried off by the Black Death while he was still a child; his wife bore him no sons; he had no influential kinsmen. No patron helped him to establish himself in Avignon, or to remain there when the Pope's interdiction fell upon all Florentine merchants. And when at last, after thirty-five years abroad, he came home, he was regarded almost as a foreigner. When a forced loan was levied by the Commune, he was among those most heavily taxed; when he required some backing in a foreign venture, he knew better than to ask for it. Except for Ser Lapo Mazzei, he had no friend whom he could trust, and even when he formed his companies abroad, his partners had neither the wit nor the character to become anything more than subordinates. All that he achieved, he achieved alone.

Thus by circumstance, as well as by temperament and the stirrings of the *Zeitgeist*, Datini belongs to the merchants of the Renaissance, and the story of his achievements is something more significant than the mere record of the enrichment of an ambitious man. In the extent and variety of his ventures, in his powers of organization, in his international outlook, in his swift adaptability to the changes of a society in turmoil, as in his own ambition, shrewdness, tenacity, anxiety, and greed, he is a fore-runner of the business-man of today.

ACKNOWLEDGEMENTS

MY GRATEFUL ACKNOWLEDGEMENTS ARE DUE TO PRO-fessor Federigo Melis for putting at my disposal all the material in the Archivio Datini and for facilitating my researches, and to Dott. Aviano Marinai for his help in research and transcription. I wish to thank Dott. Gino Corti for his assidu-ous and patient assistance in research and transcription during the early stages of the work.

I am grateful to Professor Renato Piattoli for advice and valu-able information, to Professor Raymond de Roover for his in-valuable advice with regard to the chapter on "Money," and to the Archivist of the Archivio Comunale of Prato, Dott. Rug-gero Nuti.

I also wish to make my grateful acknowledgements to Profes-soressa Cristina Arcamone, Librarian of the Biblioteca Casanatense in Rome, for facilities in consulting various manuscripts and for permission to reproduce four illustrations from the Codex Casana-tense No. 4182; to Count Vittorio Cini for permission to repro-duce the picture of *The Notary*, from his private collection in Venice; to Dott. Angela Zanini, Librarian of the Biblioteca Estense in Modena, Dott. Irma Merolle Tondi, Librarian of the Biblioteca Nazionale of Florence, Dott. Antonio Toschi, Librar-ian of the Biblioteca Universitaria of Bologna, and Professor Luciano Laurenzi, Director of the Museo Civico of Bologna, for permission to reproduce pages of codexes in their libraries.

Above all, I wish to thank Professor Gaetano Salvemini for reading my typescript and for his warm and generous encourage-ment.

To Elsa Dallolio's intuition, accuracy, and forbearance I owe, once again, more than I can express or repay.

XXX

CONTENTS

PART ONE: THE MERCHANT

PART TWO: THE HOUSEHOLDER

ILLUSTRATIONS

xxxiii

ILLUSTRATIONS

PART ONE

THE

MERCHANT

THE YEARS IN AVIGNON
(1350-83)

"Gli accorgimenti e le coperte vie
lo seppi tutte. . . ." [1]—DANTE, *Inferno*, XXVII, 76.

HE PEOPLE OF PRATO—A BUSY, FLOURISHING LITTLE city in the wide plain of Florence—are level-headed, sceptical, and practical folk whose chief concern is, and has always been, the manufacture of cloth. The mystical or chivalrous legends of Siena and Umbria have not flourished in this soil; Prato has had no Pia de' Tolomei, no Margherita da Cortona. But one story, from the fourteenth century to this day, has been told to the children of Prato: it concerns a merchant and a cat.

In the days—so the legend runs—when the adventurous traders of Tuscany were sailing to far lands, a merchant of Prato came to a remote island called the Canary Isle; and there the king of the island invited him to dinner. "And the merchant saw the table laid with napkins, and on each of them a club as long as his arm, and he could not fathom its purpose. But having sat down at table, and the viands having been brought in, the odour thereof brought

---

[1] "All wiles and covert ways I knew."

3

forth a great abundance of mice, who must perforce be chased away with those clubs, if the guests wished to eat. . . . And the next day, having returned at night to his ship, the merchant came back with a cat up his sleeve. And when the viands came, the mice also appeared; and the merchant brought the cat out of his sleeve, and she speedily killed twenty-five or thirty mice, and the others ran away. 'This animal is divine!' cried the king. Whereupon the merchant replied: 'Sire, your courtesy to me has been so great that I can only return it by bestowing on you this cat.' " The king gratefully accepted the gift, but before the merchant left the island, he sent for him again and presented him with jewels worth 4,000 *scudi*. And the following year the merchant came back again to the island, taking with him a tom-cat—and this time received a further 6,000 *scudi*. The merchant of Prato came home a rich man; and his name was Francesco di Marco Datini.[2]

This charming legend, which has also been told about several other merchants of the time, cannot seriously be fastened upon the subject of this book. Francesco di Marco never journeyed to the Canaries, nor indeed any further than Avignon; and in all his vast correspondence there is no mention of a cat. But that so persistent a tradition should have continued to connect the story with his name indicates the position that he held, and still holds, in the minds of his fellow citizens. And indeed the true story of his rise to fortune is hardly less remarkable than the legend. It begins when, as a boy of fifteen, wrapped in a crimson cloak (the only detail that has come down to us), he set forth alone from Tuscany in 1350 to seek his fortune in the great city of Avignon, and it ends only with the bequest of his whole fortune to the poor of his native town.

Of the birth, childhood, and family of Francesco di Marco Datini we know extremely little, and of his ancestors nothing but

[2] One early version of this story attributed it to Niccolao di Piero Gatti (whose family still exists in Prato), another, a century later, to a merchant called Arnaldo degli Ormanni, "in the time that our Amerigo Vespucci was discovering the New World." But the children of Prato are still told that it was Francesco di Marco.

4

their very Tuscan names.[3] A parchment laying down some bound-
aries of land near Prato in 1218 refers to a man called Accom-
pagnato, the son of Bonfigliolo; his son Toscanello had a son
called Datino, from whom the family took their surname; and
Datino's son Marco was the father of our Francesco, who was
probably born (the precise date is uncertain) in 1335. Marco di
Datino was a poor taverner, but he appears to have saved a small
sum—perhaps by lending out money (though the term "usurer"
was one very easily come by in those days)—and to have bought
a little land; we also hear of him selling the meat of his cattle in
the Prato market-place, with his boy, Francesco, cutting up the
meat. He died in 1348, the year of the Great Plague, which also
carried off his wife, Monna Vermiglia, and two of their children
—the only survivors being Francesco and his brother Stefano.
Their guardian, Piero di Giunta del Rosso, took charge of their
small inheritance—a house, a little land, and forty-seven florins [4]
—while the boys themselves went to live with a good woman of
Prato, Monna Piera di Pratese Boschetti, for whom, until the day
of her death, Francesco retained feelings of the most lively gratitude and affection. "I will do for you in life and in death," he
wrote to her in the days of his prosperity, "what I would do for
Monna Vermiglia [his mother] were she still alive." And Monna
Piera, on her side, signed her letters to him as "your mother in
love" *(tua madre per amore).

Francesco, however, was far too restless and active to remain
for long under petticoat government, even the kindest, or to be
satisfied with the six lire [5] a year which—with twenty bushels of
wheat and four barrels of wine—was all his tutor could supply for
the maintenance of the two boys. Within thirteen months of his
father's death he went to Florence, as an apprentice first in one
bottega and then in another, doubtless learning much that was
useful to him later on, and hearing, too, from Tuscan merchants

[3] The surname Datini was not used by his contemporaries; he was Francesco di Marco da Prato.
[4] See Appendix A.
[5] See Appendix A.

who had come back from Avignon, of the great opportunities offered by that crowded, corrupt, and prosperous city. His ambition and curiosity were fired, Prato and Florence no longer sufficed him. Soon after his fifteenth birthday he sold a small piece of land for 150 florins and—probably in the company of some Florentine merchants, since to travel "in the shade" of a great man (all'ombra del signore) was a poor traveller's only protection—set off for Avignon.

The town to which he came was one of the most important trading-cities of Europe. Situated on the Rhone—the chief natural artery between northern and southern Europe—it became the centre of the trade between the two most enterprising countries of the time, Italy and Flanders. Here arrived, by the valley of the Rhone, the wool and cloth of England and Flanders; by the valley of the Durance and the passes of Mont Cenis and Mont Genèvre, the wheat, barley, linen, and armour of Lombardy; by the ports of Provence and Languedoc, the spices, dyes, and silks of the Levant; by Roussillon and the Col de Perthus, the wool, oil, leather, and fruit of Spain. Above all, it was here that Tuscan merchants came—by sea from Pisa to the coast of Provence and then up the Rhone—to buy Flemish and English wool and heavy cloth, and to sell the fine finished cloth of the *Arte di Calimala*, the silks and brocades of Lucca, the veils of Perugia and Arezzo, the painted panels and gold- and silver-ware of Florence.

When young Francesco di Marco arrived there, Avignon—like most other great medieval cities—was both magnificent and squalid, but with luxury and misery in peculiarly sharp contrast. Clement VI—the Pope who held that "no subject should ever leave his Prince's presence unsatisfied"—was still upon the papal throne, and his court was the most brilliant in Europe. But the little provincial capital which had now become the centre of Christendom was far too small to hold its thirty thousand inhabitants. The gigantic papal palace which dominated the whole

town could not house even the members of the Curia.[6] Beyond
its walls lodging had to be found for the city's innumerable
visitors—ambassadors and petitioners, merchants and travellers
—as well as dwellings for all the courtiers, employers, and hang-
ers-on of the papal court, and of the smaller courts of each cardinal, which included not only guards and servants, but lawyers
and notaries and money-changers, artists and merchants. So
overcrowded was the city that special officials were appointed—
taxatores domorum—to assign lodgings to members of the Curia
and to regulate their rents. And finally, crowded together in the
heart of the town, were the low, dark dwellings of the poor—
the penniless students of the university, the builders and craftsmen by whose hands the new great palaces were rising, the servants and washer-women and sweepers and water-carriers of the
prelates and nobles, the tradesmen and artisans who supplied
their needs—and the host of adventurers, usurers, thieves, and
prostitutes. The dwellings were so close and so overcrowded,
and the narrow unpaved streets so ill-odorous, that—even in a
period when such inconveniences were accepted as a common-
place of city life—an Aragonese ambassador complained that
their stench had made him ill, and Petrarca declared that he had
been obliged to move to Vaucluse, not only to enjoy its beauties
but to prolong his life.

> *Dall'empia Babilonia, ond'è fuggita*
> *Ogni vergogna . . .*
> *Son fuggit'io per allungar la vita.*[7]

In the papal palace itself, luxury and austerity were also to be

[6] A census made in 1376 listed 1,471 citizens of the papal court (*Cives
Romanæ Curiæ*) and 2,359 courtiers. These included not only the Pope's
thirty chaplains, but his knights and squires, chamberlains and grooms,
bodyguard and jailers, servants and tradesmen. In addition, each cardinal
had a large court of his own: in 1321 one of them required fifty houses to
lodge his dependents. Mollat: *Les Papes d'Avignon*, pp. 442–5.

[7] "From this impious Babylon, from which all shame has fled . . . I, too,
have fled away, to save my life"—*Le Rime*, LXXVIII.

7

found side by side. Except for the chapel and the consistory, the windows were not glazed, but closed with waxed cloths; the floors of the scantily furnished rooms were covered (except for the audience hall) only with straw mats, or bestrewn with rushes or lavender, and at least one Pope—Urban V—chose to sleep only on bare boards. But the banqueting and audience halls were hung with heavy woollen and silken hangings from Italy, Spain, and Flanders, while the table-services and ornaments were of silver and gold. Even the tasting-goblets, used to ensure that no poison had been put into any prelate's wine, were of fine metals and adorned with serpents' tongues—since these were supposed to possess a miraculous power of revealing the truth. The cardinals' mules and horses had golden bits and gold upon their trappings—soon, Petrarca wrote, they would even be shod in gold!

No less sumptuous—and costing, under John XXII, no less than seven or eight thousand florins a year—were the garments of the papal servants. Twice a year, in spring and autumn, new clothes were distributed to all the members of the papal court, while the Pope did not hesitate to buy for his own use forty pieces of cloth of gold from Damascus for the immense sum of 1,276 florins. Above all, fabulous sums were spent on furs—even though the use of these was restricted to prelates and members of the papal court. For his personal wardrobe alone, Clement VI used no less than 1,080 skins of ermine, while John XXII even trimmed his pillow with them.

Of the artists and craftsmen living within the papal city, a very large proportion were Italians. A list made in 1376 of the members of the Confraternity of Notre Dame de Majour, who were almost all artisans or tradesmen, mentions, in a list of 1,224 names, over 1,100 Italians, of whom 70 were wood-workers or carpenters and over 40 jewellers or goldsmiths, besides many weavers and leather-workers and some armourers, stone-masons, and sculptors. The great Sienese painter Simone Martini, who had come to Avignon at the Pope's bidding, had died six years

8

before Datini's arrival there, but many of his pupils were still working in the new chapel of St. John, and the official painter of the papal court was an Italian, Matteo Giovanetti of Viterbo. Moreover, most of the artisans were Tuscans, in particular the goldsmiths, who made the great reliquaries and chalices for the churches, and the silver plates and goblets for the prelates' tables. Originally most of these articles had been brought to Avignon by Italian merchants or money-changers, but before long some Sienese goldsmiths settled in Avignon, bringing the tradition of fine Tuscan craftsmanship to the banks of the Rhone. It was they who made the golden and silver chalices and processional crosses encrusted with precious stones, the exquisite golden rose (with a sapphire at its heart and rubies in its leaves) which was carried in procession through the town twice a year by a great prince of the Church, and the great golden reliquary ordered by Clement VI in the shape of a church.

Even more numerous than the artisans were the Italian merchants and tradesmen. They monopolized the luxury trade and (with a few Jews) the banking-tables. They dealt in wheat, wood, cheese, and vegetables; they imported horses, cloth, armour, and spices; they were taverners and middlemen, and they lived in a tight little community of some six hundred families, under the jurisdiction of their own consuls, forming their own confraternities and keeping their own feast days. A few of these merchants were Lombards or Piedmontese, but most of them were Tuscans, and so were their apprentices, their clerks, and their craftsmen. There were even some booksellers and doctors, and various eminent teachers and monks of the Curia. The Pratesi enjoyed the protection of their own cardinal, Niccolò da Prato —born of "*piccioli parenti*"—who became, owing to his role in the election of Pope Clement VI, one of the most powerful men of the Curia, and of their own grammarian, the simple old scholar Convenevole da Prato, whose favourite pupil was Francesco Petrarca. They even had their own doctor, Maestro Naddino Bovattieri of Prato, who had set up practice in Avignon and

9

become one of the physicians of the Pope, but who later on wrote to Francesco to discourage one of his colleagues at home from following in his footsteps—partly on the grounds that life in Provence had become too dear, and partly because, in his opinion, clients there required too high a standard of learning from a country doctor.

> Life here has become too costly. I have strictly examined his plan and verily, journeying at his own cost and setting himself up in the same manner, I trow he could spend no less than 2,000 florins. I say this of my own knowledge. And touching these gentlemen, I wyst not how to put him in touch with them, for the great men in power are already supplied; and furthermore, they would have doctors in physic. All day they question you, both in medicine and philosophy. I know it well—and though I have read much, were it not for my great studies both by day and night, I could not hold my own with them.*

Whether indeed the general level of culture in Avignon was as high as Maestro Naddino maintained must remain uncertain. Certainly some of the cardinals were men of brilliance and learning who bought rare books and gave fine parties. But Petrarca's final verdict was one of superficiality and frivolity, and it would appear that Provence in the fourteenth century was not so much the centre of an indigenous artistic or intellectual movement, a pre-Renaissance, as a place to which, for a short period and for purely accidental reasons, the talent of other lands was drawn. A Petrarca, a Simone Martini lived and worked there, but put down no roots. Certainly, however, these Italian artists and merchants brought to Provence their fine workmanship and fine tastes and a most lively intellectual curiosity—and, at the same time, made their own fortune.

The shrewd and enterprising young Francesco, on arriving in this city, must at once have realized the vast opportunities it offered. To import goods for this almost inexhaustible luxury market was a swift road to fortune. But how he succeeded in raising a small capital to start with is not known. Perhaps he worked first as an apprentice with one of the Florentine merchants whose firm was already established; perhaps some "fine cloth" which was sent to him in 1356 by his guardian, by means of a wandering friar, formed the basis of his stock. All that is certain is that he did not send his tutor any requests for money, and that by 1358 he was doing sufficiently well for his brother to join him in Avignon. In the same year he returned to Prato for a short visit, sold another piece of land for 138 florins, 14 *soldi*, and 2 *denari*,[8] persuaded his tutor to entrust him with the 100 florins which were his brother Stefano's share of their inheritance, and, with this small capital, went back to Avignon.

By 1361 he was securely established as a merchant, in partnership with some other Tuscans, Toro di Berto and Niccolò di Bernardo, a nephew of Monna Piera's.

At first he dealt chiefly in armour—a choice no doubt influenced by the presence in Avignon not only of the knights of the papal court, but of the Soldiers of Fortune, both English and Breton, who—after the truce of Bordeaux of 1357—were infesting the whole of southern France. Innocent VI, indeed, unlike his predecessor, had been obliged to spend the revenues of the papal treasuries not on works of art, but on fortifications against these wandering brigands, and on one occasion—in 1360, when the great company of Bertrand du Guesclin was encamped at Villeneuve—was able to avert the menace to the papal city only by the payment of 30,000 gold florins.

Francesco, however—like other dealers in arms before and since—seems to have felt no scruples about providing arms simultaneously to both sides. In 1368 his books mention a sale of arms worth 64 *livres* to this same Bertrand, a lieutenant of Messire de Turenne, and in the same year a sale of 50 "cuirasses for brigands" (the usual term for infantry), 50 *cervelières*, 12 bassinets, and 12 pairs of gauntlets to the Commune of Fontes

[8] See Appendix A.

11

—presumably for defence against these companies. An inventory of his shop in 1367 includes 25 bassinets, 3 "iron hats," 10 *cervelières*, 60 breastplates, 20 cuirasses, 12 coats of mail, and 23 pairs of gauntlets, as well as some mailed sleeves, cuissards, etc.[9] These arms were chiefly imported from two firms of armourers in Milan, Basciamuolo of Pescina and Danesruollo of Como.[1] The armour was carefully wrapped in straw and packed in canvas bales, which were then carried on mule-back across the Alps— the journey by Pavia and Avigliana taking about three weeks.

It is amusing to note in this connection that already in Datini's time Milan was considered the most flourishing trading-city of Italy. "Milan," he wrote in 1378, "is a fine city and at the head of our trade." * But he would also sometimes send one of his partners to buy *harnais de jambes* or bassinets "in the latest fashion" in Lyons,* and in 1382, having heard of the rout of a Company of Free Lances in Liguria, he promptly instructed his agent in Pisa, Stoldo di Lorenzo, to hasten to Genoa and buy up all that he could. "For, when peace is made, they are wont to sell all their armour." *

Comparatively few swords or daggers are mentioned in

[9] The bassinets Datini sold were very tall, with a protruding visor which opened and shut; they mostly came from Milan, but some were made in Avignon by Milanese workmen. The most expensive had a circular bib of iron, protecting the shoulders; they were lined with silk and contained an inner hood of leather or sheepskin. Fashionable ones from Milan cost 4 or 5 florins each, or even as much as 21 florins. The "iron hats" were round iron helmets, much less expensive. The *cervelières* were low iron hats without a rim, protecting only the skull, worn by the infantry; in 1369 they were worth 33 *soldi* each. The price of these coats varied according to the quality of the mail, between 3 *livres* and 14 *livres*. The *coretto* was a coat of mail with short sleeves, sometimes decorated with metal studs. It is difficult to make out of what material the *cuissards* and *harnais de jambes* were made; some seem to have been of iron and some of leather, studded with iron nails. The gauntlets in fashion in 1367 were of iron, studded with rows of tin nails and lined with leather. One pair of luxurious gloves was of white chamois, lined with white kid and sewn with vermilion silk. Brun, *Notes sur le commerce des armes à Avignon au XIV⁴ siècle*, pp. 217–25.

[1] A single delivery of armour from Basciamuolo, in 1370, consisted of 11 bales, worth 744 *livres*, while in 1371 and 1372 another firm sent no less than 47 bales. Brun, op. cit., pp. 210–11.

Datini's books; those which he did import came chiefly from
Florence, and some from Viterbo and Bologna. The only lances
mentioned also came from Florence; and there are many orders
for spurs, often gilded, which came mostly from Florence,
Nîmes, or Lyons, but were also sometimes made in Avignon.
Datini presented a pair worth 1 *livre* 16 *sous*, in 1368, to a member of the papal court, and in 1372 another pair, worth 2 *livres*
8 *sous*, to Messire d'Aigrefeuilles.

Finally, Datini also dealt in the metals and accessories required for making arms: he sent to Pisa and Genoa sheets of
iron for visors and *harnais de jambes*, and even some sheets of
copper and tin—the latter coming from Cornwall and costing
12 florins a quintal.* He imported from Milan great quantities
of wire and belt-buckles and thousands of tin studs for shields
or cuissards. And there are orders for blades from Germany
and for scabbards and handles from Italy, which suggest that
the weapons were then assembled in the shop in Avignon. His
inventory included a box of tools and some emery, and he employed a Belgian craftsman, Hennequin of Bruges, who made
coats of mail. He did not disdain even to hire out arms to in-
digent noblemen in exchange for a pledge: in 1369, for instance, the Sieur de Courcy borrowed a bassinet and an old pair
of gloves.

From all this it is plain that Datini's trade in arms developed
swiftly, and it was continued, though on a smaller scale, even
after his return to Tuscany. In 1394 his branch in Avignon was
sending two sample bales of Milanese armour to Barcelona—
containing chiefly coats of mail, brass, and iron spurs, iron buckles, iron gauntlets with brass borders—to discover whether they
could fetch a good enough price on the Spanish market to justify
further shipments. "The price here [Avignon] would be 263
fiorini correnti and 3 *soldi provenzali*. And we deem that from
Milan to there [Barcelona] should bring in a profit of 15 per
cent or more, considering the time and the risk." *

And in the following year the branch in Avignon was inquiring of the one in Barcelona if it could supply steel to a Milanese firm in Pinerolo.

Long before this, however, Datini had opened up many new lines. His first shop in Avignon, in Piazza dei Cavalieri, was bought by him in 1363 from another Pratese for 941 gold florins, plus 300 florins for the customers' goodwill—and above this shop he took up his own lodging. How swift and large his profits were is shown by his own statement that on July 13, 1363, he and one of his partners, Niccolò di Bernardo, each put into the business the sum of 400 florins and by the following January each of them had made a profit of 200 florins.

The first steps in the foundation of Datini's fortune were probably the hardest, but he was swift to follow them up with further ventures. In 1367 he renewed his partnership with Toro di Berto, and now on a much larger scale. Each partner brought into the business a capital of 2,500 gold florins, and they now owned three shops, for which they paid rents of respectively 37, 35, and 30 florins a year.[2] At much the same time he also entered into partnership with another Tuscan, Tuccio Lambertucci, and so greatly did their affairs prosper that in a letter written some years later Datini states that 800 florins put up by himself and his partner had brought in, in the course of less than eight years, no less than 10,000 florins.*

It must, however, be emphasized that none of Datini's companies ever rose to the level of the great international trading-companies in Avignon—such as the Malabayla of Asti, the Alberti *antichi* and *novi* and Soderini of Florence, the Guinigi of Lucca, or Andrea di Tici of Pistoia—who were the Pope's bankers and merchants, his couriers, and his information service, and through whom the dues of the whole of Christendom reached the apostolic coffers. Datini, in comparison with these, was one of the minor merchants of Avignon; his companies con-

[2] The deed of partnership of this company is printed in full by Bensa, *Francesco di Marco da Prato*, Doc. I.

sisted of no more than two or three partners, and though he imported a large variety of goods, it was all on a comparatively small scale. But in Avignon there was room for the small companies as well as the great ones, and their trade covered quite as wide a field as that of their rivals. They, too, dealt in cloth, silks, and spices which had come from thousands of miles away; they, too, kept full and elaborate accounts and corresponded with other companies abroad, often no larger than their own; they, too, contributed to the luxury and prosperity of the great city. It is as the record of the achievement of one of these smaller men that the Datini papers have an especial interest.

The variety of his activities during the next few years is truly remarkable. In 1376 he began to trade in salt, though apparently unprofitably at first, since in 1378 he complained that he had kept 5,000 florins immobilized in this trade for two years, and had lost 1,500. "Yet I will be like unto a mariner who, though he be much afraid, will not cease to sail." *

In the same year—in spite of the fact that there were already fifty official money-changers in the city—he set up a money-changer's counter, which a *"Maestro Steve dipintore"* adorned with a golden fleur-de-lis on an azure ground. It is probable that here he dealt not only in the exchange of currency, but in silverware and works of art, since this was a customary sideline of most money-changers and one of his friends and associates, Bonaccorso di Vanni, was both a money-changer and a goldsmith. The Datini papers, indeed, contain an inventory of Bonaccorso's shop in 1335 which shows what very valuable works of art and silverware passed through his hands. It includes two large crucifixes worth 285 florins each, "an image of Our Lady, with a crown and Child" worth 180 florins, a mitre worth 280 florins and another, "not so good," worth 80, two gold angels "with pedestals and wings and holding crystals in their hands" worth 250 florins—besides innumerable silver and gold candlesticks, chalices, bowls, basins, goblets, cups, plates, salt-cellars, forks and spoons, a metal apple, silver-gilt, "for warming the hands," and a fine collection of sapphires, emeralds, and garnets.*

It was at about this time, too, that Datini began to export to Florence some of the fine French enamels, on a gold ground, which were in fashion for the adornment of ladies' gowns and especially for the silver or golden garlands they wore as head-dresses. Such enamels, in the Paris market, were worth 5 gold francs an ounce, and were so easy to carry that in a single year (1370-1) Datini was able.to export no less than 1,328 of them, in various sizes, to Florence.

The variety of goods he dealt in continued to increase. He opened a wine tavern and also a draper's shop, and in 1382 he mentioned in a letter that he had no less than 4,000 florins' worth of saffron in hand, "betwixt what I have in the house and what is on the way . . . all paid for in cash."

Apparently all these ventures did well, for in 1380 he was sending two of his factors to Naples with 2,000 florins to spend, but unfortunately without specifying in what merchandise. In the same letter, however, he wrote: "It is in my mind, to put into wool of Arles all that I can purvey, beyond what I need in the shop," adding that very valuable goods should be shipped to Nice, but coarser goods to Marseilles or Arles. "And if many galleys are sailing, send without insurance." *

It is interesting to note that all Francesco's partners, then and later, were Tuscans like himself—as, indeed, was inevitable at a time when traders in foreign parts formed a tight little community, dealing and associating almost exclusively with their fellow countrymen, under the rule of their own consuls. This was partly because—at a time when each city had its trading customs and often also its own currency—it was more convenient to deal with one's fellow countrymen. "As you know," wrote a Florentine merchant in Paris, "those Lucchesi conduct their companies in a diverse manner from our folk, and we cannot understand them well." But in addition this custom was favourable to the integrity of trade, since—in view of the generally accepted custom of reprisals, by which any merchant in a foreign land might be held responsible for the debts of a defaulting fellow citizen—the whole merchant community had a direct interest in the honesty of each of its members. It need hardly be said, however, that the custom of *rappresaglie* constituted a peculiar menace for merchants abroad, since a completely innocent man, on arriving in a strange land, might suddenly find himself held responsible for the misdeeds of a dishonest fellow citizen.[3]

Francesco's main shop in Avignon displayed a fine variety of wares. In addition to the armour we have already mentioned, and some Florentine silver belts and gold wedding-rings, a customer could find leather hides, saddles, and mules' harness imported from Catalonia, and household goods from various parts of Italy: white linen from Genoa, fustian from Cremona, scarlet *zendadi* from Lucca—and from Florence white, blue, and undyed woollen cloth, sewing-thread and silk curtains and curtain-rings, table-cloths and napkins and large bath-towels (this has a very modern sound). In addition Datini also imported from Florence the fine painted coffers which were an indispensable part of every bride's dowry (and generally contained her linen) as well as strong travelling-coffers and little jewel-cases. In 1384 the firm sent an order to Florence for a pair of such coffers:

. . . of medium size or a little larger, if you can find them, for a lady, painted on a vermilion or azure ground, according to what you can find. Let them be handsome and showy, and of good workmanship and made of dry and light wood.

[3] The custom of *rappresaglie*, which dated from the ninth century, had become a recognized institution; in 1164 the *Breve dei Consoli* of Pisa had established that if a Pisan citizen had been defrauded abroad (and had failed to obtain his dues on applying to the Rector of the foreign city) he might *ricolligere suum* from any fellow citizen of his debtor who came to Pisa. Private citizens, however, could exercise this right only through letters of reprisal (*lettres de marque*) issued after investigations by their own Communes. (In some cities, including Florence, a special official was appointed for this purpose.) Various categories were exempted from *rappresaglie*: ambassadors, pilgrims to the Holy Land, students of the University of Bologna (by a special decree of Frederic Barbarossa in 1158), and, in some cities, merchants.

Spend on them 7 or 8 florins a pair, as you think best; the finer and better they are, the better I can sell them.*

The same letter also ordered "two lady's travelling-coffers, for riding . . . with seven clasps and two hinges and locks, light and well made." Smaller coffers, used as jewel-cases, were lined with silk ("we will take no camlet,⁴ for they are meant for objects of great value"); * while some bridal caskets, "all of fine gold and painted in fine azure with figures of ladies and knights," came from Barcelona, together with six walnut chessboards and "boards for the game of nine." *

Among Datini's most valuable goods were richly embroidered stuffs for priests' vestments, which came from Lucca. One bale received in Avignon in 1371 included a fine piece of embroidery for a cope, representing the Passion, which was worth 43 florins; another, of the Nativity, worth 33 florins; and one representing the martyrdom of the Twelve Apostles, worth 30½ florins. Moreover, a little later on, in 1396, the firm was involved in the somewhat dubious transaction of forwarding to Paris, to be sold there, a great altar-cloth, worth at least 3,500 gold florins, which had been ordered in Florence by Charles VI of France but had never been paid for, and which apparently had also proved unsalable in Avignon. It was packed in a box hidden in a bale of sheepskins and carried on mule-back to Paris—where Datini's agent was told to "show it to whoever was likely to buy it," but secretly, because "the people who reside in the courts of great men are more apt to be evil than good." *

Another most profitable "line," which Datini continued to develop even after he had left Avignon, was the trade in religious pictures. The first bale arrived on February 8, 1371, from Florence, by sea: "a panel painted in fine gold, with no doors but with a base at the foot" (i.e., a *predella*), painted "with figures and niches," worth 6 florins, and two smaller pictures worth 3½

⁴ The Italian word is *camelotto*—a rough cloth of little value.

18

florins each. In June two more panels arrived, and in September four more—two worth 7 florins, and two worth 3 florins.* Plainly they sold well, for orders for similar ones were soon sent off.

Most of these pictures were objects of very slight artistic merit—hardly greater, indeed, than those sold in Florence for a similar tourist market today. Their value depended on their size rather than on the artist's skill—for that came very cheap, while paint was dear. Very little, too, was left to the artist's own taste. He was told what subjects to paint, and how many figures he might put into the scene—and was also often supplied with the precise measurements.⁵ An order sent on July 10, 1373, to Niccolò and Lodovico del Bono of Florence, gives a good idea of what was required:

A panel of Our Lady on a background of fine gold with two doors, and a pedestal with ornaments and leaves, handsome and the wood well carved, making a fine show, with good and handsome figures by the best painter, with many figures. Let there be in the centre Our Lord on the Cross, or Our Lady, whomsoever you find—I care not, so that the figures be handsome and large, the best and finest you can purvey, and the cost no more than 5½ or 6½ florins. Also a panel of Our Lady in fine gold, of the same kind, but a little smaller, the cost 4 florins, but no more. These two panels must contain good figures: I need them for men who would have them fine.*

The price of works of art, however, appears to have gradually risen, for ten years later, in 1384, the firm in Avignon was ordering very similar pictures, "of the usual type," for which it was prepared to pay as much as 8, 10, or 12 florins each. It is only very seldom that a painter's name is mentioned, but on March 6,

⁵ One order asks for four square pictures, "of the size of a medium-sized folio," which was, according to a fourteenth-century inscription in Bologna, 0.51 × 0.34 cm.

1386, there is a record of the arrival of "four panels of fine gold, with good figures of Our Lord and Our Lady and several Saints, without flowers, by Jacopo da Cione." [6]

More expensive works of art seem sometimes to have passed through the firm's hands, but only when they had been specifically ordered and paid for in advance, for the partners never bought any picture unless they were quite certain of making a handsome profit.

> You tell me [wrote Boninsegna to Florence in 1387] you can find no pictures for the money we will pay, for there are none so cheap, and therefore we bid you, if you find no good things at a fair cost, leave them, for here there is no great demand. . . . They should be bought when the master who makes them is in need.*

The same letter relates that the partners, having sold three out of five of the pictures in the last shipment, had received 10 gold florins for each of them—and this, they had to admit (since it was double what they had paid for them), was "a very good profit." Yet when one remembers the length and hazards of the journey, the large sums to be expended on taxes and toll-duties, and the uncertainties of the market, it is perhaps hardly too high.

By the age of thirty-five Francesco di Marco was a man of substance, and, moreover, one who did not deny himself any of the pleasures of the curious city in which he lived. "A man who has known all delights of the body" was the description given of him later on by his friend Mazzei, and elsewhere he called him "a man who kept women and lived only on partridges, adoring art and money, and forgetting his Creator and himself." *

It is from this date onwards—1371—that Datini's private letters have been preserved; and through them we at last have a glimpse of his private life. The first folder contains his correspondence,

[6] A younger brother of Andrea Orcagna. He entered the painters' guild in 1368-9 and painted the *Coronation of the Virgin* now in the Accademia of Florence. Cf. G. Meiss, *Painting in Florence and Siena after the Black Death*, p. 169.

between 1371 and 1382, with his foster mother in Prato, Monna Piera di Pratese, and with her neighbour Niccolozzo di Ser Naldo, to whom she dictated her letters or who wrote on her behalf. In Francesco's letters much of his character is displayed: arrogance and pride in his self-made fortune, shrewd common sense, a truly Tuscan sententiousness, a generous if masterful kindness towards his foster mother—and a firm determination, now that his fortune was made, to return home and settle down at last.

> Since God has granted me more than I deserve [so the first letter begins], I will not be ungrateful. I intend to set my life in order, in one manner or another. And therefore I have told Tuccio [his partner] to go to Prato before he leaves, and if you need ought whatsoever, to give it to you, and I have commended you to him. . . . I will strive to be with you as soon as may be, and bring you the Pope's indulgence.

We have not got Monna Piera's reply, but from Francesco's answer it would seem that she reproached him for his dissipated life, imploring him to bring his affairs in Avignon to an end and come home.

> I obtained your letter [Francesco replied] by means of certain pilgrims from Prato, and was right glad. Touching your words, I trow they are true; and it weighs upon no one in the world so much as on me, since I know that I do wrong. But sometimes one cannot do better. Man proposes and God disposes [*L'uomo propone e Dio ordina*]. Sometimes it is needful, when one is dancing, to finish the measure, and there is a women's proverb: "Struggle a little longer, and give birth to a male child." Thus I, too, purpose to struggle a little longer, and content myself and the folk who love me. Our Lord grant me grace in His mercy, to do what is best both for body and soul.

Then followed a passage in which Francesco firmly told his foster mother that this time he would come home, not as her adopted son, but as master of the house. "This time I shall seem to you another Francesco." Monna Piera had been left in charge of the kitchen and the garden, and perhaps, on other occasions, had fed Francesco with a truly Tuscan frugality, but this time, he wrote, he would require very different treatment.

> Place not garlic before me, or leeks or roots. Let it seem a Paradise to me. . . . I will not still be treated like a boy, and will not feed on half a pound of kid in a little pot meet for small fish; this time I would have the great cooking-pot.

Nor was it only in the kitchen that he required his desires to be satisfied.

> Tell me if you would have me send you a slave or another wench. . . . But if you say: "Send me an old woman," I like not their cooking and they cannot bear heavy toil. Moreover, I would not remain with a dry mouth. If you would have a slave, I will send you a fair and young one, skilled in every matter, who will not bring shame upon the house.

He added that he would also bring with him "two or three more beds and benches and stuffs and silver spoons and fine brass candlesticks, and many other things. And you shall see if I will be content to live like a mere boy!" *

Doubtless, after receiving this letter Monna Piera set to fattening the capons and cultivating vegetables, but in the autumn Francesco had not yet come. "Monna Piera is well," wrote Niccolozzo, "but it seems to her a thousand years until you are here; she thinks not she will see the day." *

Francesco did not come, but instead sent back to Prato a young man in his employ, Stoldo di Lorenzo (who later on became one of his factors in Florence), with a list of instructions which plainly shows how much attached he still was to his old friends at home. "The first is Monna Piera di Pratese, beside your own house . . . and you shall treat her as you would my mother. And whatsoever she bids you, do it, whether it be paying out money or aught else." *

In the following spring Francesco really seems to have intended to make the journey, for he was again sending instructions to Monna Piera about the cooking. "Look to it that I find fowls in abundance, for I purpose not to live as I did before. Capons please me better than cockerels, so you will not err in setting hens in good time to hatching." *

There was another year's pause—while Francesco went on making money in Avignon and his old friends went on fattening his poultry and waiting, month after month, for his coming. Their letters now held a great urgency: the time had come, they wrote, for Francesco not only to come home for a visit, but to settle down for good. "Pray hasten to find a wife," wrote Niccolozzo, "for the time is ripe, that some memory may remain of you, and some fruit of your labours be bequeathed to your lawful heirs." *

Francesco replied on other subjects, but a year later Niccolozzo returned more firmly to the charge. His letter reveals traits which are to this day deeply characteristic of the Tuscan mind: a piety conventional in expression but deep in feeling; a shrewd appreciation of the value of this world's goods, coupled with a natural sense of moderation; and a cult, almost equal to that of the Chinese, of *la famiglia*. All a man's labour is fruitless if he has no sons to whom to transmit what he has earned.

You know God has granted you to acquire great riches in this world, may He be praised; and you have borne, and are bearing, great burdens. Pray toil not so hard only for the good of strangers; let some remembrance of you remain here and someone to pray God on your behalf. Crave not for all: you have already enough to suffice you! If you would still trade, do as other men: take a wife, leave your partners there [in Avignon] and buy something for yourself here. . . .

23

How long will you wait to take a wife? Until you are old? Then must you leave your children—if God grants them—in the care of guardians, and God knows how such are treated, and you yourself have known it.[7]

This time Francesco did not delay his reply. "That I should get myself a wife," he wrote to Monna Piera, "it is not needful to remember me. . . . I would avise you all, I wyst well it is time and more than time; yet verily have I had lawful excuses, which, were they known, would bring me forgiveness. . . . Night and day I think only of how to come to you and order all my matters, when God wills." The pleasantest passage in the letter is the one in which he expresses his unchanged affection for his old foster mother.

In naught have I ever made a difference, nor shall I, betwixt you and me, even as I would not betwixt me and Monna Vermiglia [his mother], were she now alive. You will find me until my death—if you yourself live so long—the same Francesco you knew up to my fourteenth year. This I say to you, once and for all time: you may do with me and with my possessions as with your own, for that is how I reckon them, and ever have. Demand of me any monies you require, and they shall be given you; and do with them what you will, and I shall be glad, even as if I did it myself—and let this suffice.*

It is not surprising that Monna Piera liked such letters to be read to her often. Soon afterwards she asked Francesco to address to her directly and not to Niccolozzo, "For then I bid someone read them to me divers times. Verily Niccolozzo reads them to me once; but I would hear them many times." *

Francesco, however, had returned to his old ways in Avignon.

[7] The last sentence does not seem to apply to Francesco's own experience—at least no record remains that his own guardian, Piero di Giunta, ever treated him unfairly.

He even appears to have had, at about this time, an illegitimate child, for a letter from Monna Piera, written in January 1375, inquired after his son and sent the child a thousand blessings, while another from Niccolozzo congratulated the father less whole-heartedly. "We rejoice as greatly as may be in the son whom God has given you, and Monna Piera in especial is joyful. Yet we would remember you to beget some lawful children, which will be more to your honour before God and the world." *

A later letter, however, from Monna Piera in the same year lamented that the child had gone to Paradise.

The preceding year (1374), moreover, had been a bad one for Francesco. There had been an outbreak of plague in Avignon and he had not escaped; indeed, according to a letter to Monna Piera, he had been on the point of death. And when he recovered he had to pay, "with great melancholy," 260 florins to the Pope "as a loan, or whatsoever it may be." "I have been put among the rich men," he complained to Monna Piera, "though I am not."

His losses inclined Francesco towards domesticity again, and he now asked Monna Piera to look for a suitable wife for him in Prato. But she firmly refused. She would start looking for a bride for him, she wrote, but only if he then came to see the girl for himself. "There are some that please me, and some that please me not. I know you better than any, and because I know you, I pray you see the goods for yourself. These are not goods you can sell or invest!" *

Another six months passed, and still Francesco would not leave his business in Avignon.

> Endeavour [wrote Niccolozzo] to place your eggs in two nests. Well do I know that, even if you would, you could not take all away [from Avignon] at once. But this much I say: purvey something here, and leave your shop there well furnished, and you come and go. And come home and get a wife and beget heirs, that all these riches you have earned

with such toil may be bequeathed to them, in love and delight.

In every letter the same pressure continued. Francesco, his friends insisted, must take a wife from his own birthplace, not only for the obvious reasons, but because if he should die and leave young children in France, "where our florin is not worth a quarter of theirs—think how they [the children] would be served!" Moreover, Niccolozzo added: "You need not money: you need what is right for you. And Solomon himself said: 'Go with your own people.' " *

At last all this advice bore fruit. Francesco did not, indeed, return to Prato to find himself a wife, but he chose one among the Italians in Avignon: a Florentine girl of sixteen named Margherita di Domenico Bandini.[8]

"Methinks," he wrote to Monna Piera when he gave her the news, "God ordained at my birth that I should take a Florentine as my wife." His bride's father, he said, Domenico Bandini, "had his head cut off in Florence some time ago, being accused of wishing to hand over Florence to our Lord [the Pope]." One of her sisters was married in Florence to Niccolò dell'Ammannato Tecchini, and her mother, Monna Dianora, with two other sisters, was living in Avignon. "I know them and they know me . . . wherefore I have been more content, since I knew what I did." *

For once Francesco's instincts as a merchant gave way to simpler human feelings: his wife brought him no dowry but youth, good looks, and good breeding. Her family, on her mother's side, belonged to the small Florentine nobility, above the merchant class—and later on, in times of conjugal dissension, she was to remind her husband of the fact: "I feel the blood of the Gherardini in my veins."

The marriage was celebrated during Carnival, on a scale suita-

[8] Guasti gives her age as eighteen, but a letter of Francesco's eight years later, in 1384, shows that she cannot have been more than sixteen, for he says then: "You will soon be entering your 25th year."

ble to the bridegroom's fortune. The list of food for the wedding-banquet included 406 loaves, 250 eggs, 100 pounds of cheese, 2 quarters of an ox and 16 quarters of mutton, 37 capons, 11 chickens, and 2 boars' heads and feet for jelly—besides such small items as pigeons and sea-fowl. And it is pleasant to read that, as well as the fine vintages of Provence, Francesco supplied his guests with wines from his native Tuscany, with Chianti from Filettole, and the "sparkling Carmignano," which, according to Redi, it is a sin ever to mix with water.

So now, at last, Francesco di Marco had found a wife. His friends in Prato doubtless hoped that this would cause him to come home the sooner, but, on the contrary, its first effect was to settle him more securely in Avignon. His prosperity, according to his own account in a letter written many years later, continued to increase. "I was richer then," he wrote, "than I am now, for I found myself able to make as much money as I would." But he prided himself on having gone on working as hard as ever, and above all—unlike his other partners—on having kept his young wife at work, too. "Tieri [his partner]," he wrote, "let his wife go with other women to make merry in the pleasure-gardens and at every little feast; but mine was sewing helmets." *

His warmest human feeling still seems to have been his affection for his foster mother, and only a few months after his marriage he was trying to assuage her chagrin at his absence by asking her to spend her last years with him and his wife in Provence. Perhaps even, he added with transparent guile, she would be able, in the end, to achieve what no one else could— to bring him home to Prato.

Verily I wyst [he wrote] I shall never find any to whom my honour and comfort are of such concern as to you, or who so greatly desires to see me wed and joyful. Furthermore I vow, by all the love there has ever been betwixt you and me, you alone could induce me to come home. But if

27

you come not, I shall never go home, leastwise not until much later . . . so you see what power you have to do me great good or great harm.

Moreover, I shall never be at ease until I have rewarded you with as much love as you have bestowed on me. And I know not what reward I can offer you, save to spend long years of our life together, with each of us pleasing the other. And let it not enter your head to say: "But he has a wife!" For had I a hundred, it would not keep me from ever bearing myself to you as to my mother. But if you do not as I ask, I shall say you neither love me nor have loved me, or you would live and die where I abide.

Under the affection and masterfulness, one perceives that Francesco was surprised at having to plead so hard. "Consider what folk would say, if they knew I have besought you so much! For you know that they have ever said, you would go to the end of the world for my sake. Call them not liars." *

This is the last of Francesco's letters to Monna Piera that have come down to us. For all his coaxing, the stubborn old country-woman remained in Prato; her bones were too tired, her ways too set, to carry across the Alps. Her letter of refusal is lost, but from this time onwards all her letters and Niccolozzo's monotonously repeat the same urgent refrain—come home, come home! "Monna Piera is amended, praise God, and beseeches you heartily that she may see you before her end, for she is old."

Another six months passed, and Francesco had not come. "Again we remember you: may it please you to make ready your return and hye you home to rest in your own country with your kinsfolk and your friends and neighbours, and not end your days in other men's lands. . . ."

Yet another year went by. Messer Francesco still delayed, and still had no sons; and Monna Piera was growing weaker.

I read your letter to her [wrote Niccolozzo]. She was much comforted, and prays you to hye you home before

she dies, that she may go to God more joyfully. She is old
and sickly, and she needs a cloak; but until she saw your
letter she would not we should beg the money of Niccolò.
She thinks she will never see you more. She sends a hundred
blessings to you and your wife. . . . [And again the letter
ended with a warning:] Give thanks to God, for you already have enough. Crave not for all, crave not for all! *

What was it, indeed, that delayed Francesco for so long? His
wife's Florentine relations were convinced that it was her fault.
"I marvel greatly at Bita [Margherita]," wrote her brother-in-
law, Niccolò dell'Ammannato, "that she will not come home to
her own people, since she could come in such a wise as to live
honourably, according to her degree."

Francesco replied that, on the contrary, Margherita was
constantly beseeching him to go back to Italy, but Niccolò
would not believe him. "Love will make one say even worse
things than lies, and it assuredly is a sign of love, that you make
excuses for her. But tell her from me, if she knew how weighty
a matter this is for her, she would strive harder, not with *Gherardiname*, but with coaxing and wiles." [9]

Moreover, Niccolò expressed great anxiety about Francesco's
intention of leaving a large part of his capital behind him in
Avignon. "I will tell you my thought: leave no more than a
third; for wherever your person is, there should be two thirds
of your goods." *

Datini, in the end, followed this advice; but at the time more
immediate problems were weighing upon his mind. He was one
of the very few Tuscan merchants still safely established in
Avignon, and that he was still there at all was—in view of the
events of the past six years—a remarkable testimony to his agility.
In 1374 he had written to a friend in Pisa: "I am like a bird upon
a tree, who knows not which way to fly," * for the trouble which

[9] By *Gherardiname* Niccolò meant the family pride of the Gherardini,
from whom both Margherita and his own wife descended—a fact which
they apparently impressed on their bourgeois husbands.

had been long brewing between Florence and Pope Gregory XI was at last coming to a head, and he foresaw that all Tuscan merchants in Provence would suffer in consequence. In the summer of 1373, after an unusually bad harvest, Tuscany was stricken by famine, but the Papal Legate in the Romagna, Cardinal Guillaume de Nollet, forbade the exportation of any wheat from the Romagna to Tuscany, while at the same moment the dreaded "White Company" of Sir John Hawkwood descended like a flock of locusts into Florentine territory. The exasperated Florentines, who for a long time had been dreading the extension of the Church's powers all over central Italy, delayed no longer; they created an emergency government called the "Eight of War" (who later on were nicknamed the "Eight Saints"), declared war on the Pope, and persuaded most of the central Italian cities to join with them. In the course of 1375 Orte and Narni, Città di Castello and Montefiascone, Viterbo and Perugia, and finally Bologna, each in turn defeated and expelled their Papal Vicars: in a few months the Church lost a considerable part of her Italian domains.

It was not long before the Pope's retaliation came: on March 31, 1376, he not only laid his interdict upon the whole city of Florence, decreeing that her citizens were henceforth to be treated as heretics, but ordered all Christian rulers to expel Florentine merchants from their lands, and to confiscate their property. "And, moreover," wrote a contemporary chronicler, "[the Pope] said it was licit to rob any Florentine merchant without God's displeasure. . . . And so in many places . . . they were robbed. And, moreover, Florentine cloth and other wares made in Florence were also interdicted, like the men. . . . And this is what one gains by going against God and the Church!" [1]

The dismay which this decree awakened in Florentine merchants, both at home and abroad, can be easily imagined. More-

[1] *Le Croniche di Giovanni Sercambio Lucchese*, ed. S. Bongi—Ist. Stor. It., *Fonti per la Storia d'Italia*, vol. I, p. 216.

over, among the humble and God-fearing artisans of Florence it hardened a long-standing resentment against the avidity and arrogance of the high prelates of the Church, and a conviction that they, the *popolo minuto*, were (as they had long liked to call themselves) God's own people, *il popolo di Dio*. "In the city and the territory of Florence today," wrote an anonymous chronicler belonging to this class, "Mass is no longer said, nor is the Body of Christ imparted to us citizens and peasants. But we see Him in our hearts, and God knows we are neither Saracens nor Heathens, but true Christians chosen by God, amen." [2]

The Florentine merchants in Avignon were, of course, the first to be hit by the decree: the whole prosperous colony of some six hundred merchants was dissolved, and many took refuge in Genoa, which city—as a punishment for sheltering them—was also placed under a partial interdiction. Francesco, however, avoided being included among the banished, since, as he himself explained, the Pope decided to apply his ban only to Florentines and not to citizens of Prato—a city which he hoped, in view of an insurrection which had recently taken place there, to bring under the rule of the Church. A tradition has survived that, on their departure, many of the Florentine merchants entrusted to Francesco all their wares in Avignon and the management of their affairs, and that it was thus that he so speedily became a rich man—but no document has remained in proof of this.[3] It is certain that he stayed on, turning a deaf ear to the persuasions of all his friends in Italy, but by 1381—when the Pope relented to the extent of allowing Florentine merchants to come back and

[2] *"Diario di Anonimo Fiorentino"* in *Documenti di Storia Italiana,* vol. VI.

[3] There is no evidence for Professor Sapori's assertion that Francesco "forgot his own country in his own interests . . . and passed over entirely to the side of Gregory XI, furnishing him with funds to fight against his own country." Professor Sapori quotes a letter of Francesco's (dated January 10, 1377) complaining that he had to pay the Pope 260 florins "for a loan, or whatsoever it is called." But this was merely a general tax levied by the Pope on all residents of Avignon, as is shown by the next sentence, "I am put among the rich, and am not." Cf. Sapori, *"Economia e morale alla fine del trecento"* in *Studi di Storia economica medievale.*

trade in Avignon for a period of five years—he was ready at last to wind up his affairs. And indeed he felt uneasily that the time had come to go. "Methinks," he wrote to Stoldo, "this place is like to see change every day . . . and I can think of naught save of getting my matters sped." And he characteristically added: "I would keep my foot in both stirrups." *

His uneasiness was not unfounded. Not only was the political situation extremely insecure, but the return to Rome in 1378 of the Pope and his court had already partially deflected the current of the luxury trade to Italy. How swiftly merchants acted when they saw that the tide was turning is shown in a letter from a Florentine merchant to his Pisan correspondent in the very year of the Pope's return, telling him to send some Catalonian coffers —"rich and fine and painted with the story of King Priam"—not to Avignon but to Rome.*

Francesco took note of such straws, and decided to delay no longer. In the following spring he besought Stoldo to come to Avignon without delay, to help him wind up his business. "Here I am with water up to my chin, and at night I go to bed so worn out, that I can bear no more. . . ." When Stoldo arrived, he wrote, he would hand over all his papers to him and two other clerks. "And you shall never go forth, until all my matters are in order. And then we shall do what the times will counsel. If God keep us in health and destroy not the world, we shall have men and money to suffice us." *

Before leaving, Francesco handed over his affairs in Avignon to Boninsegna di Matteo—a man who had worked in his shop as his salaried *garzone* for over eight years, and whom he trusted more than any other man in Provence. "For assuredly," he wrote to Stoldo, "I have reason to praise him more than any man in the world." Before leaving, he drew up a deed of partnership with him and another Pratese, Tieri di Benci, who had also been working with him for several years. The deed of partnership stated that the capital—3,866 gold florins—was Francesco's but that Boninsegna and Tieri might trade with it "as they think best," while half of the profits were to go to Francesco, and of the rest, two thirds to Boninsegna and one third to Tieri.*

Thus, at last, on December 8, 1382, Francesco di Marco was able to set off for home. He sent some of his household goods by sea, via Arles to Pisa, but he himself, with his wife and servants, rode across the Alps—a company of eleven persons. To travel in a large company, indeed, was still the general custom—the highways being so dangerous that often a prosperous merchant would ask the rulers of the lands through which he passed for an armed escort, or else would spread false reports beforehand about his route. "If you go to Siena," advised Paolo da Certaldo in his *Book of Good Manners*, "say you go to Lucca; and you will travel free of evil folk." [4]

On this occasion, however, Francesco seems to have accomplished his journey without running into any danger. It took just over a month: a fortnight for crossing the Alps, by Sisteron to Milan, where the travellers arrived on December 23 and rested for a week; and then another ten days to take them on, by way of Cremona, to Prato, where they arrived on January 10, 1383.*

After thirty-three years abroad, Francesco di Marco had come home. But for the person who was awaiting him most eagerly, his return came almost too late. Monna Piera had often said that when she had her foster son again she would be ready to fly, "like an arrow," to Paradise; and now Messer Domeneddio took her at her word. For a few days after his return she was able to enjoy Francesco's company; but then he was off again to Pisa to see about the new warehouse he wished to open there; and only a few days after his departure bad news followed him. "Monna Piera is ill," wrote his factor, Monte d'Andrea, on January 29, "methinks with a rheum. I have been to her, offering money; she says she will take it when she needs it."

A postscript two days later said that she had made her will. "She leaves you her house [which Francesco had given her],

[4] Paolo da Certaldo, *Libro di buoni costumi*, para. 96.

with which you are to pay the funeral, and she leaves 4 *lire* to God [for charity]. And she is very ill."

That same evening the end came.

Tonight, between the first bell and midnight, she passed from this life. God, in His grace, receive her in His glory. And this morn we buried her in San Domenico, as she desired. And her burial was honourable, for your family and I, too, resolved to pay her honour, for love of you, thinking you would fain have it so, were you here. All the priests of the city paid her honour, and the bells rang out, and there was a sufficiency of candles, and all that was needful.*

Thus, only a few weeks after Messer Francesco's return to his native land, one of the closest ties that bound him there was severed.

CHAPTER TWO

PRATO AND
THE CLOTH TRADE

"I thank God and ever shall
It is the sheep hath payed for all." [1]

T WAS AN OLD SAYING IN PRATO THAT IF A MAN cared to look beneath the foundation of the city walls he would find there a tuft of wool. Certainly from the twelfth century until the present day the city's fortunes have waxed and waned with the cloth trade, although the wide valley in which the city lies is not a sheep-farming district and the wool of the sheep in the neighbouring hills of the Pistoiese is, like their pastures, both coarse and poor. Possibly the first impulse towards the manufacture of cloth came from the Longobardi of Lucca by whom, according to one tradition, the little *corte* of Borgo al Cornio was founded on the site where Prato now stands, for Lucca was the Tuscan city in which the *Arte della Lana* first flourished.[2] Perhaps, too, a reason may be found in the presence close by, on Monteferrato, of a very dark slimy earth, suitable for fulling.

[1] Motto in the window of the new house built by a rich English stapler, John Barton of Holme.

[2] A manuscript in Lucca, containing instructions for dyeing cloth, dates from the seventh century.

35

What is certain is that in 1108, only seventy years after the first known reference to the *"terra di Prato,"* there was already a fulling-mill on the banks of the River Bisenzio—a mill fifty-six years older than the oldest one in Florence.[3]

At this time the little town consisted of two main groups of buildings: one clustering round the old fortified court of the Borgo al Cornio, the other round a wide meadow—*prato*—from which the town got its name. But the city's main characteristic, which it has retained until this day and which probably contributed to the development of its chief trade, was its great abundance of water. In the twelfth century the waters of the Bisenzio were made to flow through the city in a network of little canals, providing water for its fulling-mills and dyeing-establishments,[4] and the narrow streets already bore the names which still reveal the trade of their inhabitants: *Via dei Lanaiuoli* (wool merchants), *dei Cimatori* (clippers), *dei Tintori* (dyers), and close beside them (as was always the case wherever ready money was likely to be required) the *Via dei Giudei*. Little groups of skilled wool-workers from Verona and Lombardy settled in Prato, bringing with them—as the Umiliati did in Florence—the secrets of their craft.[5] The *panno pratese* became a recognized type of cloth, like the Florentine or the Lombard. And by the beginning of the fourteenth century the *Arte di Calimala*—the guild of cloth-finishers—also had a street of its own, beside which, on the banks of the Bisenzio, a market-place was built, the *piazza di Mercatale*, and here great wooden frames for stretching and dyeing cloth were set up—*i tiratoi dell'arte*. The square was

[3] *Statuti dell'Arte della Lana di Prato* (fourteenth to seventeenth century), p. 1. The statutes of the fullers of Prato in 1285, the *Breve dei Gualchieri*, are still preserved in the Archivio di Stato, Florence.

[4] Repetti, *Dizionario geografico-fisico-storico della Toscana*, vol. IV, p. 654. The name of one of the gateways of the first circle of the city walls, *Capo di Ponte* (recorded in 1105), shows that there was already a bridge there then, over one of these canals.

[5] A document exonerating from taxes any *Veronesi* or *Lombardi* who had settled in Prato as wool-workers or dyers testifies to their presence there in 1243, and possibly sooner. *Statuti dell'Arte della Lana di Prato*, Introduction, p. 3.

surrounded by arched porticoes and little shops, in which cloth and wool were displayed and sold—and on September 8—the feast-day of the *Madonna della Cintola* —a great annual fair was held, which brought wool and cloth merchants to Prato from all over Europe. The *Arte della Lana* built its hall in the main square, beside the church of its patron saint, S. Giovanni, whose lamb, as in Florence, was the wool merchants' emblem; and when, a few years before Francesco di Marco's birth, the city's oldest church, the Pieve di S. Stefano, was rebuilt, the new ceiling above the choir was erected at the guild's expense, and decorated with its shield.

The rich, well-watered lands of the Pratese territory and its flourishing trade were viewed with envy by both its powerful neighbours, the Priors of Florence and the Bishop of Pistoia. But until the end of the thirteenth century Prato succeeded in maintaining her independence, and was still, at the very doors of Florence, a free and self-governing little Commune.

However, at the beginning of the century in which Francesco was born, this state of affairs came to an end. "The history of Prato in the first half of the *trecento*," writes Professor Nicastro, "is that of a slow death-struggle, the death of freedom." [6] The century began with the occupation by the Florentines of the city's ancient fortress, *"il castello dell'imperatore"*—on the pretext of "safeguarding it for the Commune of Prato"; and thenceforth in fact, if not yet in law, the smaller city came under the rule of the greater one. The Pratesi were obliged to fortify their city at the behest of Florence, though at their own expense; to accept officials appointed by the Florentine Priors; to send men, arms, and money for Florentine wars; to open their gates, without exacting a toll, to Florentine goods; and, moreover, they were largely dependent, for the sale of their own wares, on the merchants of the larger city. The cloth of Prato was largely sold in Florence, or, further afield, by Florentine merchants; and it was

[6] Nicastro, *Sulla storia di Prato dalle origini alla metà del secolo XIX*, p. 115.

on Florence and Pistoia that Prato depended for the purchase of salt.

In 1312—the year of the descent into Italy of Henry of Luxemburg—the Pratesi, in the hope of finding a stronger protector, placed themselves under the protection of the head of the Guelph party in Italy, Robert of Anjou, King of Naples—but only to find that they had acquired an even harder master. And in 1351, after the death of King Robert, his grand-daughter and heir, Queen Joanna—at the instance of her Grand Chamberlain, the Florentine merchant Niccolò Acciaiuoli—sold the whole city and territory of Prato to Florence, for the paltry sum of 17,500 florins. Even before this purchase had taken place, however, Florence had built a new fortress at the Porta S. Marco, joining it to the old one with a double row of walls, the *cassero*, from which they could dominate the city. It was while its walls were rising that Francesco di Marco set off for Avignon—and when, thirty years later, he returned, it was to find his fellow citizens completely subject to Florentine laws and Florentine taxes, while their cloth industry was in danger of being swallowed up by that of their rich neighbour. Moreover, especial privileges had been offered by the Florentines (who were short of skilled artisans) to the Pratesi, and many of the most enterprising were beginning to move their shops and looms to the larger town.

What did Francesco see when he rode down the pass over the Pistoiese hills and caught a first glimpse, after thirty years in Avignon, of his native city? First he saw two great castles—the old and the new.[7] They were united by the double row of fortified walls which encircled the city—the *cerchia antica* of the twelfth century and the new fortifications of the Florentines— broken by watch-towers and by the great stone gateways after which the various quarters of the town were named: Porta Fuia, S. Trinità, Gualdimare, S. Giovanni, Serraglio, and Capo di Ponte. In the centre of the town the ancient Pieve of S. Stefano, com-

[7] Each fortress was under the command of its own captain, who was forbidden ever to leave it and who had to set down, on his appointment, a bail of no less than 10,000 florins. Nicastro, *Storia di Prato*, p. 143.

The Cloth Market

MATRICULA SOCIETATIS DRAPERIORUM

pleted and adorned at the beginning of the century according to the design of the celebrated Giovanni Pisano, stood before a square which still preserved the irregular shape of the original *prato;* close by stood the Palazzo Pretorio, where the Priors sat in council; and several other fine churches, monasteries, and hospices cared for the souls and bodies of the faithful.

In spite of those noble public buildings, however, the general impression was not of a great town, but rather of a fortified village, an overgrown *castello:* poor little brick or wooden houses in dark, narrow streets were intersected by green canals with fulling-mills or dyeing-sheds upon their banks, while nearly half the space within the walls was given up to orchards and gardens. The list of Datini's possessions in Prato, indeed, twenty years after his return, shows that—in addition to his own fine garden of orange trees and pomegranates—almost every one of the twenty smaller houses he owned had an *orto* or *orticino.* One of them possessed "a court with a few apple trees," another a threshing-floor, yet another "a court with a canal, to make wine," and yet another "a court and four big orange trees and a pergola." * Everywhere the country thrust its tendrils into the town: little square plots of green onions and leeks and beans grew at the foot of the battlements and in the spaces between the city walls; a pergola of vines shaded the tavern door; window-sills and stairways were adorned with pots of sage, mint, and parsley, of basil and rosemary. Every day, too, country produce poured in by the city gates (though not without paying heavy tolls). Long trains of mules and donkeys carried in sacks of wheat, barley, and oats, and flour from the water-mills of the Commune. Peasant women brought in their baskets of vegetables and fruit, fishermen their buckets of carp or tench from the river, or eels from the shallow ponds. And there was hardly a stout friar or shrivelled nun who passed through the city gates without a trussed fowl or a handful of beans, well concealed in wide sleeves or ample habit, to evade the toll. In the autumn the pungent smell of must, arising from the cellars, filled the whole street, and a little later on, when the olives had been gathered, the acrid odour of newly made oil.

The aspect of the private houses, too, contrasted greatly with that of the churches and public buildings. Many were still of wood, and even those of brick had few architectural pretensions —their chief features being generally a steep outer staircase and, next to the street door, a low, wide arch which let the light into the owner's shop. Moreover—since it was only recently that it had been made lawful for two adjacent houses to have a party wall—a small open space between the houses (called a *quintana*) was often used as a rubbish heap or latrine, giving forth such a stench that the phrase "to stink like a *quintana*" became proverbial. The principal streets had been paved at the expense of the families which lived there, but they were still, like those of Siena and Florence, so narrow that Sacchetti told the tale of a young nobleman—"a haughty youth of scant courtesy"—who, when he rode through the city with his feet stuck out in his stirrups, took up so much of the street that the passers-by were perforce obliged to polish the points of his shoes! [8]

Within these narrow streets (as, indeed, in many a little Italian town today) life was lived almost entirely in public. All the shops were open to the street; the cobbler, saddler, tailor, goldsmith, barber plied their trades in the public eye; the weaver sat in a doorway with her loom. Before the butcher's shop a sheep's throat was cut in the open street while the purchaser stood by, bargaining for chops; the fruiterers and fishmongers sold their wares at open booths (but at nightfall the Commune's officials saw to it that no stale fish should be sold next day by scattering all that was left on the ground, to be scrambled for by the poor). Often cooked foods, too, could be bought at these booths: roast pigeons and geese and partridges (though these were only for the rich), and many fish, especially roach, tench, and eels. On market-days there was a succulent roast pig on a spit, with a spray of rosemary in its mouth. Before the communal oven the baker drew out his hot loaves, marked with the Commune's stamp

[8] Sacchetti, *Novelle*, CXIV.

to show that a tax for the use of the oven had been paid. The tanner spread out his skins in the street to dry—but not, by statute, too near any spring or fountain; the tenterers hung up their cloths in the market-square. In the canals the fullers and dyers washed their cloth and wool—except during the vintage, when all the water was needed for wine-making—though the statutes obliged them to stretch a rake across the canal, so that the wool should not clog the watercourses. The town crier, *il banditore*, hurried from one street corner to the next, to spread the day's news: births and weddings and deaths, bankruptcies and emancipations, lists of lost property and lost cattle, even applications for wet-nurses—while more important official news was imparted by three trumpeters on horseback, dressed in the colours of the Commune, who blew a treble blast on their trumpets before announcing the sentences of the courts of law—banishments and fines, and sometimes executions. And such penalties of course also became a public show: thieves and prostitutes were birched naked through the streets, and forgers or heretics dragged at the cart's tail, to be burned alive in the open square.[9]

Always there was something to gape at—for the city's festivals, too, all took place in public. The great *loggie*, indeed, which now were added to some of the richer houses (one of the first was that of Francesco's house) were built precisely for this purpose: so that each private festivity could be enjoyed by the whole town. At a wedding the bride and bridegroom walked in procession through the city, attended by their relatives and friends, and sometimes also by trumpeters, mountebanks, and strolling players, to the church steps where the notary was waiting to read aloud in public the marriage contract. A funeral, too, was hardly a less fine show. For the dead man—not concealed in his coffin, but dressed in his best and borne on the shoulders of his friends—would be carried at dusk through the town, while the torches cast a flickering light in the dark, narrow streets, and

[9] This was the punishment awarded, too, to a man who tried to steal the Virgin's holy relic, her girdle, from her own chapel in the Duomo. Nicastro, op. cit., p. 132.

the cowled and veiled members of the confraternities walked behind him, chanting hymns and prayers.

If a member of one of the guilds was raised to knighthood, that ceremony, too, took place out of doors, and the subsequent feasting—to which each member of the guild contributed his share—sometimes lasted as much as a week. And though we have no record in Prato of an artisans' *"brigata di divertimento,"* such as there was at San Frediano in Florence, we do know that each of the city's quarters had its own committee, which organized mock battles in the squares, and that Francesco di Marco, soon after his return, was appointed one of the captains of Porta Fuia.[1] The parchment still remains, containing the formal challenge sent by the "unafraid fighters" (*non-paurosi combattenti*) of Porta S. Trinità, with their glove, to "the noble and illustrious Messer Piero de' Rinaldeschi and the famous and virtuous merchant Francesco di Marco, Master of the Battle of the Men of Porta Fuia," asking them to choose twenty or thirty men of their Porta "to give proof of their strength and valour . . . against whom we are prepared to fight, in the customary form of battle." * "One saw skirmishes and advances, retreats and ambuscades, tricks and feints fit for children, which gave great pleasure and delight, and castles were built like fortresses, defended with moats, towers and a bastion—and they were attacked by a veritable army encamped around them . . . and men of note came to see it."

There were also other, more brutal sports, even more pleasing to the crowd. In one of the squares a pig was enclosed in a wide pen and beaten to death by armed men as he ran squealing from one to the other, "among the loud laughter of those present"; in another, a live cat was nailed to a post and killed, in spite of her desperate clawing and biting, by men who, with shorn heads and

---

[1] These mock battles—of which we find the first mention in Ravenna in 692—were popular in every medieval town, but in some cities (notably Perugia and Siena) were forbidden in the second half of the thirteenth century. Their traces still survive in the *Gioco del Ponte* of Pisa and the *Gioco del Saracino* of Arezzo.

bound hands, drove the life out of her by buffeting her with their heads, "to the sound of trumpets." [2]

These, with the accompanying jests and boasts, bleeding backs and broken heads, were rare pleasures. But every day there were the gatherings of muleteers and women by the city fountains and washing-troughs, with long hours of chatter and laughter intermingled with the clap-clap of the wet cloth on the stones. And on summer evenings the men would sit for hours on the long stone benches beneath the Palazzo Pretorio—a custom that gave rise to a new verb, *pancheggiare* (from *panca*, a bench)— while the gossip of the town ran rife. Every man's business was also his neighbour's—and, most of all, the concerns of such a man as Francesco di Marco! When one of his ships went down off the Catalonian coast, or his maid-servant gave birth to a child who, it was whispered, was Francesco's own, or Messer Filippo Corsini of Florence came to stay, the whole city knew of it.

The whole city—but what, indeed, did it amount to? Prato in the fourteenth century appears to have numbered some 12,000 souls within the walls—with about 10,000 more living in the forty-eight villages and hamlets of the surrounding territory.[3] But though, by the standards of the time, a fair-sized city, it was a little world. The few Pratesi who had distinguished themselves in law and letters and the Church, had left their native city for a wider field: both Cardinal Niccolò da Prato and the greater humanist scholar Convenevole, whom Petrarch was proud to call his master, spent the greater part of their lives in Avignon. At the time of Francesco's return the most able young man in Prato was a young jurist, Messer Gimignano Inghirami, who later on attained such distinction that the phrase "*sentenza di Gimignano*" became synonymous with one against which there was no appeal;

---

[2] Giovanni Miniati da Prato, *Narrazione e disegno della terra di Prato* (1594), pp. 45-7. The writer is describing the sports of an earlier age, though with a gusto which shows that they were still popular.

[3] This figure—which is of course only approximate—has been inferred by local historians from their knowledge that at the beginning of the fourteenth century the city contained 3,000 houses.

but he, too, soon went off to the law-courts of Paris, Bologna, and Rome. For the rest, the city to which Francesco returned held one young captain of fortune, Bartolomeo Boccanera (who met a violent death in 1397, beneath the walls of Arezzo); one eccentric old writer and architect, Giovanni di Gherardo; a handful of lawyers, notaries, and doctors; and several flourishing religious congregations.

But the vast majority of the population, then as now, consisted of merchants and craftsmen. Every citizen, as he reached manhood, enrolled himself—if he could pay the entrance tax of 5 *soldi*—in one of the city's fifteen guilds, swearing to submit to its laws and to come to the assistance of his fellow craftsmen. Through the guilds, and only through them, could a man hope either to share in ruling the city or to make his fortune: to be fully a citizen you had to belong to a guild.[4] And no other could rival, in numbers or in riches, the cloth guild, the *Arte della Lana*.

This, then, was the chief characteristic of Prato in the *trecento*: it was a city in which rich and poor were welded together by the bond of a common trade. From this arose, not an equality of fortune (for a wide gulf lay between the rich *lanaiuolo* and the poor spinner or weaver), but a complete identity of interests and a great familiarity in daily intercourse. The humblest spinner called the rich *lanaiuolo* by his Christian name; the master dyer worked at the vat beside his apprentice; and all were equally subject to the rules of their guild.

The "Book of Privileges" of the *Arte della Lana* of Prato, which contained a list of "all documents resulting in any direct or indirect benefit to the Guild," began with a vital concession: the right granted to them in 1351, when Prato came under the domination of Florence, to maintain their independence in the

---

[4] The guilds of Prato were the following: Judges and Notaries, Wool Merchants, Wool-workers, Money changers and Goldsmiths, Apothecaries (which included the doctors), Blacksmiths, Cobblers, Butchers, Grocers, Vintners, Tailors, Bakers, Millers, Barbers, and Carpenters.

exercise of their craft.[5] The guild's statutes—which, despite their independence, were closely modelled on those of the *Arte della Lana* of Florence—were certainly quite as vital to the city's general welfare as the Commune's laws, and indeed, after the first years of the *trecento*, the guild's four consuls were no longer nominated by its own members, but by the city council.[6] The duties of these consuls—who took a solemn vow of honesty and fidelity on assuming their office—included the imposition of fines on anyone who broke the guild's rules, the settlement of quarrels between its members, and the recovery of stolen goods. They held their inquiries and issued their sentences twice a week in the guild's main hall. The other officials of the guild were a treasurer, a notary, several brokers, four "measurers," and several "appraisers of damages." The brokers were entrusted with the purchase and sale of the guild's cloth; the measurers were responsible for the correct measuring of the cloth on official yard-sticks; and the appraisers looked into complaints about ill-woven or ill-dyed cloth or yarn, or wool that was not up to sample. When a foreign merchant came to Prato to buy cloth, the whole procedure was mapped out for him. He could not buy from any firm he pleased, but was obliged first to visit the consuls. Then, in their presence, he drew out of a bowl the name of a broker, who took him to make his purchase and, when the transaction was completed, wrote down the quantity, price, and colour of the cloth and marked it with the guild's stamp.[7]

Special clauses in the statutes referred to each of the types of craftsmen employed in the various processes of the trade: first came the sorters, washers, pickers, and dyers of wool; next the

[5] *Riforma della terra di Prato deliberata nei Consigli della Repubblica di Firenze*, February 28, 1351. Printed by R. Piattoli, "Documenti per la Storia dell'Arte della Lana di Prato," in *Arch. Stor. Pratese*, A. XXXVIII, 1952, pp. 6–7.

[6] *Statuti dell'Arte della Lana di Prato*, a cura di R. Piattoli e R. Nuti, drawn up between 1315 and 1320, with a few alterations and additions in 1333 and 1371.

[7] *Statuti* VIII, X, XIV, XV, XVIII, XIX, XX, and XXI.

wool-combers, who also greased the wool and placed it on the distaffs for spinning; then the carders and spinners and the men who measured off the warp; and finally the weavers. Last of all came the various stages of finishing the cloth, each with its own specialized workmen: burling, scouring, fulling, tentering, teaseling, clipping, dyeing, then napping and shearing a second time, pressing, and, at last, folding for packing.[8]

In the early days of the *Arte della Lana*, in Prato as in Florence, many of these craftsmen had been independent—especially the weavers, carders, spinners, and dyers—and there had also been some small entrepreneurs, the *lanivendoli* (wool-sellers), who acted as intermediaries between the merchants and the craftsmen, buying up the raw wool and selling it to the *lanaiuolo* (wool-merchant). At that time, too, there were independent dealers in yarn, the *stamaiuoli*, who bought this wool from the merchants, made it into yarn, and sold it back to them again. But by Francesco's time all these minor branches of the trade had become absorbed by the *Arte della Lana*. The trade was now run on completely capitalistic lines: the *lanaiuolo* had become an entrepreneur on a big scale who employed (sometimes in partnership with other members of his family) a great many different kinds of craftsmen. The poorest and least independent (since they did not even possess the tools of their trade) were the washers and carders—known by the clogs they wore in the wash-houses and sheds as *I Ciompi*. Immediately above them, and enjoying at least a partial independence, were the spinners, warpers, and weavers (almost all of them women), most of whom worked at home at their own distaffs, warps, and looms—though even upon these, great economic and moral pressure was sometimes brought to bear. The dyers, too, who at first had had a guild of their own, had been gradually absorbed into the cloth guild and were subject to its rules. Only the finishers (fullers, clippers, menders,

[8] Cf. F. Edler, "Steps in the Manufacture of Woollen Cloth in Italy" in *Glossary of Medieval Terms of Business*, pp. 324-9.

and folders) who had their own workshops and tools still retained a partial independence.

But in the last resort it was always the capitalist *lanaiuolo* who, by means of the guild's statutes, controlled the cloth production —and, consequently, the lives of all the people engaged in it. How detailed and meticulous this control was is plainly shown by the guild's statutes. Some craftsmen—notably the fullers and folders—were required to put down bail before the cloth was given them, while the dyers (since they showed dangerous tendencies to independence) were bound by a number of special precautions: they swore an oath of fidelity and obedience to the consuls, bound themselves to bring back all the cloth and yarn entrusted to them and never to dye any stuffs except the guild's, and were even told precisely what dyes they might use, and which sorts of cloth might be dyed with woad or black. Even the type of cover for their vats was regulated.

A great many of the statutes dealt with the "penalties" incurred by those who infringed the guild's rules: such as a man who took a foreigner (i.e., someone who was not a Pratese) as a partner or even employed one in his workshop, any member of the guild who damaged another, any merchant who went back on his bargain, or, among the craftsmen, "a weaver who weaves linen that is not supple," a workman who made cloth on his own account, a tenterer who did not keep his cloth well taut, or an unpunctual workman. The men in the sheds or wash-houses were bound to be there "before the third stroke of the bell," under penalty of a fine of 5 *soldi*—and any man who was dismissed was refused employment by any other member of the guild.

Finally, the statutes firmly enforced the guild's religious duties. Feast-days—and how many of them there were! including, of course, the day of St. John the Baptist, the guild's patron—were to be observed not only by abstention from work, but from selling, or even showing, one's goods. And when, at the end of his

47

laborious life, a member of the guild died, all the others were bound—as was the custom in every corporation—to follow him in procession to his last resting-place.[9]

So life unrolled itself in Prato—a society of industrious, God-fearing, law-abiding, thrifty men—and also of men timid and unadventurous both in body and in mind. "I feel," wrote another Pratese who returned there a few years later, after having lived in the wider world of Padua and Ferrara, "as if I had come back into the land of the Philistines. All gladness in life is quenched, and meseems, the men who live here feel shame to be alive." *

It was into this world that, after thirty years in the cosmopolitan, luxurious city of Avignon, Francesco di Marco returned—a man whom the Pratesi remembered only as an ambitious boy of fifteen, but now an established, portly, self-assured merchant with a pretty young wife and a formidable temper. A man whose achievement (by which they meant his riches) the Pratesi at once respected—and whom they never really came to like.

II

We do not know much about Francesco's first month in Prato. He received a warm welcome from Monna Piera and Niccolozzo, as well as from the whole family of his tutor, Piero di Giunta. But the Pratesi, on the whole, kept aloof, as Francesco did from them. He was elected Councillor of the Commune and—a few years later—was appointed as one of the *Gonfalonieri di Giustizia;* but, both in Prato and in Florence, he made it plain that he was not interested in public office, and he took no part in the constant party strife of the town. Moreover, he clearly showed that he did not think much of his fellow citizens, and though he did sometimes lend money to the Commune—on one occasion, 10,000 florins to buy some wheat from Florence *—he was

[9] *Statuti* XXII, XXIII, XXV, XXVI, XXVII, XXVIII, XXXVI, XLI, LI, LIII, LXXXVIII.

quick to complain that his generosity had been received with insufficient gratitude, and thus swiftly destroyed any popularity he had at first enjoyed. "You came back from Avignon," wrote one of his partners, "with a repute as high as ever a man brought back to our city, and were beloved by every faction, and thought to be a man of means. . . . But you must have complained to some man, for he has told one here that you have spoken ill of him. Beware of whom you trust." *

Certainly in one respect Francesco followed this advice: he kept his own counsel about his trade, and never satisfied his neighbours' curiosity about the extent of his fortune. Indeed, except for the fine new house which he had already begun to build before his return, and which was steadily rising before their eyes, he showed few outward signs of prosperity. "He has come back from Avignon," wrote the puzzled tax-collectors of Prato in their report for 1383, "and is said to be rich. Here we see naught of it, save some houses—so, to make no error, we set no value on his property." Three years later Francesco declared his possessions in Prato alone to be worth 3,000 florins—"but what he owns elsewhere," wrote the officials, "may be worth more or less. We know not, but God does!" The common folk of Prato, however, had no doubt about the matter: they called him "*Francesco ricco*." *

His next act confirmed their opinion. While his new walls were still rising, he planted before the house, not a vegetable-plot or orchard, but a pleasure-garden—32 *braccia*¹ by 14—"full of oranges, roses and violets and other lovely flowers." He himself considered later on that this had been "a great piece of folly," for it cost no less than 600 florins. "I would have been wiser to put it into a farm." * Yet it is pleasant to know that—at least once in his life—Francesco spent his money on something that could bring in no profits.

At the foot of the garden stood his new warehouse, also built in the same year, in which he opened his office, painted grass-

¹ See Appendix A.

green and containing several chests, a cupboard, and four writing-desks—one "covered by a carpet" and one "by a black cloth, with a little chest on it in which Francesco keeps his writings." This desk also had on it "two baskets for letters and a bowl for cash." And at the head of one of his new great ledgers, after the customary formula—"In the name of God and of the Virgin Mary and of all the Saints of Paradise, that they may give us grace to do right both for body and soul"—his factor, Monte d'Andrea, wrote out the Ten Commandments.* Not always to be observed, perhaps—but there, at the head of the ledger, they stood.

This became Francesco's central office, in constant correspondence with each of his other branches in Italy and abroad. And soon great bales of foreign ware began to arrive in Prato: not only the fine Spanish or Provençal wool so badly needed for the cloth industry, with alum, soap and gall-nuts, Flemish madder and Lombard woad, but also linen from France and Germany and leather of all kinds—buffalo-hides and sheep-hides from Pisa, and fine white skins from Córdoba. Soon, too, Francesco began to receive the materials he needed to complete his new house: ultramarine blue and "*azzurro d'Alemagna*" and gold leaf for the use of his painters; painted coffers and curtains to furnish his rooms; and velvets, samites, and brocades for Monna Margherita's clothes and his own. Perhaps the most impressive of all, to his fellow citizens, were the rare foods and wines: cheeses from Pisa, Sardinia, and Sicily, barrels of tunny-fish, oranges and dates from Catalonia; besides sugar, pepper, and all sorts of spices—cassia, clove, ginger, and saffron. And sometimes, too, a crate of exotic creatures for the new garden would be unpacked before their startled eyes—"a monkey, a porcupine in a cage, two peacocks (male and female) and a sea-gull." *

It was natural that, in a city whose fortune depended upon the making of cloth, Datini should have promptly associated himself with this industry. Before doing so, he carried out a plan he had already formed before leaving Avignon: he made sure of his trading-channels by opening a branch in Pisa, so as to be able to import his wools and dyes from abroad. Then in 1383 he was formally enrolled in the *Arte della Lana* and entered into partnership with the cloth-maker Piero di Giunta, his old tutor, and with a distant kinsman, Francesco di Matteo Bellandi. In the following spring he formed another company for *L'Arte della Tinta* with Piero's son, Niccolò, a master dyer, and ten years later (after Piero's death) entered into partnership with Niccolò's son, Agnolo. The understanding was that Datini was to supply both the foreign wool and the rough cloth which needed "finishing," while the Pratesi undertook "to work the stuffs for him and for ourselves." *

The company to which he brought his capital was a modest family business, in which the grandfather and grandson were the *lanaiuoli* and Niccolò the dyer; they sold their cloth in a little shop in Florence which Niccolò had opened a few years before. "Our shop," Piero had written to Francesco before his return, "is held to be one of the best wool-shops in Florence and there is no dyer so beloved by all the merchants as your Niccolò. He has begun well—a good merchant and a good dyer in woad and every other colour."

What they lacked, like most other firms in Prato, was capital. "I have 300 florins in the wool and dyeing," Piero had written in 1378, and had added that if only he could raise a little more capital he would do well, since the profits were high. "We make our own coloured cloth at various prices, some at 2 florins a rod, and some at 1½. I reckon they cost us 12 to 16 florins each [i.e., for each piece of cloth] and we make a profit on each of 6 to 8 florins" (i.e., of 50 per cent).*

The firm was run along the traditional lines which we have already described: the *lanaiuolo* buying the wool, which he then distributed to the various types of workmen, while Niccolò saw to the dyeing. The names of the men who worked with him are written down at the beginning of one of the firm's ledgers: "Here below we shall write down all the fullers and dyers and every other person who will full or dye the stuffs given by us, Francesco di Marco and Piero di Giunta and Francesco di Matteo Bellandi, partners in the *Arte della Lana*, beginning on August 21, 1384." *

And every transaction—so the scrivener affirmed—would be carried out "in the name of God and of profit."

That Niccolò himself actually worked with the other dyers, turning over the woollen cloth with poles in a large circular vat, is shown by a description in one of his letters of an explosion of this vat, in which he and five others only narrowly escaped being scalded. But the man who was feeding the fire was badly hurt— "so that for two months he can do nothing, and he has nothing, and the cauldron is broken."

Niccolò was known as a *tintore di guado* (woad) because he was a master dyer who used chiefly woad and indigo. Woad was cultivated at the time in certain parts of Tuscany, notably the Val Tiberina, but not apparently in quantities sufficient to meet the demand, for in 1385 Niccolò was asking Francesco's branch in Pisa to get him some from Genoa, "for there will be a great scarcity, and some cloth-makers have come here from Florence, asking me to dye for them." A later letter in the same year added: "I have no more woad, save that we bought, and can work no more, except you send me some." Later still, in 1388, he wrote that he would go himself to Lombardy, "or whereso-ever woad is grown," and complained about some he had received from Bologna, saying that the woad from Genoa was "more supple." *

Woad was used not only for dyeing blue (in particular, the best deep blue called *perse*) but as a foundation for other colours; madder (*robbia*) served for a tomato red, while the two together produced the various shades of dark red and purple so often seen in medieval stuffs: violet, "sanguine" (blood red), and burnet (almost black). But the colours admired above all others were the reds obtained with the rarer red dyes—brazil, vermilion, and, above all, *grana* (grain), the brilliant and lasting dye obtained

52

from the small grain-like Mediterranean insect *coccus ilicis*.[2] This was mostly used for the fine cloth called scarlet; so that gradually the name of the cloth came to be applied to the colour itself. Yet other dyes in common use were the lichen called *oricello* (orchil), which Francesco imported from Majorca, and saffron, which at that time was grown near San Gimignano in the Val d'Elsa and in the Abruzzi, but which Francesco also imported from Catalonia. Lotus, also mentioned in the company's books, was used only for cheaper stuffs, for local consumption. And finally, through Francesco's branch in Genoa, the company was able to import from the Black Sea alum, the indispensable mordant for fixing the dyes.

The greatest advantage, however, derived from Francesco's partnership was that it was now possible to import foreign wools. The coarse local wool called *romagnolo* was used only for the rough undyed cloth worn by the poor, *bigella*, the finer cloth being made either with the Spanish, African, or Minorcan wool generally called *lana di garbo*[3] or *di San Matteo* or with English wool. But it was only the international merchants, whose varied trade enabled them to command comparatively cheap and swift transportation, who could afford to import this foreign raw material and who could subsequently dispose of the finished cloth in foreign markets. It was for this reason that Francesco's entry into the *Arte della Lana* of Prato gave a fresh impulse to his city's industry—for which the Pratesi are grateful to this day.

One of the first entries in the books of the new company records the arrival of "12 bales of wool from Arles in Provence," * but it would seem that at first the Pratesi were rather chary about making too much of the finer cloth, for fear of not

[2] Brazil was derived from the West Indian tree *Cæsalpinia sappan*. Vermilion was made with a crystalline substance found on the shores of the Red Sea.
[3] The word *garbo* came from *Algarve*, the southern province of Portugal, from which some of this wool came, but later on the term was applied also to wool from Northwest Africa and Catalonia. San Matteo was a village in Catalonia which became a collecting-centre for Spanish wool.

being able to dispose of it. "I would see how things go," wrote Niccolò in 1385, "before we make cloth with any more wool beside that we have already. If you are pleased with our profits, we will make as much as you please—if not, we will make no more." *

It is plain that Francesco was not an easy man to work with. "I am so much afraid to do what does not please you," wrote Niccolò, "that I would rather give up work entirely, than cause you any displeasure." Moreover, it would appear that even with Francesco's backing, it was difficult to compete with the long-established Florentine *lanaiuoli*. A letter from Niccolò some years later to Datini's company in Barcelona shows the difficulties that small companies had to meet. He wrote to ask whether it would be possible to sell some of his better cloth in Catalonia, because it was no longer possible to dispose of it either in Prato or in Florence, owing to the merciless competition of the Florentine merchants and the high duties. He had sent his correspondent, "by way of Venice," three sample bales of cloth, "pale, unbleached, and of other colours"—and they are of the finest quality, and so well made that perchance even in Florence they would not be better. Now you will see them, if God wills, and tell me your intent." He added that he thought he could make about 100 cloths a year.*

The finest and most expensive wool of all was the English,[4] which came mostly from the Cotswolds (referred to in the Datini papers as "Chondisgualdo")—in particular, from Northleach ("Norleccio") and Burford ("Boriforte"), and from the great abbey lands of Cirencester ("Sirisestri") and Winchester ("Guincestri"). Unlike his great predecessors—the Bardi, Peruzzi, and

---

[4] According to a list of prices of the Prato cloth company, the dearest wool was English wool from Cotswolds, for which the maximum price was 51 *lire a fiorino* for 100 lbs.; next came the *lana di Minorca* at a maximum of 39, 3s., *lana di Majorca*, 25, 30s., *lana francesca*, 22.3.0; *lana di San Matteo*, 21.0.6; *provenzale*, 18, down to the *romagnolo* and *barbaresco*, which varied between 21 and 18 *lire*. Cf. F. Melis, "La formazione dei costi nell'industria laniera alla fine del trecento" in *Economia e storia*, I, p. 36, n. 20.

Frescobaldi—Datini never opened a branch of his own in England nor did he send any of his own men there to buy wool, but depended for this purpose on Tuscan firms already established in London—especially the Guinigi, Mannini, Alberti, Dini, and Caccini—who sent their buyers riding round England to collect wool from the monastic houses or individual farmers, or else to buy it from the local woolmen. Research in the Enrolled Customs and Subsidy Accounts during the years in which Datini was importing English wool (1382–1410) has discovered frequent shipments to Italy by each of these firms, and the constant repetition of the same names, over a period of years, in different combinations, shows the close connection between all these family groups of Italian merchants abroad.[5]

Here is a typical letter to Datini's firm in Florence from Giovanni Orlandini and Neri Vettori & Co. in London, acknowledging one of his orders:

[5] The following firms are mentioned in the Datini papers as sending him wool from England: Gherardo degli Alberti & Co., wool and cloth merchants; Agnolo Cristofano & Co.; Piero Marchi & Co.; Francesco Tornabuoni e Domenico Caccini & Piero Cambrini; Gherardo Davizi; Dino Guinigi & Co.; Fazzino di Giovanni & Co.; Francesco e Giacchetti Dini; Marco Mercati; Francesco Ardinghelli; Francesco di Filippo de' Neri; Luigi and Salvestro Mannini & Co., merchant-bankers; Giovanni Orlandini & Co., Florentine cloth merchants. Shipments from all these firms are mentioned in the lists of the Exchequer Customs Accounts in the Public Record Office during the years that Datini was importing English wool (1380–1410), but we do not know what proportion of these shipments went to him or to other merchants. The names quoted are: Francesco Guinigi (17 shipments in November and December 1380 and 27 shipments in 1381), Pietro Marchi (13 shipments in 1384 and 1385), Agnolo Cristofano (4 shipments together with the Guinigi firm in 1381 and 1390), Antonio Mannini (2 shipments in 1390), Giovanni Dini (6 shipments in 1390), Pietro Mercati (1 shipment in 1390), and Marco Mercati (2 shipments in 1397 and 6 in 1398). In 1404, 2 shipments from Filippo Alberti and Domenico Caccini, in 1410 "shipments of *cloth*" from Gherardo Davizi and Filippo Alberti and one from Gherardo Davizi, Filippo Alberti, and Marino Cristofani. All these shipments were from London or other Thames ports, but there are also some of cloth from Southampton: 2 in 1390 and 2 undated from Neri Vettori, Alamanno Mannini, Gherardo Alberti, and Cecco Cristofano, 2 in 1403 from the same, Marco Mercati, and Domenico Caccini, and 2 in 1403 from Giovanni Vettori and Giovanni Orlandini. Public Record Office: Exchequer L.T.R. Customs and Subsidy Accounts, London and Thames Ports to Gravesend; and Southampton, Wool Subsidy, and Wool Subsidy and Petty Custom.

You say you have writ to Venice to remit us 1000 ducats with which, in the name of God and of profit, you would have us buy Cotswold wool. With God always before us, we will carry out your bidding, which we have well understood. In the next few days our Neri will ride to the Cotswolds and endeavour to purvey a good store for us, and we will tell you when he has come back.

Apparently the firm continued to act as Datini's agents, for two years later there is a letter confirming another order:

We went to the farm and purveyed some very fine, perfect and good wool, at the cost of 11 marks. Please God these countries of ours will be at peace, that trade can flow once more.*

It was, of course, exceedingly important to avoid any delay in buying up the clip. At the beginning of the century the papal tax-collectors who purchased English wool from the great abbeys often reserved the amount of the clip they wanted, even before the sheep were shorn, and this custom apparently still survived in some places, for there is a letter to Datini from Francesco Tornabuoni and Domenico Caccini & Co. of London apologizing for some wool from Cirencester which had proved unsatisfactory by saying that he had been obliged to buy up the clip before seeing it. "For one must buy in advance from all the Abbeys, and especially from this one, which is considered the best." * But apparently other firms waited to buy until the summer fairs, for a letter from Mannini & Co. tells Datini that the best time to buy is around St. John's Day (June 24) "for it is then that the Cotswold fairs are held, and that those who want good produce should purvey it." *

The wool—which was classified as "good," "middle," or "young," was exported either in sacks of shorn and wound wool from the clip or as wool-fells (i.e., sheepskins with the wool still on them, collected after the Martinmas slaying)—240 wool-fells, for purposes of taxation, being considered equal to one sack. The wool was brought in to the great barns of the sleepy Cotswold villages, weighed and valued and packed and corded and sold, after much hard bargaining, to the highest bidder, and was then loaded on pack-horses and brought to London, where it was weighed for custom and subsidy, and shipped off with the next merchantman who set sail for the Mediterranean.*

The amount of English wool which was handled by Datini's branches for the Tuscan market cannot, unfortunately, be estimated precisely. That it was considerable, however, may be deduced from the fact that in a single year—1397—his branch in Genoa alone records the arrival of 38,749 pounds. Not all, however, of the wool he imported was for his own use; the Prato company was too small and the English wool too dear. A small proportion of it was undoubtedly retained by him for his company's workshops in Prato, but what proportion we do not know, since only a single record remains in his books: 1,080 pounds in 1397.* Another, relatively small, proportion was bought on commission or in common with other firms. But by far the greater part was sold by him, as soon as it arrived, to established Florentine *lanaiuoli*.

The years in which Datini was importing English wool were those in which its export was decreasing, while that of English cloth (whether exported by English or alien merchants) was greatly on the increase, and was indeed competing seriously with the cloth-making industries of Flanders and France.[6]

Datini imported to Tuscany not only wool but cloth—which may at first sight seem surprising, since he had a cloth-manufacturing company of his own. It must, however, be remembered that English cloth was not only good, but cheap, since English manufacturers had the great advantage over their Italian or

---

[6] In 1350–60 England had exported an average of 32,000 sacks per annum: in 1390–9, an average of only 19,000, while her cloth-export increased from an average of 5,000 cloths to 35,000. Cf. E. Carus Wilson, *Medieval Merchant Venturers*, pp. xvi–xviii and p. 248.

Flemish competitors of first-rate raw material on the spot, and since the English export tax on cloth was then only about 2 per cent, while that on wool was about 33 per cent. Moreover, fine English cloth seems also already to have been fashionable, for we find Datini (in spite of the *scarlattino* he made in Prato) buying "6 scarlet *berrette*, dyed in England" for his own use. The types of cloth he imported were Essex cloth (*"panni stretti di Sex"*) in various colours, Guildford cloth (*"panni di Guildiforte"*) in various colours, and unbleached cloth (*"panni bianchetti"*) from the Cotswolds and Winchester, while there is also one record of two bales of "Scottish cloth" sent from Bruges to Majorca.*

By English law, all wool exported for the European market was obliged to go first to Calais, where the staple was fixed—the only two exceptions being some wool from the northern counties which might be shipped straight to the Netherlands, and wool for Italy. Some Italian merchants, it is true, continued to purchase English wool in Calais and then either shipped it to Italy from Sluys, or took it across France and the Alps by land. But the Datini records show that none of the firms with which he dealt made use of these routes, but shipped their wool (as was increasingly becoming the custom) the whole way by sea. The great bi-yearly fleet of Venetian galleys generally sailed straight to Italy from Sluys (the harbour of Bruges), only touching England at Sandwich or Dartmouth, while the Genoese or Pisan merchantmen only touched Flemish ports if driven there by storms, but otherwise sailed straight from London or Southampton [7] (called "Antona" or "Suantona") to the "Straits of Marrock" (Morocco). In the Mediterranean, the Genoese ships generally skirted the Catalonian and Provençal coasts, calling at the chief ports, while ships bound for Pisa or Venice called also at

[7] Both London and Southampton are frequently mentioned in the Datini papers, while Sandwich is mentioned only three times (with regard to Venetian galleys bound for Flanders), Dartmouth ("Daramundo") once, and Bristol once. It was not till the second half of the fifteenth century that Bristol began to play a large part in the Mediterranean trade.

Ibiza and Majorca. Some of the cloth and Cornish tin which they carried was disembarked in Spain or Majorca,[8] but the wool all went straight on to Italy—and a large proportion of it for the Tuscan market.

The ships listed in the Customs Accounts as sailing from the Thames ports mostly have English ship-masters (engaged by the Italian merchants), though a few are Venetian or Genoese, while those sailing from Southampton are all Genoese vessels, with Genoese ship-masters. The ship-masters mentioned in the Datini papers are almost all Venetian or Genoese, but there is an occasional Catalonian and also one Englishman.

"This is to advise you," wrote the firm of "Alamanno & Francesco" from London, "that we have chartered, together with Niccolò di Luca and Francesco di Giovanni, ⅓ of a ship made in this country, and it is a noble vessel, and owned by one of the greatest knights in the land. His name is Sir Thomas di Presi [Duplessis?] and he has an English Master, who is a valiant seaman. And the said ship will be accompanied by 50 good men, furnished with arms and cross-bows . . . and it will be in Southampton, on the 5th of November." *

The presence of cross-bowmen was no luxury, especially for ships bound for the Mediterranean, for the constant menace from pirates was by no means confined to Moorish or Saracen ships. In the great Italian sea-republics war by piracy—*la guerra di corsa*—had long been a recognized institution. The word "corsair" carried no stigma, and the seas were full of privateers—Pisan or Genoese, Catalonian or Greek—who, if they chanced to meet an unarmed merchant-man, would attack and capture it, subsequently demanding a fat ransom for the persons and goods on board. Some seas, indeed, were so habitually infested that it was thought prudent not only to provide a cargo ship with guards,

[8] File 664. Giovanni Orlandini & Co. in London, January 31, 1404, inform Francesco di Marco & Co. in Florence of the departure of two "carracks" from Southampton, laden with 1,770 sacks of wool, 339 bales of cloth, and 521 pieces of tin for Majorca.

but to make inquiries beforehand "to discover the position of the corsairs"—and, if necessary, alter the route.[9]

Similar dangers, though for a shorter voyage, attended the ships carrying the wool which Datini imported from the western Mediterranean: the *lana di garbo* and *lana di Minorica*. In Spain the chief collecting-centre was the Catalonian borough of San Matteo, whence the wool was taken to the little port of Peniscola; in the Balearics, Palma di Majorca (then called simply Majorca). The ships generally skirted the Catalonian coast as far as Barcelona, after which some of them would call at the Provençal ports (Nice, Marseilles, Aiguesmortes) before proceeding to Genoa (whence the wool was either sent on by sea to Pisa or overland by Lucca to Florence and Prato), while others sailed straight to Porto Pisano. Subsequently the finished cloth was sent back to the markets of Spain and North Africa by similar routes —except at such times (all too frequent) when Pisa was closed to Florentine trade, or Visconti's Soldiers of Fortune were harrying the Tuscan countryside. Then it was safer, and nearly as cheap, to send the bales from Florence across the Apennines to Bologna and Ferrara, proceeding by river to Venice, and thence down the Adriatic and all the way round the toe of Italy to Majorca.

It is plain that journeys such as these could not be swift ones, and indeed one of the great disadvantages of the cloth trade, especially for a small firm, was the amount of time which necessarily elapsed between the first expenditure of capital and any

[9] The following declaration, signed in Bruges on January 13, 1396, gives a full picture of the cost of chartering an armed ship to carry wool from England to Porto Pisano:

"We, Diamante and Altobianco degli Alberti & Co. declare to you, Niccolò degli Ammannati and Tano di Ghinoffo & Co. . . . that Francesco of Arles and his company chartered storage to Lucca from Luca del Biondo on the three ships that he took last year to Porto Pisano for the wool and cloth which Bernardo di Jacopo loaded on the said ship. . . . And Luca promised that all the goods that the said Bernardo loaded would cost 6 florins a sack for wool and 8 florins a sack for cloth, that is for freight, and besides there would be the customary expenses, according to the Spanish usage, and the cost of 30 bowmen, whom they all agreed would be needful, on board, and the cost of the pilots of Antona [Southampton] and of five guards, who by his consent and that of the other merchants were aboard." Bensa: op. cit., Doc. CIII.

return. A detailed study of the whole process, in one typical instance—from the first order of wool in the Balearics to the final sale of the finished cloth—shows that no less than three and a half years were required to complete the transaction. Its various stages are perhaps worth recording, since they show some of the difficulties that a merchant had to overcome.

The first stage—the wool's voyage from Majorca to the workshops of Prato—took fourteen months. An order was transmitted on November 15, 1394, by Francesco's company in Florence to its branch in Palma di Majorca. In the following May, when the sheep were shorn, an agent was sent to Minorca, who bought 29 sacks of Minorcan wool and wool-fells and chartered a Spanish ship, which, owing to storms, reached Minorca only at the end of July, but then set sail for the port of Peniscola in Catalonia, and thence along the Catalonian coast to Barcelona, where it crossed the open sea to Porto Pisano. As far as Barcelona (which was considered the most perilous part of the journey) the ship was escorted by two others; but from Barcelona to Porto Pisano she sailed alone, so it was thought necessary to place twelve archers on board for her protection. The voyage from Barcelona to Porto Pisano took seven weeks (September 2 to October 22, 1395). From Porto Pisano the wool-fells were sent on to Pisa by land, on mule-back, but the sacks were sent by sea and river. At Pisa the wool was repacked into 39 bales, of which 21 went to a client in Florence and 18 to Francesco's warehouse in Prato, where they arrived on January 14, 1396.

The next stage—which required six months—was turning the wool into cloth. The wool was beaten, picked, greased, washed, combed, carded, placed on the distaff and spun (in this case by ninety-six different peasant women on their farms), then it was measured off the warp and woven, then burled, shorn (while still damp), stretched out to dry, teaseled and shorn again, handed over to the dyers (in this case to be dyed blue), napped and shorn again, and at last pressed and folded—each of these processes requiring a different set of specialized workers. At the end of July six cloths (of about 36 yards each) were ready, and (together with five other cloths, also of Minorcan wool) were packed into two bales, to be sent back for sale, via Majorca, on the markets of Spain or Barbary.

This was, however, one of the occasions when the Tuscan ports were all closed to Florentine trade, so on July 14 the bales set forth on mule-back across the Apennines, via Bologna and Ferrara, to Venice, where they were embarked on a Venetian ship and reached their destination, Palma di Majorca, on September 1. This journey took only seven weeks.

Then the last stage—and not the easiest—began: the sale of the finished product. The market happened to be in a stagnant condition, after an unusually severe outbreak of plague, and, moreover, it appears that the cloth's colours were not liked. All the cloth was sent on to Valencia, and subsequently part of it—which could not be disposed of there—to Barbary; but of this, too, a portion came back to Palma. It was not until the spring of 1398, three and a half years after the ordering of the wool, that they were at last all sold.

And at the end of all this, we may well ask, what return did Francesco and his partners receive? After deducting all the costs —purchase of raw material, packing, transportation, duties, insurance, taxes and tools, manufacture, and sale—the profits came to no more than 8.92 per cent.[1] A small return, indeed, for so great and prolonged an effort! When we consider, moreover, all the imponderable hazards—from shipwreck, piracy, land robbers, dishonest agents, closed ports, pestilence, and deterioration of wares—we may conclude that the medieval draper well deserved his profits!

It need hardly be said that the management of such a firm as

[1] F. Melis, "*La formazione dei costi nell'industria laniera alla fine del trecento*" in *Economia e Storia*, Nos. 1 and 2, 1954. Of the costs, Professor Melis has calculated that 15.24 per cent should be assigned to the purchase of raw material, plus 0.28 per cent for collection and loading. Transportation accounted for only 5.37 per cent, plus 3.51 per cent for packing, 6.08 per cent for insurance, and 0.62 per cent for warehousing. Duties came to the large amount of 10.69 per cent and sales costs to 3.08 per cent. Manufacture came to 40.61 per cent.

this entailed a great deal of very complicated book-keeping, as is testified by the ledgers and account-books of the Archivio Datini. No less than 84 of these have been preserved. Ten of them, from 1395 to 1399, are given up to the accounts of the cloth-making firm of Francesco and Agnolo di Niccolò. They enable us to follow every stage of the process. Some books record the purchase of raw material and tools, others the sales, and yet others the various kinds of workmen employed—noting the name of each, and the amount of wool and other materials assigned to him and returned, while there is also an account-book for petty cash, and one devoted to salaries, loans, etc. Finally, there is the firm's main account-book, which summarizes the costs of each separate process and records the final cost of each piece of cloth, from the spinning of the wool to the final pressing and folding of the finished cloth.*

It is possible that a realization of the slow and small profits of cloth-making, as compared to most of his other enterprises, discouraged Datini from taking any larger part in this industry. His contribution to it, as we have seen, was some capital and the good English and Spanish wool which his money bought. But the management of the business remained entirely in the hands of his partners, and after the death from the plague of both Niccolò di Giunta and Francesco Bellandi in 1400 (the business passing into the hands of Niccolò's son, Agnolo) the amount of wool which Datini bought for the company gradually diminished— though he continued to import considerable quantities of foreign wool on behalf of other merchants. In one year (1402), indeed, the whole amount he bought in England, 11,566 pounds, was immediately sold to Florentine *lanaiuoli.**

Long before this, however, Prato had become too small for Francesco. Florence—a town as rich, busy, and open to enterprise as Avignon itself—was only fifteen miles away. By 1386— four years after his return to Tuscany—Datini had made his decision: he would build his fine house and keep his wife in Prato, but would start trading again in Florence.

CHAPTER THREE

TRADE AT
HOME AND ABROAD

"Believe me, sir, had I such venture forth,
The better part of my affections would
Be with my hopes abroad. I should be still
Plucking the grass to know where sits the wind,
Peering in maps for ports, and piers, and roads;
And every object that might make me fear
Misfortune to my ventures, out of doubt
Would make me sad."

SHAKESPEARE, *The Merchant of Venice*, I, i

HEN, IN THE SPRING OF 1386, FRANCESCO DI MARCO decided to move to Florence and establish himself there, his decision was partly due to the fact that this city had just come under the rule of a few powerful families—rich bankers, merchants, and professional men—whose laws he thought likely to be favourable to trade. Their rise followed upon a long period of social and economic trouble. In the first third of the century Florentine trade had reached a zenith of prosperity, but this had been followed, for a period of over forty years, by a long series of calamities. The bankruptcy, between 1343 and 1376, of the greatest Florentine banking-houses, the Peruzzi, Acciaiuoli, and Bardi—largely caused by the default of their chief debtor, Edward III of England—had resulted in the collapse of almost every smaller trading- and banking-company in Florence. Abroad, Flemish cloth had begun to rival that of the *Arte della Lana*, French *"lettres de foire"* enjoyed as good credit as Italian *"lettere di cambio,"* Catalan sea-captains and merchants were successfully competing with Italians in the Levant. At home, the brief tyranny of the French soldier of fortune, the Duke of Athens, called in by the magnates of Florence to command their troops against Pisa, had ended ignominiously in his banishment. Then came the Black Death of 1348, carrying off about one third of the population. Among the survivors, according to the unanimous accounts of contemporary chroniclers, the rich had lost their taste for enterprise and the poor for hard work; labour became scarce and dear; trade languished; the fields remained untilled.[1]

Moreover, year after year, the scanty harvests were plundered and destroyed by the recurrent passage through Tuscany of the Free Companies, who, on whatever side they might be fighting, left destruction behind them wherever they went. The Priors attempted to replenish the city exchequers—further depleted by a succession of minor wars—by levying exorbitant taxes, increasing the discontent of the rich and the misery of the poor. Moreover, the old struggle between Guelph and Ghibelline and between the major and the lesser guilds were further complicated

---

[1] "Men surrendered themselves to a most shameful and disordered life, such as they had not led before. For roaming in idleness they gave themselves up to the pleasures of gluttony, in banquets and taverns, delighting in delicate viands and amusements, giving way to an unbridled lust, and discovering strange and unfamiliar fashions for their raiment, and unseemly manners. . . . And the poor folk, because of the abundance of all, would work no more at their old trades . . . and servants and vile women wore the beautiful fine garments of honorable dead women." M. Villani, *Cronaca*, vol. I, chap. 1.

and intensified by the emergence of the class which in every crisis had suffered most, since its members never had more than a bare margin between them and starvation—the *popolo minuto*.

In 1368 a widespread prophecy—which perhaps came from one of the Franciscan *Fraticelli*—spoke of a day when "the worms of the earth will most cruelly devour the lions, leopards and wolves; and the blackbirds and small fowl swallow up the greedy vultures. And at the same time the common and little folk will destroy all tyrants and false traitors. . . . And there will be great famine and pestilence, wherefrom some evil folk will die, and the churches will be despoiled of all their temporal goods." [2]

Such sayings—at first only whispered by a few, but gradually spoken louder and spreading further—indicate the gradual destruction of an idea which had supported the whole economic structure of the preceding two centuries: a blind respect for authority and, in particular, for that of the guilds. The statutes of the guilds—so they had always affirmed—reflected God's will; and this belief was so widespread that in 1333 the consuls of the cloth guild could even persuade the Bishops of Florence and Fiesole to hold a threat of excommunication over any poor spinners who failed to carry out their orders. [3]

But as, during the absence of the Popes in Avignon, the corruption and weakness of the Church increased and in many cities the temporal power of their Vicars was overthrown, the authority of the guilds, too, began to decline. The workers were no longer wholly docile: they began to form associations of their own, they protested and rioted. In 1343, during one of their riots, twenty-two *palazzi* and warehouses of the Bardi were sacked, causing damage to the value of 60,000 florins, and in 1360 a similar insurrection was led, among others, by Margherita Datini's father, Domenico Bandini, who was executed as a rebel.

[2] "*Diario di anonimo fiorentino*" in *Documenti di storia italiana*, ed. by *R. Deputazione di Storia Patria per le provincie toscane*. The writer was a Florentine working-man of the second half of the *trecento*.

[3] Rodolico, *La democrazia fiorentina nel suo tramonto*, p. 55.

Finally in 1378—four years before Datini's return to Tuscany —the general discontent took shape in the famous insurrection of *I Ciompi* (so called from the name given to the lowest class of the wool-workers, who took the chief part in it). "Down with the traitors who allow us to starve!" they cried as they rioted before the palace of the *Signoria*, demanding the right to form their own guilds, and a guarantee of a minimum yearly output of 24,000 pieces (though even this was only one third of the production in 1338). Three new guilds were formed—the Dyers, the Doublet-makers, and the *Ciompi*—who styled themselves the Guilds of God's People (*le Arti del popolo di Dio*); and though the insurrection was quelled with swift and merciless reprisals, two of these guilds continued to form part, for over three years, of a coalition government—the most genuinely "democratic" that Florence had ever known. It did not, however, succeed— partly because many of the rich merchants shut down their workshops—in restoring the prosperity of trade, and a counter-revolution, in 1382, restored to the full the power of the *popolo grasso*.

Thus when Datini decided to move to Florence, it was to a city governed by a small, reactionary oligarchy, which was to remain in power for the next forty-two years. But though, under this rule, trade revived, the events of the previous half-century were not easily forgotten. Well did Datini and his fellow merchants know that the social unrest which had stirred up the insurrection of the *Ciompi* was not confined to Tuscany alone. Three years later Bonaccorso Pitti was writing home to describe a similar insurrection in Paris, while in the same year the streets of London were filled with rioting peasants singing: "When Adam delved and Eve span, who was then the gentleman?" Moreover, all over Europe other hazards complicated and slowed down the revival of trade. Fresh epidemics of the Black Death, hardly less destructive than the first, broke out every few years; the Hundred Years' War in the north and a succession of small wars between rival cities in Italy blocked the trade routes and paralysed investments. Even when a merchant did succeed in establishing himself in a foreign city, he well knew that it was only on sufferance. In his youth, as we have seen, Datini had only narrowly escaped being banished, together with the Florentine merchants, from Avignon, and later on, in Spain, his trading-permit depended only on the King of Aragon's caprice. He conducted his trade, in short, with the knowledge that every venture was precarious, and every achievement at the mercy of events beyond his power to control.

It is this conviction—often reflected in Datini's letters—which makes him seem curiously akin to some business-men of our own time. His nerve had been irremediably shaken; he lived in daily dread of war, pestilence, famine, and insurrection, in daily expectation of bad news. He believed neither in the stability of any government nor in the honesty of any man. "You are young," he wrote to one of his factors in 1397, "but when you have lived as long as I and have traded with many folk, you will know that man is a dangerous thing, and that danger lies in dealing with him." * It was these fears which caused him to distribute his fortune in as many places as possible, never sinking too much in any single company, never trusting too much to any partner, always prepared to cut his losses and begin again, to recover in one field what he had lost in another. And it was by this caution, this unceasing vigilance, that he made his fortune. But it was a weary life.

It is interesting, too, to see in these papers how this precarious state of affairs affected other merchants of Francesco's time. Certainly in some respects they were smaller men than their predecessors. Francesco's generation holds no pioneers like Marco Polo, and even no international merchants of the calibre of the Bardi or Peruzzi. "The volume of trade," Professor Sapori writes, "had not shrunk; what had shrunk was the spirit of the traders." [4] But indeed there were some heroic virtues which the

[4] Sapori, *"Economia e morale alla fine del trecento"* in *Studi di storia economica medievale.*

68

times no longer required. The "epic period" of Italian trade had come to a close; the trade-routes to the Far East and the Black Sea, to the coasts of Asia Minor and Africa and Spain, had long since been opened and established. The greater security along the roads had enabled merchants not to travel themselves with their goods in armed caravans, but to entrust them to carriers, while the invention of the bill of exchange made it possible to transfer purchasing power without the shipment of actual coins. It was thus that Datini's first youthful venture needed to take him no further than Avignon, and in his later years his agility was only of the mind. Moreover, like most other merchants, he took no part in the defence of his republic, or even in its government. The time was past when the citizens of Florence were also her soldiers; now her battles were fought by mercenaries under the leadership of foreign *condottieri*, while her government and that of her expanding territory had come into the hands of a small group of officials. The bureaucracy which from that day to this has been the curse of Italian political life was already in the making.

In this new order of things, most merchants remained aloof from politics, concerned with the affairs of the republic only in so far as they affected the course of trade. The only office they cared to hold was that of Prior—which, apart from the prestige attached to it, enabled its holder to have a say in the decrees most vital to trade: those concerning the city's budget, and its taxes and levies. But all minor offices were so unwelcome that it was found necessary to draw by lot the names of their holders, and to impose large fines on those who refused the appointment.[5] How necessary such measures were is illustrated in a letter among the Datini papers, in which a Florentine merchant, Andrea di Maestro Ambrogio, said that his name had been drawn on two successive days, first as *Castellano* of Serravalle and then of Pescia. "Today I shall refuse both the one and the other; it is

[5] Piattoli, "*L'origine dei fondaci datiniani di Pisa e Genova*" in *Arch. Stor. Pratese*, 1927–30.

69

not for me, nor for those of my standing, to take on charges such as these." And he went on to speak of a more ambitious friend, whose wife was pressing him to accept "such hours and offices." "Methinks, if he seeks such things, he will destroy both body and soul." *

These views were Datini's own. The only public office he ever held in Prato was that of *Gonfaloniere*, and in Florence he remained completely aloof from politics. But if anyone had accused him of indifference to the public good, he might well have replied, not only that every hour was taken up by the press of his own affairs, but that the real power in Europe was still held, not by priors or *castellani*, but by merchants like himself. It was with their money that wars were waged and allies purchased; it was their friendship that foreign princes sought. Like wily old spiders in the corners of their webs, these sedentary merchants still controlled, from the warehouses of Por S. Maria and Calimala, the fortunes of Europe. As for Datini himself, it is true that he never became either as rich or as powerful as the greatest merchants of the *dugento* and early *trecento*. The interest of his story lies rather in the fact that it was possible for a man like him, with little capital and no backing, to obtain a firm footing in international trade at all.

A mere glimpse at his vast correspondence shows how wide his net was flung, and how very frequently, in spite of war, plague, robbers, and bad roads, even the smaller trading-houses of the fourteenth century managed to communicate with each other across the whole of Europe. The files of Barcelona and Valencia, for instance, show not only an almost daily exchange with the Majorcan branches and with other Spanish cities, and frequent letters home, but dealings with Paris and London and Bruges, Nice, Arles, Perpignan and Aiguesmortes, Lisbon, Rhodes, Alexandria, Tunis, and Fez. There are letters in Latin, French, and Italian, in English and Flemish, in Catalonian, Provençal, and Greek, and even a few in Arabic and Hebrew. Moreover, all these letters have one thing in common: every event they report—a battle or a truce, a rumour of pestilence, famine or flood, a Pope's election or a prince's marriage—is noted only with a view to its effect upon trade. When Visconti's troops descended upon the fields of Tuscany just before the harvest and it was plain that a famine must ensue, Tuscan merchants were not concerned with the defence of their territory, but with swiftly buying up Genoese wheat.* When peace was at last signed, the merchant who sent the good news did not so much rejoice at the deliverance of his city from Gian Galeazzo's ruthless rule, as at the thought that "God be thanked, journeying will be safe again." * When, further afield, the Hundred Years' War was interrupted in 1408 by a three years' truce between England and Flanders, Datini's Florentine correspondents in Bruges lost no time in sending him the good news: "Now many English merchants will tarry here, and we shall trade much more with them." * But when, two years later, hostilities broke out again, the repercussion on trade was immediate. "The fair here took place on the seventh, but never was there so sad a one; and all for default of the English, who ever spend most at this fair and who may not journey here, because of their war with the French." *

Yet even war could sometimes be turned to good account. When a new campaign was about to open in northern France, Milanese cuirasses and Toledo blades were hastily packed into bales and forwarded on mule-back from Avignon to Paris. And when, after a victory, public rejoicings were foretold in London, a member of the Barcelona company hastily set forth from Spain to England, carrying with him a precious load of rubies, diamonds, and pearls.⁶ So vital, indeed, was it to merchants to receive such tidings before their competitors that Paolo da Certaldo warned them always to master the contents of their own letters from abroad before giving to their fellow merchants any-

⁶ A letter from Paris to Valencia specified that it was only worth while to send jewels of a high quality, for there was no market for cheap ones, of which there was already a glut. Moreover, it was an unfavorable time of year, "*Perchè ora sono passate les estrene*" [*les étrennes*].

thing that had come from them under the same cover. "For those letters might hold matters that would injure your trade, and thus the service you had done to a friend might turn to your own disfavour." [7]

These letters bear witness not only to Datini's own activities, but to those of many other Tuscan firms abroad, particularly in Spain, Flanders, and England. In addition to wool, these firms traded chiefly in cloth, spices, jewels, and works of art, and one of their most important "colonies" was in Bruges, where the Florentines (like the Venetians and Genoese) had their own fine consular house in the Place de la Bourse. Many of these firms were in close touch with Francesco's companies, especially with the one in Barcelona, which they often used as an agent for their Spanish trade. Datini's most frequent correspondents were Deo Ambrogio and Giovanni Franceschi & Co., dealers in spices, whose main house was in Montpellier and who also had a branch in Paris; Luigi and Salvestro Mannini & Co., dealers in wool and cloth and the luxury trade (with branches also in London and Paris); Giovanni Orlandini & Co., Florentine cloth merchants, with a prosperous branch in London; and the Alberti brothers, who had branches also in Avignon, Seville, and Rhodes. All these were merchant-bankers who dealt in money as well as goods, and the Datini Archives contain many bills issued by them, and paid by Francesco's branches in Italy or Spain. [8]

In the letters from these merchants we can follow the perilous voyages of the Genoese and Venetian galleys from the Levant across the Mediterranean and up the Atlantic coast to Flanders, bearing spices of every description, besides the grain and brazil indispensable for dyeing Flemish cloth, and alum for fixing the dyes. The galleys were generally due in July, and their arrival was followed by a drop in prices. But accident or delay sent prices up with equal speed: hardly had the news reached London of the shipwreck in the Channel of a Genoese ship carrying

[7] Paolo da Certaldo, *Libro di buoni costumi*, para. 251.
[8] *Vide* chapter v, p. 150.

Prato in the Fourteenth Century

THE FIGURE ON THE RIGHT REPRESENTS FRANCESCO DI MARCO
PRESENTING HIS *Ceppo* TO HIS NATIVE CITY.

Bartering Wool for Cloth

Bartering Wheat for Wool
CODEX BIBLIOTECA RICCARDIANA 2669

alum and cotton when these commodities soared to double their usual price, while in another year—1384—when the galleys were delayed until the end of August, the price of grain and brazil went up by 20 per cent.

Other calamities, too, sometimes arrested the course of trade. In 1404 trade was brought to a standstill by severe floods which covered all the plains on the Flemish coast, drowning over two thousand persons and casting ashore all the trading-ships lying in the harbour of Sluys.* A few years earlier, in 1400, there had been an even greater calamity: an outbreak of plague in Bruges had carried off over twelve thousand persons, "and the greater part of the merchants went away." * So Flemish drapers were able to sell only a small portion of their scarlet cloth, and, consequently, in the following year they bought up from the Italian trading-ships only a quarter of the usual amount of *grana*, the scarlet dye.*

In Paris the most profitable goods, then as now, were those for the luxury market, and in this Francesco's companies in Avignon and Spain took an active part, exporting to Paris Tuscan silks, embroideries and pictures and Spanish jewels, armour and leatherwork, and buying Parisian fine enamels, inlaid in gold, Flemish or French painted stuffs for bed-curtains and wall-hangings. One new firm to settle in Paris in 1401 was that of the Aldobrandini. "God give grace to us all," one of them exclaimed, "for the more of us there are, the more we shall achieve!" But the Italians complained that the Parisian shop-keepers showed little enterprise. "This is a city where we must be well purveyed with everything and then wait for the demand. These apothecaries will never take anything until they are assured of its sale, according to the demand. They will never buy on chance." [9] It was the Italian merchants who, more flexible and more shrewd, were prepared to take risks—and often successfully.

But sometimes fortune was against them. The Mannini, for instance, emboldened by success, agreed—like the Bardi and Pe-

[9] Brun, *Notes sur le commerce florentin*, pp. 90 and 92.

ruzzi before them, though on a much smaller scale—to act as bankers to an English king. In 1395 they were advancing money in Paris for the wedding in the Sainte Chapelle of Richard II with Isabella, the daughter of Charles VI, "a pretty creature." And—no more fortunate than their predecessors—they shared, four years later, in Richard's downfall.

> Because of the deeds in England [wrote their rivals, the Orlandini, after Richard's abdication and murder], the said Mannini must needs give up their trade—and thus the world goes. Had there been no revolution in England, they might have become great, but no man ever allied himself with great lords, without losing his feathers.*

Another Tuscan firm, however, that of Deo Ambrogio, thought it might still be possible to turn the situation to their advantage. They took over the Manninis' company and—before Richard was cold in his grave—were speculating on the chance that Henry of Lancaster would take on Richard's child-widow —or if not her, some other bride.

> Whomsoever he may wed, there will be great feasting in England; and silken stuffs and jewels will go up in cost. . . . Wherefore I would advise and praise any who have fine jewels, to send them here.*

II

It is naturally with the foundation and expansion of Datini's own branches that these papers are chiefly concerned. His first step was to establish himself firmly in Florence. As soon as he arrived there, in 1382, he opened a warehouse in Via Porta Rossa, of which he at first entrusted the management to his brother-in-law, Niccolò dell' Ammannato Tecchini—an experienced merchant but, as his letters show, a foolish man. In the

following year Datini formed a company with a Florentine who
had already been in his employ in Avignon and Pisa, Stoldo di
Lorenzo, and with a third partner, Falduccio di Lombardo, and
this partnership was not dissolved until 1404, when Francesco
formed a new company with Francesco di Benozzo and with a
man whose qualities Mazzei described as being "of 24-carat
gold," Luca del Sera—this time with a capital of 12,000 florins,
of which 6,000 were Francesco's. These companies dealt especially in wool from Minorca, Catalonia, and Provence, cloth
from Florence, Prato, and Perpignan, and silks and velvets from
Lucca and Spain, as well as in Córdoban and Sardinian lamb-
skins and other hides (to be worked by the Florentine fine
leather-workers), wax, tar, spices, wine (both the common Tuscan and Spanish malmsey), and even Provençal wheat. Moreover, in 1387 Francesco also entered into partnership with
another Florentine, Domenico di Cambio, for the export and sale
of silk and cotton veils (mostly made in Perugia). "Forasmuch
as God gives us grace to furnish Avignon with veils," wrote
Domenico to Francesco, "we shall have honour and profit, too.
And whensoever Boninsegna [the partner in Avignon] would
have our goods better than other men's by 3 or 4 per cent, we
shall send him some that are better by 10 per cent; let us see if
that will satisfy him!" * This company, too, flourished, and was
only dissolved seventeen years later, in 1404.[1]

At the time of his arrival in Florence, Francesco did not belong to any of the Florentine guilds, but in 1388 he joined the
Arte di Por S. Maria,[2] the guild of the silk merchants who lived
by the church of St. Mary at the gate—a choice which can easily
be explained. In Prato he had joined the cloth guild because, according to the city statutes, he would otherwise have been cut
off from taking any part in the cloth trade. But in Florence he
wished to develop a more varied export trade, and it was the

[1] *Iscritta della Compagnia di Francesco e Domenico,* February 1, 1387.
Bensa, op. cit., Doc. X.
[2] Arch. di Stato, Firenze, *Arte della Seta,* No. 4, p. 5. Francesco became
one of the consuls of this guild in May 1403.

75

Guild of Por S. Maria which specialized, not only in the manufacture and sale of silk, but in the purchase, sale, and export of any sort of cloth (excepting only the *panni franceschi*,[3] which were the speciality of the *Arte di Calimala*). Moreover, this guild also included a great many subsidiary trades—goldsmiths, armourers, wood-carvers, chisellers, workers in silk and feathers, mattress-makers, quilters, doublet-makers, and tailors—many of them craftsmen from whom Francesco had already ordered goods when he was still in Avignon.[4]

He started by opening, in Por S. Maria, a shop in which he sold not only cloth, silks and velvets, tablecloths and table-napkins from Cremona and veils from Perugia, but the various wares of a mercer's shop: scissors, needles, thread, hammers, table-knives, metal clasps for books, and "soft soap." His shop was—according to Domenico di Cambio—"the finest *fondaco* in the finest street in Florence," but its equipment was probably no more elaborate than that of the shop of Francesco del Bene & Co., a cloth-finishing company with a *bottega* in Via di Calimala, of which the full record remains in that company's books. Its walls were lined with pine-boards (since it was important, according to Pegolotti, to keep stuffs where they were neither too damp nor too dry), and in the inner part a great studded cupboard, called an *arca* (ark), was set up for the most valuable materials, while the others were folded on open shelves. For furniture there were only a row of rough benches against the walls, a desk with a stool, and two smaller tables "for showing silks

<hr />

[3] These included not only French cloth, but any cloth bought in France —i.e., often also English or Flemish.

[4] The variety of crafts included in this guild is shown in the list of its members, according to the Statutes of 1335, which lists (after the merchants of all sorts of cloth not reserved for the merchants of the *Arte della Lana* or *Calimala*) "all those who trade in doublets, blankets, quilts, mattresses, dyed linens, cottons, capes, hose, new hats, felt, *zendadi* (fine silk) samite . . . cloth of gold, purple, coats of mail, carpets, serge hangings, foreign chairs or benches, banners, basins, yarns from across the Alps, Irish serge, tablecloths, table napkins, French surnapes, raw and dyed silks, scarlet cloth, woven gold and silver, and emery."

from Como," while the rest of the equipment consisted merely of a money-box, two ladders, two pairs of scissors, a yard-stick, a copper pail, and an iron lantern. In addition—since the statutes required that someone ("the one of the apprentices who is considered the best") should sleep in the shop at night, an old trestle-bed, bought in a junk-shop, was set up in the back and provided with two mattresses, three pillows (one of feathers), two blankets, and three pairs of sheets. Both the windows and the door were given strong bars and bolts, and outside the shop, above its ensign, an awning was stretched in summer.[5]

In a secluded corner, in front of a cupboard containing his account-books, sat the scrivener or accountant—often with a mirror on the wall to reflect the scanty light on to his ledger—and beside him on a table stood a large square counting-board, with some bowls or little sacks containing counters of various colours. This board was the medieval merchant's *abbaco*, and was used for keeping his accounts, as smaller similar boards were used for teaching arithmetic in schools. The board was divided into seven columns: the counters representing *denari* (pence) were placed in the first column on the right, the *soldi* in the second, and the *lire* (pounds) in the third, multiples of *lire* extending up to the seventh column, that of the tens of thousands. The merchant or accountant sat at the table, while a boy handed him the counters he required, and other apprentices crowded round to watch him and *"far pratica."* [6] At other tables, nearer the front, the wares were displayed and measured. (The yard-sticks, as the city statutes required, were frequently controlled by the guild's officials.) In the doorway a group of merchants bargained and argued and discussed the news of the day; sometimes a dusty and weary courier arrived, with his bag of

[5] Sapori, *Una compagnia di Calimala ai primi del trecento*, pp. 43–4. This shop was opened in 1319, but those of Francesco's time (to judge by pictures of the period) were not equipped any more elaborately.

[6] Sapori, *"La cultura del mercante medievale italiano"* in *Studi di storia economica medievale*, pp. 302–10.

77

letters at his belt—and then merchants from other shops, too, came crowding round, to see if there was anything in his bag for them.

Francesco's outstanding trait as a merchant is the variety of his activities. First an armourer and then a mercer in Avignon, he had become a cloth-maker in Prato and was now again a shop-keeper in Florence; next he founded a flourishing import-and-export business, and became the chief partner of a number of different trading-companies: he dealt in wool, cloth, veils, wheat, metals, and hides, in spices and pictures and jewels. In 1404 he joined yet another guild—that of the cloth-finishers, the *Arte di Calimala*.[7] He even took over, for a short time, the city tolls for meat and wine in Prato; he did some under-writing; and finally (against the advice of all his friends) he set up a bank.

Such varied ventures were entirely characteristic of his time, when the fundamental distinction between the international merchant and the "little man" did not consist in whether his trade was wholesale or retail, or even in the quantity of his mer-chandise, but rather in the outlook of two different kinds of men.[8] The local merchant was still, in his way of life, his lack of enterprise, and his parsimony, a man with the outlook of a crafts-man—trading with a number of familiar clients, strictly subser-vient to the rules of his guild, taking small risks and expecting small profits. The international trader—whether he was the chief partner of a great company like the Alberti's, or a small one like Datini's—still retained something of the enterprise and au-dacity of his ancestor, the travelling pedlar; he was prepared to take great risks, but diminished them by spreading them over the widest possible field; he acquainted himself with foreign lan-guages and foreign ways, adapted himself to the needs of for-

[7] Arch. di Stato, Firenze, *Mercatanti in Calimala*, Reg. No. 6.

[8] That the distinction between these two types of merchants was then already recognized is shown in the two forms of Venetian citizenship—*de intus* for men who took part only in local trade, and *de intus et extra* for men who traded abroad, especially with the Levant. Cf. Luzzatto, *"Piccoli e grandi mercanti nelle città d'Italia del Rinascimento"* in *Saggi di storia e teoria economica in onore di G. Prato.*

78

eign markets, was both merchant and banker, dealt simultaneously in both wholesale and retail trade. As the Bardi had continued to run a draper's shop in Via di Calimala even while they were exporting enough wheat from Puglie to feed a whole city and financing the English campaigns in France, so Datini, even at the time of his most successful foreign ventures, never closed his little mercer's shop in Por S. Maria.

But to his timid Florentine partners the variety of his enterprises was most alarming; they could not forget how many other great trading-houses, in recent years, had ended in bankruptcy. The following letter from Domenico di Cambio is typical of their warnings:

> Francesco, I have heard you would embark on a new enterprise. Before God, I beseech you, open your eyes wide and look well to what you do! You are rich and at ease, and not a boy any more, that you should need to undertake so much—and bethink you how we are mortal, and the man who does many things will assuredly meet with disaster. . . . Bethink you how Donato Dini must feel, who is now over seventy, and because he has tried to do too much is bankrupt, and gets only five *soldi* in the *lira!**

But Francesco did not heed. The opening of his new branches followed each other swiftly; first the Pisan *fondaco* in 1382, the Florentine in 1386, and the Genoese in 1388. Then came new branches in Spain and in the Balearic Islands in 1393 and 1394, while at the same time the company in Avignon prospered and trade with both the Black Sea and the Balkans increased.

The process of opening a new branch was always much the same. In spite of his refusal to take part in politics, Datini plainly had a good political sense, a shrewd flair for the moment in which a city's power and prestige were in the ascendant or in decline. He would first choose a flourishing town in which other Tuscan firms had already obtained trade agreements; then he began to deal with one of these firms; next he sent one of his own agents

79

on the spot to look into local conditions; and only then (often several years after his first approach) did he form a "company" of his own with one of his own partners or *fattori* in charge of the new branch.

In the second half of the fourteenth century it is possible to distinguish several main currents of Mediterranean trade. The first and principal one was from the Far East and the Levant to Italy, southern France, and Spain, and vice versa. Venetian, Genoese, Tuscan, and Catalan sailors and traders brought back from Constantinople, Famagusta, Antioch, and Alexandria (to name only a few of the chief ports) the produce of the Levant, and exported in return wool, cloth, armour, and wood.

Then there were the great trade-routes between the Mediterranean and northwestern Europe, by which many of the wares of the Levant and Italy reached the markets of England and Flanders, while these countries dispatched to the Mediterranean their English and Flemish wool and cloth, French linen and tapestries, and even furs and metals from the Baltic.

Finally, two minor trade channels, though of lesser importance, were extremely active in Datini's time. One was between Italy and the Balkans, the other between Italy, Spain, and Barbary. Ships from the Balkans and the Black Sea brought to Italy —in return for wool, cloth, oil, wine, and salt—the furs, metals, cattle, wax, sandalwood, alum, and slaves of the Crimea and "Roumania." [9] And, equally, Italian traders bought in the ports of Catalonia, Majorca, and North Africa, Spanish and African wool and fleeces, and Spanish wine, fruit, leather, and ceramics —taking back in return their Tuscan cloth and silk and many articles for the luxury market.

It was after the foundation of his companies in Genoa, Spain, and the Balearics that Datini began to have an interest in each of these main currents of trade—but especially in the one between the Balkans and the western Mediterranean.

[9] The term "Roumania" was then employed for most of Yugoslavia, Dalmatia, Albania, and Bulgaria.

The books of the Pisan company record dealings with southern France, Spain, the Balearics, and Africa, and also with Flanders and England; the Genoese books, trade between Spain, Africa, and the Balkans. The port of Genoa also served for the export of Datini's Tuscan goods whenever, for political reasons, the port of Pisa was closed to Florentine trade; he then sent his goods to Genoa overland, by Lucca, or else from the minor Tuscan ports of Talamone, Motrone, or Pietrasanta. Sometimes, too, he sent merchandise to Spain by the longer but safer Venetian route: on mule-back across the Apennines to Bologna and Ferrara, then on by river to Venice, and finally down the Adriatic and round the toe of Italy to Majorca or Barcelona. And yet another secondary route was by Lucca to Milan, then across the Alps by the Mont Cenis or Mont Genèvre to Avignon—and then down the Rhone, to be embarked for Spain at Marseilles or Aiguesmortes.

The development of Francesco's two companies in Pisa and Genoa is so closely connected with the political events of the time that it can be described only against this background. In addition to the blow which had fallen upon Florentine merchants in consequence of the Pope's interdiction and the "War of the Eight Saints," the peace of Tuscany was constantly threatened by the ruthless attempts of the Duke of Milan, Gian Galeazzo Visconti, to extend his rule from Lombardy over the whole of northern and central Italy. The passage of his Freelances, or of the mercenary troops called in by the cities of central Italy to defend them, brought fresh perils to every traderoute. Merchants adapted themselves to these events as best they could, providing their ships with armed escorts, and transporting their wares by roundabout routes when the direct ones were closed.

When Francesco decided to return to Italy in 1382 and to ensure his trade-routes by opening a branch in one of the great Italian trading-ports, his choice lay between Genoa and Pisa. Genoa was the larger and more prosperous city, but her trade was in a parlous condition, since war had again broken out with her old rival, Venice, who had found an ally in the Duke of Milan. Lombardy was thus closed to merchandise from Genoa, Visconti's troops infested Liguria, and Tuscan merchants established there were hastily transferring some of their goods to Pisa. Here the faction favourable to Florence was temporarily in the saddle; Florentine goods passed freely through the port, and were accorded especially favourable tariffs. (A list of these—written out on a long scroll which probably hung in the branch's office—is in the Archivio Datini, and testifies to the variety of the wares, as well as showing that a special bank [cassa] in Pisa was at the disposal of Florentine merchants for the payment of their dues.) *

It was therefore natural that Francesco should have chosen Pisa as the site of his new branch even before leaving Avignon, and as soon as he got home he carried out his plan. He had already been dealing for some time with the Pisan company of Andrea di Maestro Ambrogio and Agnolo degli Agli, and early in 1383 he took over this company (in conjunction with two partners, Stoldo di Lorenzo and Matteo di Lorenzo) under the name Francesco di Marco & Co. Early in the following year he opened his new branch—with an expenditure of less than 9 florins, since the furniture, apart from some bare boards for shelves, consisted only of two desks, "one new chest with a lock," and "one framed mirror," while the rest of the equipment was one ledger and one money-bag, some "painted bags for letters," needles and thread, ink, and 7 ounces of scarlet sealing-wax. Later on, however, in 1406 Francesco rented for this branch (at a cost of 100 florins for three years) "a house with a court and a little kitchen-garden" which Mazzei described as "the most pleasing house in which I have ever dwelt, so rich in land and stables and loggias; and on the upper floor, too, furnished with every virtue and comfort a house can have." *

The chief fattore employed by the company was Cristofano di Bartolo da Barberino, who later became one of Francesco's

partners in Spain, and under him worked Manno di Albizzo degli
Agli, a young kinsman of a partner in the original company,
Agnolo degli Agli. The young man proved "industrious and
alert" (*curoso e sollecito*) and, after ten years, asked to be taken
into partnership.

> Now he is grown and become a man [wrote his kinsman
> Agnolo] and would greatly desire to improve his condition,
> with your help and counsel. . . . He says he would gladly
> work with you, he giving his person [his services] and abid-
> ing here, and taking the part you think fit of the prof-
> its. . . . Wherefore I pray you, in love and favour, let him
> be commended to you.*

So in 1392 a new company was formed—into which Francesco and the other senior partner, Stoldo di Lorenzo, each put
3,000 gold florins and Manno only 300, but Manno undertook
to give all his services and live permanently in Pisa. Profits and
losses alike were to be divided in the following proportions:
three quarters to Francesco and Stoldo between them, and one
quarter to Manno; and this arrangement lasted until, in 1400,
Manno was carried off by the plague.[1]

The Pisan correspondence is larger than that of any of Datini's
other branches—not only because Pisa was the point of arrival
and departure of so much of his merchandise, but because this
company, like a modern shipping-firm, dealt not only in its own
goods, but in commissions for other merchants. The 130 files of
papers (from 1382 to 1402) record dealings not only with Francesco's other branches in Avignon, Spain, and Majorca, but with
southern France (in particular, Montpellier, Aiguesmortes,
Arles, Marseilles, Nice, Perpignan, and Tarascon), with Lisbon
and Tunis, with Paris and Lille, and especially with Bruges and
London. In good years the books show a turnover of as much as
21,000 florins.

To follow the company's vicissitudes within the next few

[1] Bensa, op. cit., Doc. VII.

years is to realize under what precarious conditions Tuscan trade was conducted. At first it seemed as if a short period of prosperity might be hoped for, for in 1389 Gian Galeazzo Visconti was persuaded to form a three years' league with the principal Tuscan cities, during which truce all the league's members undertook not to invade each other's territory, nor to impede the safe passage of merchandise.[2] For a few months trade prospered, and Datini's firm shared in the general activity. But Visconti merely employed the time in stirring up a faction favourable to himself in Pisa, and by the following harvest his troops were once again harassing the territory of Florence. The exasperated Florentines decided to carry the offensive into the enemy's own country, and, having secured at great expense the services of the great English *condottiere* Sir John Hawkwood, sent him to attack Visconti's men in Verona. But in the spring Visconti's troops again descended into Tuscany; again Tuscan ports were closed and Tuscan merchants harried. "Stoldo says," wrote Domenico di Cambio to Francesco, "that there is an armed ship in Porto Pisano, at the Count's [Visconti's] behest, to rob Florentine wares, and that two days ago a courier was captured, who came from Genoa with many Venetian letters. God in His mercy confound him, for he causes too much travail to merchants." *

The files of this year are full of similar letters. One advised a correspondent in Spain that all the wares he had sent to Tuscany were likely to be lost, "for men have been held and robbed both on the road from Pisa to Florence, and from Pisa to Lucca." Another, two years later, described the sinking of a wheat-ship by a pirateer under Genoese command. "May God confound him and all other pirates and keep us and our friends out of their hands." One ingenious merchant who wished to send two silver belts from Genoa to Pisa decided to hide them in a loaf of marzipan—but then, in a post-script, thought better of it: "We are not sending the said marzipan." Perhaps he was right, for another letter in the same year describes the misadventures

[2] Piattoli, op. cit., Doc. IV, October 8, 1389.

that overtook a Florentine merchant in Genoa, called Galvano, who attempted to sail from Portofino to Pisa with his wares. At the mouth of the Arno a first encounter took place, in which two armed ships (presumably in Visconti's pay) were put to flight. The galley then, confident of safety, proceeded up the Arno to the music of trumpets and bagpipes, "with the sailors in their shirtsleeves and the archers also at the oars." But their troubles were not yet over. "When we were within a mile of Pisa, by the order of Ser Jacopo . . . , thief and traitor, divers bowmen were concealed in houses or in thickets on the banks, and, as we came up, they began to shoot with their arrows and bombards." The traders defended themselves as best they could, but soon part of the population, too—delighted to have a chance of a blow at any Florentine—came down to the shore and joined the firing; so the ship turned back to the river's mouth, "having received much damage and inflicted little," with three men killed and fifteen wounded.*

It is hardly surprising that merchants should have embarked with some reluctance on journeys such as these. Every incident in the long tedious campaign is reflected in these letters. When Visconti's troops were threatening Livorno, the Florentine merchants in Pisa were required to contribute the sum of 500 gold florins for that harbour's defence. Francesco di Marco & Co., no doubt most reluctantly, gave 56 florins. When at last, in January 1391, Visconti's troops retreated northward and peace was signed, hope and activity at once sprang up again: "Much merchandise is being sent to Pisa, bread and other goods for our Florentines; be assured that one can forward to Genoa at any hour." * But when, only a few months later, Piero Gambacorti —the leader of the party favourable to Florence—was murdered in Pisa by a traitor in Visconti's pay, the short respite was over. Angry crowds rioted round the Florentine warehouses in Pisa, crying: "Down with the Florentines!"—and Manno degli Agli saved his life only by hiding in the shop of a Pisan friend. Then the wind veered again: the new ruler of the city decided to make peace with Florence; honeyed words were exchanged, trading-facilities were again granted to Florentine merchants.

But now Francesco had had enough. Manno had been so badly frightened that he begged to be sent to another city; Francesco was weary of paying huge taxes which were swallowed up by the wages of mercenaries. Moreover, the news from Genoa indicated that the situation there had changed: trade was prospering and most of the city's banks were already in Florentine hands (the Medici and Strozzi were already established there). For a short while Francesco played with the idea of selling up all he had in Tuscany and establishing himself permanently in Genoa. From this his Tuscan friends dissuaded him, but he nevertheless decided, and rightly, to transfer at least a part of his trade to the Ligurian port. For some time he had been dealing with the Genoese firm of Ambrogio di Meo, Andrea di Bonanno, Luca del Sera, and Jacopo di Giovanni (indeed, Luca del Sera's name suggests that perhaps some of Datini's capital was already invested there), and early in 1392 he formed his own company, under the name of Francesco di Marco, Andrea di Bonanno & Co. Thenceforth the greater part of Datini's merchandise for the western Mediterranean—especially goods from the Balkans or the Black Sea—passed through Genoa and was forwarded from there to Majorca, Barcelona, or Valencia.

III

The Genoese company lasted only till 1400, when Andrea di Bonanno was carried off by the plague and the company's affairs were wound up. But long before this time Francesco had decided to take another step—to extend his trade to Spain. Following up the investigations of two of his Florentine *fattori* some ten years earlier,[3] he sent to Barcelona, in 1393, his ablest Floren-

[3] In 1382, the year of his return to Tuscany, Datini sent his Florentine partner, Falduccio di Lombardo, to look into the possibilities of the Spanish market, while six months later another of his men, Matteo di Lorenzo, was travelling on his behalf between Barcelona and Perpignan.

tine partner, Luca del Sera, and in the following year he founded
three Spanish companies: in Barcelona, Valencia, and on the island of Majorca. Subsequently another small agency, in connection with the Majorcan branch, was opened on the little island
of Ibiza,[4] and yet another at San Matteo, a small borough which
was then one of the chief collecting-centres of the Catalonian
wool-clip. The merchandise that passed through his Genoese
fondaco now increased both in quantity and variety, as is shown
in his *libri di mercanzia* and *libri di balle*—ledgers in which all
goods entering or leaving were set down, together with the
names of the senders or recipients, and the cost of carriage and
tolls.* According to these books, Datini's chief imports from
the Black Sea and the Balkans were iron, wax, alum, sandalwood, resin, gall-nuts (used for both dyeing and tanning), furs,
the rough woollen cloth called *schiavina*, which was used for
blankets and pilgrims' robes, and (though never in large numbers) slaves. From the Iberian peninsula his largest import was
wool, both African and Spanish, as well as lamb-skins and wool-
fells from both Majorca and Catalonia, but information about the
many other kinds of merchandise on the Iberian markets is also
provided in a list of prices current in Barcelona in 1385, as well
as in a letter quoting prices of goods available in Malaga in 1402.*
Among the goods which Datini's correspondent recommended,
the chief two were silk and saffron, but also leather and wax
from Barbary, Moroccan vernice and grain (*grana*) from both
Spain and Barbary; and he added that a great deal of both silk
and saffron was also sent to Flanders. In return, Datini's companies in Italy sent Florentine cloth to the Spanish markets as
well as Lombard woad and the dyes and spices of the Black Sea
and the Levant. The lists of dyes and mordants supplied by his
branches include indigo, orchil, brazil, Indian lak, realgar
(*risogallo*) from the Red Sea, and erpiment (yellow arsenic),

---

[4] The branch in Ibiza was managed by two Florentines, Giovanni and
Tucci di Gennaio, who were already settled there, trading on their own
account.

as well as gall-nuts from Roumania, rock alum, and red and white tartar. The spices include pepper, cinnamon, clove, ginger (both green and "ripe"), nutmeg, *galinga* (a bitter Chinese root), cassia, incense, aloes, zedoary, camphor, cardamon, spikenard, myrrh, and resins such as Arabian gum, mastic, galbanus, and "dragon's blood." Three kinds of sugar are mentioned: one from Damascus, one from Alexandria, and the "*zucchero mucchero*," which Pegolotti called "the best there is"; the name came from the Arabic words *al mukarrar*, refined sugar.[5] Pepper was, of course, one of the most expensive, but nevertheless was imported in large quantities. A single ship, for instance, from Alexandria, brought to Genoa over 300 pounds of pepper from Cyprus, as well as "much ginger and cotton," and the news that "another caravan from Mecca was soon expected." And on another occasion we are told that the whole Genoese fleet ("18 galleys, 2 *galeotti* and 12 trading-ships") was held up in Rhodes, during the absence of the Grand Master of the Knights of St. John, while the Saracens were already in sight, "and the admirals do not agree amongst themselves. And therefore pepper has gone up to 160 *lire*." *

Foodstuffs, too, often appear in these lists—especially wheat, which mostly came (as did also tunny) from Sicily and Sardinia, but sometimes also from Alexandria, Rhodes, or Tunis,* and there are also frequent shipments of rice, almonds, and dates from Valencia, raisins and figs from Malaga (raisins being already a monopoly of the Genoese trading-house of the Spinola),[6] apples and sardines from Marseilles, and olive oil from both Gaeta and Catalonia. Moreover, the little island of Ibiza, where Datini had an agency, possessed some flourishing salt-mines, from which salt was sold not only to Venice, Genoa, and Pisa, but even to Germany. "Two German ships," wrote Datini's agent in Ibiza,

[5] Evans, *Glossary* to Pegolotti, *La Pratica della Mercatura*, p. 434.
[6] These [the raisins] belong to *casa Spinola* and none can take them out of this kingdom, save they." (File 893. *Carteggio Malaga-Barcelona*, December 17, 1402.)

"arrived on the 13th from Flanders, and load salt for Germany.
. . . All here marvel at their coming—so long a road, only for
salt!" * Provence produced hemp, both woven and in the yard,
and also canvas and ropes. Finally there were all the Spanish
and African products for the luxury market: fine leather from
Córdoba and Tunis, Toledo blades, Valencian soap, ivory tusks
and ostrich-feathers and ostrich-eggs from Barbary, ceramics
from Valencia and Majorca, and maps from Barcelona.

Ceramics or *maiolica* were a speciality of the Moorish craftsmen of Valencia, and it was here that Francesco ordered a whole
dinner-service "from the Saracen who makes them"—"soup-
bowls, both large and small, plates, and a few fine big dishes,
very well made." And the results were so pleasing that Ser Lapo
Mazzei asked if he might copy one of the plates—"like the one
we had, the evening we ate the swifts." They were all engraved
with Francesco's arms, but when, three years later, he sent another order for his house in Florence, his partners in Valencia
had "forgotten what these arms are like" (this must have annoyed him greatly) and were obliged to write to Florence to
ask for a model. This later order was executed in Majorca—so it
would appear that this kind of pottery owed its name to having
been made on the island, as well as shipped from there.*

Cartography, too, was a speciality of Barcelona, and the Datini
papers contain some letters to Simone d'Andrea from the Florentine ivory-worker and jewel merchant Baldassarre degli Ubriachi,
who made a journey to Spain, Bordeaux, England, and Ireland
with some jewels for sale, and while he was in Barcelona ordered
some fine maps from two expert Jewish cartographers. These
he proposed to present to the Kings of Aragon, England, and
Navarre, in gratitude for granting him a free passage through
their dominions. They cost the large sum of 111 florins and
were made by Maestro Giame Riba, "*cristiano novello, maestro
di carte da navigare*," and Maestro Francesco Bene, "*dipintore di
carte da navigare*," and were stored in the Barcelona *fondaco*,

89

"secretly and well wrapped, so that no man can see them." [7]

It is after the opening of the Spanish and Genoese branches, too, that we find reference to yet another line—the slave trade, of which the Balearic Islands were then the chief centre in the western Mediterranean. This trade was, of course, nothing new. In the eleventh and twelfth centuries Spain had been the great slave-market of western Europe, and as early as 1128 traders from Barcelona were selling Moslem slaves in the markets of Genoa. But it was the labour shortage after the Black Death of 1348 that suddenly caused a demand for domestic slaves to revive, and brought them to Italy not only from Spain and Africa, but from the Balkans, Constantinople, Cyprus and Crete, and, above all, from the shores of the Black Sea. In Florence a decree of the *Signoria,* issued in 1336, officially authorized their importation—provided only that they were infidels, not Christians, and they were also soon to be found in most prosperous Genoese and Venetian households.[8] Many of them mere children of nine or ten, they belonged to a great variety of different races: yellow-skinned, slanting-eyed Tartars, handsome fair Circassians, Greeks, Russians, Georgians, Alans, and Lesghians. Sold by their parents for a crust of bread, or kidnapped by Tartar raiders and Italian sailors, they were brought from the slave-markets of Tana and Caffa, of Constantinople, Cyprus, and Crete to the Venetian and Genoese quays, where they were bought by dealers and forwarded to customers inland. By the end of the fourteenth century there was hardly a well-to-do household in Tuscany without at least one slave: brides brought them as part of their dowry, doctors accepted them from their patients in lieu of fees

---

[7] "And by the King of Navarre I was granted leave to go through his kingdom with my jewels and goods in safety, paying naught either at coming in or going out, and methinks I will go on towards Bordeaux and thence by sea to England and thence to Ireland, where the King is." (*Carteggio di Barcelona,* Baldassarre degli Ubriachi to Simone d'Andrea Bellandi, July 14, 1399.)

[8] Arch. di Stato, Firenze. Cl. XI, Dist. 81, n.81. Cf. also I. Origo: "Eastern Slaves in Tuscany in the Fourteenth and Fifteenth Centuries" in *Speculum,* vol. XXIX, July 1955.

—and it was not unusual to find them even in the service of a priest. They were employed, too (as we shall see), in Francesco's own household, and he would sometimes oblige Tuscan friends by selecting one for them through his agents in Genoa or Venice; but the most active part in this trade was taken by his branches in Majorca and Ibiza, where both African slaves bound for Italy and Eastern slaves bound for Spain were collected and sold.

Many letters in these files bear witness to these transactions, though they did not take place on any large scale; the most frequent entries refer rather to a few slaves included in a shipment of other assorted wares. The bill of lading, for instance, of a ship arriving in Genoa from Roumania on May 21, 1396, listed "17 bales of pilgrims' robes, 191 pieces of lead and 80 slaves." Another ship, sailing from Syracuse to Majorca, carried 1,547 leather hides and 10 slaves, and one sailing from Venice to Ibiza "128 sacks of woad, 55 bales of brass, 15 sacks of raw cotton, 5 sacks of cotton yarn, 4 bales of paper, 3 barrels of gallnuts, and 9 Turkish heads." The "9 heads" were then forwarded to Valencia to be sold, with a letter stating that one of them was a woman who could "sew and do everything," and who was therefore, in the writer's opinion, "too good for the people of Ibiza"— "for they are like dogs." "Your money," he added, "will be well placed in her." *

Duty had to be paid on these slaves (as was also the case in Italian cities) both on entering and leaving the Balearics, as well as a sales-tax, and apparently sometimes, if these dues were not met, the owner's other merchandise was confiscated. "The goods of the Genoese have remained here, because the Flemish ships would not pay the duty on the Moors they took to Alexandria, and it is said that a slave was taken away from them." Sometimes, too, a trader in Majorca who had sold some slaves to a Spanish buyer would attempt to charge him for their board during the time they had been on the island; but in at least one case the buyer protested. "You kept our slaves there . . . to load and unload merchandise and to work in your warehouse, and instead of [word missing—"paying"?] for the use of these slaves you add a charge! Think me not so simple, that I cannot see through this!"

Sometimes, too, slaves were procured by the simple method of raiding the coast of Barbary. "A brig has sailed from here," says a letter from Ibiza. "It has gone with a Majorcan ship [*liuto*] and ten men to trade in Barbary, and has brought back 4 heads." *

Very often these "captives" tried to run away, but generally without success. "We hear from Ibiza that Ser Antonio Delio has arrived there, with many Moorish captives on his ship, and twelve of them ran away with his rowing-boat. . . . But because of the weather, the said Moors came here [Majorca] and for the present have been imprisoned, which has been a great piece of good fortune." How far indeed a master's hand could reach, and how great the solidarity between the trading-companies was, is shown in a letter in Catalan from Barcelona to Boninsegna di Matteo in Avignon, asking him to catch two runaway slaves who, he thought, might possibly have made their way to Provence. "One of them is named Dmitri, a big man and very handsome. His flesh is good, fresh and rosy"; the other "lacks a tooth in front and has rather greenish skin. . . . I pray you, *señor*, have them caught, let them be strongly fettered, and send them back by boat to me." *

Apparently, too, slaves sent long distances were sometimes insured, like other goods, against the perils of the voyage, for the Datini papers contain the insurance policy, dated May 9, 1401, of a Tartar slave named Margherita, sent from Porto Pisano to a Catalonian buyer in Barcelona, and insured for the sum of 50 gold florins against "any risk from the hand of God, the sea, human beings, barter or her master," but not against any attempt at flight or suicide, "if she throws herself into the sea of her own accord." * Tragic human merchandise, tossed hither and thither by the seas!

It need hardly be said that no sentimental feelings hampered the dealings of any of the traders. Sick or well, wounded or pregnant, the slaves were merely goods, whose value might increase or deteriorate. Pregnancy, in particular, was regarded as a mishap as inconvenient as it was frequent, since it reduced the mother's market value. The following letter is characteristic in tone:

The slave you sent is sick, or rather full of boils, so that we find none who would have her. We will sell or barter her as best we can, and send you the account. Furthermore, I hear she is with child, two months gone or more, and therefore she will not be worth selling.

A few weeks later the same slave is referred to:

No man will have her. She says she is with child by you, and assuredly seems to be. The pother she makes is so great, she might be the Queen of France.*

And here is another brutal letter about a woman who declared her pregnancy to be due to the priest who had been her previous master.

We spake to the chaplain to whom your slave belonged and he says you may throw her into the sea, with what she has in her belly, for it is no creature of his. And we deem he speaks the truth, for had she been pregnant by him, he would not have sent her. . . . Methinks you had better send the creature to the hospital.*

IV

One fundamental question still remains unanswered: which of all these ventures brought in the profits that made Datini a rich man? Professor Melis's detailed analysis of Datini's cloth-making company in Prato shows, as we have said, that his profits there came to only just under 9 per cent—a figure which is confirmed

93

by the data about several other Tuscan cloth-making companies.[9] Undoubtedly a similar examination of the account-books and correspondence of Datini's other companies would throw much light on his profits in other fields, but the information at present available is too fragmentary for generalizations to be of any value—and, moreover, the only useful figures are, of course, those covering several consecutive years, since the fluctuations of the market were so great that figures for any single year may be misleading. Francesco himself has set down that the first company he formed in Avignon, with Tuccio Lambertucci—to deal chiefly in armour and household goods—made, in the course of eight years, no less than 10,000 florins, with an initial capital of only 800 florins. But he added: "Now matters go not in the same fashion." * The company which he founded in Florence with Domenico di Cambio for the veil trade (manufactured in Perugia and sold in Avignon) seems to have brought in—during the seventeen years of its duration—about 28 per cent.[1] But for many of his other companies we have nothing but a large number of —as yet—unanalysed figures.

The truth is, indeed, that the whole question of medieval trade-profits is still somewhat obscure. Professor Renouard, in his brilliant study of the commercial and banking companies of the Popes in the fourteenth century, has surmised that "the activities of these companies in certain regions must necessarily add up to a chronic deficit." How, he asks, could any cargo of wheat or cloth sailing from the western Mediterranean to the Levant ever equal the value of one of silks and spices in the opposite direction? [2] (We must remember that the cargo of a

[9] Professor Sapori estimates that profits in the Florentine wool trade oscillated between 7 and 15 per cent, while money invested with banks or commercial firms brought in between 6 and 10 per cent a year. Cf. Sapori, *Il commercio internazionale nel medioevo, Una Compagnia di Calimala ai primi del trecento,* and *L'interesse del danaro a Firenze nel trecento.*

[1] *Iscritta della compagnia di Francesco e Domenico.* Bensa, op. cit., Doc. X.

[2] Renouard, *Les relations des Papes d'Avignon et des compagnies commerciales et bancaires de 1316 à 1378,* pp. 72–3 and 84.

single galley of spices to Venice from the Levant could be worth as much as 200,000 ducats.)

We may, however, hazard a surmise that Datini made his fortune, not so much by a series of brilliant *coups,* as by an infinitely patient accumulation of small profits—an avoidance of dangers, quite as much as a seizure of opportunities. Moreover, it is not difficult to see why he succeeded—unlike so many of his contemporaries—in avoiding bankruptcy. The great trading-companies of the first half of the century—and, to a slightly lesser extent, of his own time—had taken part in every field of human enterprise: trade, industry, banking, and politics. The immense prestige and power that these merchants attained rested almost wholly upon credit: there is a startling disproportion between the capital at their disposal and the yearly turnover of their various enterprises. Moreover, it was hardly possible for them to keep out of politics: they could not well deny a loan to a foreign prince who could at any moment expel them from his dominions, or refuse to pay the mercenary troops called in by their own city to defend its walls. Thus, they were the first to suffer from the repercussions of political or military disasters; one could almost say that the greater and more powerful a company was, the more certainly was it doomed to failure.

A man like Datini could, and did, avoid these perils. Though Ser Lapo Mazzei and Domenico di Cambio were astounded by his daring, he was in truth a very prudent man. His little trading-companies, unlike the greater ones, kept out of politics. He made no loans to kings or prelates; he helped to finance no wars; he even—no easy matter at that time—had no share in party strife at home. The only credit he granted was to solid merchants like himself, to other trading-companies like his own. Thus, while he never attained a position equal to that of the heads of the great companies of his time—the Alberti or the Soderini, the Malabayla or the Guinigi—he was affected only indirectly, as any merchant must be, by politics and wars; he kept his vessel sailing through every storm.

CHAPTER FOUR

THE TRADING-COMPANIES AND THEIR MEMBERS

"*S'agrada pregio aver a Mercatante,*
drittura sempre usare a lui convene;
e longa provedenza li sta bene,
e che impromette non venga mancante.
E sia, se può, di bella contenenza,
secondo a che mestiere orrato intenda;
e scarso a comperare, e largo venda,
fuor di rampogne con bell'accoglienza.
La chiesia usare,
per Dio donare,
il cresce in pregio; e vendere ad un motto,
ed usura vietar tôrre del tutto,
e scriver bello, e ragion non errare." [1]

—Dino Compagni

[1] "A merchant wishing that his worth be great
Must always act according as is right;
And let him be a man of long foresight,

96

T BEFITS A MERCHANT," WROTE LEON BATTISTA Alberti, the great architect who was also the head of one of the chief trading-companies of Florence, "always to have ink-stained hands." Datini was of the same opinion. While the heads of some firms left much of their correspondence to their *fattori*, he insisted, even in his old age, on writing every letter with his own hand—often working at night, with only four hours for sleep, and sometimes not leaving his desk for several days on end. "It is the ninth hour," he wrote to one of his partners, "and I have not yet eaten nor drunk, and tomorrow I shall do the same." * In vain did his wife, his friends, and his doctors unite in begging him to transfer some of this work to one of his partners, or at least to keep a young scrivener by him, to whom he could dictate. "You injure yourself greatly," wrote one of his partners, "forasmuch you would keep all matters in your own hands. Wherefore will you not keep Simone or another beside you, to write what is needful? . . . Remember you, one bad night now is more harmful to you than twelve when you were younger. Come closer to God and let Simone do the writing!" * But Francesco would not heed. "It is my intent," he wrote, "to be ever a common scrivener, like an old horse in harness." *

In addition to his interminable daily letters to his wife and his *fattori* and to his peasants, masons, tradesmen, and artists—for no

---

And never fail his promises to keep.
  Let him be pleasant, if he can, of looks,
As fits the honor'd calling that he chose;
Open when selling, but when buying close;
Genial in greeting and without complaints.
  He will be worthier if he goes to church,
Gives for the love of God, clinches his deals
Without a haggle, and wholly repeals
Usury-taking. Further, he must write
Accounts well-kept and free from oversight."

("Song on Worthy Conduct," translation in R. S. Lopez and I. W. Raymond, *Medieval Trade in the Mediterranean World.*)

sack of flour could be moved, no grape picked, no brick laid, no button or box of comfits bought without his specific orders—he would write every week to the managers of each of his branches. "Veritable Bibles" was his own term for these long missives, a strange medley of business instructions, paternal homilies, and scoldings—which he called "caning" or "biting." "And ever I say I will be brief, and then I write a whole Psalter." *
No detail was too small to deserve his notice, no omission or extravagance slight enough to escape his reproof. In return he required his partners or managers to send him equally detailed reports, and woe betide the man who was either dense or careless! "You cannot see a crow in a bowlful of milk!" he wrote to one stupid underling, and to another, who had sent him a confused report (was the writer referring to thirteen sacks of wool, or only to ten?), he wrote: "You have not the mind of a cat! You would lose your way from your nose to your mouth!" If a man could not trust his memory, he told him, he should follow Francesco's own example, and take daily notes. "For even the wisest man in the world must bethink him, by day and night, of what he has to write, lest he forget it. But I see well that you only read my letters once and reply heedlessly . . . and then sit by the fire, dreaming of the great profits you will make!" *

Fortunately most of his other *fattori* were more diligent, and their letters were carefully filed and docketed by Francesco himself, in his Florentine office. "I would look over each of my papers," he wrote in 1398, "and set them in order and mark them, that I may be clear about each man with whom I have to do." *

What did all these letters look like, and how did they reach their destination? They are written on sheets of paper folded in three, closed by passing a small cord through holes in the edges and sealing it at each end. The side containing the address was marked with the same trade-mark which was placed on

Francesco's bales of merchandise.[2] Each bundle of letters was then wrapped in a waterproof canvas and enclosed in a bag or purse called a *scarsella*, sealed by the merchant and worn at the messenger's belt.

The choice of messenger was of vital importance. From the earliest days of Tuscan trade most great companies had their own couriers: in the thirteenth century the *Arte di Calimala* was sending two messengers *a day* from Florence to the great fairs of Champagne, and in the fourteenth century the Venetian Republic maintained a regular postal service between Venice and Bruges, which took only seven days. Smaller firms entrusted their letters to the post-bags of the great companies, or made use of the professional couriers who were to be found in every big trading-city, ready to set forth in any direction, but who were seldom engaged as regular employees. (A letter of Datini's from Avignon, for instance, mentions two couriers—one of whom was in Lyons on his business, and the other just setting off for Pisa —but neither of these men is ever referred to again.) Sometimes, too, a messenger could be picked up at the city gates, where travellers changed horses: letters could be entrusted to a monk or an envoy going abroad, or even to a casual traveller, but this entailed a risk, for—in spite of official agreements between many Communes to guarantee the inviolability of each other's posts —letters were often sequestrated and read on the way, with serious consequences for the writer. One indiscreet Florentine merchant, for instance, Ambrogio di Meo, got into trouble in 1391 for sending his partners in Genoa an account of the state of affairs in Florence—high loans exacted by the Commune to pay their mercenaries, attacks on merchants on the roads, and harvests destroyed by Visconti's Freelances. His letter was sequestrated at the gates of Genoa, and copies of it were sent to

[2] Such trade-marks, of course, were then in general use. Each merchant or craftsman had his own, and if two of them entered into partnership, another monogram was generally formed, embodying the designs of both. Datini's is on the binding and the title page of this book.

Visconti and to the *Signoria* of Florence; whereupon he was summoned by the Priors, and was fortunate to escape with only a severe reproof. "It were better," commented Francesco's informant, "to keep silence than to send tidings, and in especial not to speak against a man's own Commune." *

Francesco made no such mistakes. He warned his *fattori* never to write down anything that should be kept private— "For there are many who strive to seize letters that pass through their hands, to read them. . . . It were wiser," he added, "ever to hold some letters in readiness, and when you find a friend about to set forth, deliver them unto him, saying: 'Give this into the hand of such a one, and of no other.' " *

Sometimes, too, he sent one of his own partners or *fattori* to travel between his branches, carrying his instructions and sending back reports. And that it was far from unusual for a merchant thus to ride about the world on his company's business, without even a change of horses, is shown by a letter of Mazzei's in which he boasted about a horse whose previous master "left Barcelona and went to Paris and then round Flanders for his Company, with the animal covering 1400 miles." *

Finally Francesco, like other merchants, also guarded against loss by having several copies made of his business letters and sending them by different routes. "Bid them write oft to you," he instructed one of his managers, after having sent two of his men from Avignon to Naples with 2,000 *fiorini di camera* to trade with, "and also to write in every other place, that I may get their letters. They are two; let one, that is Tieri, write a letter, and Checco make 3 or 4 copies and send them in every direction." *

The speed with which these couriers travelled varied, of course, according to the regions and season, and depended on whether they were on foot (as was most usual) or on horseback. Francesco wrote that he once sent one of his men from Florence to Genoa in three days, and that it usually took six days from Florence to Venice.* But his contemporary Bonaccorso Pitti boasted that he had ridden from Florence to Padua in little more than two days, and that once, on a secret message for the Duke of Orleans, he had covered the ground from Asti to Paris in only nine days! [3] Letters to England, of course, had often to wait for wind and tide at the Channel ports, and those bound for Majorca and Spain were subject to similar hazards, as well as those of piracy. But a glance at Francesco's files is enough to show that a great many letters did reach their destination safely and even speedily. It is through them and through the business documents and account-books of his branches—for he told his *fattori* to preserve them all—that we can follow the growth and formation of his companies.

II

Partnership was, of course, characteristic of most forms of medieval trade, but whereas the trading-associations of the great sea-republics were mostly of the type called *commenda*—a short-term sleeping partnership, in which one merchant stayed at home and supplied the capital, while the other travelled abroad and conducted the business—the Tuscan ones were *compagnie:* each of the partners supplied both capital and management, and was liable to third parties for any debt contracted by any of the others. The structure of these companies, their methods, and the immense credit they came to enjoy are best understood in the light of their origin. The *compagnia* was originally a small family partnership—between father and son, or several brothers —men who lived in the same house, who broke the same bread (as the word *compagno* implies), whose interests were identical, and who therefore found it natural to accept unlimited liability for each other's actions. The partners received, of course, no salary, and it was on their skill and activity that the company's prosperity depended. A *compagnia* was as stable and secure as

[3] Bonaccorso Pitti, *Cronica*, pp. 42 and 55.

the family whose name it bore, and its credit rested, at least in part, on the solid landed property which that family owned. Subsequently these companies were extended to include members outside the family circle (although generally they were still controlled by members of the original family) or were formed by men unrelated by blood.

Datini's companies were of this last kind, but they still retained the main characteristics of the old family partnerships: many passages in his letters show how deep-rooted the tradition was that the tie between partners should be as close as a family one, a truly fraternal bond.

> What comfort and gladness and contentment there is [he wrote in his old age] betwixt two good brothers and good *compagni*, bound to each other and abiding in trusty friendship. . . . I myself [he added] am one of those who hold that two partners or brothers who come together in the same trade and demean themselves as they should, will make greater profits than each of them would separately, and that their life is as different [from that of a man working alone] as white is from black.

Moreover, he considered that the obligations implicit in such partnerships were in themselves good.

> When I formed a company with Toro di Berto in Avignon many laughed at me, saying: "You were free and have now made yourself a servant; you could rise and go to bed when you pleased, and now you must follow your partner's bidding." I replied I was glad to have a partner for divers reasons—first, to have a brother, and then, to have someone to keep me from the follies of youth.*

To Stoldo di Lorenzo, who had been his partner for over twenty years, and in whom, he said, he placed all his hopes, he even declared that the bond between two partners could be closer and more secure than any family tie. "One sees brothers betray each other every day; but good friends do not thus." *

It can hardly, however, be denied that in some respects Francesco treated his partners with less consideration than is generally a brother's due. The lion's share was almost unfailingly his own. "*Et la raison, c'est que je m'appelle Lion.*"

In many companies the senior partner—called "*capo*" ("head") and sometimes, even when there was no blood-tie, "*padre*"—still held the position of the head of a great family; it was he who decided the company's policy, and on his audacity and wisdom its fortunes largely depended. But Datini, in his own companies, went somewhat further than this. Though only a few of his contracts have been preserved, it is plain that, wherever they varied from the norm, it was to increase his own authority and power.

The main points established by these contracts—which were drawn up by a notary whenever a new company was formed—were generally much the same:

(a) *The shares due to each partner, in proportion to the capital supplied or services rendered by each*, and the consequent repartition of profits and losses. As was customary, the capital of each company—known as *il corpo della compagnia*—consisted of the contributions of each of its partners, each of whom received, when it was dissolved, a dividend proportionate to his share. In addition, however, each member could pay in further sums, which constituted what was called *il fuori corpo* (or *sopra corpo*) and on which a fixed interest of 7 or 8 per cent was generally paid, and similar deposits were also accepted from people who were not members of the company. These last, in great trading-companies like those of the Bardi and Peruzzi, often came to enormous sums, but none of Datini's companies were on this scale. In the first of his contracts, drawn up in 1367 with Toro di Berto in Avignon, each of the two partners contributed 2,500 florins and shared equally in the profits or losses, both agreeing "to employ their persons in the said Com-

pany, without any salary."[4] But in the next company—of which
the contract was drawn up in 1382, before Datini's departure
from Avignon, with the two men whom he left in charge of
his business there—the whole of the capital was Datini's, while
the other three partners (Boninsegna di Matteo, Tieri di Benci,
and Andrea di Bartolomeo) merely contributed their services.[5]
Half of the total profits were to be Datini's, the rest was divided
between the other three partners.

(b) *The time limit for the company's duration*—generally
two or three years—during which period the *corpo della compagnia* was tied up, and any partner who drew on it for his
own purposes had to pay a fine of 20 per cent. This short
duration was the general rule; most companies lasted only two
years and none more than twelve, so that in speaking of such
companies as those of the Bardi or the Peruzzi, which lasted over
seventy years, it would be more precise to say that they were
constantly renewed over that period. It was only when a company was dissolved that any member could draw out his own
share or decide—if the company was renewed—to put it
in again. In the contract of Datini's Pisan company, however—
drawn up in 1396 between Datini, Stoldo di Lorenzo, and Manno
d'Albizzo—it was stated that only Manno, the junior partner,
was bound for the full two years of the company's duration
(remaining steadily in Pisa, at the company's service), while
Francesco alone could dissolve the company or dismiss either
of the other two partners whenever he pleased.

(c) *The rule that no member of the company should belong
to any other company or guild, or do any trading except for
his own company.* This rule (which was also laid down by the
city statutes) was customary in even quite small firms—as is

---

[4] October 25, 1367. The company was to be of three years' duration, during which period the capital was to be used "for the three shops in Avignon," and neither partner could trade elsewhere without the other's consent. Toro was to live over one shop and Francesco over another. Bensa, op.
cit., Doc. I.
[5] For other similar contracts, see Bensa, op. cit., Docs. I–X.

Order for Velvet and Brocade
(SEE TRANSLATION, APPENDIX B)

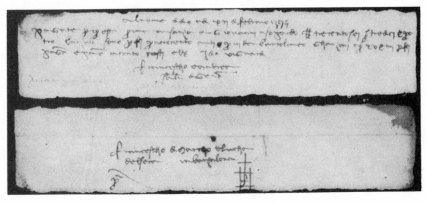

Bill of Exchange, Fourteenth Century
(SEE TRANSLATION, PAGE 150)

The Trader's Departure

Shipwreck
CODEX 492, BIBLIOTECA RICCARDIANA

shown by another deed in the Datini archives, drawn up between two manglers of Prato, of whom one, Betto di Giovanni, was also the town trumpeter. A clause stipulated that Betto might "serve the Commune of Prato with his trumpet and his person," but only on condition that he put half of his earnings back into the mangling.

But here, too, Datini made his own rules, for he was himself a member of several different companies, and controlled the management of each of them. Whereas it had previously been the custom for a *compagnia* to have one central office which controlled a number of dependent branches in other cities, Francesco, in addition to his main office in Prato, formed a separate company in each place in which he traded. Each company had different partners; he alone belonged to each, and controlled its management. This arrangement, as Professor Sapori has pointed out, marks an important step in the history of trade—its logical outcome being the "holding company" of the Medici.

Moreover, Datini sometimes even reserved to himself the sole right to dispose of the profits of one of his companies. In 1398, for instance, we find him writing to Luca del Sera:

> I am disposed, if you do well, to satisfy you by not taking out of your hands the profits made last year, and also next year's; but reckon on naught else, for it is my intent not to give way until I have put together 10,000 florins, to use as best I please.*

Well might Domenico di Cambio exclaim to the men who envied him for being one of Francesco's partners: "If Francesco has any money, he keeps it for himself!"

In short, it is plain that Datini always kept the control of his companies in his own hands, the other partners being little more than shareholders without a vote.

Each of Francesco's companies, like those of the Medici later on, was an independent enterprise, and each, in dealing with one of the others, would charge commission and interest.[6] The only common link was Francesco. The various branches, however—whose members referred to each other as "ours" (*i nostri* of Pisa, Valencia, Majorca, etc.)—promoted each other's business as much as possible. When, for instance, the wool-dyeing company of Francesco di Marco and Niccolò di Piero in Prato sent some cloth to the company of Francesco di Marco and Stoldo di Lorenzo in Florence, to be sold in Venice, the cloth was consigned to Bindo di Gherardo Piaciti, the company's Florentine correspondent in Venice, who, instead of selling it, exchanged it for pearls belonging to Messer Andrea Contarini (108 strings of 74 pearls each), and these were then insured and forwarded to the company of Francesco di Marco and Luca del Sera in Valencia, to be sold in Catalonia. When the transaction was completed, the Florentine branch credited the amount due to the company in Prato.[7] Thus, three of Francesco's companies and one of his correspondents were involved in a single transaction.

Finally, in most important trading-cities in which he had not got a branch of his own, Francesco had correspondents (*commissi*) working on a commission basis. These were sometimes, as in Venice, agents who carried out his instructions, sometimes (as in Bruges, Paris, and London) one of the Italian trading-companies already established there.

Whether Francesco's partners resented his high-handed ways must remain a moot point; but they certainly had to put up with them. Two years after entering into partnership with him, Domenico di Cambio sent him a letter of complaint in which he plainly set forth his grievances:

[6] This commission was generally a small one, as is shown by a letter from Datini to his manager in Barcelona, saying that a commission of 1½ per cent was too high. "If you yourself had trade to give, whom would you prefer, the men who demand enormous charges, or reasonable ones?" (File 1111. To Simone d'Andrea, February 10, 1406.)

[7] Piattoli, *Un mercante del trecento e gli artisti del tempo suo*, pp. 33–4, quoting a letter from Francesco's branch in Florence to Agnolo di Niccolò di Pietro, July 9, 1398.

It is now two years that I am your partner, and I tell you, since then I have known not one joyful day, and further-more, know not even now how much I earn. When I was with Benavini I had six months of the year for myself, and at the year's end I had made 150 florins. But with you I know not yet what will fall to me; so I pray you, when May comes, settle this account, that you and I may be clear with each other and I may get some comfort from my life.*

Nevertheless, the partnership lasted for fifteen more years, apparently without any improvement in Domenico's position, for when the company's affairs were wound up, Domenico grumbled that Boninsegna had once kept back 400 florins of his share to supply Francesco with funds in a moment of crisis, and that when the money was returned he [Domenico] had lost 48 florins on it. "You never had a partner," he commented, "who bore greater burdens in a company than I, and yet have I borne them all without strife." *

III

In all these companies, a great deal of the work which would nowadays be a clerk's was done by the partners, and, above all, by Francesco himself. Nevertheless, each company also had its salaried employees—*fattori*, notaries, accountants or cashiers, mes-sengers, and *garzoni*. Each of these groups of underlings had its own duties. At the bottom of the ladder were the unlettered *garzoni* (shop-boys, office-boys, and messengers). According to the books of the Compagnia de' Bardi, a *garzone's* salary, at the beginning of the fourteenth century, was seldom more than 5–7 florins a year, and was sometimes partly paid in food and clothing, and often irregularly. But a young shopman who hoped to become a *fattore* or an accountant received a regular—and slightly higher—salary. The Datini papers contain, for instance, the contract of a young Pratese, Berto di Giovanni, who was to serve in Avignon for three years at a salary of 15 florins the first year, 20 the second, and 25 the third, plus all his expenses, and there is also a receipt for the salary of a young accountant, who was paid 12 florins a year. It is characteristic of the times that in both these cases the salary was paid not to the young man himself, but to his father or mother. The number of these underlings naturally varied according to the size and prosperity of the *fondaco*, but it does not appear that any of Datini's companies employed many men. Shortly before leaving Avignon he wrote that he had eighteen people "in the house," but this probably included servants as well as employees, and he added, moreover, that one of them was ill, one "rather itchy in the hands," and all were very inexpert. "I must put the bread into the hands of each one of them [i.e., teach him his business] for they are new." *

On the second rung of the ladder came the scriveners and accountants or cashiers, sometimes called *fattori-scrivani* or *contabili* or *chiavai*—the men who kept the ledgers and held the keys of the safes and the boxes of petty cash. Boninsegna di Matteo, who afterwards became Francesco's partner in Avignon, was one of these, and how arduous his day's work sometimes was is shown in one of Francesco's letters. "He does naught but write, day and night, yet cannot do half of the great writings that have piled up during his time away. But he shall not get up from his seat, until all is done." *

To cast one's eye over the five hundred account-books and ledgers of Datini's companies is to realize how very highly evolved book-keeping had already become. Up to the beginning of the fourteenth century merchants had kept somewhat rough-and-ready accounts, which were often little more than memorandums of entries of credit, without any record of cash transactions, and indeed it would appear that in Prato, even in Datini's time, account-keeping was hardly more advanced. He complained, after his return there, that the Pratesi kept their books only in their heads, "like the carriers who reckon up their accounts twenty times along the road. . . . And God knows how they do! For four out of six of them have neither book nor ink-well, and those who have ink have no pen." But he was honest enough to add that "just for that reason, they call things to mind better after four or five years than most men would after a month!" *

Most of the great Florentine companies, however, as well as the Venetians and Genoese, already used the system of book-keeping by double entry which was then known—since only Italian merchants were acquainted with it—as "the Italian method"; and in each of Datini's companies he insisted on its use.

His account-books are of a great many different kinds. Some are merely rough copy-books called *quadernacci di Ricordanze*, in which each day's intake and outlay were set down pell-mell, together with notes and memorandums of various kinds, and even fragments of the day's news; others, called *Memoriali*, set forth in a more orderly fashion the information in the *Ricordanze*; and, finally, each company had its *Libri grandi*—kept in double entry—handsomely bound in vellum or leather, and marked with Francesco's trade-mark and with a progressive letter of the alphabet. The first page of these is almost invariably headed, as was customary, with a religious formula: "In the name of the Holy Trinity and of all the Saints and Angels of Paradise" or "In the name of God and of profit!"

In addition there were books entitled *Libri d'entrata e d'uscita*, or *Debitori e creditori*—the books setting down the outlay of petty cash—which were then summarized, in their turn, in the *Libri d'entrata e d'uscita della cassa grande*. In the *fondaco* in Avignon there were boxes for petty cash which were controlled every evening, their contents being transferred into the "great cash-box," of which Francesco alone held the keys. Both Francesco and Margherita, however, were obliged to apply to their cashiers for petty cash, and on one occasion we find Margherita complaining of being left so short that she had been obliged to borrow three *lire* to get the day's marketing done!

There were also the books of the various warehouses (inventories, receipts, bills of lading, etc.), the account-books of partners and employees abroad, the inventories of real estate, the lists of salaries, and also the twelve ledgers of the cloth-making industry of Prato. And, finally, there were Datini's private account-books, "*di Francesco proprio,*" in which he set down his personal and household expenses, and the "secret books," containing, in particular, the deeds of partnership, the accounts showing the amount of each member's share, and the balance sheets. A merchant's right to keep these books private was so well established by custom that when, in 1401, the tax-collectors of the Florentine Commune demanded to examine *all* Datini's books, Mazzei commented: "It is the Commune's need that drives it to this dishonest deed."

So important and responsible was the cashier's work that when Ser Lapo Mazzei heard that his son Piero was to be given this position in Barcelona, his first feeling was one of anxiety rather than satisfaction. "I fear me, he may be forgetful, and if you make an accountant of him and he is not well endowed with memory, he may fail, with loss and shame. . . . Yet you might try him with little sums, and see how he does." *

In a later letter he suggested that whenever the boy had forgotten to write down any sum he had paid out, he should be fined one *soldo,* "And before he has paid ten *soldi,* he will be cured for ever. And also before he takes in any money, let him write it down before he takes it. This is a blessed rule, sound and well proven." *

The company's notaries, too, had an important rule, since it was they who drew up deeds and contracts, and sometimes also acted as advocates, pleading on the company's behalf in the courts. Datini, however, did not pay any notary a regular salary, but made use of the best men on the spot: Ser Lapo Mazzei in

Florence, Ser Amelio Migliorati and Ser Schiatta di Michele in Prato, and, abroad, one of the notaries who settled wherever Italian merchants went.

Finally, at the top of the tree came the *fattori* proper, the men who carried out the instructions given them by the partners and who often became the managers of foreign branches. They received a salary "for the donation of their time," but no share in the profits. Unfortunately, no list of their salaries has survived in the Datini papers, but we know that, in general, a good *fattore* was well paid, receiving between 100 and 200 florins a year. These men were often given very full powers of attorney, but they were always the company's salaried servants and *not* partners. In some companies, such as the Bardi's, they also often received a handsome bonus ("*gratifica*") for the hazards and discomforts of living abroad, and that there is no record of any such payment to Datini's *fattori* is probably due to the fact that several of them swiftly became his partners—partly, no doubt, in virtue of their experience of local trading-conditions, but chiefly, one suspects, because he was thus able to retain complete control of each company.[8] And, finally, there were some young apprentices—*discepoli*—such as Piero Mazzei and Maso dell'Ammannato, who hoped to become partners or at least *fattori* later on.

All these men formed a large family—sometimes harmonious and sometimes not, like other families, but always held together, especially abroad, by a strong bond of common interests and common dangers. Sometimes, too, the tie between the members of a branch was actually a family one. In Avignon, for instance, one of Datini's first partners was the nephew of his foster mother, Monna Piera, and later on, when he formed a company with Matteo di Boninsegna as his partner, he decided

---

[8] Thus, Matteo di Boninsegna, employed in Datini's shop in Avignon, became his partner when he returned to Tuscany; Manno di Albizzo degli Agli rose from *fattore* to partner in the Pisan company; and Cristofano di Bartolo and Simone d'Andrea followed the same course in the Spanish branches.

to find a place there for one of Boninsegna's nephews, because, he wrote, "I would gladly do good to Boninsegna and all his kinsfolk." * In Florence, Datini employed his brother-in-law, Niccolò dell'Ammannato; in Prato he entered into partnership in the cloth trade with the son and the grandson of his old guardian, Piero di Giunta. And there were family connections, too, between Tuscany and most of the members of the Spanish branches.

All these ties gave a patriarchal character to these companies, and this partly accounts for the filial obedience that Datini required from his subordinates, though this was also a survival from the paternal relationships of an earlier age, between master and apprentice. "We gave you Manno as your son," wrote Agnolo degli Agli about the young kinsman he had placed in Francesco's company in Pisa. "You know that he is your plant, and a farmer has great gladness when his plant bears fruit." *

In illness Francesco watched over his employees with a quasi-paternal solicitude.

> My Checco went to Paradise a few days ago [he wrote from Avignon about one of his *garzoni*]. It was not from lack of care, for two good doctors were always at his bedside and all in the house, both men and women, were at his service day and night. . . . It is a great grief to me; he was a good young man and faithful.

And here is a letter written several years later to Monna Margherita, bidding her to comfort "the mother of Simone"—a young man who had died abroad in his service.

> When you receive this, send speedily for Simone's mother, and do her honour and comfort her in her affliction and offer her all there is in the house, and let her consider the house and all that is in it as her own. . . . And furthermore, say to her every good word you know of, for it is needful to comfort the afflicted.*

It must, however, be admitted that while Francesco's subordinates were still alive his tone was considerably harsher. The virtues that he required of them were those enumerated by his contemporary Paolo da Certaldo: he expected them to be "humble, loyal, solicitous, steady, honest and orderly." [9] And, indeed, this formidable list of virtues was no more than what was required by statute. A *fattore*, according to the statutes of the *Arte di Calimala*, might not work for any firm save the one that employed him, nor trade on his own initiative even for his own company's benefit; he was expected to render a detailed account of all his dealings, and it need hardly be said that the slightest breach of honesty was severely punished—both by immediate dismissal and by imprisonment. His private life was subject to a strict rule; he might not take a concubine—with the exception, indeed, of one of the household slaves, whose role was tacitly admitted—nor take part in any game of hazard, especially *zara*. "Even to mention such a thing," wrote Mazzei, "is horrible!" *

Since it was the *fattore* who ordered the day's work of a whole *fondaco*, it was necessary for him to possess, not only industry, but a clear head.

> See to doing whatever is needful [Datini wrote to a new *fattore* in Pisa] and think day and night of what you have to do. And put not so many things into your head, that one makes you forget the other, and make a note of what you cannot keep in mind, for it is not possible to remember all that one has to do, but one should always keep one's eye on what is most needful. . . ." *

"Three things," writes an anonymous contemporary of Datini's, "are needful for a merchant: sense, experience and money." [1] And he went on to define the meaning he gave to these terms.

[9] Paolo da Certaldo, *Libro di buoni costumi*, para. 1239.
[1] *Cod. Magliabechiano*, Biblioteca Nazionale, Florence. Cl. VII, n.1377. Published by G. Corti, *Arch. Stor. Ital.*, 1952, disp. 10.

By money he meant that it was desirable to trade with one's own capital and not with other people's. "For what is done with other men's money, comes to cost too dear to produce profitable trade."

By experience he meant a thorough knowledge of the quality of one's own goods, "whether they are good or mediocre or bad or false or genuine or fit to be preserved, and for how long." A merchant must know when to buy his merchandise, how to store it, and "how to keep and repair it and show it off, or if you will, falsify it, so that it is more pleasing." Much of this information was to be found in the numerous trading-manuals of the time, of which the most famous was Francesco Pegolotti's *La pratica della mercatura*, compiled by a *fattore* of the Bardi's trading-company who had lived and traded for many years in Cyprus. This manual was often consulted by Datini's *fattori*. "Would to God," wrote one of them, "that Boninsegna would for once praise the wares I send him! But he follows the rule of Pegolotti, who will never praise anything." *

Much else besides was necessary, however, to become a successful merchant abroad. Such a man had to speak one or more foreign languages (in particular, French), to make himself familiar with foreign currencies, to be capable of reporting on the prices of commodities, the rates of exchange, and the fluctuations of the market.[2] He had to keep on good terms with foreign rulers and rivals, to adapt himself to local customs and laws, and often to take sudden decisions on his own responsibility. Court mourning would increase the demand for black or purple cloth; a coronation send up the price of jewels; while the disbanding of a Free Company might bring a glut of arms upon the market.

A *fattore* abroad, in short, had to possess not only quickness and elasticity of mind, but a high degree of shrewdness.

> *Vestir basso color, esser umile,*
> *grosso in aspetto ed in fatto sottile:*

[2] Most of the letters from Datini's foreign branches end, as was customary, with a quotation of current exchange rates.

4. THE TRADING-COMPANIES

male sia all'inglese se t'atterra!
fuggi le cure e pur chi ti fa guerra.[3]

His "*senno*"—according to this Florentine adviser—would appear in "controlling and ruling every action—that is, in knowing what should be seized and what given up, not spreading oneself too far, nor undertaking more than one's purse can bear." A wise merchant would avoid "disordered and immoderate spending on clothes or other things," for "nothing weighs upon the mind so heavily, as to wish to hold too great a state"; but, on the other hand, he should also know that at times it is true prudence not to be penny-wise. "It is not always damaging to pay more than what is due—for instance to masters and middlemen." Moreover, money is always well spent that is bestowed on judges or arbitrators, for, in the words of the Scriptures, "gifts blind the eyes of the wise and alter the words of the just." [4]

Above all, *senno* is to be found in the man who is always on his guard. Any document should be judged not literally, but with discretion, "as the time and place and degree require," and "not according to its text but its intention." Any deal must be regarded with initial suspicion, "for many are the snares and malicious devices used to attract a merchant, and every man thinks that rubble will turn into gold in his hands." Friends should be chosen only for what can be got out of them—"It is good to have friends of all kinds, but not useless men"—and even with prosperous friends a man should always be on his guard. "Remember," wrote Paolo da Certaldo, "envy is more general in all men's hearts, than is commonly believed . . . and so you will not err in ever keeping your business secret and not making a show of it and not speaking in your shop of your profits or your riches." Secrets, of course, should be kept to one-

[3] Dress in a dull colour and be humble, coarse in your aspect, subtle in your dealings; woe to the Englishman who defeats you! Avoid both those who flatter and attack you." First lines of some verses addressed by Giovanni Frescobaldi "To those who take passage for England."
[4] Deuteronomy 16:19.

self: "To confide in a man is to turn yourself into his slave." But if, indeed, you have a matter you must confide, make sure first that no one is hidden behind a curtain, and speak low, so that you cannot be heard through the wall, or, better still, "Go and speak of your secrets in an open square or a meadow or sandheap or open field . . . and beware of hedges and trees and caves and walls and street-corners, and all other places where a man or woman, big or small, might hide and hearken to your words." [5]

The writer—a successful merchant himself—went so far as to say that it was wiser not to place one's *whole* trust—*la tutta fidanza*—even in one's children. And with all these sentiments Francesco cordially agreed. "The earth and the sea," he wrote to one of his partners, "are full of robbers, and the greater part of mankind is evilly disposed." * And in another letter: "Were I to be born again, with the small store of wisdom that the Lord has now lent me, I should beware of men even more than of the Devil. . . . Go about the Company's business," he added, "in shoes of lead!" *

With such a view of human nature, it is not surprising that the underlings of the great trading-companies should have been strictly supervised and disciplined. "You are my son," wrote Francesco to young Piero Mazzei, whom he had brought up as a boy in his own house. But he added: "Do your duty well, and you will acquire honour and profits, and can count on me as if I were Ser Lapo [the boy's own father]. But if you do not . . . it will be as I had never known you." *

Moreover, Francesco's paternalism towards his underlings included, as was plainly the custom, a father's duty not to spare the rod. "Chastise him in every way you can," he wrote to the head of the branch in Barcelona about his nephew Maso on one occasion when the boy had misbehaved himself, "and wear yourself out in doing so. You will acquire merit for it from God and men, for no good thing is ever lost." * Even the gentle Ser Lapo

[5] Paolo da Certaldo, op. cit., paras. 87 and 333.

Mazzei, in commending his own son to Cristofano di Bartolo, advised similar methods. "Let him not lose Mass on Sundays; let his clothing be coarse, but fit, so that he may work well in it. Let him have the stick speedily when he needs it, and make him do every low office both indoors and out, that he may ever hang his head low." *

The standard of industry, too, was relentlessly high, since it was to be equal to Datini's own.

> In May it will be two years since I have slept at ease for more than four hours a night. And so take an example. And if you would reply, "You are old and cannot sleep, and we are young and could sleep even on bare boards," I will say that I, too, would take pleasure in lying warm abed. . . .*

As to the loyalty that he required of his subordinates, he wrote that he could best describe it by an *"assempro,"* a parable. There were once, he wrote, two cardinals in Avignon who were at strife with one another, and one of them had two Florentine grooms. These decided to assassinate the other cardinal "for the great love they bore their lord." But their attempt failed, and after a while the two cardinals were reconciled—whereupon the cardinal who was to have been stabbed sent for the two grooms and told them they would always be dear to him "for the faithfulness and love that I see you bear towards your lord." Francesco did not actually urge his *fattori* to commit murder for his sake—for, he remarked, "not all men are like those two grooms, or like that Cardinal"—but he did conclude that "any man who works for another, is bound to place that man's interests before his own." *

It is, perhaps, hardly necessary to add that very few of Datini's *fattori* succeeded in serving him to his entire satisfaction. "Save for Boninsegna and Tieri," Margherita wrote to him, "you have no man who does not betray you twelve times a day!" In all his long years of trade there is only one man for whom he never had anything but praise: his first underling in Avignon, Bonin-

117

segna di Matteo, who rose to be his partner, and who, when Francesco went back to Tuscany, remained in charge of the Provençal branch for the rest of his life. He too, like Datini himself, had come to Avignon from Prato as a penniless apprentice—*humilis pauper et miserabile servus*—and, like him, had attempted to set up business in Provence. But—less fortunate or less shrewd—he had failed in all his ventures, and had been obliged (after a period of imprisonment in the Pope's dungeons) to take service in Francesco's shop. "For eight years," his master wrote later on, "he dwelled with me at a fixed salary, wherewith he bought his own clothing and food, living in great straits and sharing half his bread with his brother Francesco and his children, whom he loved better than himself, like the best and most loving brother in the world. And then he was my partner for twelve years, without adding even a penny that was not due to him to his share of the profits." Moreover, even when Datini's fortunes began to prosper and Boninsegna shared in these profits, his first thought was to pay off his old creditors. "For he desired neither riches nor advantage, but only what was needful to pay back 20 *soldi* to the *lira*, and he would not rest until each man was satisfied. And he has neither house nor land nor office, in Florence or elsewhere. . . . I reverently commend to you," Francesco concluded, "such a citizen"—and even after his death he referred to him, in a phrase which shows how rare such disinterestedness was considered, as *il santo Boninsegna.** Yet even with him Datini appears to have indulged in some sharp practice, for, after his death, his mother sued Datini, demanding an examination of past accounts of the branch, and the Florentine courts awarded her no less than 1,000 florins in damages! *

IV

It is about the life of the three *fondachi* in the western Mediterranean that we have the most information; partly, no doubt, because in Datini's later years the most important part of his trade was centred there, but chiefly because it was to his partners in these companies that he wrote the longest letters. Moreover, we have some of his partners' replies, and also the anxious letters of Ser Lapo Mazzei to his young son Piero, and about him. From all these papers a great deal of miscellaneous information may be gathered, and also a vivid, if fragmentary, picture of some aspects of a trader's life.

As we have already said, Datini's western *fondachi* were three: one in Majorca, with a small subsidiary agency on the island of Ibiza; one in Barcelona; and one in Valencia, which was connected with another smaller agency at San Matteo, the collecting-centre for Catalonian wool. At first Luca del Sera—the partner "worth 24-carat gold"—took charge of the branch in Valencia and Cristofano di Bartolo of the one in Majorca, while Simone d'Andrea, a young kinsman of Francesco's from Prato, was employed as the managing *fattore* in Barcelona. After only a couple of years, however, Simone began to complain of his salary and demanded to become a partner. "There are men," Francesco tartly replied, "who, forasmuch as they have fasted two days a week, think by the end of the year they have deserved Paradise! And thus, methinks, are you, who have only been there two years, and already would be made a partner." Shortly after, however, he relented: Simone was made a partner and put into the company 300 florins, which Francesco himself advanced. "You need not beg for them, nor be obliged to any man, for I myself will serve you." And Simone was to receive as his share "one-fifteenth of all we earn there [Barcelona] and in Valencia and Majorca." * It was Luca del Sera, however, whom Datini appointed as his managing partner—"consider Luca as if he were myself"—and who traveled to and fro between the various Spanish branches, and after 1403 the two branches of Valencia and Barcelona were fused into a single company, with a capital of 10,000 florins. Each of the branches, of course, also had its underlings—accountants, scriveners, *garzoni*, and couriers, as well as two young *discepoli*—Datini's own nephew, Maso dell'Ammannato, and Ser Lapo's son, Piero Mazzei. All these men were Tuscans: Luca del Sera, Piero Mazzei, and Maso dell'Ammannato Florentines, and Simone d'Andrea a Pratese, while Cristofano di Bartolo came from a village between Florence and Siena, Barberino di Val d'Elsa. For what sort of world did they exchange the gentle hills of Tuscany and the familiar arcades of the Mercato Nuovo? And what life did they lead?

The centre of their life, as for every merchant in foreign trading-settlements, was their own *fondaco*—the group of buildings which was at once shop and office, warehouse and dwelling. If at home, in Calimala or Por S. Maria, a *fondaco* was often merely a merchant's counting-house and shop (above which, perhaps, he lived), in settlements abroad it still kept much of the character of the Arab *funduk* from which it took its name. Originally built, no doubt, to shelter merchants and their wares from the assaults of wild desert tribes, these *fondachi* still had something of the aspect of fortified castles. In their great inner courtyards the long trains of pack-animals were watered and stabled, the slaves assembled for inspection and sale, and the bales of merchandise unpacked and stored, while the buildings served as offices, warehouses, and dwellings. Here, under the jurisdiction of their own consul (or, if there were no Tuscan in the city, with the advice of the consul of the Venetians or the Genoese) the merchants could safely transact their business according to their own laws, and pray to their own God. Here they penned the long reports they sent home, and received Francesco's rare praise and frequent "canings"; here they tried to teach their Moorish slaves the rudiments of Tuscan cooking; [6]

[6] The account-books devoted to the household expenses of the Valencian branch in 1395 record the daily fare of its members. Bread and wine were bought every day, and meat on every day but the two fast-days—Friday and Saturday—when there were fresh fish, eggs, cheese, and salad. On Sundays there were also sausages and rice (a product of Valencia). There were oil for cooking and spices (unspecified), and the fruit and vegetables mentioned are oranges, figs, apples and nuts, cabbages, beans, aubergines, chickpeas, and onions. Bensa, op. cit., Doc. CXLII.

here they kept their concubines, and sometimes, in spite of Francesco's reproofs, their little bastards. The *fondaco* was, in an alien land, their home.

The cities in which Francesco's *fondachi* were placed were already well established as flourishing trading-ports—Barcelona numbering some 35,000 inhabitants (about half the size of Florence at the same time), Valencia and Palma di Majorca somewhat smaller. At this time the kingdom of Aragon and Catalonia not only included the whole of these two states and that of Valencia, the Balearic Islands, and the little kingdom of Roussillon, but extended, through its possession of Sardinia, Sicily, and the Duchy of Athens, across the greater part of the Mediterranean. Catalan merchants and sea-captains, who had long possessed an undisputed monopoly of the trade of Northwest Africa, had now taken full advantage of the long years of strife between Genoa and Venice to become serious competitors of the Italian sea-republics in the Levant. Moreover, the Italian demand for Spanish and North African wool was greatly increasing, in consequence of the diminished exportation of English wool during the Hundred Years' War. In business technique, too, Catalan merchants were fully equal to their Italian rivals and made use of very similar contracts, while the Bank of Barcelona was probably the first public bank in Europe.

In the *Casa di Contratacion* of Barcelona—the magnificent loggia, built in 1382, in which, as in the *Loggia dei Mercanti* in Bologna, merchants met to bargain and extol their wares—Datini's Tuscan partners jostled with Moorish and Spanish merchants and Venetian and Genoese rivals, with Flemings and Frenchmen, Jews and Levantines and Greeks. A list, among the Datini papers, of prices current in the Barcelona market in September 1385 shows which goods were generally available—spices, dyes, and metals being the most conspicuous.

These lists suggest a prosperous and civilized society in constant need of fine wares. But the impression is misleading, for the veneer of civilization was still rather thin. Unlike Tuscany, where a hundred smaller cities and villages copied the way of life of Florence and Pisa, the cities of the Catalonian water-front had behind them only a bare, poor countryside inhabited by a few great lawless nobles and their hungry peasants. Moreover, the standing of Italian traders in Spain was still very precarious. The cities in which Francesco founded his new companies were among the few in the kingdom of Aragon in which Tuscan merchants were permitted to trade at all. Permits granted by the kings of Aragon to a previous generation of merchants had several times been revoked, and though special privileges were still conceded to the Pisans and Genoese, all other Italian merchants (*"Fiorentini, Viniziani, Lucchesi, Sanesi, e Piemontesi e altri qualsivoglia italiani eccitto Genovesi e Pisani a quali è già promisso"*) were only permitted to "dwell and trade in wool" in the cities of Barcelona, Valencia, Tortosa, Perpignan, and in the islands of Majorca and Ibiza, but in no other part of these dominions. These restrictions were repeated in a decree issued by the King of Aragon in 1402, of which a copy exists among the Datini papers: * they might buy only from Spaniards or Majorcans, not from other Italians, and might load their wares only upon Spanish ships. They might buy only wool which was already shorn (i.e., *boldroni*, not the unshorn fleece), and they were forbidden to make any investment in other Spanish cities. Florentine merchants, in short, like the Jews, pursued their trade in the Iberian peninsula only on sufferance—within clearly defined limits, and always subject to banishment or prohibitive taxation. According to a letter of Luca del Sera's from Barcelona, there was even a moment in 1394 when all Italian merchants in Catalonia were in danger of being called to trial, "with the Pope's consent," by the King, on the pretext that they were guilty of "usury," but with the real object of collecting an exorbitant fine. "But," Luca added, "I shall come out of it as well as the others or better, thanks to the friends we have made." *

Under such precarious circumstances all that merchants could do was to form a tight, autonomous little community with their fellow citizens, lending each other both material and moral support and submitting to the authority of their consul. This man—generally elected by all the members of the merchant community—was the true representative of the faraway Commune at home. It was he who dealt with any trouble with the local authorities, who had jurisdiction in disputes between one merchant and another, and who could be called upon for help in times of need. In Majorca, however, where the Genoese and Venetians had been established long before the Tuscans, there was no Florentine consul, and Datini's men were obliged to turn instead to the consul of the Genoese. "Trust no man there [Ibiza]," Datini wrote to Giovanni di Gennaio, "for they are evil folk. The best man is the Consul of the Genoese; if you need counsel, turn to him." *

Trade in Majorca at this time was largely in the hands of the Jews and of the Moors, who traded peacefully with the Italians in the island, even though at the same time Moorish and Italian vessels on the high seas were busily sinking each other's ships and seizing each other's wares. The great importance which the Balearic Islands came to assume in Mediterranean trade was due not so much to their produce—except perhaps for the wool called *lana di Minorica* (Minorca) and the salt of Ibiza—as to their position: they had become, as we have seen, a centre for the collection and forwarding of both Spanish and African goods to Italy, and of goods from Italy, the Balkans, and the Levant to Spain, England, and Flanders. Ibiza was a regular port of call of the great Venetian trading-fleet on its bi-yearly expedition to Flanders, while Genoese trading-ships plied their way between Majorca and the ports of the Catalonian coast, and Catalan ships touched there on their way home from the Levant. Thus these little island ports were thronged with traders of every Mediterranean race, as well as with the 12,000 local sailors who manned the armed trading-ships of the island, and a great underworld of slaves—Berber and Ethiopian, Tartar and Greek. So large, indeed, was this part of the population that in 1374—after a slave insurrection which ended in the hanging of fourteen Saracen and Tartar slaves who had tried to set fire to Majorca—a special official was appointed by the King to keep order among the slaves, and ferocious measures were taken to prevent them from running away.[7]

To this strange and alien world some of Datini's men, as their letters show, never became reconciled. "This land is pestilent," wrote Giovanni di Gennaio from the rocky little island of Ibiza, "the bread is bad, the wine is bad—God forgive me, nought is good! I fear me I shall leave my skin here." * But the men sent to the flourishing cities of Catalonia held a different view—indeed, they became, in Datini's opinion, only too well acclimatized. One of the chief characteristics of the Italian foreign *compagnie* had been that their members did not settle permanently abroad. No member of any of Datini's companies took a foreign wife, and though Francesco himself got married in Avignon, it was, as we have seen, to a Florentine. These men, like most Italian emigrants in later centuries, regarded their years abroad as entirely provisional—to be endured only with an eye to their eventual return home, when a new generation of younger men would take their place.

The young Tuscans in Francesco's Spanish companies, however, did not follow this tradition; they liked their new life so well that they had no wish to leave it. Luca del Sera did indeed return to Tuscany after ten years to become Francesco's partner in Florence, but Simone d'Andrea and Cristofano di Bartolo showed no desire to follow his example. Hardly had they discovered the warmth and freedom of Catalonia when they cast off, according to Mazzei, their Tuscan parsimony and honesty, and became "young madmen, mastered by their desires and hot blood." Simone kept, in the *fondaco* in Barcelona, a Moorish slave-

---

[7] Cf. Verlinden, *L'esclavage dans le monde ibérique médiéval*, and *Esclaves, fugitifs et assurances en Catalogne*, pp. 308–10.

woman who acquired so much power over him that she became the real mistress of the place, and from whom he contracted a disease which shortened his life. In vain did Ser Lapo remind him "how swiftly this body of ours fades and turns to nought," adding that assuredly the gout which already afflicted him had been sent "to diminish your vigour a little!" * In vain did Francesco complain that Simone and Cristofano told him nothing in their letters and point out the example of Boninsegna, the model *fattore* in Avignon, who, he said, never kept anything secret from him, "not even the first night he lay with the maid!" * In vain did he peremptorily order Simone to keep a male servant and dismiss his mistress; "I require no women in such places!" * The young man, secure in the breadth of the Mediterranean between him and his exacting master, continued to live as he pleased.

Cristofano di Bartolo was no better. "It pleases me not," wrote Francesco, "to have a partner who keeps his eyes as much in the kitchen as you do." Not only did Cristofano keep a succession of slave-women as his concubines, but he insisted on bringing up his little bastards in the *fondaco* instead of sending them out to nurse. This, indeed, appears to have been the aspect of his conduct which Francesco thought most unseemly.

> Let every *compagno* of mine get it out of his head [he indignantly wrote] that in any place I have to do with, he can boast of keeping a woman in the house or a child at the breast—for in good faith I know not, had I one of my own, if I would keep it with me. Even in Prato and Florence there are few men who keep a child at the breast in the house, even among the very rich. . . . You once said to me, you would like to be the head of a branch, to show your ability; but I now believe . . . you spake thus to do what you please and to live at ease and make merry and have much pleasure and beget bastards. . . . Perhaps, had you

ruled yourself according to my counsels, you would now have several children and be ruled by the hand of a wife, and not of a slave.

He added, however, that on this subject he would write no more "Bibles"—"for I have lost all hope that you will draw nearer to God."

The line in Francesco's mind between licit and illicit pleasures was firmly drawn: it lay between what did or did not interfere with a man's business.[8] He himself, he admitted, had not despised the pleasures of the flesh and of society, but he had never let them take him away from his shop for a single hour, and he had demanded an equal concentration of his wife. "Margherita never made herself agreeable to anyone, nor I either . . . as many women do, and many men who have a wife, so much was my mind held by the matters of my shop." *

Not only did these *fattori* disappoint their master; their influence also corrupted (at least for a time) Ser Lapo Mazzei's sixteen-year-old son, Piero, who was placed in the charge of each of them in turn. When Piero arrived in Catalonia, he was—according to a Tuscan friend of Francesco's who saw him in Barcelona—"a most amiable youth, courteous as a damsel and quick as a boy can be." * His father's letters explained that all his hopes were centred on him: he would one day be "the head of the family, and a light to illuminate all the others," and from the first his character must be shaped to this end. "Woe betide the family whose eldest son is bad!" Ser Lapo hoped, of course, that Piero would do well, and perhaps one day rise to be a part-

---

[8] It was the improvidence of his young partners that most aroused Datini's anger. "By God's grace you have made much money . . . but methinks all of you, each worse than the other, wot not how to keep it. . . . And the few letters I have had from you show me that you are like the Cardinal who, when he was still a boy and an apprentice, was wont to fast, but when he became a Cardinal, fasted not a single day. . . . For he said he had fasted on the eve of the Feast-day, but now that he had reached the state he had always desired, would fast no more!" (File 1110. Francesco to Cristofano di Bartolo, undated.)

ner himself—"Put him forward when you can do so in fairness," he wrote—but he cared far more that his principles should be sound.

> He will do you honour if you cause him to be straight, faithful and without fraud (this will be easy,) and comfort him with the love of God, rather than of riches, for which I care naught. . . . It is enough for me that the boy be honest and well-mannered, working day and night, and be taken away from the corrupt customs of Florence.

All the father's letters reveal a naïve belief that the principles of the man he was addressing were the same as his own. "I commend him to you," he wrote to Simone, "for meseems he is too far away from me, and still such a child [sì fantino]. But I shall be fully comforted if only you make him good; and if he obey you not well, beat him like a dog, and cast him into prison, as if he were your own." * He transferred, in short, to his son's employers his own absolute paternal authority, by which an unruly grown-up son might be not merely beaten, but even cast into prison.[9]

It was only after Simone's death that he learned that his son's mentor had spent his days "in wrangling, gambling and whoring," and that the Moorish slave-girl who had shortened Simone's life still continued to live in the fondaco. Then, indeed, the good notary took alarm and implored Francesco "to turn out and sell the evil and guilty woman who had caused Simone's death. Let them keep instead," he pleaded, "an old woman or man or

---

[9] One of Antonio Pucci's sonnets summed up a father's duties:
Quando il fanciul da piccolo scioccheggia
gastigal colla scopa e con parole
e passati i sett'anni, sì si vuole
adoperar la ferza e la correggia.
E se passati i quindici e folleggia
fa col baston, chè altro nogli duole . . .
E se da venti in su ti fa la fica
deh mettilo in prigion, se te ne cale,
e ivi un anno e più magro il nutrica.

boy to cook for them—that, because of your lenience, your boy and mine be not destroyed. . . . We both know what happens to a spark, when it is set close to another. . . . If I indeed believed that Piero was being corrupted by evil folk in Barcelona, I would beseech you to fetch him home again, and let him be your factor and servant for ever." *

Francesco, however, had no intention of removing a promising young apprentice. He contented himself with sending the boy a paternal homily—and a fresh letter of reproof to Cristofano. Year after year, his long chiding letters went off, useless as he knew them to be. "Did you not bite me in each letter," wrote one of his *fattori*, "you would feel you had done no good."

His reproofs were not confined to his partners' moral conduct: their management of the business, too, came in for constant criticism. A letter addressed to Cristofano di Bartolo in 1396 may be quoted as typical of many others. "You shall have such a caning from me," it begins, "as leaves a mark!" Cristofano, it appears, had committed "a great error": he had lent 700 *reali* to a Venetian sea-captain, and was likely to get no more thanks for it "than the man who set himself out to save a drowning sailor, and was then drowned himself." "A rescued man," Francesco wrote, "once on dry land, will assuredly refuse to save his deliverer, saying, 'Lo, he is well rewarded for holding my life dearer than his own!' "

The heinousness of Cristofano's behaviour lay in the fact that each of his partners was liable for any loss he incurred. This was, of course, customary in all *compagnie*, but Datini now threatened to break the arrangement.

> I tell you once for all, beware lest such things hap once more, for they will be set down to your own account; and the first thing I shall set into the company's agreement, will be this clause. I mean to bind you in such a manner that if one of you demeans himself as you have done here, it will fall upon himself.

Then followed a long list of Cristofano's other misdeeds. He had sent four bales of cloth to Alexandria, on the ship of Luca del Biondo, without any written order or surety—which was as good as throwing the cloth away. "Now go and prove to Luca del Biondo on which ship our cloth was, and what he did with the said cloth, and prove that he has received money or goods for it!" He had omitted to pay his share of the taxes at home, at Barberino, and Francesco had had to pay them for him, "that your people at home be not molested every day." And, finally, he had embarked on a foolish transaction, not fully explained, about some ostrich-feathers, and this, too, without consulting any other partner. "You mean to earn 16 per cent for yourself—let the others earn what they may!"

Francesco made it clear that he had no intention of being involved in such dealings. "I intend not to lose what I have, for I need it greatly, to make a little more. And wise merchants say, it is sometimes wisdom to wait and see, and perchance money is worth 10 or 20 per cent, merely kept in one's coffers."

"By my troth," he ended, "I vow if you and Luca beware not of causing me so much vexation, I will speedily withdraw from the trade in Catalonia!" *

This threat—of removing from the firm his capital, experience, and prestige—was Francesco's only real hold over his partners, and he did not scruple to use it. But indeed he was quite as dependent on these men as they on him, for without them none of his foreign branches could have been set up or maintained.

Owing to the slowness of the posts and the need for immediate decisions on the spot, Datini reluctantly provided his partners in Spain with very full powers of attorney—to sell, buy, barter, or otherwise dispose of any goods on the company's behalf, to load them upon any ship, to borrow or lend on the company's surety, to contract negotiations with other companies, to collect all monies due (with a right to demand the arrest and imprisonment of any debtors), and to represent the company in any law-suit, "under criminal, canon or secular law." [1] It was on their enterprise and shrewdness that he depended, to meet any emergency. After reading these letters, a strong impression remains that the real heroes of Italian trade were no longer the heads of the great companies, who sat at home, but their obscure partners and underlings in foreign parts. These were the men who had to live abroad for the best part of their lives, striving against the mistrust of foreign rulers and the competition of foreign trade—without home or family—and, when one of the dreaded epidemics of plague broke out, with no one but a black or yellow slave to nurse them. Fear of the plague hung heavily over all these little colonies of traders—and not without reason. It had been a galley from the Black Sea, with slaves on board—or so at least it was believed—that had first brought the Black Death to Italy in her hold,[2] and certainly it was observed that the arrival of a new shipload of slaves was often swiftly followed by an outbreak of *la moría*. In 1393 we find Francesco writing to warn his wife that he would not be able to get her a slave from Roumania that year, as the plague had broken out there "and those who come, die on board. It would be bringing the plague into our own home." * But the *fattori* in the *fondachi* could not protect themselves so easily. "God grant her a true pardon and protect us a little!" wrote one of them from Valencia when one of his own slaves had been carried off. "We are afraid because they are so close to us, but we are holding up our strength as best we can." *

Ser Lapo Mazzei, who had seen the ravages of the Black Death in Florence and had lost two of his children, lived in constant terror that Piero, too, would succumb, abroad and alone. Hardly

---

[1] Power of attorney made out by Francesco in favour of Cristofano di Bartolo, May 23, 1397. Arch. di Stato, Florence, *Diplomatico, Ceppi di Prato*. The same files also contain several other powers of attorney made out to Francesco's partners in Spain and Pisa between 1400 and 1404.

[2] It was believed that the Black Death had first broken out among the Tartars who in 1347 were besieging the Genoese merchants in Caffa, and who flung their infected corpses into the beleaguered city, thus spreading the disease among the defenders—the first known instance of "bacteriological warfare."

had the boy arrived in Catalonia when there was an outbreak of the Black Death—and at once Ser Lapo wrote to Francesco in deep dismay.

> Even the dread, in an inexperienced youth, may suffice to make him perish. . . . I leave it in your hands to do what you will, in your love for me, for I am still a father. Write a word to Simone, to look to Pieraccino, and if he sees him too much afeared, or if many other such as he are dying, send him back at my expense to Genoa.

The epidemic died away and Piero stayed on, but five years later it broke out again, and this time Ser Lapo was stricken by panic. Desperately he wrote to Francesco to implore that Piero should be sent away from Barcelona.

> I told you [he wrote] of Piero's good intention to abide where he is, and to obey, and not fear the plague and accept death when God shall please to send it. But I beseech you, in despite of his words, if fear should seize hold of him, permit him to go away for a fortnight or a month to some place near by. . . . Perchance he is already dead, and in pleading for him, I am in a dream. Alive or dead, God keep His hand upon him; my blessing I have sent to him, and send him still.*

Finally these merchants, year after year, had to face the perils of travel, both by land and by sea—crossing the Apennines and the Alps, or tossing across the Mediterranean on small unsafe little ships. Since they generally had some merchandise with them, they mostly travelled on the low, broad sailing-ships called *cocche* or *navi*, more stable but slower than the long, narrow war-galleys which were manned by oars as well as sail. Most of these *cocche* were not built to carry more than about 30 tons, but it appears that they were often greatly overloaded, to the peril of both goods and men. We hear, for instance, of a ship due to sail from Majorca to Venice in the autumn of 1400 which was proposing to carry "twenty-nine persons, large and small," although, the writer affirmed, "whosoever would sail that ship with twenty-nine men on board, runs into great peril." Francesco's informant, his *fattore* in Ibiza, commented that it was all the fault of "those Venetians." "When they have hoisted the banner of St. Mark, they deem they must carry at least fifty men." *

Merchants were set down, in ship's papers, in the same class as pilgrims, since the maritime laws, which were not interested in men's purposes, recognized only one kind of traveller: any men who were not sailors were either merchants or pilgrims—that is, "men who pay a charge for their person or possessions." In 1400 in particular—when the best part of Christendom was flocking to Rome for the "Great Pardon"—we find several references to mixed cargoes of pilgrims and merchandise, including a Genoese ship sailing from Majorca to Gaeta "whose cargo will be pilgrims and salt." A merchant was distinguished from a pilgrim merely by the amount of space he chartered. "What weighs less than 10 quintals is not merchandise, and no man is a merchant who pays less than 20 *pesanti*." [3]

Apparently, according to a memorandum "of all the things that are required at sea," most travellers, in addition to their wares, took their own food and cooking-pots with them. The list (which does not specify the number of travellers or the length of the journey) includes 3 large oil-jars, 6 bowls, 6 basins, 2 earthenware saucepans, 2 pewter cups, 12 glasses, and 6 knives, while the food consists of 250 white loaves for making biscuits, 1 sheep, 2 shoulders of salted meat, several pairs of fowls, 50 eggs, 1 lb. of salt, 4 lbs. of sugar, 1 little flask of oil, 2 flasks of strong vinegar, 100 sweet oranges, ½ lb. of spices, 1 lb. of cassia in beans, 2 lbs. of comfits (*tregea*), 1 lb. of rosewater, and an unspecified amount of onions, garlic, saffron, pepper, clove, and

---

[3] The laws quoted are those of the *Consolato del Mare*, in a Catalonian copy of the fourteenth century. These laws were recognized internationally, and were translated into almost every European language. Wagner, *Seerecht*, p. 66.

ginger. And, finally, to keep up the traveller's courage, there were 2 barrels of red wine and 2 flasks of "good Corsican"—and the list ended with 2 lbs. of wax candles and "comfits to set the stomach right." [4]

Certainly travellers must have needed all the courage they could muster, both by sea and by land. The roads of medieval Italy, after centuries without a centralized government, were in a far worse state than they had been in Roman days; often they were little more than a track—*l'endroit où l'on passe*. Between the comparatively safe territories immediately surrounding a city or great abbey stretched great areas of wild forest or swamp, the home of the outcast and outlawed, whence bands of brigands would swoop down on any unarmed traveller. Sometimes a band would take possession of a whole mountain village, and woe betide any merchant who passed that way!—as one may see in the complaint lodged before the *Signoria* of Florence by Ser Neri Micci of Borgo San Sepolcro, who, on his way home with some merchandise, was set upon by robbers. "*Accurre, accurre homo!*" the wretched merchant cried. "I am attacked by robbers, *devastatores stradarum!*" But though the whole village heard his cries, no one dared stir a finger to help him. [5]

To guard against such dangers, wise merchants travelled in large parties with an armed escort—or else, as Paolo da Certaldo advised, lied beforehand about their destination.

> *Ne saccia alcun andando*
> *Qual via fai camminando.* [6]

The stretch of sea between Catalonia and the Balearics was well known to be perilous, and the correspondence of those branches contains many references to narrow escapes. "The gal-

---

[4] Livi, op. cit., p. 33. The list, dated 1393, is entitled "Remembrance of all the things that are needful for us at sea."

[5] Davidsohn, *Forschungen zur Geschichte von Florenz*, III, pp. 189–90.

[6] Nor let any know, when you leave,
  By what road you mean to pass.
    —FRANCESCO DA BARBERINO, *Reggimento e costume di donna.*

ley from Peniscola is in these seas," a typical letter runs, "and they say she is bound for Majorca. God sink her speedily. I have goods to send to Majorca and Barcelona and they cannot sail on account of her." And, indeed, three days later the pirate-ship had seized "an armed ship with twelve oars, carrying salt—very rich, worth more than 4,000 florins, loaded with silver and cloth. The goods belong to Jews and recently converted Christians." *

On one occasion Tieri di Benci, Francesco's partner in Avignon, fell into the hands of Corsican pirates and had to be ransomed, together with the goods on board—the ransom, of 2 *soldi* per pound, being shared by the ship's captain and the company.[7] On another occasion, it was a ship bearing Tieri's young wife, who, together with the wife and three small children of Dr. Naddino da Prato, the Pope's doctor, was attacked by a Genoese ship at the mouth of the Rhone as the women were sailing to join their husbands in Avignon. No one was injured, but the ship's merchandise and equipment were stolen, the captain despoiled and left in his tunic (*"in giuppone"*), while the women lost all their jewels and money and had to make the rest of the journey on foot.*

The most dreaded fate of all was capture by the Moors—and this was a not infrequent occurrence. One letter contains the appeal of an unfortunate young Tuscan, Jacopo di Giovanni Franceschi, who had been captured off the African coast and had fallen into the hands of the "worst dog in Barbary." He implored "all the Florentine merchants in Majorca" to pay his ransom of 190 *dobre*, charging it to his former master, the consul of the Catalonians in Pisa—"and I will come to your place and stay with any of you whom you will." *

And an even stranger story is implied in a document drawn up by a notary, presumably for the captain of a ship bound for Tunis, asking him to inquire "whether there is anywhere in Bona, Neri di Ser Lodovico of Florence, captured as a slave." This was a young Florentine who, having sailed as a scrivener

[7] Bensa, op. cit., Doc. CIII.

sixteen years before, had been captured by Moors and sold in the markets of Tunis. After ten years the Venetian consul there had sent news that the young man had become "the slave of a miller," and that he (the consul) would ransom him and bring him home. But the consul had died, the young man had run away "into the Kingdom of Garbo," and his father "could never get any news of him, and would pay 100 florins to have him back, and would like to know whether he is alive or dead." *

Such were the journeys and such the risks by which the countries of Europe were gradually united in a tight network of trade. If the brains were those of the great merchants at home, the risk and the daily toil were those of their anonymous, forgotten servants.

CHAPTER FIVE

MONEY

"Tal fatto è fiorentino, e cambia e merca." [1]
—DANTE, *Paradiso*, XVI, 61

N THE LAST TEN YEARS OF THE FOURTEENTH CEN-
tury Francesco di Marco achieved all that he
had set out to do. He finished his fine house
in Prato, bought land, and built himself a villa;
he became a member of the cloth guild of Prato
and of the silk guild of Florence; his *fondachi*
at home and abroad were firmly established; he was a rich and
respected man. And he never knew a peaceful hour. Day after
day, night after night, he brooded over the perils that might
overtake his ships and his merchandise.

I dreamed last night [he wrote to his wife] of a house
which had fallen to pieces, and all my household were
therein. . . . And the meaning of this dream gives me much
to ponder on, for there are no tidings of a galley that left
Venice more than two months ago, bound for Catalonia;
and I had insured her for 300 florins, as I did the other ships
for Domenico di Cambio, which perished the next day. . . .

[1] "One who is now a Florentine, and changeth coin and wares."

5 · MONEY

I am so vexed with many matters, it is a wonder I am not out of my mind—for the more I seek, the less I find. And God wot what will befall. . . .*

In the fourteenth century it was not customary for trading-companies to own ships of their own; they either sent their goods on a ship chartered from a ship-owner for a specified period, or—in the case of smaller consignments—paid for carriage on a vessel which also carried other cargo.[2] When a merchant or one of his underlings travelled himself with his goods, the consigner often merely made an entry in the ship's log, but generally the goods of Datini's companies were sent, as had become the custom, unaccompanied, with a bill of lading and sometimes also a separate letter of advice, stating their amount and value, and giving instructions for their disposal.[3] The contract of charter generally specified that half the price of the shipment was to be paid before departure, and the balance within a specified time of delivery. This was consistent with Pegolotti's advice: "Let merchants be warned not to pay the dues, in whole or in part, to the ship's master, not to lend him any money." But he added: "Let the merchant avoid this *if he can* . . . but let him act according to the need he has of the vessel.[4] This

---

[2] The terms proposed, for instance, for the charter of three galleys in Nice or Marseilles were 1,300 florins per month. In case of capture the ransom would be divided equally by the merchants and the ship-owners. The galleys were to be of twenty-nine benches, and provided with archers. For various types of carriage contracts see Bensa, op. cit., Docs. LXXX and CXXVI.

[3] The following is a typical letter of advice: "In the name of God to a safe passage. The bearer is Pietro di Sarro d'Ardignone, master of the ship named *S. Giuliano*. By the said ship I am sending you 105 *salme* of wheat loaded in Termini and it is fine wheat, the finest on the place; and the said master is to deliver the said wheat to you within eight days and is to have 5 *tari*, 12 *grane* for each *salma*." Bensa, op. cit., Doc. LXXVIII. August 17, 1388.

[4] Pegolotti added that a wise merchant would take care to choose a rich shipmaster, for a poor one often borrowed such large sums before sailing, on the surety of his cargo, that he preferred to let it sink rather than pay up! *La pratica della mercatura*, ed. Evans, p. 323.

advice certainly suggests that the need of trading-ships was greater than the supply, and that sometimes merchants in a hurry had to give way to inordinate demands, in order to be able to ship their wares at all.

Contracts of charter generally contained clauses stating whether the ship's master assumed full responsibility for the goods they carried, in which case the goods were said to be sent *"salvi in terra"* (delivery guaranteed), or disclaimed this responsibility, when the merchandise was said to be sent *"ad risicum et fortunam Dei, maris et gentium"* ("Subject to the hand of God and to hazards of the sea and of [hostile] people").

Regular convoys of trading-ships, escorted by war galleys, were sent out several times a year to the chief ports of the Mediterranean and the Black Sea from Genoa and Venice (supervised and sometimes subsidized by the governments of these cities), and a prudent merchant like Francesco would spread his merchandise over several ships, so that, in case of shipwreck or piracy, something at least might be saved. But it would appear that sometimes these convoys merely facilitated the pirates' task, for in 1393 Francesco wrote to his wife that he expected some of their ships to be captured, because

> there are many ships at sea and only one trade route, by which some sail in one direction, and others sail back. . . . We have divers galleys at sea [he added] and we know naught for certain yet. . . . We have much merchandise therein and it is all insured, but we are not like to escape save with great loss. May God be praised for all! *

It was Datini's rule, as this letter shows, to insure all his merchandise, even though some of his correspondents thought this expense unnecessary. "We would not insure these five galleys for even a groat," wrote Bindo Piaciti from Venice in 1401; "meseems we would cast away the money spent on this, for the passage is safe." * But when Datini's own partner in Genoa once failed to insure some goods bound for Barcelona, he drew upon himself a sharp reproof, even though the ship had already safely arrived.

> Touching your saying now, the ship has reached Barcelona safely, you are no prophet—and if some evil *had* come to her, it would have been the worse for you. . . . For you have our orders never to send any merchandise of ours lacking insurance, and let this be said to you once for all.*

It appears, however, that insurance monies were not always easy to collect, for on one occasion, when Datini had goods worth 3,000 florins on a galley sailing from Venice to Catalonia, he wrote to his wife that, if it went down, he would lose at least 500 florins. "For when they insure, it is sweet to them to take the monies; but when disaster comes, it is otherwise and each man draws his rump back, and strives not to pay." *

The successive stages by which the insurance contract reached its modern form have given rise to some controversy as to what trading-cities first made use of them, but certainly by the fourteenth century unmistakable insurance contracts—involving under-writers who were not the same persons as the ship-owners —were in use both in Genoa and in Tuscany. Datini's companies not only caused their own goods to be insured, but did some under-writing—in particular, the Pisan company, which kept a record of some of the policies it had issued in a note-book dated 1384, which has been preserved. On its cover is written: "This is the book of Francesco of Prato & Co., partners abiding in Pisa, and we shall write in it all insurances we make on behalf of others. May God grant us profit, and protect us from dangers." [5] The goods insured included wool from Catalonia and Minorca to Porto Pisano, cloth from Porto Pisano to Tunis and Palermo and Naples, silk and fustian from Porto Pisano to Barcelona, and malmsey (in a Genoese ship from Cadiz) to Sluys and South-

---

[5] Bensa, op. cit., Doc. CXXVII. These notes are translated into English in Lopez and Raymond, *Medieval Trade in the Mediterranean World*, pp. 263–5.

ampton. The premiums varied from 3½ per cent to 5 per cent, except for the malmsey, for which the premium was 8 per cent.[6] Each of these records ends with the note: "Arrived safely."

Another policy, dated 1385 and drawn up in the form then customary in both Florence and Pisa, enumerates the risks for which the insurers assumed liability: "from act of God, of the sea, of jettison, of confiscation, of princes or cities or any other person, of reprisal, mishap or any other impediment." Usually a time-limit was set for a ship's arrival—after which, if no news was forthcoming, the insurers had to pay full indemnity.[7] When a ship was lost, the insurers' approval was required for any attempt of the owner to recover his goods: there is, for instance, a letter from Teramo and Tommaso Cattaneo, Genoese insurers, authorizing Andrea di Bonanno to recover, if he could, 22 sacks of wool, insured for 200 florins, from a ship captured by pirates off the coast of Elba.[8]

II

One of Datini's salient characteristics was his ability to draw advantage even from misfortune. When any of his ships was lost, he told his wife not to keep the news secret, but to spread it abroad: perhaps he might then be thought a poorer man, and so reduce his taxes!

Let every friend know [he wrote] how I am placed. . . .
Say that four or five of our galleys, which have been captured at sea, held half of all we possess, and, except God

---

[6] These were low premiums, for Giovanni da Uzzano considered a fair premium to be as much as 12 or 15 per cent.

[7] Insurance policy of Francesco di Marco & Co., in Pisa, for 400 florins on goods loaded on a Provençal ship, from Arles to Porto Pisano, July 11, 1385, and insurance policy of Francesco di Marco and Domenico di Cambio for 2,100 florins on *merci sottili* from Motrone to Aiguesmortes, July 10, 1397. Bensa, op. cit., Docs. XI and XIV.

[8] Ibid., Doc. CXXXIX, November 3, 1394.

help us, we shall be destroyed. Let not your mouth dry up, in saying such good words.*

His dread of taxation was certainly justified. If in Prato he had been able to conceal the size of his fortune from his fellow citizens, in Florence his fellow merchants were well aware of it. When his partner Domenico di Cambio was called upon to pay a tax, he wryly remarked that he hoped Francesco's "tender care" would do him as much good as the mere fact of being his partner had already injured him. "For every man deems me up to the neck in gold, forasmuch as I am with you." *

Now, it was the custom of the Florentine Priors, when the exchequers of the Commune were empty, to levy a high tax— thinly disguised by the name of a loan, *prestanza*—on the inhabitants of the territory of Florence (to which, of course, Prato belonged), and they sometimes also exacted the immediate payment of a large sum by one of the rich merchants trading inside the city—especially if, like Francesco, he was not a Florentine citizen. Generally, however, a man was not taxed on both accounts: he paid his tax either in the country or in the town. In 1393 Francesco—according to his letters to his wife and to his partner Stoldo di Lorenzo—had paid the customary tax in Prato, and great was his indignation when in the following January he was called upon for another large sum. "Those who pay in the country cannot be called upon for a loan, unless indeed they have brought the trouble upon themselves, by becoming citizens," he wrote to Stoldo, adding bitterly that this was his reward "for all the money I spent on this blessed house, to do honour to Florentine citizens!"

> Will they not remember [he cried, in Shylock's very accents] how much I have paid out and the courtesies [loans] I have rendered to my own Commune and to many others? . . . And furthermore I pay in Avignon, and have been taxed in many other fashions . . . and shall all this count for naught? I will not pay in more than one place! Will

they make a new law, only for me? I am half out of my mind, pondering on all these matters! *

At the same time, too, he was writing to his wife:

> I am in as great tribulation as ever a man was, touching the great injury that beseems is being done to me: Never have I had tidings that grieved me so. These members of the *Gonfalone* fight against me with all their wits; and they are so strong, I fear me force will prevail over justice.*

He was determined, however, to fight, and to find some strong friends to back him. "As you know," he wrote to Stoldo, "justice sometimes fails through lack of support, and I have been advised to cause every friend to come to my succour." He himself, he said, was writing at once to Ser Lapo Mazzei, his friend and notary—"who has been the *procuratore* of our Commune and knows all these things better than anyone"—and to Filippo Corsini and Guido del Palagio (both Priors of the city), "commending this matter to them, that they should see to it, and I suffer no injustice." At the same time he sent Stoldo a long list of other men to whom he must appeal: Messer Francesco Rucellai, "who men say is the most obliging man in the world," and Matteo Strozzi, and six or seven others. "Every good man," he wrote, "must take pleasure in doing what is just for his friend. . . . Read this to them all . . . and make a note of whatever parts you think best. And forsake me not at this point, for never has aught grieved me as this does." And the letter is signed "Francesco di Marco in Prato, with toil." *

In spite of all these efforts, Francesco was summoned in April before the *Signoria*, and was told he would be detained there for some days. He decided at least to make a fine appearance. "Send me," he wrote to his wife, "my gown lined with taffeta and my scarlet hood and a pair of black silk hose, with the slippers and the scarlet cloak." *

It was at this point that Francesco was saved from disaster by

142

two of his friends: Lapo Mazzei, his notary and his closest adviser, and Guido del Palagio, who had recently been appointed as *Gonfaloniere di giustizia*—a man of such high character and standing that to have his support was almost a certificate of honesty. He appears, indeed, at first to have hesitated to take Francesco's part, saying to Mazzei: "Be very sure the man is in the right." But when once he had made up his mind, he did not stint his support. "Guido said," wrote Mazzei, " 'Whatever befalls, I will do my best to save Francesco, with as little loss as possible, and as much honour!' " And Mazzei added a warning, which reveals what the general custom in such cases was, that Francesco should refrain from attempting to reward Guido with any gift: "For should you endeavour to pay him even a groat, he would ne'er be your friend or well-wisher again." *

Margherita, too, was well aware of the importance of Guido's support. "Though I be but a woman," she wrote to Mazzei, "I well know what we owe to Guido. I trow, had Guido not been there, this matter had been so grave that Francesco would have been sent out of this city, or else his life here would have been short." *

Yet in spite of these influential friends, the case dragged on. "Were I to sum," Datini wrote, "all the cares I have ever known, they would not be as great as the dread which now casts me down." *

At the root of his anxiety lay the fact that, except for Ser Lapo Mazzei (and perhaps, to a lesser extent, Guido del Palagio), he had no real friend in Florence. Like other merchants who had spent the best part of their youth abroad, he had become almost a foreigner. "Say not," was Paolo da Certaldo's advice to the merchants of his time, " 'I will send my boy to France and let him be brought up and taught to trade there," for when he comes home he will never be a good member of the guild: . . . and always his heart will remain in France!" [9] Moreover, Datini was not even a Florentine citizen by birth, but a member of the

[9] Paolo da Certaldo, *Libro di buoni costumi*, para. 252.

class which had been regarded with hostility and distrust by the Florentines since the days of Dante—the men of the *contado* who had established themselves in town, and had gradually taken possession of most of Italy's trade.[1] He felt that he was considered an outsider, a yokel, and an upstart.

> Here, I have a hold upon none [he wrote to Margherita] and the things that please them, please me not. It is no marvel that no man will intervene in my matters. And justice is dead, and mercy and pity and faith and honour. Every man goes straight to what he deems to his advantage. In words they are all grieved and say a more shameful thing than this has never been done in Florence; but no man stands up to say, it must not be allowed.*

In his resentment, he began to regret that he had ever left Avignon.

> I left a good place and good people [he wrote] and have fallen among devils. Assuredly, if I live a little longer, I had better go and fulfil my penance where I committed my crime [i.e., in Avignon]. I would rather be a little less at ease there, than prosperous here. . . . Never shall I rest until I have drawn out the greater part of what I have here, and placed it elsewhere. I would have my riches in Avignon or Catalonia, and—if my friends will permit it—myself, too, with all my household.*

These plans were never carried out—perhaps, even, never fully intended—but certainly if Francesco expressed these sentiments to his Florentine friends, it cannot have increased his popularity. Only men who, like him, had once lived and traded in Avignon could share his views.

[1] It was of these men that Dante wrote:
> lo puzzo
> *Del villan d'Aguglion, di quel da Signa,*
> *Che già per barattare ha l'occhio aguzzo!*

("The stench of the yokel from Aguglion or Signa, whose eye is already sharp for barter.") *Paradiso*, XVI, 55-7.

144

5 . MONEY

I see and understand from your letter [wrote Giuliano di Giovanni, who had also just come back from Provence] you would fain be in Avignon, for there I trow you will never be glad. Even as you wish yourself back again [in Avignon] even so do I, and nineteen out of twenty other men who abided there. . . . For here greater injuries and slights are done to merchants than, to my belief, elsewhere in the world, aye in Saracinia, or Pagania or Turkey, or the place where the Jews have their reign. . . .*

In the end, the question of Datini's taxes was settled by a compromise. The case was dismissed, but he had to pay 800 florins into the Florentine exchequer—an enormous sum for those days. "And be assured," he wrote to his wife, "that had it not been for Guido, they would have eaten me up alive!" What rankled, he wrote, was not only the money, but the injustice—"a grief that has destroyed both my body and soul. For all Florence knows of the injustice that has been done to me."

Moreover, he foresaw that unless Florentine citizenship was granted him, such a tax might at any time be repeated, and once again it was the support of Mazzei and Guido del Palagio which enabled him to obtain his wish.

This evening at eleven [wrote Mazzei] I was called before the *Collegi*[2] and when the audience was over, I heard the Twelve speak very well about our matter. Guido supported our cause very well, after I had spoken. And the end of it is, they all unanimously approved your being released from the *estimo* and from every tax in the *contado*. May God be praised and thanked, for I feared me we should lose.

The victory was Francesco's, but he soon discovered that his new position did not exempt him from the other forced loans

[2] The assemblies of the *Gonfalonieri* and of the twelve *Buonomini* of Florence were called *collegi* because it was there that the representatives of the people (*Buonomini*) discussed the city's affairs with the members of the *Signoria*. Mazzei, June 27, 1394.

which at frequent intervals were levied by the harassed Commune.

> Last night [he wrote to Margherita] four loans were voted, which methinks will be published today. Tell Barzalone [his *fattore* in Prato] he will no longer feel like making merry, and will don his week-day coat on a feast-day. . . . God help and counsel us, for we shall need it.

Before he had finished his letter, the news had been proclaimed.

> The four loans are announced for April, and I know not where to find a *denaro!* I shall abide in prison until we can pay, and shall be in good company there, for methinks a great many others will have to go there, too.*

This was not the last of these impositions. The levying of *prestanze* continued to be the Commune's main resource in any crisis, and no rich merchant could hope to escape. How much pressure, indeed, was laid upon this class of citizens throughout the whole of the fifteenth century is shown in the words addressed to them by Savonarola: "When you see," he cried, "that the city needs some money, come to her succour with all you can! Lend your private means to save the public good . . . and I bid you, lend not to the Commune on interest [*ad usura*], but for naught." [3]

Datini, however, never fully resigned himself to these exactions: on each occasion he felt freshly aggrieved and indignant.

> Bethink you how merry I am [he wrote to Cristofano di Bartolo] forasmuch as since I became a citizen I have paid 6,000 florins in six years, and now they [the taxes] are doubled. . . . I shall see torn from me in my old age all that God has lent me, and all I have earned in fifty years with so much labour. . . . I have reached such a point that

[3] Fra Girolamo Savonarola, *Prediche*, ed. G. Baccini, Firenze, 1889, p. 563.

methinks, if a man stabbed me, no blood would issue
forth! *

The taxes to which this letter refers were fifteen loans levied
in 1401, to raise the enormous sum of 500,000 florins for the
German Emperor, whom the Commune was imploring to defend Tuscany against the troops of Gian Galeazzo Visconti.
Francesco himself was in Bologna at the time, and Ser Lapo
urged him to remain there, saying that if he were at home it
would hardly be possible to avoid showing the officials his account-books, and the full amount of his fortune would be revealed. But in his absence Ser Lapo could fight and lie for him,
"saying and unsaying, promising and vowing and preaching, and
living as in Hell, a devil among devils." Undoubtedly on this
occasion the good notary allowed his friendship to get the better
of his honesty, or considered (as many others have done) that
statements made to revenue officers are in a field apart, for he
prepared a draft for Francesco of a letter to the assessors, in
which Francesco not only stated that his affairs in both Avignon
and Catalonia were going so badly that he was daily proposing
to withdraw from them, but added that all his property, apart
from his houses, was not worth 2,500 florins—a lie so blatant as
to be hardly worth refuting, but accompanied by most pious
protestations of patriotism, and of a wish to pay "even 22 *soldi*
in the *lira*." *

Francesco got off with the payment of 775 florins, but in the
following spring he was called upon to pay another 106 florins,
and noted sourly that this was no less than the thirteenth "*prestanza piacente*" (willing loan) that had been demanded of him.
It need hardly be said that his chagrin was extreme—and now
Ser Lapo, having done all he could to protect him, took up his
pen and advised him to take comfort in the thought that many
others had suffered more than he.

Look you, Francesco, you should comfort yourself about
the loan and all else that has befallen to the whole city . . .

for this is not an injury done to Francesco, but to every citizen. . . . Incline your thoughts rather towards the men whose bed has been taken from under them, who suffer from the cold or have to give up buying wine, and, in the name of God's charity, weep for them, rather than for yourself! *

III

An accusation which it would scarcely seem fair to levy against Francesco is that of neglecting his trade. But he himself apparently considered that during the first ten years after his return to Tuscany he had often allowed a frivolous preoccupation with building to distract him from his real business, and it was in the tone of a man turning over a new leaf that early in 1398 he announced his intention of giving up building and farming, and devoting all his energy again to his affairs. "Meseems it were better to give heed to my trade, than to build and plough up the hills." * He ordered some tables and shelves for a fine new office in Florence, and rearranged all his papers; he went over his account-books. Misunderstandings had arisen because he had not kept in sufficiently close touch with his branches abroad—especially with those in Spain. "But now I shall demean myself so, that we shall all understand each other, and each man shall have his own task; and one man shall not say: 'The other has done this to me,' and the other cry: 'He lies!' For I shall keep so close to these matters, I shall at last see the truth." *

In the same year he entered into partnership with another Pratese, Bartolomeo Cambioni, and opened with him a bank in Florence, and in the following spring—on March 4, 1399—he joined the Florentine money-changers' guild, the *Arte del Cambio*.[4]

---

[4] The registers of the *Arte del Cambio* of Florence record both Datini's entry into the guild and his partnership with Bartolomeo di Cambio. "*Fran-*

5 · MONEY

This step was, at this stage of Datini's career, an entirely natural consequence of his previous activities. Throughout the later Middle Ages the avocations of merchant and banker were very closely connected.[5] Traders in money could be divided, roughly speaking, into three classes: the petty money-lenders or pawnbrokers, often called *lombardi*,[6] who offered loans at a high interest in return for a pledge (mostly small sums to poor men) —thus performing, in spite of all the odium attached to them, a necessary social function; the money-changers, who dealt in the actual exchange of coins and the trade in bullion and precious stones, and who occupied a respectable and authorized position in every city, being largely responsible for the regulation of currency and the detection of counterfeit coins; and, finally, the great international merchant-bankers, to whose ranks Francesco already belonged. The essence of their business was its diversity: as the member of the *Cambio* traded also in jewels and precious stones and sometimes in works of art, so the merchant dealt not only in goods, but in bills of exchange. If one year he lost money in trade, he could make it up in his exchange dealings, supplying his clients, through his foreign branches, with money or goods abroad (without any real transfer taking place, but always taking a commission *pro portaggio e cambio*). The Datini papers show that Francesco often took part in such transactions, and although the claim is erroneous that he was actually the inventor of the modern bill of exchange—an informal letter, as opposed to the formal deed drawn up by a notary which had been in use until

ciscus Marci de Prato, Bartholomeus Francisci de Cambionibus, iuraverunt et promixerunt ut supra et dixerunt se esse socios et alios socios non habere." Arch. di Stato, Firenze, *Arte del Cambio*, Matr. 12 (1385–1598), March 4, 1399, and Reg. 14, April 10, 1399.

[5] In the twelfth century the *Arte del Cambio* and the *Arte di Calimala* formed part of a single guild.

[6] Professor R. De Roover, in *Money, Banking and Credit in Medieval Bruges* (pp. 345–6), has pointed out the confusion arising from the two different meanings attached to the word "lombard" in medieval documents. Sometimes the word was used as synonymous with "caorsino" or pawnbroker; sometimes (as in the case of the lombards of Lombard Street) it described any merchant from Lombardy, or even from other parts of Italy.

then—it is certainly true, as is testified by more than five thousand of these bills among his papers, that he made a free and constant use of them; and it is with a sheaf of them in his hand that his statue stands in the main square of Prato.

The following bill of exchange (see plate facing page 104) is a typical one:

> In the name of God, the 12th of February 1399 Pay at usance,[7] by this first of exchange, to Giovanni Asopardo £306 13s. 4d. *Barcelonesi*, which are for 400 florins received here from Bartolomeo Garzoni, at 15s. 4d. per florin. Pay and charge to our account there and reply. God keep you.
>
> Francesco and Andrea, greetings from Genoa.
> Accepted March 13.
> Set down in Red Book B., f. 97

[on back]
> Francesco di Marco and Luca del Sera in Barcelona (first of exchange) *

In this bill, as was then usual, four parties were involved: (1) the borrower or drawer (*prenditore o traente*), Francesco and Andrea (di Bonanno) in Genoa; (2) the payer or drawee (*trattario o pagatore*), the Barcelona branch of Datini's firm, to whom the bill was addressed; (3) the payee (*beneficiario*) in Barcelona, Giovanni Asopardo; and (4) the deliverer or remitter (*remittente*), Bartolomeo Garzoni, who bought the bill and gave consideration for it. The bill was made out on February 12, 1395, and accepted on March 13.[8]

---

[7] Usance was the time customarily allowed for the payment of a bill of exchange. The usance between Genoa and Barcelona was 20 days.

[8] For the whole question of bills of exchange I have followed Professor De Roover (*Money, Banking and Credit in Medieval Bruges*, chap. IV), who has based his conclusions largely on material in the Datini papers, clarifying once and for all the use of these somewhat complicated terms. Cf. also De Roover, *L'évolution de la lettre de change* and *Le contrat de change depuis la fin du treizième siècle jusqu'au début du dixseptième*.

Profits on the purchase and sale of such bills—which always involved an exchange, as well as a credit transaction—were generally recognized to be high, if precarious. "I would rather earn 12 per cent with our merchandise," wrote Domenico di Cambio, "than 18 per cent on exchange dealings." * But it was precisely the precariousness of the profits that caused these transactions to be approved by the Church, on the grounds that, since the bills were bought and sold at a fluctuating price determined by the unpredictable variations of the exchange, the banker's profit was not—like interest on an ordinary loan—"a *certain* gain," and therefore not "usurious." That large sums, however, were often involved is shown by many letters in the Datini papers, in particular in those of the Spanish branches, since Francesco's correspondents in Bruges often used their credit balances with his branch in Barcelona to make remittances to Italy, and vice versa. For instance, in a letter dated January 9, 1400, we find the Orlandini firm of Bruges instructing Datini's branch in Barcelona to remit 1,000 florins to Genoa, 1,000 ducats to Venice, and 1,000 florins to Florence, covering these transactions by drawing on Bruges. And on February 21 of the same year the firm Bernardo degli Alberti of Venice drew a bill of 400 ducats at 16s. 8d. *Barcelonesi* per ducat on the Datini branch in Barcelona, requesting them to charge the amount—£333 6s. 8d. *Barcelonesi* —to the Alberti Co. of Bruges.*

The purpose of the bank which Datini now opened in Florence was neither to break into a new field nor to take over the exchange dealings of his various branches, but rather to co-ordinate and centralize these previous activities. The bank's ledgers show the names of some of the same correspondents whom we have already encountered in Datini's trade dealings: Giovanni Orlandini and Neri Vettori & Co. in London, Giovanni Orlandini and Piero Benizi & Co. in Bruges, and Deo Ambrogio in Paris and Montpellier—as well as Datini's own branches in Italy, Avignon, Spain, and Majorca, and other companies in Venice, Bologna, Lucca, and Rome. In addition, the bank had a number of independent clients—mostly wool-workers of Florence or artisans of Prato—who had deposit or current accounts on which regular interest was paid, and who were also granted loans.

The contract between Datini and Cambioni, at the time of the company's foundation, has disappeared, and the books do not record the amount of capital contributed by each. But since the firm bore Datini's name and trade-mark, it would seem probable that, as in every other company founded by him, his share was the largest, and that Cambioni contributed a smaller sum, in addition to his services. It was he who managed the bank, and its chief ledger, the *Libro dei debitori e creditori*, is kept in his hand.*

The bank offered its clients a variety of services: acceptance and issue of bills of exchange, loans (though only to other trading-companies or private clients, not to princes, Popes or Communes), endorsements (*avalli*), guarantees (*fideiussioni*), and correspondence accounts in one or more currencies. For payments to third parties, cheques, which were only just coming into use, were freely accepted.

During the first two years of its existence, the bank was extremely active, and undoubtedly it would have extended into a still wider field, had it not been for the renewed outbreak, in 1400, of the Black Death. All business came to a standstill: debtors and creditors alike fled from the diseased city, and in the summer Cambioni—whose son had already escaped to Bologna with Datini and his family—followed them there. But it was too late; he had already been afflicted by the contagion and succumbed a few days later.* After his death the company was gradually liquidated—two "arbitrators" deciding on the distribution of the profits on exchange dealings, of which, in the end, three quarters went to Datini and one quarter to Cambioni's heirs.* The bank had lasted less than three years, but was already, in its technique and in the instruments it employed, one of the most advanced in Europe. Professor Melis, indeed—who has devoted a whole section of the Datini exhibition to the merchant's banking activities—has declared that it was in some respects more advanced than the one then considered to be the first bank in Europe, that of Barcelona.[9]

This phase of Datini's career gave rise to a letter which is of peculiar interest to the social historian, since it provides a curious glimpse of the attitude of the common man to the whole business of banking and money-changing.

> Divers men have said to me, Francesco di Marco will lose his repute as the greatest merchant in Florence, by becoming a money-changer; for there is not one of them who practices no usury in his contracts. I became your advocate, saying you mean still to be a merchant as before, and if you keep a bank, it is not to practise usury. But they reply: "The world will not speak thus: they will say, he is a *caorsino* [usurer]!"[1] And I reply: "He does it not to be a usurer, forasmuch as he will leave all he has to the poor!" But the other replied: "Think not he will ever again be as great a merchant as he was, or in such high repute." You have been badly counselled over this! *

Finally, the writer said that this step was not only wrong, but inexpedient. "Wots not Francesco that, if the Commune need money, it will weigh upon him to enter into exchange dealings on its behalf, and he cannot say them nay? For Francesco's shoulders are not as strong as those of some other citizens, who can say nay to the Commune."

As to this last point, the writer was certainly right: Francesco, who had only recently become a citizen and who was already marked down for heavy taxation, was in no position to deny the Commune anything it asked. To state, however, that

---

[9] At the *Mostra dell'Archivio Datini* parallel current accounts of the Barcelona bank and Datini's bank showed that Datini's was the more advanced of the two.

[1] The origin of the word *caorsino* is uncertain—possibly it is derived from the merchants of Cahors, who were also bankers. In the later Middle Ages it was used, like "lombard," as a synonym for usurer.

by joining the *Arte del Cambio* Francesco would necessarily draw upon himself the stigma of "usurer" shows how great a confusion still reigned in men's minds as to what a usurer really was. "Usury" was forbidden by statute and condemned by all honest men—but it was a very wide and ill-defined term. According to the strict rule of the Church, as we have said, it was usury to take not only excessive interest, but any interest at all, from a loan. "*Quidquid sorte accessit, usura est.*" This view was unquestioningly accepted, for instance, by Francesco's most trusted adviser, Ser Lapo Mazzei, as is shown by the answer that he gave about one of Datini's loans. Ser Lapo wrote that he would have no part in the transaction, "for meseems it would be against the laws and statutes of God—which are, that no interest should be taken on a loan of money." And a few days later he added: "Methinks you are bound to give back that money to Ludovico, as arising from a *contratto usuraio;* and meseems I, too, should confess and make penance." *

Even St. Thomas Aquinas, however, had included, in his definition of "the just price," that any damage caused to the seller might be reimbursed to him, and it followed that if a creditor could prove that some damage had been caused him (for instance, by slowness in repaying a debt) it was licit for the debtor to pay him compensation.[2] This net proved to have a very wide mesh, since in practice it served to authorize the taking of interest under the name of compensation (or sometimes of a gift).

But the confusion in men's minds only increased—as well it might, when even their spiritual leaders could not dispel it! "There are certain cases," wrote Fra Jacopo Passavanti, a celebrated preacher of Francesco's time, in his *Mirror of True Penitence*, "touching which even wise and lettered men are in doubt . . . such as usurious contracts, which are so many . . . one can hardly understand them. And some men conceal and excuse them

---

[2] "*Hoc enim non est vendere usum pecuniæ, sed damnum vitare.*" *Summa*, 2.2.978, art. add. 1.

154

under the names of exchange or interest, and others with those
of deposit or savings. Some call them purchase and sale, or profits
involving hazards or deferred payments, and yet others say they
are investments, companies, associations, and other abominable
profits." [3] In short, the good friar, in his confusion as to what
deals were licit or illicit, ended by condemning practically any
form of trade!

The common man, moreover, did not attempt to grasp any
subtle distinctions: he confused all men who dealt in money
with the *lombards*, the pawnbrokers. He remembered a scene that
was often before his eyes: a little man (very often a Jew—since
Jews, not being bound by the Church's laws, were free to exercise the execrated profession) seated from dawn to sundown in
the market-place behind a table with a little cloth, noting down
his odious accounts in his ledger, demanding an interest of 20,
30, and even 40 per cent, and—for a pledge was necessary—
taking away from a poor man his patched tunic, from a widow
her cloak or bed. [4] Nothing was too bad to be believed of such a
man. In the depositions during the trial of some usurers in Pistoia
at the end of the thirteenth century, one of them was referred to
as a heretic (twice branded as such with a cross, on his chest
and thighs) and others as blasphemers, liars, drinkers, and whore-
mongers. True or false, these accusations show the usurer as he
appeared to his contemporaries: Shylock with his pound of flesh,
the personification of cupidity and avarice. In foreign cities other
Italian merchants would not associate with the *"lombards"*; they
were excluded from the Sacraments and they were even denied
burial in holy ground. Fra Filippo degli Agazzari told, indeed,
in his *Assempri*, the horrifying tale of a usurer whose corpse was
placed in a mortuary chapel that his heirs had built for him, but
on the night after the funeral "all the devils of Hell surrounded
the chapel wherein he lay, with so much noise and clamour that

---

[3] Fra Jacopo Passavanti, *Lo specchio della vera penitenza*, p. 23.
[4] Sapori, *"L'interesse del denaro a Firenze nel trecento"* in *Studi di storia
economica medievale*, pp. 96–115.

for miles around no man could sleep; and in the morn it was seen that the chapel had been uprooted and cast into the river near-by." [5]

Certainly the odium attached to the usurer's trade is not difficult to understand: the poor debtor had had a great deal to bear. We may form some idea of the rates of interest demanded of him when we recollect that Giotto, though he depicted the allegorical marriage of St. Francis and Our Lady Poverty, did not scruple to hire out looms to poor weavers at a profit of no less than 120 per cent. [6] And in the University of Bologna, in the middle of the thirteenth century, even the professors of jurisprudence lent money at a high interest to poor students who had to buy codices for their studies—and then, when the books had found their way to the pawn-shop, the jurists bought them back again at a great profit!

To wipe out the usurer's sins alms were not enough: he could obtain pardon only by full restitution, in his lifetime or at his death, of every penny of his illicit gains. An instance of such a restitution, which took place when Francesco was already living in Florence, was shown in the will of a Florentine usurer, Bartolommeo Cocchi, who laid down (to the chagrin of his heirs) that every groat earned by him unrighteously was to be given back to those he had wronged, before any other bequests were paid.

Such wills were far from uncommon; they testify to the ever increasing divergence between the moral law and general practice. But it is characteristic of this time of transition that, in spite of all the differences in standing between an international merchant-banker like Francesco and a wretched usurer like Cocchi, the common man still uneasily felt that *any* transaction concerned with money, as opposed to goods, must have the taint of

[5] Fra Filippo degli Agazzari, *Assempri*, XI. Christian burial was denied to *usurari manifesti* by the Lateran Council of 1179, and this was confirmed by the Second General Council of Lyons in 1271. "Their bodies," wrote Fra Filippo, "should be buried in ditches, together with dogs and cattle."
[6] Davidsohn, *Firenze ai tempi di Dante*, pp. 414-15.

The Money-Lender
CODEX DE SPHÆRA

usury—so that the best defence Domenico could find for his friend was merely "all his goods will be left to the poor."

In actual fact, the only transactions of Datini's which did sail, by the standards of his time, rather near the wind were two forms of exchange in which his Spanish companies, at least, certainly did deal—*cambi a termine* (with deferred payment) and *cambi secchi* ("dry exchange"), both of which were strongly condemned by the Church. The former were transactions involving deferred payments, which often contained concealed interest, owing to fluctuations in the exchange in the interim between the ordering and payment of the goods; while the latter—*cambi secchi*—were really concealed loans (sometimes made with the connivance of an agent abroad) by which a man could procure money by making out a bill on a foreign market on which he had, in actual fact, no credit—his correspondent merely redrawing at the prevailing rate as soon as the bill was due. Thus, no real exchange transaction ever took place, and the operation became what the Church called a usurious exchange.

How plainly such practices were condemned by the theologians of the time is shown in a curious little treatise written, at the request of Savonarola, by Fra Santi Rucellai, a Florentine banker who in his old age had joined the Dominican order and who was requested by Savonarola to set down, as a practical man, his views as to what was, or was not, licit. His treatise was indeed strictly practical, but his condemnation of *cambi secchi* was unqualified. With regard to other exchange dealings, he rightly commented that the real point at issue was "the good or evil intention." "For human malice, when a man would conceal or disguise his dealings, may circumvent all obstacles placed in its way. But from God, who searches our hearts, it cannot be hid." [7]

The Datini papers plainly show that Francesco's Spanish com-

[7] "*Il trattato di Fra Santi Rucellai sul cambio, il monte comune e il monte delle doti*" (1495-7). Published by De Roover in *Arch. Stor. Italiano*, 1953, Disp. I.

panies, at least, did deal both in dry exchange and in transactions with deferred payment. "These exchanges," wrote the honest Ser Lapo in dismay, "which you make at hazard, without any letter or [transfer of] coins, are as bad as playing at dice. . . . If ever I hear that Piero has done such a thing, I will cut him off from me, as one lops off a rotting arm." * Luca del Sera, too, Francesco's partner in Valencia, appears to have been uneasy about these transactions, not so much on grounds of morals as of experience, since some other Italian merchants who had taken part in them had been arrested by the King of Aragon.

> Methinks you have already heard from our men in Genoa that the King has brought the usurers to trial, and has had leave from the Pope to do so. They consider those who sell with deferred payment to be usurers, and if it be their intent to pursue them all, they will ruin this city.

He added that so far he had been left alone. "But I tell you plainly, henceforth I will not trade, save in ways wherein I cannot be molested." *

Simone d'Andrea in Barcelona, however, was less prudent or more greedy, and continued to take part in exchange dealings, in spite of repeated orders to desist.

> I have told you ere now [Francesco wrote in 1400] that for no man on earth will I agree to the company's exchange dealings. Once for all, I would have you a merchant and not a banker. If you are not so disposed, you will see how swiftly any agreement between us can be brought to an end.

Apparently, however, Simone did not change his ways, for two years later he was warned again. "I have told you," Francesco wrote, "these *cambi* please me not at any cost . . . and for several reasons. The first and chief is, they are not licit, and the second, I would not run into such dangers." But Simone was incorrigible, and four years later Francesco again threatened to break with him. "If you feel inclined," he wrote in 1406, "to buy

or sell money on the exchange, and attend to the business of
many money-changers . . . find someone else who is of a like
mind, for I will not be caught to satisfy your hunger, nor dwell
in constant fear." *

Francesco, in short, never allowed his cupidity to overcome his
prudence—nor was he, by the standards of his time, a dishonest
trader. He repeatedly boasted—even in his private letters to his
wife—that he had always kept his word, had indulged in no
sharp practice, had never made illicit profits. Yet in all these
protestations there is a flavour of uneasiness, and undoubtedly
his love of money and his indefatigable, implacable pursuit of it
were so great as to be remarkable even in the loving-money
society to which he belonged. It dismayed and alarmed all those
who had the welfare of his soul at heart. "Crave not for all!"
his foster mother had warned in his youth. "Sappiti temperare" [8]
was his wife's constant refrain. "In Christ's name," warned Fra
Giovanni Dominici, "beware of rising too high: that snare has
caught some very big birds." * Even his business partners joined
in the chorus. "Let me remember and beseech you," wrote
Domenico di Cambio, "clutch not at every bird that flies. . . .
Be content with what God has given you, and strive to keep it."
And, in another letter: "In good faith, Francesco, a man must
think of earning money, but also of taking pleasure with his
friends. But you think each man is like unto you." *

But, above all, it was Lapo Mazzei who, from the first years of
their friendship, gently and unceasingly poured counsels of moderation into Francesco's ears.

> It grieves me [he wrote] that you should take these en-
> terprises of yours . . . with so great an avidity, desire, so-
> licitude and anguish. It is not good. A wise man should
> learn to bridle himself . . . and not thus follow his desires,
> but demean himself with moderation and temperance. . . .
> You know men are not pleased with a house wherein the
> maid rules her mistress; even so the soul wherein reason is
> ruled by the will, is displeasing to God.*

[8] "Learn to temper thy desires."

159

Here Ser Lapo was merely setting forth the teaching of the Scholastics: that virtue lies in "the just mean." "Sin lies in exceeding this mean." From this it followed that to possess a fair share of this world's goods was justifiable, or at least enough to meet a man's needs and his family's, with a margin for charity; what was wrong was to make the pursuit of money the main object of one's life.

Laymen, no less than churchmen, unquestioningly subscribed to this doctrine, and thought poorly of those who disregarded it. For—apart from the teaching of the theologians—this view of life was entirely in harmony with the Tuscan temperament. To be free from excess—in art and in life—is what the Tuscan truly admires. "Courtesy," wrote Paolo da Certaldo, "is naught but the mean—and the mean endures." [9] In all matters a man should choose the middle way, "wherefore you will be praised and accounted wise"—and if there should be a choice between too little and too much, a wise man will always prefer the former. This is the trait which has produced all that is finest in Tuscan art and life: a moderation extending from material matters to a true sobriety of soul. And it was, in the highest degree, the virtue practised by Ser Lapo Mazzei—both because it came naturally to him, and because he believed that this was what God required. "Measure is God's demand, and no immoderate thing was ever pleasing to that eternal equity."

It was this tradition that Francesco offended and yet was ashamed to offend. For in this respect, at least, his temperament was singularly un-Tuscan. Perhaps he had been affected by the pomp and show of the papal court; perhaps he was merely acquisitive and ostentatious. It is certain that he liked, not only money, but all its trappings: fine clothes, large houses, great banquets, guests with titles to their names, and a crest to put over his doorway. He was, in short, very much the typical *parvenu*—boastful and ill at ease.

Again and again in his letters his inner discomfort was re-

[9] Paolo da Certaldo, op. cit., para. 375.

vealed in a promise so often repeated that it seems a vow to himself rather than to his hearers. He protested that he would moderate his desires, wind up his worldly affairs, have time for thoughts of God. "May God give me grace, if it be His pleasure, to lead a better life than in the past, for it is a dog's life—and it is all through my own fault."

Sometimes, indeed, he felt so vexed with himself that he tried to lay the blame on one of his partners.

Because I ruled myself ill and did not what I could and should, in all this Lent I have heard only six sermons: that is a fine and good life, for one of my standing! . . . And therefore I remember you, at no price will I go on leading the life I have led. And I will no longer work so hard, and will no longer wait for King Arthur's coming [1] and demean myself as if I would live to be a hundred! This I say to you, that you may take heed not to undertake anything new, for at last I will wind up what I am doing and lead a better life.*

But then a ship would come in from Catalonia, or a new loan would be issued by the Commune, and every resolution was forgotten. The shrewd, grasping merchant was at the helm again.

[1] "King Arthur's coming"—the millennium.

PART TWO

THE

HOUSEHOLDER

CHAPTER ONE

HUSBAND AND WIFE

"Donne, col capo basso! È la donna che regge la casa!" [1]
—S. Bernardino da Siena

OR THE FIRST SEVEN YEARS OF FRANCESCO'S MARriage, his young wife is only a shadowy figure in the background of other people's letters. But with the couple's return to Tuscany, Monna Margherita, too, enters upon the scene—and thenceforth, at least in domestic matters, holds the stage.

After seven years the couple was still childless, and this was the rock on which their marriage foundered. Francesco, as we have seen, had already had at least one small bastard in Avignon, but what he sought in marriage was an heir, to whom he could leave his riches "in love and delight." For this he chose a bride who, though dowerless, was young and handsome, and who was one of a large family—and his friends at home approved his choice. But when the first years passed and no child arrived, their anxious tongues began to wag, their curious eyes to peer. "Come home!" cried Monna Piera. "With God's grace, you will get a child here. He has granted you riches there [in Avignon].

[1] "Women, bow your heads! It is the woman who rules the house."

Here he will give you a family." * Six months later Niccolozzo
wrote:

> Monna Piera desists not from praying, by day and night,
> to God to give you an heir, to make you glad. But she also
> says, if you come back here, you will find an air that will
> drive away your cares: and gladness is fertilizing, and too
> much grief the opposite.*

Margherita's own relations advised a similar remedy: the couple must come home. "These lands," wrote Margherita's brother-
in-law, Niccolò dell'Ammannato Tecchini, from Pisa, "are male
and fertilizing" (*maschili e multipricativi*), and he added in a
later letter that the air of Fiesole, too, was said to be "*multipri-
cativa*"; he had met some Genoese who had been unable to have
any children in Genoa but who, having moved to Tuscany, had
at once been blessed with a family. His advice must have been
particularly galling, since *his* wife, Francesca (Margherita's sister), had just presented him with a fourth son. "May God be
praised and thanked, and may He grant them grace to grow up
good men." Francesca even, later on, offered to lend one of
these boys to Margherita, but could not resist, at the same time,
a sisterly dig: "She says she will only lend, not give, them, since
she [Margherita] knows not how to make them herself." *

This theme is the *leit-motiv* of Francesco's and Margherita's
letters. In 1385 the rumour spread in Prato that Monna Margherita was pregnant at last, and one of Francesco's partners
wrote to ask him if it was true.[2] But of course it was not, and
for some years we hear only of vague fevers and pains of an
unspecified nature. In 1395, however, Datini's friend, Dr. Naddino Bovattieri of Prato, who had set up practice in Avignon,
wrote from there to say that if, as he believed, Monna Margherita's case was similar to that of another patient of his, who

---

[2] "It has been told us," wrote Niccolò di Piero di Giunta, the son of
Francesco's tutor, "that Monna Margherita is with child. That were good
news indeed . . ." —May 24, 1385.

suffered from "pains every month before her purgation," he could cure her. His other patient, he wrote, had been so much benefited that "not only was she freed from her pains, but she made a male child, and this year she has made a female one; and they are all alive and well." * His prescription is unfortunately lost, but it was plainly ineffective, for several years later Margherita's sister in Florence, Francesca Tecchini, was suggesting another remedy.

> Many women here are with child [she wrote] and among them the wife of Messer Tommaso Soderini and many others. I went to inquire and found out the remedy they have used: a poultice, which they put on their bellies. So I went to the woman and besought her to make me one. She says she will do so gladly, but it must be in winter. . . .
> She has never put it on any woman who did not conceive, but she says it stinks so much, that there have been husbands who have thrown it away. So discover from Francesco if he would have you wear it. The cost is not great. And may God and the Virgin Mary and the blessed St. John the Baptist grant you this grace.*

Whether or not Francesco rejected the evil-smelling poultice the letters do not tell, but certainly it, too, failed—for two years later Niccolò dell'Ammannato was sending her, on behalf of his wife, another remedy.

> She says it is to be girded on by a boy who is still a virgin, saying first three Our Fathers and Hail Marys in honour of God and the Holy Trinity and St. Catherine; and the letters written on the belt are to be placed on the belly, on the naked flesh. . . . But I, Niccolò, think it would be better, in order to obtain what she wishes, if she fed three beggars on three Fridays, and did not hearken to women's chatter.*

This disappointment, constantly renewed, gnawed away at the core of Francesco's and Margherita's marriage. It is hardly necessary to look any further to explain the strain and exasperation that their letters reveal. Here is reason enough to account for Margherita's self-defensive petulance at first and her resigned sadness later on, and for Francesco's irascibility and frequent absences. The couple returned to Prato together, but very soon afterwards, as we have seen, Francesco went to Pisa, to start a new branch there, and most of the next sixteen years of their life—from 1384 until their journey to Bologna in 1400—were spent apart. Francesco spent most of the year in either Florence or Pisa, looking after his business interests in both these cities. Margherita sometimes joined him, but mostly remained in Prato, looking after his house, his servants, and his adopted daughter, sending him shrewd accounts of what was happening at home, seeing to his washing, and supplying his table.

It was this separation which—in addition to their childlessness —caused the chief trouble between husband and wife during the next twenty-six years. Margherita was never able to resign herself to it, and Francesco frequently repeated that he, too, deplored it; but when, later on, Margherita came to live in Florence, it was he who went away, spending much of his time in Pisa or Prato. It is to these frequent separations that we owe the long, detailed letters that the husband and wife exchanged—and the picture of an unhappy marriage.

The relationship shown in these letters was from the first a difficult one, but—even though Margherita was childless and impatient, and her husband irascible, restless, unfaithful, and cross —the marriage was not devoid of either affection or mutual respect. From Margherita's letters a strong and simple character emerges. It does not, however, conform to either of the recognized feminine types of the period: she was neither Beatrice nor Griselda. We see a girl married at sixteen to a man who was already tired and soured, and who required from her, most of all, what she could not give him: a houseful of children. A woman exasperated by her failure to perform this elementary function, and by the unceasing good advice of friends and re-

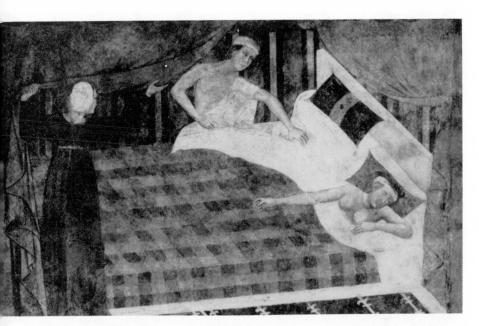

The Bed

The Bath
FOURTEENTH-CENTURY FRESCO

Tartar Slaves
BY PIETRO LORENZETTI

Evenings at Home
CODEX CASANATENSE 4182

lations; but also a full-blooded and quick-tempered girl, bored and exasperated by her husband's nagging and by his constant business worries, but making the best of a bad job—taking her sister's child to live with her for company, enjoying the laughter and gossip of a few other young women of her own age, and at last, when she had given up all hope of having a child of her own, agreeing to adopt and bring up her husband's bastard, even though its mother was a slave. A woman who, as she grew older, showed herself as shrewd in business as her husband and an admirable housewife, fully capable of standing up to Francesco and of berating him soundly—and, in his last years, attempting more gently to lead him towards the pious thoughts which had become her own chief consolation.

The correspondence begins in 1382, at the time of Francesco's first move to Pisa. Apparently his intention was for his wife to join him, and his first letter enumerated his reasons.

> Methinks [he wrote] if I am to achieve my ends, I cannot abide here for less than three months or more . . . and meseems we should all abide here together, rather than one here and the other there. We should have to spend in both places, and I should have poor comfort here, and you but little there.

He added that he expected to die of starvation if his wife did not come soon.

> I eat naught that pleases me, and they are not things to my liking, and the bowls are coarse. Were you here, I would be more at ease. And perchance this is the last time we shall have to tarry away from home, and it is good to endure it; our own bread at home will taste the sweeter.*

Margherita's reply was all that a husband could desire.

> Meseems it would please you to have me there with the whole household, and yet you leave the choice to me. This you do of your courtesy, and I am not worthy of so much

169

honour. I have resolved to go not only to Pisa, but to the world's end, an it please you.

In spite, however, of all these good intentions, the couple remained apart, and their letters during the next few years set forth Margherita's grievances and her husband's attempts to placate her. Not only did she resent his prolonged absences, but she complained of his writing long letters to Simone d'Andrea Bellandi (a young kinsman in Prato who later on became one of Francesco's *fattori* in Barcelona) and not to her; she felt she was being treated like a servant or a child. "Methinks it is not only on business that you send him these scrolls, day after day. You must be confiding to him some dis-ease of mind. But methinks he is not to be trusted more than any of the others. . . ." *

To these complaints Francesco replied with surprising meekness. Once, indeed, he exasperated his wife by suggesting that her last letter must have been dictated by someone else, because it was "beyond the fashion of a young female." Perhaps, he added half-ironically, it presaged an early death. "For there is a saying among the vulgar, when a child does or says a thing beyond his years, 'That child is not meant to live!'" But he went on to admit that much of what she had said was "as true as the Lord's Prayer." "Assuredly I have sinned in many things, and they weigh greatly upon me. But believe it to be as true as death, it is now my intent to live in another wise."

> As I know not in whose hands this will fall, I will not reply to all; but in speech I will open my heart to you. . . . For yourself, strive to be of good cheer and do what you can for your part, and leave the rest to *Messer Domeneddio*. In one manner or another He will grant us to live together until our death, and perhaps as well as our neighbours. For there is no man in this world, great or small, who has not some ill-fortune, and some things that please him not.

The letter broke off, but later in the day a postscript was added: "Ne'er have you been so joyful touching many matters, as you will be on my return. It has pleased God to soften my heart about many things which used to grieve you—and you were right, and I never said you were not." *

This was, surely, a most conciliatory letter. But Margherita was not mollified. The suggestion that her letters were not composed without help wounded her deeply.

> You must hold me even cheaper than I weened, to think I should let my letter be dictated for me. . . . Francesco, I trow I wrote to you too boldly, and showed too much pride in speaking the truth. Had I been with you, I would have spoken with a smaller mouth. . . . Yet I am still for ever speaking the truth to you, in so far as I know it. I have written naught that I have not said leastways once a month when you are here, when perchance I say it not so fitly. For each day I see you doing things that make me swell up a dozen times.

On such occasions, as she herself admitted, she was unable to resist the taunt that her husband was of humble birth, while noble blood ran in her own veins. "I have a little of the Gherardini blood, though I prize it not overmuch; but what *your* blood is, I know not."

Margherita's next letter, too, showed that she was still nursing her grievances.

> You bid me make merry and be of good cheer. I have naught in the world to make me merry; *you* could do so if you would, but you will not. . . . Each night, when I lie abed, I remember me you must wake until dawn. And then you bid me be of good cheer!

Then follows a passage that cannot be interpreted with certainty, but appears to have been dictated by jealousy.

> I believe no word you write. On every other matter I would take my oath that you would never tell a lie; but as

171

to your keeping a w——[the page is torn], as to this, I would vow that you never spoke the truth.

As to your making peace with me, I am glad: for I was never at war with you. I know not what gift you will bring me; that I cannot understand, but when I get it I shall say grammercy. You are not wont to bring me too many gifts when you come home.

As for Francesco's good resolutions, she replied that she did not believe a word of them. "We shall both live a long time, and always in the same fashion." *

While these letters were being exchanged, Francesco and Margherita seem to have kept up, in the sight of their friends, the façade of a happy marriage. "Methinks there are few women," wrote Lapa, the wife of Niccolò di Giunta, who had formed a close friendship with Margherita, "who love their husbands as you do yours. I know not well," she added, a little doubtfully, "what his demeanour is to you. I ween it is the same, for you deserve it."

Nevertheless, it would seem that Margherita—still a very young woman, and high-spirited as well as quick-tempered—plainly showed that she was more at ease with these friends of her own age than with her cross, elderly husband. "Francesco says," wrote Lapa, "you never laugh heartily save when you are with me, and I, for my part, only laugh heartily with you. And Francesco says in his letter that he would fain have you love him, even as you do me." *

Francesco's own friends and partners, too, could not fail to become aware of the bickering that went on in *casa Datini*, and those who were themselves more happily married were not slow to point out the contrast.

Verily [wrote Domenico di Cambio] I eat roast chestnuts every morn before I set forth, but that is because my wife pampers me, as I do her. Not like unto you, who are always wrangling with yours; and yet you say: "I am a good husband!" Leave that rather to me, who give mine both words and deeds.*

Niccolò dell'Ammannato was of the same opinion. When Margherita refused to accept some cloth for a new gown, Niccolò wrote to Francesco:

> Methinks there are some secrets between you, which you will not have bandied in other men's mouths. Well, go with God. I live more simply with my Francesca, and what her will is, is mine too.*

Very swiftly the tone of Margherita's letters changed; soon little was left of the docility with which she had declared herself willing "to go to the end of the world" so that her husband might be well served. A year later she was telling him instead that, if he chose to stay away, he must put up with some discomfort.

> It grieves me that all things are not as fit for you there as here, but sometimes it is well to experience a little dis-ease . . . for what seems so to us, would seem comfort to many. But assuredly, if you alter not your manner of life and give up a few things of this world, and look to your soul as well as your body, I fear all will turn against us.

A little consideration to his servants, too, would not be amiss. "Try to eat at the appointed hour, for your own sake and that of your household: they will be better pleased."

As the correspondence proceeds, we can watch the couple drawing further apart, and the wife's tongue becoming sharper.

> As to your staying away from here until Thursday [she wrote in 1389] you can do as you please, being our master —which is a fine office, but should be used with discretion. . . . I am fully disposed to live together, as God wills. . . . And I am in the right, and you will not change it by shouting!

Methinks it is not needful to send me a message every Wednesday, to say you will be here on Sunday, for I trow on every Friday, you repent. It would suffice to tell me on Saturday that I could buy something more at the market: for then at least we would fare well on Sundays! *

Again Francesco's reply shows his belief that soft words cost nothing. "When you come here, and hear from all men concerning my demeanour, you will be satisfied. . . ." And the letter was signed: "Francesco di Marco in Prato, with much grief on many accounts, owing to my failure in many things." *

Why is it, we may wonder, that all Francesco's efforts at reconciliation failed? His letters are always the more yielding of the two; they are full of soothing phrases and of promises of amendment. Why was it that Margherita never believed him, or met him half-way?

One cause for discord, at least, is not far to seek: it is written in Francesco's private note-books. Since Margherita could not give him a child, he turned to other women who could—and the family was well aware of his roaming eye. "Greet Margherita for me," wrote his brother-in-law Niccolò, "and when you leave for Pisa, tell her from me to remind you of what the women of the Marches say to their husbands at parting: 'Remember your home!' And she will understand me well." *

Soon after, however, it was in her own home that Margherita had cause for jealousy, as is shown in Francesco's private note-books. Here is the entry:

> Remembrance—That on March 11, 1387, I gave in marriage Ghirigora who lives with me—that is I signed her marriage contract with Cristofano di Mercato da Prato. . . .

Ghirigora was a maid-servant listed in the census of Prato as a child of twelve at the time of Francesco's return—a girl whom Francesco himself had described to his wife as "having little sense," and who was even now only fifteen.

Another entry in Francesco's note-book, in May, recorded the loan of a plough and of a feather-bed to Cristofano, and next there was an entry about Ghirigora's wedding, stating that she had been given, for her dowry, not only the large sum of 165 florins, but two new chests filled with clothes, linen, and household goods, to the value of 45 florins.

Finally, four months later, came the explanation:

Before dawn on the 6th of September, Ghirigora of Fiviglione di Borgo da Brescia, wife of Cristofano da Mercato, gave birth to a male child, whom she says to be the child of Francesco di Marco.*

And the note went on to say that the child was baptized on the evening of its birth and put out to nurse with the miller's wife—being provided with "six woollen and fourteen linen swaddling-bands, a little cover for the cradle and a pillow."

Such an event, in a place as small as Prato, could hardly be concealed. The foster mother proved unsatisfactory, and by December 16 the baby—now frankly called "*il fanciullo mio*"—was back again, with his little bundle of clothes, and was handed over to another nurse, and then, on December 25, to yet another. In the following February, Niccolò di Giunta, who obviously knew the whole story, was writing· to Francesco in Pisa: "The child is well, and will be a fine boy. God make him a good man, if it be His will." * But three days later bad news followed. The foster mother's husband came to tell Niccolò that the child had "the accursed sickness"—and though three doctors were called in and "beaver's fat" was administered, it was in vain.

On March 6 Francesco's note-book held a final entry. "Today March 6, 1387, the child died, and rests in San Francesco, at the foot of my own tomb." *

As for Margherita, there is no doubt that she knew about it all, for another entry in the note-book, of 1 florin, 6 *soldi* for the purchase of 5 *braccia* of unbleached woollen cloth, specified that it had been given to Monna Margherita to make a cover for the child. And another entry tells of 25 *lire* given, on Ghirigora's behalf, to the nuns of the Convent of Sanmichele: "Monna Margherita took them."

The story, however, was not quite ended. Three years later, in 1390, Niccolò di Giunta was writing to tell Francesco that Ghirigora's husband, Cristofano, was dying. He asked whether Francesco would take her into his house. "For she has a child at the breast and she will need some bread. . . . You gave her a dowry and brought her here, and now I must remind you of your soul and your honour."

But Francesco refused point-blank to take her, and Niccolò's next letter shows that once again he had come to the rescue. He wrote that he would take the woman "for as long as you wish, even a year or two. . . . And I will do for her [Ghirigora] what I would for Monna Margherita, in all faith and honour." *

It is not a story in which Francesco cuts a fine figure, and it was hardly possible that the whole episode should not have been galling for Margherita; especially, perhaps, the baby's burial in the place of honour before the altar, which should have been reserved for Francesco's legitimate children. Nevertheless, the whole situation must not, of course, be thought of in terms of our own times. The Tuscan *famiglia* of the *trecento* was a far larger and more elastic organism than the modern family: not only wives, but concubines had their place there; not only sons, but bastards. Many a young bride, on arriving in her new home, might find among the maid-servants of the house some who were her husband's concubines and others who were his sisters, and not a few respectable householders, in reporting the members of their family to the tax-collector, would frankly include their illegitimate children—some of whom had slave-girls for their mothers. Sometimes, even, such a child might be legitimized by its father and treated in all respects as his heir. But even when no legal steps were taken, the little bastards—sometimes yellow or coffee-coloured, when their mothers were Tartar or Moorish slaves—grew up by the side of their half-brothers and -sisters in

the general easy-going tolerance of family life, and were even-
tually apprenticed or married off. It was only when the mistress
of the household was unusually strait-laced or jealous—or perhaps, like Margherita, embittered by her own childlessness—that
the child would be sent instead to one of the foundling hospitals
which existed in almost every city "to receive the children whom
their father and mother, against the laws of Nature, have deserted—that is, the children who in the vulgar tongue are called
castaways, *i gettatelli.*" [3]

The baby would be placed on the steps of the foundling hospital or handed in by a revolving window, sometimes with an
identifying mark or note pinned to its garments. And quite
often, when the child was a little older, it would be adopted by
a respectable family, or even be taken back again by its own
father.

This was the destiny of another of Francesco's illegitimate
children: a little girl to whom he gave the name of Ginevra, who
was born to him in 1392 by his twenty-year-old slave-girl Lucia.
We do not know what Monna Margherita said on this occasion,
but certainly she must at first have refused to bring the child up
at home, for Ginevra is referred to (in Francesco's will) as "a
certain girl who was secretly placed in the hospital of S. Maria
Nuova." But she was soon removed from there and sent out to
nurse, for the next record of her, in 1394, is an entry in her
father's account-book of 26 florins, to be paid "to the husband
of the foster mother who keeps Francesco's daughter." [*] In 1398
—when the child was six years old—Margherita relented: she
agreed that Ginevra should come to live in Prato and be brought
up as Francesco's daughter, and at the same time the child's own
mother, the slave Lucia, was married off to one of Francesco's
servants, Nanni of Prato [4]—probably with a good dowry, like
Ghirigora, for she was also remembered, later on, in Francesco's

[3] Arch. di Stato, Firenze, *Provv. di Consigli Maggiori*, Reg. III.
[4] The marriage contract, drawn up by Ser Lapo Mazzei, refers to
"Domina Lucia, who is wont to abide with the said Francesco di Marco, and
Nanni di Prato, who is also wont to dwell with the said Francesco."

will. Margherita's letter telling her husband to send the child to Prato is entirely matter-of-fact and maternal, giving a list of the clothes she is to bring with her; and her subsequent letters make it plain that she quickly became not only resigned to the child's presence, but fond of her. She wrote to Francesco about Ginevra's growth, the doctor's visit when she had a swollen face, the gown she was cutting down to make a dress for her, and the three ounces of silver buttons that were required for it. And when Francesco came home, he found not only one, but two children to welcome him—for now Margherita's niece Tina (the daughter of Niccolò dell'Ammannato) was also there most of the year, and kept Ginevra company. The fine new house in Prato had got a little warmth into it, at last.

II

The greater part of Monna Margherita's time, however, could not be given to these children, nor to any occupation of her own choosing: it was claimed by her domestic duties, which increased each year, together with Francesco's fortune and the size of his household. From the first, most of his letters had been given up to domestic instructions, and soon they came to fill every page.

The duties that fell upon Margherita in her husband's absence were both heavy and varied. If we wish to know what was expected of her, we have only to read the description of a good housewife in the sermons of the greatest popular preacher of the time, San Bernardino. "The good housewife is one who looks to everything in the house. She looks to the granary and keeps it clean, so that no filth can enter. She looks to the oil-jars, bearing in mind, this is to be thrown away, and that kept. . . . She looks to the salted meat, both in the salting and the preserving. She sweeps the house, and decides—this is to be sold, and that kept. She causes the flax to be spun, and then the linen to be woven. . . . She sells the bran, and with the profits she gets the linen out of pawn. She looks to the wine-barrels, if any are broken or leaking. She watches over the whole house."

And the good Saint went on to paint a grim picture of the unhappy man who was not blessed with such a helpmate. "If he is rich and has some wheat, the sparrows eat it, and mice. If he has some oil . . . it is spilled. . . . Know you what his bed is like? He lies in a ditch, and when he has put a sheet on his bed, he never takes it off again, until it is torn. And in the room in which he eats, the floor is covered with a melon rind and bones and salad leaves. . . . He wipes the trenchers off: the dog licks them, and so washes them. Know you how he lives? Like a brute beast. Women, bow your heads! It is the woman who rules the house." [5]

This, as is plain in these letters, was the rule in *casa Datini*, too. The house, the cellar, the kitchen-garden, the stable, the mill were all within Margherita's province; she rose in the morning before the front door might be opened, and retired only when the last careless slave had gone to bed.

Day after day Francesco's letters would bring her a long list of instructions, to be carried out immediately. Here is a typical letter, chosen almost at random:

. . . Tomorrow morn send back the branches of dried raisins and the bread, by Nanni of S. Chiara. And send the barrel of vinegar. . . . Remember to wash the mule's feet with hot water, down to her hoofs, and have her well fed and cared for. And have my hose made and then soled by Meo. . . . And give some of the millet that is left with you to the nag, and see that it is well mashed. . . . And speed the sale of the two barrels of wine in Belli's house; and empty all the other vats in the cellar, the ones with white wine, that have already been opened.

These are the instructions contained in a single letter. And here is another, hardly less varied. It began with a long list of

[5] San Bernardino da Siena, *Prediche Volgari*, pp. 261–3.

179

the linen Francesco was sending back to be washed in Prato, together with 30 herrings, a sack of capers, and 20 pounds of flour and of peas. In return, Margherita was to send him 50 oranges ("in such a manner that they are not spoiled"), 25 loaves, 2 barrels of oil ("for the monks of 'gli Agnoli' "), and a bushel of grain. ". . . And remember to do all you have to do, and look well to the barrels, and feed the beasts well; and every evening shut the door well and look to the light, and see to it that I shall not have to scold. . . ."

"Remember"—that was the word with which most of Francesco's sentences began. "Remember, as you lie abed in the mornings . . ."

> Remember to draw a little of that white wine every day, and remember to send to the mill the sack of grain that was left over. . . .
> Tell me if the mare is ready to be fetched and if she has been shod. . . . And remember to water the orange-trees as we used to do, or they will be burnt up in this heat. . . . And remember to keep the kitchen windows shut, so that the flour does not get hot.*

Remember, remember . . .

Almost daily, too, it was necessary to prepare baskets or sacks that were to go, on mule-back, to Francesco in Florence, and to count and set in order the things that he sent back to Prato. All the food grown on the farm was sent to Francesco in this manner: flour, eggs, oil and wine, capons and pigeons and geese, besides, of course, fruit and vegetables in season—beans and onions and leeks and salad, and "strong herbs for omelettes," chestnuts and figs and oranges and dried raisins—and also jellies (of pork or veal, with spices) made by Margherita herself, and carefully packed in a basin, that they might not be spoilt on the road. The bread, too, was baked in Prato and then sent to Florence—sometimes as much as thirty loaves at a time.

Sometimes Margherita tried to forestall her husband's complaints: "If we send not the things even as you would wish, be not angered, for I am but a woman, and alone with a pack of little girls, and have no help from any. I send what I deem best."

Margherita's meticulousness is not surprising, in view of Francesco's tendency to believe, on the slightest provocation, that he was being robbed or defrauded. One long letter is given up to describing her search for a lost pillow-case, which Francesco said was in Prato, while she was sure it was in Florence. She had unpacked, she said, the whole chest at the foot of the bed in the kitchen, and also her own chest. "And I think you will find it in the sheets' chest, where it has been for three years."

A more serious loss was that of Margherita's sapphire ring, which apparently was kept in a chest in her room. She was certain, she wrote, that she herself could not have lost it or thrown it into the street while shaking out the blankets, for it had become too small for her. She had searched every cranny of the house, and had even swept the road outside; she sent a man to search through the pawnbroker's shop, in case it had been stolen —"I am so grieved, I know not where I am." "Since I lost it, I have known no joyful moment, by day or night; and I thought you would comfort me, and feel compassion for me." *

But instead Francesco sourly wrote that it was irksome for him, too, to have lost a valuable ring.

Certainly he was a difficult man, either to serve or to love. What exasperated his wife beyond bearing was that, though he left the full burden of the household upon her shoulders, he never ceased, even from a distance, to supervise and find fault. "Tell me," he wrote in a letter which caused her especial pain, "if you took the water out of the verjuice [6] [*agresto*]; for you know it is your habit to let water get into it, or else to let it leak away." In addition, he accused her of having let some water leak into the cellar from the street. "Yet you have such a pack of females about you, that assuredly you might have made them

[6] "Verjuice" was sour grape juice, used for making vinegar.

carry some of the sand that is laid in front of Our Lady, and spread it before the door!" And he proceeded to compare his wife's housekeeping most unfavourably with that of the wife of his noble friend Guido del Palagio, "who, in the thirty-four years she has lived with him, has never vexed him." *

Margherita's reply, written on the same day, shows how deeply the comparison rankled. "I know not why you ask about the verjuice, for even if I told the truth, you would not believe me! If it has some water in it, it is not my fault, but is because the barrel is bad. . . ." She took breath, and came to what had wounded her most deeply.

> You tell me about Guido, that his wife never caused him tribulation. Methinks he speaks the truth; but I trow *he* has caused even less grief to her, than she to him. For Guido knows how to rule not only a woman, but a whole city! I have discovered from Ser Lapo [Mazzei] and from his daughter-in-law who came here what Guido's demeanour is in his own house. He is not to be compared to other men, and he keeps his wife as a woman, and not as an inn-keeper's wife! For it is fifteen blessed years since I first came here, and always I have lived as in an inn. . . .

And then a great flow of confused old grievances came pouring out, large and small, and ended up with the arrival in Prato, the night before, of Francesco's over-fed mule, "to whom you have given so much to eat and so much ease that she was about to burst, and at the third hour we had to have her bled. . . . Would God you treated me as well as you do her!"

Well did Francesco know, she concluded, that when he himself was at home, he had more than enough to do. "And now I have both your work and my own . . . and I am no longer as strong as I used to be. But I would endure all, if only half of what I do was known to you." *

This is the letter of an exasperated woman, but not of one who is afraid to speak her mind. And, indeed, Francesco himself, in his better moments, had come to admit that in household matters his wife's judgement was as good as his own. "Take heed to what I write," he told her, "but then do the best you can, and no more. And whatever I may have said, do what you yourself think best, and I shall always be satisfied!" He even admitted that in the past he might himself have been in the wrong. "Would God I had believed you with regard to many things in which I took pleasure, and you did not!" *

Perhaps this handsome admission may partly have been due to the influence of Francesco's closest friend, Ser Lapo Mazzei. He was in the confidence of both husband and wife, and for many years did all he could to pour oil upon the domestic waters. "The thought of Monna Margherita weighs on me," he wrote to Francesco in 1394, "for her sake and for yours; but I can do no more. God comfort her, and help both her and you." Constantly he implored Margherita to be less rebellious, and Francesco kinder. That Margherita was often impatient, he did not deny. "I wish she were as meek," he remarked, "as she is shrewd," but he also pointed out to her husband that she was "the person who has had to listen to your blessed sermons for eighteen whole years!" And he added: "Methinks if you knew how oft she refrains from replying to all your storming, you would deem her meek."

In the summer of 1395, after twenty years of marriage, matters came to a head. For some months Margherita had been entreating her husband to let her join him in Florence, but when at last she did come, he went back to Prato himself. This was more than Margherita would put up with, and she stormed so loudly that Ser Lapo came to hear of it, and warned Francesco that his wife's patience was at an end. She had threatened: "One day I shall pack up my things in a bundle and set forth home again!" Lapo added that Francesco would do well to pay heed to such threats, and to the unhappiness that caused them.

Let not the many, many letters you write, to increase your bodily welfare and your riches in this world, make you lose

your charity and love for the person to whom you are
bound by God's laws. For your rough soul and your frozen
heart need to be comforted.

Francesco did not heed, and Margherita carried out her threat;
she packed up her goods and, without a word of warning, went
home again. This, Ser Lapo wrote, was "thought too bold," but
he went on imploring Francesco to be more gentle with her.

I commend Monna Margherita to you, for she deserves it,
and God has given her to you for your companion. For my
part, I take it not amiss, when I am feeling bitter towards
mine [his wife], and a friend takes her part. And she [Mar-
gherita] has a great turbulence of spirit, which most women
are not afflicted by—and you, too, are stormy.

She was, he repeated, "a woman who has had much to bear,"
and he added that he wished he could have helped her "to become strong where she is weakest: I mean in patience." He admitted that Margherita was sometimes insolent, but, he asked,
"What have you been towards her? Had she always been patient
and humble, she would have conquered herself in more battles
than any saint!" And when, in 1400, Francesco and his family
fled from the plague to Bologna, Ser Lapo returned once again
to the charge.

I have no more to say, save to commend Monna Margherita to you. Not for love of me or of any living creature,
but solely for the love of God, whom it pleased to place her
as your companion and in your care. . . . And thus I commend to you Monna Margherita, and your own honour.*

Good advice to married couples is proverbially fruitless. But
certainly after the two stormy years of 1394-5 Margherita's
and Francesco's relationship took a turn for the better, and perhaps this was also partly due to a serious illness of Francesco's in
the summer of 1394. "Let us not deceive ourselves," wrote Mazzei

after his recovery, "you were on the point of death." * After this date some of Francesco's letters to his wife began to change their tone. Some of them still contain the old nagging worries, but others reveal a deeper melancholy, and a need of someone in whom he could confide. This is a man who has begun to look back upon the picture of his whole life—and does not like what he sees there.

> Fate has so willed [he wrote] that, from the day of my birth, I have never known a whole happy day. . . . Yet if my end be a good one, I care little for the rest. But I greatly fear it will not be, and I think of little else.

The truth was that Francesco was now over sixty, and the strain of his daily work and, still more, of the unceasing anxieties that preyed upon his mind, was beginning to tell. In 1395 he admitted that he could no longer toil all day and night as he used to do. "Yestereve I was ailing, by reason of all the writing I have done in the last two days, without sleeping either by day or night, and eating in these two days barely one loaf." *

And now Margherita's reply was more conciliatory—for she, too, was growing weary.

> I pray you [she wrote] be as little vexed as you can, and pass on to me as little grief as you can, for I can no longer bear so much. I am brought right low . . . and this summer has cast me to the ground.

At least, she begged, he might spare himself, and her, his constant interference in domestic matters. "When you are away I look to them with even greater solicitude than when you are here. I trow I demean myself in such a manner, and so rule the household, that I need feel no shame: please God it may be so."

Eighteen months later she herself fell ill with a tertian fever.

> Think not it is from over-eating, for I nearly killed myself with hunger this Lent. The doctor says my disease is from

185

weakness more than from aught else, and has told me to eat pounded chicken, and this I have done and will do, until I feel better.

Perhaps Margherita's illness was influenza, for it left behind it —in spite of the pounded chicken—a profound distaste for life.

> Were it not for love of you [she wrote to her husband] and because I am not free, I would leave all these tribulations, and stay no more in the service of this world. I am bound neither by children nor kinsfolk nor money nor merchandise; naught holds me save the two things I have writ. . . .

This letter would almost suggest that Margherita was playing with the idea of leaving her exacting husband and entering a convent. But a year later she was still at home. "I now desire naught," she wrote, "save to do what is pleasing to God, and to find peace within myself. . . ."

Certainly, in the following years Margherita's letters are less filled by her own grievances, and more with concern for her husband's welfare. "Say no more," she wrote, "touching the life you lead and your nightly watches, for I am as grieved about them as I can bear. . . . I must remember you of what I said to you long past, that the good and the evil we have in this world, are what we make for ourselves."

But still Francesco would not heed. In vain did Margherita go on pleading with him to spare himself, "for now surely you must be [word torn—"weary"?] of tormenting yourself." Her anxiety about Francesco's health led her to reflect once again about the odd separate lives they had led—not with the old resentment, but merely with sadness.

> Methinks the pain in your belly is much greater than you told me, to save me anxiety. I vow I have never been more sorrowful than now at being parted from you, for I understand more than was my wont before. I care for those

whom I need not, while the man who needs me to care for him is in an evil state, both in his health and his reputation, and no man can set this right, but you.

She could not refrain, too, from reminding him—perhaps more often than was wholly tactful—that he was now an old man, that he no longer had too much time before him. "In view of all you have to do, when you waste an hour, it seems to me a thousand. . . . For I deem naught so precious to you, both for body and soul, as time, and methinks you value it too little." *

It is, in substance, the same advice that old Monna Piera had sent to the rising young merchant of Avignon: "Crave not the whole world!" In reply, Francesco would protest that he, too, was weary of his cares, and conscious of their vanity. Let Margherita only wait until one more ship had come in, or until one more deal had gone through, and he would wind up his affairs and spend his old age in peace.

Perhaps all their last years would have been spent in this manner if—in the autumn of 1399—a shock had not come to Francesco. For an outbreak of the plague—heralded by rumours from Francesco's branches abroad—was once again threatening Tuscany. And with this menace, the lives of Francesco and Margherita took another turn.

CHAPTER TWO

"LA FAMIGLIA"

"And let them all warm themselves at the same fire, and eat at the same table."—L. B. ALBERTI

RANCESCO AND MARGHERITA, AS WE HAVE SEEN, were childless, and Francesco had no close relations. But in spite of this, the fine new house in Prato was always full of people. Its doors were open to Margherita's large family—her brothers and sister and brother-in-law and nephews and nieces—as well as to Francesco's partners and *fattori*, and it housed besides a great pack of servants, both male and female, slave and free, and sometimes their children as well. All these formed part of *la famiglia*.

Any picture of Tuscan life—now, as in the past—must start by emphasizing the strength and compactness of the family. Always strongest in the times in which the State was weakest, indeed often the only stable point of an unstable society, the *famiglia* embraced a very wide field. *Fuoco, famiglia, parentela*—these were the terms used to designate not only a man's immediate descendants, but every relative living under the same roof and eating the same bread—aunts and uncles and cousins and cousins' children, down to the most remote ties of blood. They all belonged to the *casato*, as they had to the Roman *gens*, and often the term was extended to include even people bound to the family by common economic interests or by dependence, such as partners, employees, and servants. Bonaccorso Pitti, in writing about his family at the time of the Black Death, counted no less than "40 mouths," and in 1465 Alessandra Strozzi wrote about a friend: "Giovanni Franci leads a fine life, living at home with more than 50 mouths, between *fattori* and slaves, both male and female." [1]

The family, moreover, was an economic entity, as well as a social one. Its importance, which had once largely depended on the number of its fighting men, was now chiefly assessed by the strength and variety of its connections at home and abroad, in politics and in trade. If a man acquired fame and fortune, it was for the family good, and his first duty, having increased his worldly goods, was to draw up a will transmitting them to his heirs—not from parental affection, but merely as a *restitution* to the family of what in truth belonged to it.

Since the unity of the family was more important than the happiness of any single member, its rule was hardly less strict than that of a religious order. Grown-up sons and daughters unquestioningly obeyed the orders of the head of the family, *il capo del parentado;* widowed daughters returned to their father's house, bringing back their dowry with them. There was little room left for affection or tenderness; parental authority was too absolute, too severe. Sons and daughters addressed their parents as *"Messer padre"* or *"Madonna madre";* they were forbidden to sit without permission in their presence, and, when they met them, were told humbly to incline their head when given an order, and duly tip their hood (*far riverenza di cappuccio*). "At least twice a day let them kneel down reverently at their father's and mother's knee, and ask their blessing . . . and on rising, bend their head and kiss their father's hand." The father chose his sons' professions and his daughters' husbands, and it was only

---

[1] Alessandra Macinghi Strozzi, *Lettere ai figlioli.*

189

a small, daring minority who rebelled. Even a grown-up son, so long as he lived at home, had no money of his own. And one pedagogue went so far as to say that a small child should be forbidden to keep for himself any gift of nuts or sweets, or an older boy to save up his salary. "Let them never have a savings-box, or say: 'This is mine,' so long as you [the father] are alive." [2]

On the other hand, the obligations of the head of the family towards the members of his vast tribe also extended very far: public opinion made it impossible for him not to care for his poor or feckless relatives or dependents, to pay their debts, provide work for their sons and dowries for their daughters, and take the old and feeble into his own house.

Among folk of plebeian or bourgeois stock such as Francesco's, the family structure was much less rigid than in a great aristocratic house, and, moreover, he had no legitimate children to whom to leave his name and fortune. Yet even here the pressure of the family tie was so strong that we find him taking on, as a matter of course, the full obligations of the *capo del parentado* not only towards Margherita's relations, but towards the families of his partners, managers, and servants. When one of his partners in Avignon, Bonaccorso di Vanni, left at his death four little daughters whom he had had by one of his slaves, Francesco took all four of them into his own house, and engaged a woman to look after them; when his maid-servants or his partners' daughters married, he contributed to their dowries; and the legacies in his will included not only gifts to his partners and underlings, but a dowry of 100 florins each to the four daughters of a distant kinsman, Chiarito di Matteo, " a poor and foolish man." *

Relatives were an even greater liability than dependents: their demands never ceased. Margherita's numerous kinsfolk seem to have been unusually rapacious and persistent, and, moreover, they made it clear that whatever they received was rather less than

[2] Beato Giovanni Dominici, *Regola del governo di cura familiare*, pp. 163-5.

their due: Francesco was so rich, they all agreed, that he could well afford it!

On the rare occasions when Francesco asked a favour of one of them, they at once tried to make some profit out of his request. One of the most disobliging was Margherita's mother, Monna Dianora Bandini, who had remained in Avignon after her daughter's return to Italy, but had also kept a house in Florence. When, in 1387, Francesco decided to move his family from Prato to Florence, he asked her if she would let her house to him, but she replied that she would consent to do so only if he paid her the exorbitant sum of 4,000 florins, promising also to return the house to her or to her son, whenever they could raise the same sum. "But otherwise I would that neither you nor any other should enter the house, for it is my intent to sell it, and keep the money in my own hands; for I am old and ailing, and shall never find a soul who will succour me with even a groat."

By the same post she hastened to appeal to Margherita's filial feelings, to bring pressure to bear upon her husband. "I beseech you, my dearest daughter, for the comfort and honour of us all, pray and beseech Francesco to pay me the said moneys; he will lose naught by it, and he could do more than that—wherefore I rejoice. . . ." *

But Monna Dianora's plans were unsuccessful: Francesco found himself another house.

Francesco had trouble, too, with his youngest brother-in-law, Bartolomeo Bandini, who seems to have been the family black sheep. Certainly he appears in this correspondence only when in need of help or money. On the first occasion, in 1399, he was writing to say that the little city of Fondi, where his wife and children lived, had been sacked by a company of free lances commanded by Giovanni da Barbiano, which was devastating the Kingdom of Naples. "The wheat and the vineyards have been cut down and burned; my family must be in grievous trouble. . . . So I beseech you, Margherita, in charity, aid me in some fashion to join my family." *

191

The answer to the letter is missing. But a few months later, in May, Bartolomeo turned up in Tuscany again—and was again in trouble.

> When I heard he was come [wrote Margherita to her husband] it was more grievous for me than if I had seen him dead before my eyes. . . . For he is after all my brother, and I cannot but love him. . . . And I see him old and poor and not strong and burdened with children.

Nevertheless, the family tie still held. "I beseech you," Margherita pleaded, "if you would ever do aught for my sake, let it be to purvey for him." *

To her brother himself, however, she allowed herself some plain speaking. "You have demeaned yourself in such a fashion, you and my mother, as to seal up my mouth in Francesco's presence, and I dare not speak either of your needs or of those of my other kinsfolk." *

But Bartolomeo was not so easily discouraged.

> You say [he replied] you bear a great burden, and dare not open your mouth with Francesco on behalf of your family. I would that I and your other relations were not in sore need—but since fate has willed it so, one cannot go against fate. . . . You bid me tell you what my state is. My state is this: I have lost all I had to live on, that is, my cattle. . . . All that I had toiled for, during a whole year, was torn from me all at once. But I thank God for bestowing on me a wife who can bear ill-fortune well. And I still have land and vineyards . . . which give me bread and wine for my household. And I have three children, two boys and a girl.

He then proceeded to explain his latest plan—which, of course, was dependent on Francesco's backing. The following year was to be the Holy Year, and "the Roman court will be the most perfect place for profits in every field that man has ever known."

Bartolomeo suggested that Francesco should provide him with some capital to start a company there, "and I would give my services to feed my children." *

Whether or not Francesco agreed to this naïve proposal the letters do not tell. In 1409 Bartolomeo was still living in Avignon, "working at the Customs for 6 florins a month, which is enough to live on and be clothed and shod," but complaining that it was not enough to meet the illness of his wife, "who for four years has been living on pounded chicken." * And with this Bartolomeo passes out of this record until the day of his death, when—no doubt most unwillingly—Francesco felt obliged to pay his doctors' bills and to buy mourning cloaks for the whole family.*

A more virtuous character, but in the end no less expensive to Francesco, was Niccolò dell'Ammannato Tecchini, the husband of Margherita's sister, Francesca. In him we find the prototype of the small Florentine bourgeois: God-fearing, prudent, honest, sententious, devoted to his wife and children, anxious about his health, loquacious, and slightly censorious—a good man, and a bore. His relationship with Datini might be drawn on a chart by a steadily descending curve, as Francesco's fortunes rose and Niccolò's declined. In early days, when Francesco was still in Avignon, Niccolò's letters were full of kindly but somewhat condescending advice: it was he who was the established householder, proud of his wife, his home, and his four sons, while Francesco, although rich, was still a homeless and childless exile. Niccolò presumed to advise him about the disposal of his goods in Avignon, and also—from the security of his own happy, fruitful marriage—about his behaviour to his wife.

They say it is not seemly for a man to praise his wife; I agree, if the man is boasting; but when occasion arises, me-thinks it is well and honest to speak of her virtues, only not in her presence. You praise Margherita for being respectful and obedient and without *Gherardiname*. In good faith, I can say the same of Francesca; and if any man has good reason

193

to be satisfied with his wife, I have. And since I have always kept the bridle in my hand, I have not needed to jog the bit against her teeth. She is my wife, and as my wife I love her, and this suffices both to her and to me.*

It was at this time, too, that Niccolò condescendingly offered one of his children on loan to Margherita. "If Margherita would borrow one of her boys from Francesca, she is willing; provided that when she has one of her own, she verily gives him back. Francesca has three and is great with another."

But only a few months after Francesco's return to Italy, the tone of the letters begins to change. Francesco employed Niccolò in his Florentine branch, but apparently at the same time pointed out that it was no longer suitable for his brother-in-law to address him with the familiar "*tu.*" "I have become aware," Niccolò wrote humbly, "of my fault in not saying '*voi*' to you in the past; but now I shall amend it, as you see in this letter."

Soon, too, a family coldness arose because the Datinis did not go to stay with Niccolò and Francesca for Carnival.

> You say that you are pledged to come to Florence for Carnival, and Margherita will go to a wedding . . . and, on the other hand, that you and she would have dwelt with us, if your clothes had come. In good faith . . . since Margherita goes to a wedding, she could have come here in the clothes she will wear to that wedding. . . .

This letter throws light, too, on the generous length (then as now) of Tuscan family visits. "You may stay 8 or 15 days with us now. . . . And Francesca says that, an it please you, she will then stay with you twice as long as you have stayed with her!" *

A few years later misfortune overtook Niccolò: in 1398 he went bankrupt, and turned to Francesco for help. The rich relations did all that was necessary, but without tenderness. Francesco gave 300 florins; other relations, 300 more; but Margherita firmly wrote:

2. "LA FAMIGLIA"

Francesca must earn her living now, with her own hands; Niccolò is old and ill; he has become a broker and makes his livelihood as best he may. I have taken the girl in, and must pay for her keep; and Francesco has sent the boy to Majorca. Lo, see how many burdens Francesco bears for my sake! *

It would appear, moreover, that Niccolò's daughter, Tina, was a troublesome child. On one occasion, when she was sent to a christening in Prato, she refused to go on foot, "saying that if you were here, she would not have to walk . . ." and then met a man whom she coaxed to lift her on his mule. "A man who helped her down asked whose child she was. She said she was the daughter of Francesco di Marco—brazenly—she has more pride even than you. And all this is because you wish it to be so. . . . It would be better for her to live with her own mother. Her pride would not then wax so high." *

But it was not possible to send the child home, for Niccolò was now a broken, penniless old man—"practically dead to the world, what with old age and poverty"—and his wife had been attacked by a "cruel and perverse disease." "I come home four or five times a day to order all that is needful, and complain not of the toil, but when I bethink me that her disease may not be healed, I cannot be resigned. I turn to God and pray Him to grant us His grace, and in His mercy to help her, and help and counsel me."

Two months later he wrote that his wife was already dead and buried.

Wherefore I grieve, so that I cannot eat or sleep. Death seems sweeter to me than life, when I bethink me of the companion I have lost—and here I am, old and poor and with a grown girl at home. Never have I known such grief. . . . In the church all that is seemly has been done, for the good of her soul, and for her honour and mine. . . . I vent my grief in praying to God, to open His arms to welcome her.*

195

It must not be thought that Francesco's and Margherita's only society was that of their own relatives. Though Francesco, as we have seen, had few friends in Prato, a sheaf of letters shows that during her husband's long absences Margherita was not left alone, but surrounded by a bevy of friends. There was Monna Gaia di Giunta, the wife of Francesco's old guardian, Piero (of whom Francesco wrote, when he was still in Avignon: "She is the person in the world to whom I am most beholden and whom I love best, after Monna Piera"); there were Monna Gaia's daughter, Monna Lapa, and her daughter-in-law, Simona, and Margherita's niece, Tina, and Simona's daughter, Caterina; and sometimes, too, there were visitors: Guido del Palagio's wife, Monna Niccolosa, and Ser Lapo Mazzei's wife and daughter. "*Tutta la brigata*" (the whole company) is the signature of one of their letters to Margherita, and many of them (though they were not related to her) addressed her by the affectionate name of "*sirocchia*," sister. They appear in these letters like the gay, busy groups of young women so often depicted in the pictures of the time, taking part in wedding processions or domestic scenes—following the bride in all the grandeur of their best clothes, bearing water and fine linen to a new-born child or gifts to its mother, baking, weaving, spinning, gossiping with their maids. Much has been written about the restrictions laid upon respectable young women in the *trecento*, but the picture that emerges from the Datini papers—partly, no doubt, because it was not an aristocratic family and Prato only a small country town—is of a cheerful, social, and not unduly constricted life. If a woman's days were largely spent at home, it was in cheerful company, and if there are many references to household tasks, there are also many records of pleasant, harmless little jaunts. One day there was a christening, and the child was given Margherita's name. "She will be beautiful: God make her good." * On another there was a birthday party for Simona's daughter, Caterina, and Simona asked Margherita to bring her "a bowl and an ewer, such as is customary to give to girls," as well as "three bowlsful of good comfits, made up by your own apothecary." *

In the following year Simona was planning a visit, "to cure my pains," at the Baths of Petriolo—a spring of hot sulphurous waters near Siena and a resort considered so gay that St. Catherine's parents sent her there in her youth in the hope of dispelling her vocation. And without going so far afield, there was always church-going. According to one letter from Niccolò di Giunta to Francesco, Margherita and his sister, Lapa, went together to San Francesco every evening in the Lent of 1385 to hear the Lenten sermons. "They are fasting together, for they wish to become holy," he commented benignly, and went on to reassure Francesco by adding: "they leave Simone to guard the house until they get back from the sermon." * And that such church-going was, to the young women themselves, a social occasion as well as a road to "holiness," we know from as observant an eye-witness as S. Bernardino himself. "One calls 'Giovanna!' —another cries 'Caterina!' and yet another 'Francesca!'—Lo, with what fine devotion you hearken to the Mass! . . . Here comes Madonna Pigra, and would sit before Madonna Sollecita. Cease, cease, from behaving thus! The first to come is the first to grind her flour. When you have come, be seated and let no other push in front of you." [3]

Plainly, during Francesco's absence from home Niccolò had been asked to keep an eye on the young, inexperienced bride, and his reports were most reassuring. "All are doing well, Monna Margherita looks well to the house and household. She is a sensible woman and can do well whatsoever she wills." *

Margherita appears to have been especially fond, too, of Simona's daughter, Caterina, for when, in 1390, she went to Pistoia to escape from an outbreak of the plague in Prato, she took the girl with her. "Meseems," Simona wrote, "were she in Prato and I gave her the choice, she would be fain to abide with you,

[3] San Bernardino, *Prediche Volgari*, ed. Banchi, II, pp. 109–10.

rather than with me. And not without cause; for not Caterina alone, but any girl, would lever be with folk who cherish her." *

There was, however, another child in the house to take up Margherita's attention: Francesco's little daughter, Ginevra, whom—as we have seen—Margherita had consented to bring up as her own. When, at the age of six, the child was sent home, her foster father wrote to Francesco a touching letter, saying how much he and his wife had come to love her, and begging that she might be treated kindly. "For she is fearful, and we love her dearly, and therefore we beseech you, be gentle with her." *

The foster parents need have had no fear: every reference to Ginevra in the Datini letters shows that the slave's child received as much care and indulgence as if she had been their own. Soon after her arrival, Margherita was boasting that Ginevra would mind no one but her.

"And in my presence she is the best child that ever was, but when I am not there, she will do naught she is told." "Vex yourself not about Ginevra," she wrote to her husband when the child had a sore throat, "but be assured that I look to her as if she were my own, as indeed I consider her. . . . The broken head is a trifle, but I was anxious about her throat." *

How was Ginevra brought up? This was a period in which many children received but scant attention, save that of the rod. "Bring them up on coarse food," wrote Fra Giovanni Dominici, whose sermons both Francesco and Margherita greatly admired, "with common and cheap clothing; make them walk on their own feet, accustom them to hard work, and strengthen their body so that, if needs be, little will suffice them. Let them learn to serve themselves, and to sleep, at least once a week, fully clothed with the window open, and accustom them to fast . . . and in short, treat them as if they were the children of yokels." [4]

A daughter's upbringing, moreover, was more Spartan than that of her brothers. "How you feed a girl does not matter, provided she remains alive. Keep her not too fat." Her dress, until

[4] Beato Giovanni Dominici, op. cit., p. 184.

the age of twelve, was nothing but a short, tight little tunic of coarse wool or cotton, according to the season, and her education cost nothing, since it was only if she was to be a nun that she was taught to read. After the marriageable age of twelve her life became one of the strictest seclusion. The only reason for leaving the four walls of her house was to attend Mass, and this was best done at dawn, closely veiled in her mother's company. The rest of the day was spent at home, and not in idleness.

> And teach her all the household tasks, to bake the bread and cook the capon, to put the flour through a sieve, to cook and do the washing, to make the beds and spin and weave French purses and embroider in silk and cut out linen and woollen cloth and put soles to hose, and all similar matters— that, when you give her in marriage, men say not: "she cometh out of the wilds." And they will not curse you, who brought her up.

Her mother should supervise her constantly herself, not allowing her to spend too much time with the servants, with other "silly girls" or even with her own brothers—and her father, too, should keep a perpetually vigilant eye on her. "If you have females at home, keep them always in fear and trembling." [5]

No doubt all this was the rule. But just as Monna Margherita and her friends appear to have led a freer, more amusing life than the conventional picture of young women of their time, so Ginevra was brought up more indulgently than most children. Soon after her arrival there is an entry in Francesco's private account-book of 2 *lire* 10 *soldi* to buy her a tambourine, and Domenico di Cambio spent a whole day in Florence looking for it, "so that the little girls [Ginevra and Tina] may be happy." And she certainly was taught to read, for in 1401, when she was nine years old, Francesco entered in his book "one gold florin fresh from the mint, for Ginevra to give her mistress, who teaches her how to read." *

[5] Paolo da Certaldo, *Libro di buoni costumi*, paras. 155 and 126.

She was given, as we shall see, a great many fine clothes, and long before she had reached a marriageable age the problem of her marriage played an important part in her father's thoughts. No doubt he would have liked a good Florentine *parti* for her, but her mother, after all, had been a slave, and it was considered unwise to marry a girl too high above her station. "A woman who seeks a greater station than her own," according to Fra Giovanni Dominici, "or a husband who will only take her for her money, may be said to add a further servitude to a natural yoke. So say to your sons and daughters, *ambula cum tuis*." [6] A young Pratese of not too high standing, who would feel honoured by the connection with as great a man as Francesco, seemed a more suitable choice, and apparently a candidate was suggested when Ginevra had only reached her ninth year: Lionardo di Tommaso di Giunta, a first cousin of Niccolò di Giunta, Francesco's friend and partner in the cloth trade. In the early stages of the negotiations, however, Niccolò was very cautious—partly because the young man was still rather wild. The following letter shows how warily such negotiations were drawn out. They were, of course, always conducted by a middleman—a relative or a marriage-broker. Niccolò wrote to Francesco:

> Niccolaio Martini called me into his warehouse and asked me if I would be glad for Lionardo di Ser Tommaso to take a wife, if she were a good one, and had a good dowry. I said I would be more glad if his demeanour were more seemly. And he agreed that he has bad habits and persists in them, but he said that if he [Lionardo] had a wife, his demeanour would be better.

Niccolaio then spoke to the young man himself, but this shocked Niccolò greatly: "He should have said to you, Francesco, whatsoever he would say, and not to a mere boy." *

For six years we hear no more about the matter, but then Francesco must have made up his mind, for in the autumn of

[6] Beato Giovanni Dominici, op. cit., p. 177.

The Notary
ROLL OF NOTARIES OF PERUGIA

Building
FLORENTINE SCHOOL, FOURTEENTH CENTURY

Margherita and the Vinegar

Dressmaking at Home

CODEX CASANATENSE 4182

2. "LA FAMIGLIA"

1406, when Ginevra was fifteen years old, a letter from a friend in Bologna, Niccolò Compagni, congratulated him on the engagement. Francesco remarked that many men had already asked him for Ginevra's hand—"not for her own sake, but to get my money"—but that he preferred for her "a companion who will not despise her, nor feel shame to have a child by her." "Methinks," his friend commented, "you see the truth very well—and, like a wise man, you seek to marry her so that she will be at ease, and your mind at rest. . . . And what a great boon fate has given to the man you have chosen as a son, and how ungrateful he would be, were he not always obliged to you!" *

On Sunday, April 4, Francesco solemnly promised Lionardo his daughter's hand, in the church of San Francesco in Prato, "in the presence of many witnesses." Only the fiancée herself was not present; but this was not unusual, since this ceremony —called *impalmatura*, because the representatives of both families shook hands after signing the contract—was only the first of a long series. The *impalmatura*, which marked the conclusion of the negotiations about a bride's dowry, usually took place either in a church or on the church steps, but always in public, and in the presence not of a priest, but of the notary who had drawn up the contract, the marriage-brokers, and often also, as on this occasion, many friends and relatives. The number of these was restricted, in theory, by the sumptuary laws to fifty guests from each of the two contracting families—but in practice there were often many more, for each guest was allowed to bring one companion with him, while a knight might bring four, and a judge or a doctor two.[7] Plainly, in a city of the size of Prato very few people would be left at home!

Hardly was the ceremony over when Ser Lapo Mazzei, the family notary and friend, wrote off to tell Ginevra the glad news:

May God be praised, from whom all good things come! Be advised, dearest Ginevra, your father has betrothed you in

[7] Sumptuary laws of the city of Florence, 1355. Published by P. Fanfani in *L'Etruria*, Firenze, 1852, pp. 366 ff.

201

S. Francesco to Ser Tommaso's Lionardo, a good young man with a fine appearance, in the presence of a great and honourable company from Florence and Prato. And all the town has shown singular delight. May God bless you, and pray for your loving father.*

Well might Ser Lapo refer to Francesco as a "loving father," for a parent's affection was assessed by the size of his daughter's dowry, and Ginevra, the slave's child, was given no less than 1,000 florins—more than many a daughter of the great merchants of Florence.

From this sum, however, all that Francesco spent on her trousseau was deducted, and so lavish was his expenditure that out of the whole 1,000 florins, only 161 were left! Moreover, Lionardo's receipt for the dowry stated that no object belonging to Ginevra's trousseau might be sold, pawned, or mortgaged by him without Francesco's permission, and another contract specified that if Ginevra were to die of the plague within two years of her marriage, the whole dowry, "or whatever portion of it he requires," must be returned to Francesco.*

After the public *impalmatura* came the betrothal—at which the bride's father formally presented her to the bridegroom and he placed the betrothal ring on her finger. The wedding-banquet was held and then came the bridal night—sometimes preceded and sometimes followed by a Nuptial Mass (the only religious part of these ceremonies)—and generally yet another, lesser banquet was given when, a few days after her marriage, the bride returned to her father's house for a week or so, after which she left home for good.[8]

In Ginevra's case there is no record of a betrothal ceremony; it was probably held on the same day as the wedding-feast. The details of this great occasion—which took place nearly seven months after the *impalmatura*—are fully recorded. Ginevra wore

[8] This custom probably dated from the time of child marriages, when, for obvious reasons, it was necessary for the bride to return to her father's house until she was old enough to take up her conjugal duties.

a gown of crimson samite, with a long train and a little collar of white ermine. She was girdled with a silver-gilt belt on a crimson band, with a large buckle of French enamel (such as Datini imported from Avignon).[9] On her head she wore a high, elaborate headdress called a "garland"—mounted on a crimson *mazzocchio* or support which held her hair together and supported her heavy headdress, embroidered in gold and adorned with no less than 240 carved gilt beads, golden leaves, enamel flowers, and a large bow of enamel—the whole costing over 20 florins. And in her hand she held, in a silken case, an illuminated prayer-book.*

The wedding-banquet, too, was a very fine one. A special cook, "*Mato di Stincone cuoco*," was engaged for the occasion, and was paid 4 florins 10 *soldi* for this single meal—a princely sum when we consider that a maid's wages for a whole year were only 10 florins.* Six extra servants, besides those of Francesco's regular household, waited at table, and were supplied with new tunics of scarlet cloth and new hose. 310 pounds of fish were brought "from the lake,"[1] at a cost of 14 florins, and 31 pounds of lard were used. As to the rest of the food, the sumptuary laws forbade more than three courses, even at a wedding-banquet—one of *ravioli*, *tortellini*, or *bramagiere* (blancmange), one of "roast with pie," and one dessert—and specified that there should be no more than 50 dishes for each course (allowing 20 guests for the bride and 30 for the bridegroom). But each of the 50 dishes might consist of "7 pounds of veal, or one capon with a pie, or one goose with a pie, or a couple of fowls with a pigeon, or a pair of pigeons with a fowl, or a duckling with two pigeons,"[2] and, moreover, the "pie" in ques-

---

[9] Such a belt was an important part of every trousseau, and sometimes the bride was formally girded with it, in memory of the *cestus* that Vulcan gave to Venus, which endowed its wearer with every grace. Many people believed that a marriage was not legitimate unless this rite had been performed.

[1] There is now no "lake" near Prato, but a large part of the meadow-land between there and Lucca was then under water.

[2] Sumptuary laws of 1355.

tion was itself a most ingenious way of evading the lawgivers' intent, for it was a pasty containing the greatest possible variety of ingredients: pork, chickens, ham, eggs, dates, almonds, flour, spices, saffron, sugar, and salt. Certainly none of the guests can have left the table hungry! But Ginevra herself, like every refined bride, had only a snack beforehand and did not touch the meal—so that when she dipped her white fingers in the silver washing-bowl, the water should still be clear, and the guests praise her fine manners.

Wedding-gifts were presented—*"le donora"*—musicians played, comfits were passed round, and at the meal's end it was Margherita herself who performed the symbolic act of placing a child in the young bride's arms and a gold florin in her shoe—to bring her fertility and riches.*

Finally, when the banquet was over, Ginevra, like other brides, was taken to her new home in procession by all the wedding-guests, and the narrow streets of Prato resounded to the beating of drums and blowing of trumpets, while the young bride was not spared many a ribald comment on her appearance and her bearing. Custom ordained that if she had a long way to go, she might ride on horse-back, and she was generally accompanied by six of her female friends. When they reached their destination a little ritual comedy took place: the bridegroom hiding himself in another room, while the bride's attendants told her to fear nothing, for he had ridden away.

> *Tutte confortan e pregon che stia*
> *Sicuramente, e prometton molto*
> *Che'l marito è andato lontano.*[3]

Then, with much giggling and whispering, they turned and left her, on the threshold of the wedding-chamber.

But even now the festivities were not ended: within a week,

---

[3] "They all comfort her and bid her feel safe, and vow that her husband has gone far away"—Francesco da Barberino, *Reggimento e costume di donna.*

as was the custom, Ginevra returned to her father's house, and yet another banquet was held, but apparently a less grand one, since the cook's fee was only 1 florin 12 *soldi*.* It was only a few days later that, at last, she returned to her husband's house for good.

II

Festive occasions such as these were made up for—as Tuscan tradition still requires today—by great frugality and parsimony in daily life. Nevertheless, a man of Francesco's standing required even in ordinary times a good many servants, and of these, too, a record has been preserved. In the first years after his return to Prato, Francesco's household was modest enough: according to the census of 1383, it consisted of only three servants—a man called Antonio d'Andrea, a woman named Bartolomea, and a little serving-maid of twelve, Ghirigora.* But two years later Francesco was already dissatisfied. "When I have set all in order," he wrote, "I shall need a female slave or two, or a little slave-boy, as you prefer." * In 1387 his private account-book records the arrival of "a little slave-girl of 13 from Pisa, bought by Francesco di Michele & Co. of Genoa," and the purchase of a slave called Bartolomea, "bought without a broker for 70 florins," while in the following year he bought yet another slave of thirty-six called Giovanna, who was also sent to Pisa by a Genoese slave-trader.* And in 1393 the census also recorded, in addition to these slaves, the presence in Francesco's household of a man-servant called Domenico (most often referred to by his nickname, "*Saccente*," meaning "wiseacre"), his wife, Domenica, and their little girl, Nanna; a young slave-girl of twenty, Lucia; and a blind, paralysed old woman, Monna Tinca di Simone, whom Francesco kept "for the love of God." *

But even this household was not large enough. In the same year Francesco was instructing his partner in Genoa, Andrea di Bonanno, to find yet another slave.

Pray buy me a little slave-girl, young and rustic, between eight and ten years old,[4] and she must be of good stock, strong enough to bear much hard work, and of good health and temper, so that I may bring her up in my own way. I would have her only to wash the dishes and carry wood and bread to the oven, and work of that sort . . . for I have another here who is a good slave, and can cook and serve well. . . .*

Andrea, however, was unable to find a suitable child at once, and in August Francesco wrote again: "The ships from Turkey and from [illegible] are usually in by now, and sometimes have good cargoes." *

In December the slave had not yet been found. "No ship has come in from Roumania with any aboard; but now it cannot be long before they come, and you and Margherita will be provided as you wish. Those who are here now are not worth taking, for they are second-hand wares." *

Finally, however, the child was found in the Venetian market, and on New Year's Day, 1395, Francesco's private account-book records, in a list of tips to be given for the New Year, "2 *soldi* to Orenetta, the little slave who comes from Venice." *

In addition to all these women, there were several men employed in the stables and cellars, and at least two or three messengers or carriers between Florence and Prato *—as well as a Tartar slave called Antonetto, who had been bought as a boy from some Catalonian traders for 49 florins. And, finally, Francesco's private account-books in 1405 and 1407 record the names of four more female servants—Monna Beneassai, Monna Palma, Monna Chiara, and Monna Sandra—each of whom is referred to as "*nostra servente*," while in 1408 we even meet with a French

---

[4] It was by no means unusual for a slave-girl to be so young; indeed, the greatest demand was for children of this age, and a register of slaves who arrived in Florence in 1363 shows, in a list of 357 slaves, 34 girls under twelve, and 85 under eighteen. Arch. di Stato, Firenze, Classe XI, Distr. 8, No. 81.

maid, "Monna Perronetta of Avignon." * Moreover, Margherita also seems to have had the help of several girls who came in by the day to help with the spring cleaning, the washing, and the unending baking, spinning, and weaving. "Your great pack of *femmine*" was Francesco's term for them, and Margherita herself would write of "my flock of little girls"—adding that they were incapable of doing anything without supervision. But constant supervision was precisely what Francesco considered the first of a young housewife's duties.

> Remember to go to bed betimes and rise early [he wrote to his young wife] and let not the door be opened until you are astir. And look well to everything; let them not go a-gadding. You know what Bartolomea is: she will say she goes to one place, and then goes elsewhere. Ghirigora, too, has little sense; leave her not alone without you. There is greater need of heedfulness than when I am there. . . . Now conduct yourself in such a way that I need not scold. You cannot err in watching over them well, and it will come easily to you. . . . Now strive to be a woman and no longer a child; soon you will be entering your twenty-fifth year.*

All this supervision was not, perhaps, necessary at first, for both Bartolomea and Ghirigora—according to the reports sent by Niccolò di Giunta—were good, conscientious girls. "They do well and honestly," he wrote, "all that they have to do, and obey Monna Margherita well, so that they have the best time in the world." * But when the new foreign slaves entered the house, the picture was completely altered. "They are *femmine bestiali*," wrote Margherita. "You cannot trust the house to such as they. They might at any moment rise up against you, as they did in Provence." *

The story, indeed, of the part played in Tuscan households by these Tartar or African slaves—alien, uprooted creatures, the "displaced persons" of their time—is a very strange one. Their importation, as we have said, was sanctioned by the Priors of

Florence in 1366, in view of the acute labour shortage caused by the Black Death—on condition that these slaves were not Christians, but infidels or *de partibus et genere infidelium*.[5] Thus, during the last two centuries of the Middle Ages, Florentine society came to depend—like that of Greece and Rome, though to a lesser degree—on the services of slaves. Beneath the members of the guilds (*le Arti Maggiori e Minori*), beneath even the oppressed, hungry crowd of the *popolo minuto*, the Tuscan cities held another class—formed of men without human or legal rights, without families of their own, without even a name, save that given them by their masters: the slaves. Sometimes a few of them succeeded in obtaining their freedom, but often only to form the dregs of the population who lived by robbery on the Tuscan roads, or swelled the crowd during bread-riots. Often, even after enfranchisement, they remained in their masters' houses, the necessary background of every domestic scene— waiting at every table, listening at every door, speaking a strange, incomprehensible jargon of their own [6]—and mingling their alien blood with that of their Tuscan hosts. *Domestici hostes*, domestic enemies, was Petrarch's name for these inmates of every house, so alien and yet so close, and the author of a treatise on domestic economy in Sicily was of the same opinion. "We have," he wrote, "as many enemies as we have slaves." [7]

By the end of the fourteenth century the demand for them had spread even to the smaller country towns, such as Siena, San Gimignano, Pistoia, and Prato, and sometimes Francesco would oblige a friend by procuring one for him through his agents in Genoa or Venice. "I trow," wrote one of his clients on behalf of a friend in Pistoia, called Paparo, "you will be solicitous to mark and seek out every little matter, even as if she were to be your own." Besides, he added, he could always

[5] Arch. di Stato, Firenze, Cl. XI, Distr. 81, n. 81.
[6] Ferrero, "*Linguaggio di schiave nel quattrocento*" in *Studi di filologia italiana*, Bull. Accad. della Crusca, VIII (1950).
[7] Caggio, *Iconomica*, Venetia, 1552.

get rid of the woman if she proved unsatisfactory. "I shall consider her as any other merchandise on which one sometimes loses and sometimes gains on selling again—wherefore there is naught more to be said."

Apparently, however, Francesco had omitted to mention that the girl was a handsome one, and when she arrived in Paparo's household, trouble at once ensued.

> Paparo's wife complains greatly of you [wrote the same friend] and yet more of Monna Margherita, that she should suffer you to send such a young and fair slave. She says she never would do such a thing to her, and women should take heed not to do such things to each other.*

Generally a slave's deed of sale warranted that she was free from disease ("healthy and whole in all her members, both visible and invisible") and sometimes also that she was not a thief, quarrelsome, bad-tempered, vicious, or prone to running away (*fugitiva*).[8] The buyer obtained over her *purum et merum dominium*, with power "to have, hold, sell, alienate, exchange, enjoy, rent or unrent, dispose of in his Will, judge soul and body, and do with in perpetuity, whatsoever may please him and his heirs, and no man may gainsay him." How completely, indeed, such a slave was considered a thing and not a person is shown in a list of property in the books of Datini's Pisan branch, in which a slave's value is thrown in with that of several domestic animals: "He says he has a female slave and a horse and two donkeys and three fifths of an ox. Let us put them down at 70 florins."

In spite, however, of their negligible status, these slaves, in actual practice, seem to have been treated very much like everyone else: they, too, were part of *la famiglia*. Indeed, it is impossible not to feel that slaves, servants, and children received very

---

[8] If the warranty proved false, the buyer could return the slave and get his money back.

much the same treatment: great severity in theory, and considerable indulgence in practice. Servants and children alike were subject, in law, to the *podestas puniendi* of the head of the family; they could be beaten and starved and even sent to prison at his caprice. (We have already quoted Ser Lapo Mazzei's injunction to the manager of the branch where his son was employed: "Beat him like a dog, and put him in prison, as if he were your own.") In practice, however, as these letters testify, both children and servants were often impertinent and disobedient with complete impunity—and at all times singularly outspoken and, in the modern sense of the word, *familiar*.

Let us see, for instance, what happened to Francesco's absolute authority when he was left alone in Florence, at the mercy of an ill-tempered cook.

> I brought home to dinner the Mayor and Matteo d'Antonio. She had no more to do, for the steak and the fish were already cooked. But because those two ate with me today, and because some fish was left over, and she has also got to cook two bowlsful of beans, she complains she has too much to do! So you see what maids are, when left to themselves. . . .

In the same letter Francesco told his wife that Argomento— a slave whom he himself had freed—on being reproved for not looking after the mule as he should, "took his leave, and said he would rather eat grass, than be spoken to like that!" "Therefore mark," Francesco concluded, "how like I am to be merry, when both my maids and my men hold this demeanour! I freed that numskull from slavery, and lo, this is his gratitude!" *

Antonetto, too, the Tartar boy whom Francesco had bought in Spain, appealed to the Priors of Florence for his freedom, on the grounds that he had been born free and should therefore never have been sold in the first place. But Francesco firmly testified that he himself had bought him as a slave and had sold him again to Luca del Sera in Florence (his own partner), who had always treated him as one. It is not surprising to learn that the boy's claim was not considered valid, and he was returned to his master.

It was far from unusual, too, for a slave to run away.

> This morn [wrote Francesco's partner, Stoldo di Lorenzo] when Monna Lionardo and Monna Villana had gone to church, your slave Caterina went forth and away and we cannot find her. We have been to all the doors and cannot discover that she has gone forth through any of them. . . . They say she has taken naught from the house, save the gown of *romagnolo* wool she had on her, and a little purple gown for feast days.*

Five days later Caterina came back of her own accord, "and Stoldo has come out of his melancholy, praise be to God." The chances of such a flight being successful were, indeed, very slight. Underlying the stringent penalties laid down by the statutes of every city for helping or hiding runaway slaves lay the old principle of the Justinian code: the runaway slave was also a thief, for he stole himself from his master. A proclamation cried in the city squares gave the name and description of the runaway, and it then became every citizen's duty to hunt and seize him, and to deliver him to his master. Any unknown coloured man or woman automatically came under suspicion, and so did anyone who was scarred or branded or lacking a limb. *Cave a signatis!* ran the saying. Any mark or deformity was likely to be the sign of a criminal or a slave.[9]

Even, however, when the slaves did not run away, they were

---

[9] "A slave of about 20 ran away from us this eve, of dark hair and eyes and a meet figure, that is, neither fat nor thin. She is small and her face not much like a Tartar's, but more like our fashion here, and she speaks our language not too incorrectly. Her name is Margherita. . . . She ran away from Marignolle, and took with her all her clothes, to wit, a bluish skirt, quite fresh, and a gown and a towel and other such trifles, and an old lambskin skirt with a black belt, and she is wont to wear a little cap." From Franco Sacchetti, the novelist, to one of Datini's partners in Pisa. Sacchetti then asked his correspondent to warn all the boatmen on the Arno and the brothels, "for sometimes they are taken there."

not easy to live with. They quarrelled with the other free servants and with each other, and were extremely quick with their
knives.[1] They sometimes corrupted, by their evil ways and coarse
manners, the respectable maid-servants, and even the daughters
of the house.[2] And they had even been known to use magic arts
and poison against their masters—for, indeed, in an age when
poison was a common weapon, who was in a better position to
administer it than a slave?[3]

Moreover—according to the unanimous report of their mis-
tresses—they stole all they could lay their hands on. To Francesco, with his morbid fear of being defrauded—in Mazzei's
words—"even of the shoe-buckle of the wench that serves your
slave," the dread of their thefts became a veritable obsession.
"Lock the door behind you with three keys," he adjured his wife
when she was going to Florence for the day.*

Above all, these vigorous, hot-blooded young savages were
completely promiscuous. If Margherita, as we have seen, agreed
to bring up the child born to Francesco by his slave Lucia, other
Tuscan wives were not so tolerant. One letter, for instance, from
a client in Pistoia, revealed a very awkward domestic situation.
The writer's slave had produced, "to her misfortune," a child.

> And since the father could not be found, I took it and sent
> it out to nurse. But my Monna Lucia was seized with jeal-
> ously, and said it was mine; and though I told her it was

[1] The State Archives of Siena contain the sentence of death to a slave
for having cut off—"*irato animo et malo, scienter et dolose et appensate*"—
the head of a fellow slave. Arch. di Stato, Siena, Dipl., February 6, 1433.

[2] "They sold her," wrote Alessandra Strozzi of such a slave, "because
wine was beginning to go to her head . . . and besides she was immoral,
and the wives, since they had young daughters, would not keep her in the
house." Alessandra Macinghi Strozzi, *Lettere ai figlioli*, November 2, 1465.

[3] On August 8, 1379—according to an anonymous diarist who was an eye-
witness—"the flesh was torn to pieces of a female slave who had poisoned
her master, a Bolognese." She was drawn in an open cart through the streets
of Florence, while the population watched her flesh being torn to pieces
with red-hot pincers, to the place of execution, where she was burned. Arch.
di Stato, Florence, *Capitano del Popolo*, No. 197 bis, p. 71.

only mine as a calf belongs to a man who also owns the cow, she still will not believe me, whether I vow or coax. . . . And she has won the battle, and the slave has been turned out, and we now have an old woman who is more like a monkey than a female; and this is the life I lead. . . .

The writer ended by imploring Margherita to plead with his wife "that she may not give heed to gossip, and take back the slave, or at least find another who is not an old sow." *

In view of many such comments, the only possible explanation of the continuing demand for domestic slaves is that they were cheaper—and this, indeed, was the case. All Francesco's free servants received, in addition to their board, lodging, and clothing, a regular yearly salary. In 1400 he was paying 10 gold florins a year to each of his four Tuscan maids, and 12 florins (for apparently a French maid could already command a higher salary) to Monna Perronetta of Avignon. A man-servant, Guido di Sandro, whom Francesco had taken into his household as a boy and used as a kind of superintendent, received 25 florins a year, which was afterwards raised to 30 florins.* The cost of a slave, on the other hand—even if fairly high—was paid off by a very few years' work. The Tartar boy, Antonetto, whom he had bought from some Catalonians, cost 49 florins (the same price he had paid for a young mule), and a little slave-girl of ten or twelve, bought in Venice in 1394, 50 ducats,⁴ plus 5 ducats for the purchase tax and 3 for her journey. In 1388 he paid as much as 87 ducats for an adult woman called Bartolomea, "bought without a broker, with all her own clothes and tools," and 60 for another called Giovanna.* It is plain, therefore, that even the most expensive of these slaves, Bartolomea, cost no more than a free maid-servant's wages for eight years—after which time Francesco enjoyed her services for nothing. Sometimes, indeed, after a good many years he decided to free one of his

⁴ At this time the Venetian ducat, the Genoese *lira*, and the Florentine florin were of approximately the same value.

slaves, but generally, even then, the emancipated woman stayed on with him.[5]

It must, moreover, be admitted that it was not only the slaves of their household that Francesco and Margherita found unruly; both of them loudly complained, too, about their free servants. "Saccente," Margherita wrote, "has besought me many times to lend him 40 *soldi*, and then came down to 20. If I saw him hanging on the gallows, I would not draw out a penny to ransom him, on account of his lies—for there is naught in him but lies and wiles." *

Nor does the family of Margherita's sister, Francesca, appear to have been more fortunate. "They have a fat maid," Francesco wrote, "who never gets up from her seat, and they are looking for another, to be both nurse and maid. If they find her, they will be badly served in both respects." *

Finally, in addition to all Margherita's other domestic duties, Francesco provided her with an arduous task: the choice and supervision of *balie* (foster mothers) from Prato for a number of Florentine babies. It was the universal custom to send babies out to nurse—the foster mothers generally being country girls who had had an illegitimate baby, or peasant women with plenty of milk for two—and it would seem that Prato, like certain villages of the Roman Campagna to this day, had a reputation for providing good nurses. How these women sometimes behaved to their charges may be seen in the *Cronica* of Francesco's contemporary Giovanni Morelli; his father, he wrote, used to refer to his own *balia* as "the most bestial woman that ever lived, who beat him with so many blows that even as a man, remembering them, he would gladly have killed her, had she come into his hands." [6]

---

[5] There was even a special type of enfranchisement, called *sub conditione*, by which a slave was freed only on condition of his remaining for a specified number of years in his master's house (or, after his death, with his heirs), and continuing to work without wages. Only at the end of this time was he fully free.

[6] Morelli, *Cronica*, p. 235.

2. "LA FAMIGLIA"

San Bernardino, too, did not hesitate to condemn the whole practice. "Though he be your own child, and you be wise and pretty-mannered and discreet, yet sometimes you give him to be nursed by a sow. . . . And when he comes home and you say: 'I know not whom you resemble! You are not like unto any of us!' you mark not where the cause lies—and it serves you right." And the great preacher—for he was addressing a country congregation—asked his hearers to consider what occurred when a man took a peach-stone from one of the fine peach-trees of San Gimignano and planted it in Siena: it bore thin, poor little trees. "Know you not why that is so? You have brought the stones here, but not their soil. . . . And so I say to you, women, who send your child out to nurse: he will take on the condition of the woman who feeds him." [7]

The custom, however, was far too deep-rooted to be affected by such considerations—and certainly they would not have weighed with Francesco. So many of his letters to Margherita, indeed, are concerned with finding good *balie,* that one almost wonders whether these commissions were undertaken entirely for friendship's sake, or were one more side-line of his miscellaneous business.

In any case, it is certain that most of the trouble was Margherita's. She it was who had to find the nurse, to assure herself that the woman's milk and character were really good, and to haggle over her salary, which was about 12 florins a year, or a little more than a maid's. The requisites were that the nurse should, if possible, resemble the child's mother a little, and have a fine colour and "a strong neck"—but not too large breasts, "or the child will get a flat nose, when the breast is laid over it." Moreover, since a baby was generally nursed for over two years before it was weaned—then passing without transition from milk to good Tuscan wine—it was desirable to get a woman who did not become pregnant too easily. "The *balia* could not be better," wrote Margherita, "for she never becomes pregnant

[7] S. Bernardino, *Prediche Volgari,* ed. Banchi, II, pp. 159–60.

215

again until after 28 months or more and her milk is now only two months old, so she can easily nurture a child."

The letters exchanged between husband and wife on this subject are too monotonous and repetitive to be quoted at length. Margherita's first response to each request was generally a complaint that good *balie* could not be found. "They seem to have vanished from the world, for none has come into my hands. And some I had at hand whose babes were at the point of death, but now they say they are well again." But always she ended by bustling off again on her search, or sending messengers to comb the farms. One girl, she wrote, was "a good milk-giver" but flighty; another would not do, for her last mistress had complained that "the longer she stays, the more evil she becomes—and besides, she has only one eye." Yet another was not to be trusted because she still had a young baby of her own. "Never shall I believe that when they have a one-year-old child of their own, they give not some [milk] to it."

There is a callousness in these appraisals which apparently seemed as natural to the candidate as to Margherita herself. "I have found one in Piazza della Pieve, whose milk is two months old; and she has vowed that if her babe, which is on the point of death, dies tonight, she will come, as soon as it is buried." *

The servant problem, in short, in the fourteenth century was no less trying than in any other period of the world's history.

CHAPTER THREE

THE FAMILY FRIEND

"Iddio vuol modo, e niuna cosa immoderata mai piacque a quella eterna equitade." [1]—SER LAPO MAZZEI

EARLY IN 1372, TEN YEARS BEFORE FRANCESCO DI Marco's return to Prato, he received a letter in Avignon from a distant kinsman, Andrea di Matteo Bellandi, asking him to help a poor young law-student from Prato who was studying in the University of Bologna. "The boy, according to what many men have told me, would turn into a remarkable man if he could pursue his studies, for he is believed to have a fine mind and has a great desire to study."

The writer went on to ask whether Datini could obtain a scholarship for this student in the Papal College of Bologna. "The youth might grow into a man of parts, and this would be thanks to God's goodness, and yours." Moreover, he added, "it is thus that a man may every day acquire new friends and servants." *

Andrea's prophecy came true. The student—who was then

---

[1] "Measure is God's demand, and no immoderate thing was ever pleasing to that eternal equity."

only twenty-two years old—was Ser Lapo Mazzei, who became the closest of Datini's friends during the second half of his life. Soon after Datini's return to Tuscany he was made a *gonfaloniere* of his native city, and it was then that a letter addressed by a notary to the *Otto della Signoria* of Prato [2] attracted his attention. He inquired who the writer was, and discovered him to be the man he had befriended ten years before. By then Mazzei [3]— though fifteen years younger than Datini—was already a man of standing. Though of humble birth—in which he took some pride, often referring to himself as "the shepherd of Carmignano"—his studies had borne good fruit. He had begun to practise in Florence at the age of twenty-three, had been appointed as notary of the *Signoria*, had been sent as an envoy to both Faenza and Genoa, and, finally, had become the notary of the greatest charitable institution in Florence, the hospital of Santa Maria Nuova.

He himself, however, did not think much of the class to which he belonged. "Most of us notaries," he wrote, "delight rather in heavy purses than in ardent hearts" *—and this, indeed, was the general opinion. In the early days of the Commune the notary had held a position of considerable dignity. It was he who accompanied the unlettered *podestà* and often equally unlettered judges when they were sent to administer justice in country towns or villages; and often it was he who not only whispered to them the little law they needed to know, but who drew up their official documents. [4] It was he who composed the local statutes, who arranged the election of the village officials, and who wrote any letters to neighbouring cities or princes. Moreover, he was

---

[2] The *Otto* were the eight Priors who, together with the *gonfalonieri*, formed the *Signoria* of Prato.

[3] He was born in 1350 in Prato, the second son of Mazzeo di Ghigo (a poor man whose annual taxes amounted to no more than 3 *lire* 4 *soldi*).

[4] Odofredo has described the unlettered nobles of his time, who sometimes, when the Emperor came down to Italy, succeeded in buying from him the title of judge—and who were known, from the parchment on which these titles were given, as *judices cartularii*. N. Tamassia, *Odofredo*, Bologna, 1894, p. 168.

often a man of taste and culture: [5] in the universities the studies of
the notary and of the man of letters were considered so inter-
changeable that sometimes a notary would take the course of
ars dictandi and a grammarian the *ars notaria*. And Dino Compagni, in the second half of the thirteenth century, drew up a
convincing picture of a worthy notary:

> *Se buon pregio vole aver Notaro,*
> *in leal fama procacci sè vivere,*
> *ed in chiaro rogare e 'n bello scrivere,*
> *e d'imbreviar sue scritte non si' avaro:*
> *in gramatica pugni assai, sia conto,*
> *e 'n porre accezion buon contrattista,*
> *e diletti d'usar fra buon' legista,*
> *e 'n domandare accorto, savio e pronto.*[6]

But already in Ser Lapo's day the profession was in its decline. Numerous manuals containing models not only of legal
deeds and formulas, but also of every type of high-flown pre-
amble and letter made it possible for even a man of very scanty
learning merely to copy out whatever he required (and Heaven
help his clients if, as sometimes occurred, he lighted on the
wrong formula). And as, in the cities, the number of men entitled
to act as judges increased—including, as well as the judges ap-

[5] In the thirteenth century two great notaries—Pier delle Vigne in Apulia
and Rolandino de' Passeggeri in Bologna—rose to the highest offices of
state, the former as Chancellor of Frederick II, the latter as Proconsul of the
notaries of Bologna. After Rolandino's death his fellow citizens put up to
him a fine marble tomb adorned by the emblems of his profession: pen, ink,
and paper. F. Novati, "*Il notaio nella vita e nella letteratura italiana*," in
Freschi e Minii del Dugento, p. 311.

[6] A notary who would be greatly prized
Must be of high repute in all his ways,
Write well and ever register his deeds,
Be expert and defend his learning well,
Draw up his instruments with skill and care,
Prefer to deal with valiant men of law,
And question all with shrewdness, sense and speed.
—Dino Compagni, *Song on Worthy Conduct*

219

pointed by each guild, the *Podestà*, the *Capitano del Popolo*, the Captain of the Guard, and even the Supervisor of the Customs—each judge came to be surrounded by a throng of half-illiterate, factious, and venal notaries, all pandering to the Tuscan passion for litigation, to their own profit and advancement.[7] It was with these men in his mind that Antonio Pucci declared—in a little treatise enumerating the qualities or "graces" required by each profession—that it was enough for a notary to be able to write so clearly that the word *"nolimus"* could not be mistaken for *"velimus,"* if he was also "honest and loyal and chary of taking too much wine . . . and does not mutter under his breath when he makes a contract, but speaks plainly, so that both parties can clearly understand him." [8] Nothing more was required.

Yet even these modest attainments were apparently too much for the six or seven hundred notaries who thronged the halls of Palazzo Vecchio, carrying under their arms their bundles of papers—"each folder," said Mazzei, "as thick as half a Bible." Boccaccio has rendered one of these men immortal: Ser Ciappelletto of Prato, the notary "who felt much ashamed when one of his deeds was not false" and "stole with as clear a conscience as a saint's," who "gave false witness with the greatest delight, whether he was asked for it or no," who drank and gambled and guzzled —and who yet succeeded in drawing the wool over his confessor's eyes so completely, in his last confession, that the simple friar decided he was a saint, and he was thenceforth known as San Ciappelletto! [9] Drawn by the pen of Boccaccio and Sacchetti —and, later on, by the fifteenth-century dramatists—the notary gradually became, at least in literature, nothing but a figure of fun, usually portrayed as a spare, mean little man, wearing great spectacles beneath his crooked wig, and interminably pouring

[7] It was also possible to obtain the title of notary, without any preliminary examination, from a Palatine Count, and at least one of these, Tommasino de' Bianchi of Modena, created—according to his own account—no less than a hundred notaries by a stroke of the pen, including some boys of fourteen and several soldiers of fortune!

[8] Antonio Pucci, *Zibaldone*, Codica Laurenziano Tempiano 2.

[9] *Decamerone*, Novella I.

forth in his shrill voice incomprehensible rhetorical sentences, all ending in "etc., etc."—the word which, according to a popular proverb, was "one of the nine things that will bring the world to ruin!" [1]

Ser Lapo, we need hardly say, was not a man of this stamp, but in his youth he spent ten years in Florence in the chambers of a notary who might well have sat for one of Boccaccio's or Sacchetti's portraits, Ser Paolo Ricoldi. Ser Lapo described him as an astute, violent, and godless man, so absorbed "in his rages and devilish tricks, prosecutions, writs, desires and misadventures . . . that sometimes, when he was eating, he seemed out of his senses, and had so many impediments in his head, he would forget to bring his hand up to his mouth." [2] The young man learned many tricks of the law from him, but left him as soon as he could, "preferring a poor but honest life to a rich one in which one's bread was full of worms," and joined instead the chambers of an eloquent and able lawyer, Ser Coluccio Salutati, the Chancellor of the Florentine Republic. It would appear, indeed, that during an illness of Ser Coluccio's, Mazzei acted as his substitute. But the Palazzo della Signoria was no place for him. "Freedom is so dear to me," he wrote to Francesco, "that if I remained here I would die, even as if I were in prison, and all the gold and honour in the world would not comfort me." This freedom he never renounced. "God be praised," he wrote a few years later, "I know no man who has greater freedom than I. I am fettered neither by relations nor friends nor sects. Yet I keep a yoke upon my neck, for it is thus that I desire to be." *

The yoke to which he referred, and which was dear to him because he himself had chosen it, was his work as the notary of Santa Maria Nuova—a great hospital founded by Folco Portinari, the father of Dante's Beatrice, and an institution which provided

[1] Novati, "*Il notaio nella vita e nella letteratura italiana*" in *Freschi e Minii del dugento,* p. 328.
[2] Ser Paolo died later in the same year, after an illness lasting only two days. "And how," Mazzei inquired, "after forgetting God for forty years, could he wipe out in two days the life of a beast?"

for much more varied needs than a hospital of our own time. It not only cared for the sick and for old people and foundlings, but distributed food and alms to the poor; and the men who worked there followed a rule as strict as that of a religious order.[3] Their first obligation was one of poverty. The *spedalingo* (warden), who was a priest, was bound to hand over to the hospital the whole of his worldly goods and might not receive any ecclesiastical benefices; the *conversi*, male and female, who nursed the sick, were bound to both poverty and celibacy, and to lead "a good and holy life." The hospital's administration was in the hands of the treasurer and the notary, and how varied this business was may be seen in Ser Lapo's letters. Not only did he draw up all the hospital's legal documents and deal with any purchases or sales, but—since a large part of its revenue came from pious legacies, which were often of land—he administered no less than fifty properties, frequently visiting the hospital's fields and vineyards and anxiously supervising the peasants and reckoning the harvest. With the proceeds he then distributed to the poor, in the donor's name, "monies and gowns and dowries." And, finally, he also appears to have attended to some of the hospital's supplies, for we find him ordering, through Datini, a shipment of 300 blankets for the beds. For all this he received a salary of 10 florins a month, and deprecated even this, saying that he felt it to have been earned by the sweat of the poor.

For nearly twenty years he held this office—a happy and busy man, respected by the whole of Florence, free to indulge now and then, in the hospital's behalf, in a little piece of innocent sharp practice, blessed by the poor—and delighting (it is this candour which sweetens Ser Lapo's goodness and saves it from any priggish taint) in a succulent meal at the end of the day's work, with meat and wine supplied by Francesco. "Your veal was very good," he wrote, "and I shared my part of it with the new

---

[3] The hospital's Rule was drawn up in 1329 by Fra Uberto Guidi, a Dominican monk of the Monastery of S. Maria Novella.

222

warden, to find a little comfort for the many burdens of body
and mind brought by piloting so great a ship." *

All these cares, however, did not fill the whole of Ser Lapo's
life: he also found time, as these letters testify, for the matters
closest to his heart: his friendships, his family, his poor, and his
farm.

It was perhaps to friendship that he gave the largest place. His
two closest friends, Guido del Palagio and Francesco di Marco,
were very unlike each other: the former as unworldly, pious, and
upright as Ser Lapo himself, a man who not only acted as *gonfaloniere* of Florence and as the city's ambassador on several important occasions, but who found time, in his pleasant villa near
Fiesole, for philosophy and poetry; [4] the other, the rough, restless, grasping merchant whom we have come to know. It is the
latter friendship that it is difficult to explain; but perhaps it was
founded on an attraction of opposites—the charm that an enterprising mind holds for a prudent one, the glamour of vigour
and activity for a gentle, quiet stay-at-home.

> Were I not afraid of seeming a flatterer [Ser Lapo once
> wrote to Monna Margherita] I would say he has bewitched
> me, for since reaching the age of reason I have never felt
> more fervid and warmer love for any man in the world, and
> I look to him as my second father. May the Lord grant us
> to live and endure together until the end, and to go back
> together to the home from which we came.*

It was not long before Ser Lapo became not only Francesco's
notary but his closest friend, and the bond lasted as long as
Francesco's life. It is through Ser Lapo's letters—more articulate
than Francesco's own, more literary, and also revealing a more
subtle, if less practical mind—that we may see the merchant as

[4] It was Guido del Palagio who succeeded in signing, in 1391, a peace
treaty between Florence and Visconti; and he, too, who presented to the
Franciscan friars their monastery at Fiesole. Cf. Mazzei, *Proemio*, pp. lix-
lxiv.

he appeared to his contemporaries. Moreover, the friendship which this correspondence reveals was not only delightful but rare, for it flourished in a society in which fierce competition between rival political parties and trades caused most men to regard friendship merely as a means to advancement. "It is good to have friends," wrote an anonymous Tuscan writer of Datini's time, in a little pamphlet of good advice to merchants, "but none who are not useful. If you can have them good, wise and rich, those are the best." [5] Messer Paolo da Certaldo held a similar opinion: "Spend your time always with men richer and greater than yourself." [6] And even Leon Battista Alberti, who praised in the best classical tradition the beauties of friendship, yet advised that it should be confined to members of one's own clan, so that individual friendships within it would contribute to the strengthening of the family tie and the family fortune.

Mazzei held very different views. To him, almost alone among his contemporaries, friendship was "a union of similar natures and similar tastes"—a bond founded on disinterestedness and candour. "Vile is the friendship contracted for the sake of trade," he wrote to Francesco. "You will understand me, for you have had many of them; and I think that I, too, knew it well, and pretended to be an owl." He himself was wholly free from this taint. "I look not to a man's semblance or family," he wrote, "but only to his nature"—and in a letter to one of Francesco's partners he affirmed: "He loves me more than any of his friends . . . for I seek neither gold nor silver from him, but only love."

When one of Francesco's letters arrived, Ser Lapo's wife complained that there was no speaking to him until he had read it; and on one occasion, when Mazzei had laughed over one of these letters at dinner, she sourly remarked: "You are two great buffoons; an you may enjoy each other, you care for naught else." * But Margherita was thankful for anything that relieved her hus-

---

[5] *Cod. Magliabechiano*, Biblioteca Nazionale, Florence. Cl. VII, n. 1377. Published by G. Corti, *Arch. Stor. Ital.*, 1952, disp. 10.
[6] Paolo da Certaldo, *Libro di buoni costumi*, para. 111.

band's black moods. "Pray tell Francesco some of your japes," she wrote, "that they may bring solace to his melancholy." * When Francesco had made some new wine or oil, or had a fat hare or some venison, he would at once send for Ser Lapo, and sometimes the notary, too—though a poorer man—would have a couple of partridges and some "sparkling Carmignano" to offer in his little farm at Grignano. "There will be a fire to sit by and good wine to drink, and we will speak of Venice and Genoa and other matters—and if we are disturbed, we will go out riding." * When Francesco sent his wife a basket of oranges or a bucketful of tench from the river, he told her to be sure to share them with Ser Lapo's wife, and also to send her "a little jar of dried raisins. . . . For methinks we owe Ser Lapo so much, I can never bestow on him all he deserves, and he is a good man to have for a friend." *

Although a poor man, Ser Lapo did not feel any false pride about accepting such favours. "I use you and your possessions," he told Francesco, "like unto my own," for he held that "a man who maketh not a friend's wishes his own, is neither courteous nor a friend." * Nor did he object to jogging Francesco's memory, when necessary, as is shown by the following charming request for some of the new oil from Il Palco:

> Were you made as I am, you would say: "Ser Lapo, I have some good oil, and perchance yours is not so sweet." . . . And you would say: "It is in such or such a place; and I have commanded it should be given you." . . . And I would use it, like unto my own. For I deem myself not a paid labourer, but a servant of love.

But when Francesco, with the lavish ostentatiousness which alternated with his stinginess, sent far too much of the requested gift, Ser Lapo's pride and taste were both offended. "Think not that sweet oil, bestowed by a friend, pleases me not. But, in faith, too much is not a pleasure."

But Francesco could not learn. Once he sent Ser Lapo so big a

225

load of cheese that his friend wrote: "I deem myself a notary turned cheese-monger," and twenty years later he was still protesting:

> The peasant who prayed for a little water for his millet was not pleased when a flood came into his house. And neither was I, when, having asked for a couple of melons, I received a whole load, and enough wine for a month." *

Thus, in spite of his friendship with men like Francesco and Guido del Palagio—the one much richer than he, the other better born—Ser Lapo kept his own sturdy independence. "For though I am yours and Guido's as I am, yet I have kept my soul and mind for a greater Lord than you, and I study to keep them for Him, as He gave them to me." *

Though most men at that time sought out powerful godfathers for their children, he preferred that his own (and there were fourteen of them) should be sponsored by poor and obscure men, "thinking thus to please God by going against a bad custom," and it was only after several years that he reluctantly allowed Francesco to stand godfather to one of his younger sons. "Meseems it is not needful," he wrote, "where there is trusty love, to add the kinship of *compare*." The condition he laid down was that the rich godfather should come to the christening without any of the customary gifts,[7] "but like a poor pilgrim—and thus will I respectfully take you as my *compare*, and in no other wise." *

The bond between the godparents of a child and his own parents (and also of two godparents to each other) was considered almost as close as a blood-tie. But even before then Lapo had often addressed Francesco as "my father" or "my elder brother," or "most dear, as if you were my father."

[7] Francesco was told by Domenico di Cambio what gifts were customary, "to make a child a Christian." "The cost varies according to how much a man would do himself honour. The custom here is to send a fine comfit-cake of about 8–10 lbs., and a sponge cake of 6–8 lbs., and a box of white comfits and one of red comfits of 8–10 lbs. each, and a bunch of candles and little torches of 15–20 lbs." (File 1092. January 20, 1390.)

3. THE FAMILY FRIEND

I rejoice to say what I feel [he wrote in one of his first letters] to the folk I love; others perhaps would mock at me. But I trust you, for you have granted me your friendship. How dear it is to me, God knows; my heart is silent, since it knows not how to tell it.

Nevertheless, with the quiet sense of proportion that never deserted him, he did not lay claim, even in friendship, to heroic virtues foreign to his nature.

Francesco, my feelings for you are not those of Damon for Pythias nor of Orestes for Pylades, who would die for each other, for friendship's sake. . . . But neither am I one of the milk-and-water friends you encounter today; and were you in trouble, I would not be the first to flee.*

It was not long before Ser Lapo's affection for Francesco was extended to Monna Margherita, too, and he became her trusted counsellor. "You may demean yourself towards me," she wrote in 1394, "as to your younger sister, for I love you as my elder brother. Methinks there is no man to whom I am more beholden than to you, and I never disremember it." * It was Ser Lapo who taught Margherita, when she was over thirty, to read and write, so that she might be able to communicate with her husband directly, and who, while she was still a beginner, took the trouble to write to her (the letter may still be seen) in large print, as to a child.

He complained to Francesco, however, that his pupil did not write to him often enough to show off her progress. "Tell Monna Margherita I shall write no more to her, save she herself write to me; for I would see how apt she has become." "My disciple," he called her, and "comare carissima." "It is assuredly a marvel at your age, when other women are more apt to forget what they already knew." Moreover, he was at pains to tell her that her letters were not only well written, but entertaining.

227

Your letter was placed in my hand when we were at table, and Tessa my wife was there; and I vow, my pleasure and merriment caused me to change countenance, so that my wife was consumed with curiosity touching what I read.*

But Francesco was not equally delighted. Though certainly some clever women knew how to read and write, it was still regarded as an exceptional accomplishment, and rather a dangerous one—and, moreover, he did not wish his wife to waste on it the time due to her household duties!

Purvey for your household in such a fashion as to do you honour [he wrote] and pay not so much heed to reading that you do all other things ill. Order all other matters that they go well, and then you may read as much as you please.*

The reading of most ladies, even when they had mastered the art, was generally confined to their Missal or other works of devotion. But from a letter written by Domenico di Cambio, it would seem that Margherita was more ambitious: she tried to read one of the old merchant's business letters to her husband, and found it too difficult.

I marvel not [he wrote] that she belongs to the race of the priest who could not say the Office, save from his own book. . . . But if Monna Margherita would indeed read merchants' letters, tell her to study a month to do so, even as she has already studied her own book for six months.*

Margherita's letters to Ser Lapo are as spontaneous as those to her husband, and are also largely concerned with domestic matters. One long letter is all about some vinegar which she had promised to Ser Lapo but which, she wrote, "that madman Cristofano" had allowed to run away. "He drew it by the spout, and made too great a hole, and then stopped it up with sawdust . . . and one night, when we were at Il Palco, mice nibbled at the sawdust—and it all run away!"

228

3. THE FAMILY FRIEND

And Margherita went on to moralize, in Ser Lapo's own best manner: "And it is now three years since I put up this vinegar, and every day I was wont to say: 'Pay good heed to the vinegar!' But I was not so heedful about going to church. Now I shall no longer need to say: 'Take heed! take heed!' " *

II

It was not, however, only in the family circle that Ser Lapo's friendship showed itself. Not only did he help Francesco to reduce the exorbitant taxes laid upon him by the *Signoria* and to become a Florentine citizen, but in innumerable other ways. He drafted the merchant's business letters and contracts; he advised him about the purchase of land; he helped him to make his wine, to cure his ailments, and to choose his books, his horses, and a husband for his daughter. And, above all, his counsels—always on the side of moderation, kindliness, and patience, sometimes suggesting a timely gift, sometimes a smooth word—saved Francesco from making many an enemy.

One feeling ranked even above Ser Lapo's friendship for Francesco: his love for his large family. This consisted of his mother, Monna Bartola, his wife, Monna Tessa, and fourteen children, and it was with his mother that he felt the closest bond. Monna Bartola—a simple, pious countrywoman who had been early widowed—spent her old age at her son's little farm in the hills above Prato, at Grignano, and here, riding up on his old mare, he visited her once or twice a week. Yet, when she died, he felt that he had failed her.

When I visited her, she was lifted up and brought to the fireside to sup with me, when suddenly crying out: "Oh, God, help me!" she drew two long breaths, and gave up the ghost in my arms. . . . She died at the hour at which, for over thirty years, she was wont to say a hundred Hail Marys. And God granted her to die where she could be buried beside her husband, for that was all she asked. . . . She departed in peace, and left me, ungrateful and weak as I am, most disconsolate. For during her sickness, not thinking her near death, I was not humble and courteous as I would I had been. Had I but slept and talked beside her for a single night, and comforted that poor little old body!—and persuaded that tired spirit to depart gladly, towards God, our home.*

Like many other sons of good mothers, Lapo formed his standard of feminine perfection upon her—and his wife, Monna Tessa, did not come up to it. "You must know that I, too, am often vexed by Tessa, your *comare*," he wrote to Francesco, and in another letter he admitted that he was "often sharp" with her. The portrait that emerges from his letters is of an ailing, complaining woman (perhaps the fourteen children had something to do with it) always asking for pounded chicken or capon, and, when she was ill, refusing to eat it unless her husband actually spooned the food into her mouth. Ser Lapo wrote that on one occasion, when he had gone to Grignano for a single night to see to the hoeing of his vineyard, "she would not eat, save that her daughter and son-in-law with their four children came to sleep in the house—that she might receive Holy Unction if she died while I was gone. . . . And we are at this Holy Unction," he exclaimed in pardonable exasperation, "every day!" "The spirit in me is willing, but the flesh is weak," he added, "and I am never at ease, save when I have left the house." And yet he tried to love his wife, and even to make a companion of her. "A mother," he said, "is the ship's mast," and in another letter he wrote: "When folk say: 'You should love her, because she has borne you so many children, or because you have need of her,' I think it not well said. But ever I have it in mind to love her, because she is the companion whom God has given me." *

Ser Lapo's children, too, were a source of mingled joy and grief. Of the fourteen borne to him, only five grew up, but this was so common a misfortune that few parents dared to complain, and the pious felt bound to rejoice. "It goes very ill with my second boy," wrote Ser Lapo when one of them was at death's door, "or rather well—since he is leaving the folly, snares and dreams of this world, before he has been caught by them."

Sometimes it seemed to him as if the burden of his great family was more than he could bear. "Here am I with eight children," he wrote, "to bring up and clothe and shoe and correct, alone with no servant, male or female, and with a wife who is carrying two more, I am certain, and has little health."

There was a constant struggle in him between the severity which custom and precept enjoined on conscientious parents, and the instinctive gentleness of his own nature. He told with approval the story of a father who, when he was a boy, used to come into his school in Prato to beg the master to chastise his son mercilessly because he was wasting his time in gambling. "And this father was praised by the master and by the whole school." But it is difficult to believe that Ser Lapo's own blows were very heavy ones. Though he sent off his children to a peasant woman in the hills to be nursed, as was the custom, on the day after their birth, he could not conceal his delight when they came home again. "Your godson," he wrote to Francesco, "whom I have only seen once before, has come back to me from his wet-nurse in the hills, the finest little curly badger that I have ever had. Pray God for him."

One boy—"our pet, the only one who was nursed at his mother's breast"—had epileptic attacks every month, and Ser Lapo took him to sleep in his own bed. And on winter nights he read aloud to the children, by the fireside, the stories in San Francesco's *Fioretti*, borrowing them from Margherita, "who keeps them shut away in her chest. . . . For the little boys will delight in them in the evenings." *

It was, however, Ser Lapo's eldest son, Piero, who was the apple of his father's eye, "the swiftest to obedience of all my children," and for him, too, he sought the patronage of his prosperous friend. The boy was apprenticed, when he was only eleven, to Francesco's business in Prato and was sent to live with the Datinis. "Methinks," Ser Lapo wrote, "God would approve your helping me to train him up thus, with the sweat of his own brow." Yet when he discovered that Piero was being given no time to go to school and learn his *abbaco*, he intervened. "If you take him now from his *abbaco* he will have forgotten everything in a month." * And a little later he pleaded for the child to be sent home again for a while, so that he might go back to school.[8]

> I tell you it is reasonable for boys, when they are real boys, to give vent to their foolishness at school with other children. . . . And methinks, had I to train a colt, I would rather take the advice of a simple man who had broken in fourteen of them, as I have, than that of a wiseacre who had none. *

III

The third affection in Ser Lapo's heart was his love for "God's Poor." Himself a man of moderate means, he had not much to spare; but when he begged for others from richer men, it was not in an apologetic tone, but with a warmth and assurance that is still moving. In his choice of good works, as in the rest of his dealings, he followed no extravagant flights, but was content to practise the four chief "works of mercy" hallowed by custom, which we find depicted in the pictures of the time: clothing the naked, feeding the hungry, visiting the sick, and succouring prisoners. As the notary of the hospital of Santa Maria Nuova, he not only distributed the hospital's alms, but was often visited by rich merchants who entrusted to his kindliness and shrewdness the portion of the year's profits which they had set aside for

---

[8] When Piero had learned to write, his proud father could not resist sending Francesco one of his copies. "I send you an example of how my son writes, with the old ox in front of him [i.e., copying a model, like a young ox ploughing behind an old one]. I never had a boy who learned better than he."

charity, "that they may be *good* alms." "I tell them," he wrote, "there are so many poor persons, and so many girls to be married off, that it would move a stone"—and sometimes the need was so great that he himself added to the rich men's gifts a few crumbs of his own bread.

It was very early in their friendship that Ser Lapo urged Francesco to follow the example of these other rich merchants. "For I dread lest you may not render a fit account to God, in the other life, of the things he has placed in your care (I say not yours, for they are not any man's) if you have not given part unto the poor."

Above all, he besought Francesco to perform the simplest of a rich man's duties: to feed the hungry.

> Oft do I hear of your great banquets, for men and women rich in the vain things of this world; and that is good. . . . But forget not to let the poor, too, sometimes see your fine house, and be filled and nourished by your food, that God may not reproach you, saying: "Had you but once asked *my* friends to the house I had given you!" *

Strong as Ser Lapo's Christian compassion might be, and his genuine tenderness for the poor and oppressed, there was also another side of his nature: a craving for solitude and detachment. "Believe me, believe me," he wrote to Francesco quite early in their correspondence, "I live in the world, but I am not of it. I dare not say, I serve God . . . but of this I am very sure, to serve the world is an evil thing."

As the years passed, his delight in solitude grew upon him. "I am alone at home," one letter begins, "both in bed and in my study, with as great delight as the good hermits felt in their mountains, and I feel no breeze blowing, either from the right or the left."

There was one place where he could be certain of undisturbed solitude, his little farm at Grignano, and it was here that he spent his happiest days. A countryman by birth who liked to boast that he had been a shepherd in his boyhood—"and I think," he added, "I could be one still"—he remained for ever a country-man at heart.

> I was glad [he wrote in one of his first letters] you took pleasure in my little kitchen-garden. I call it so, because so small a thing cannot be called a farm, but to my mind, which desires but little, it is great enough. And this absence of desire seems to me the height of wealth.

Small as his farm was, it had all that he required: a house in which to lodge his mother (probably no grander than the little farm in the plate facing page 265), a few olive trees to provide him with oil (and Francesco would always send him some more when that was finished), a wheatfield or two, and a threshing-floor. So great was his haste to get there—escaping, no doubt, not only from the cares of the hospital, but from the complaints of his ailing wife and the lusty shouts of his children—that he would skirt the walls of Prato without entering ("for within there are only snares and evil talk") and then urge his old mare up the gentle slopes of the hills, once even forgetting, in his hurry, to pick up the eel intended for his mother's dinner. And when at last he arrived, he would stake and tie his vines with his own hands. But the best times of all were the clear, still evenings of high summer, when the harvest was reaped and the granaries filled. Then, with his city robes and shoes set aside, he would sit at ease, as when he was a small shepherd boy, beside his threshing-floor—and write with a glad heart of the pleasures of solitude.

> Here I am barefoot, in the light and sparkling air, and the sound of bagpipes lulls me to sleep and the bare clean thresh-ing-floor invites me to leap and jump like a tumbler on the great mountains of grain which my empty granaries are awaiting. Here there are no cicadas or gad-flies or tarantulas, such as grieve me at Il Palco. I am alone and barely awake, and there is no one to molest me at the door. I hear that Francesco toils and I rejoice. . . .

And the letter, which is addressed to "Monna Margherita of Francesco di Marco, my dearest mother," is signed in jest: "Your second *fattore*." *

Even when he was in Florence, Ser Lapo felt little desire for companionship, and after the death of Guido del Palagio in 1395 he retired more and more within himself. "I have no companion left and no friend," he wrote. "On feast-days I stay at home or go forth to Mass with a little old man, my neighbour. And in avoiding merrymakers I enjoy the world."

Though he made no boast of asceticism, enjoyed a good glass of *vernaccia* as much as ever, and still performed all his duties for the hospital and his private clients, there were now few hours in which he was not aware that "our whole life is but a race towards death."

> I live content [he wrote] in the state to which God has called me, save for certain attacks of melancholy. . . . But this grief has become my companion, and says to me: "Flee from here; trust not even your wife nor her faithfulness; watch not over your children, who can live well alone; go no more even to Grignano; eschew the love of your fellow-citizens. . . . But come with me . . . for so will you reach eternal rest.

Some of his time was now spent in sermon-going, and some in reading books of devotion: the *Letters* of St. Jerome and St. Gregory, the *Laudi* of Jacopone da Todi, the *Fioretti* of San Francesco. Yet he commented that although he had read much "in God's books," he had not really drawn much from them. "But I have found three windows through which one can speak to Him: to forgive one's enemies is one; to be humble, the second; and to love all men as one's brothers." The book from which he received most spiritual sustenance was the *Revelations* of St. Brigid of Sweden—because, he said, she had written that the only services that Christ desired were those performed "with a free spirit, and in the charity of love." *

235

No better description could be found of Ser Lapo's own life. Yet there was one anxiety that still weighed upon his mind: had he indeed succeeded in softening the heart of his closest friend? Even in his youth he had never been blind to Francesco's failings, nor reluctant to enumerate them. "A friend," he maintained, "has licence to say what he likes to his friend, or he is but a fearful fellow." He was, indeed, probably the only person who dared to speak the truth to Francesco—and he did so often. "To make money," he told him, "is what every man can do; but not every man knows how to work, and then leave go and lose."

Blandly, persistently, unceasingly, during the thirty years of their friendship, he attempted to persuade Francesco to find room, in the midst of business cares, both for human affections and for pious thoughts—"To treat God as a master and the world as a servant—that is a thing we can and must do." And always these counsels were given gently and humbly, "from your younger brother," "from the shepherd of Carmignano"—from a little man to a great one. "Your great estate requires great wisdom, as a great ship a great sail; *my* little boat would go with a servant's sheet." * Even Francesco—prone as he was to lose his temper and "begin to shout"—could hardly take offence.

It is impossible to quote all his letters of good advice; but one written very early in their friendship sets the tone for them all.

> Francesco, I have considered your state a hundred times, on my walks, and in bed, and in my study, when I was most alone. And charity constrains me to tell you the truth, which I think a most precious thing among friends. . . .
>
> I have already known, from your letters, of your tribulations and the hindrances caused to you by the things of this world; but now that I have seen them with my own eyes, they are far greater than I deemed. When I think of the cares of the house you are building, of your warehouses in far-off lands, your banquets and your accounts, and of many other matters, they seem to me so far beyond what is need-

ful that I realize it cannot be that you should seize an hour from the world and its snares. Yet God has granted you an abundance of earthly goods, and has given you, too, a thousand warnings, to awaken you; and now you are nearly sixty, and free from the cares of children—and are you to wait until your death-bed, when the door-latch of death is lifted, to change your heart?

In short, I would you should wind up many of your matters, which you yourself say are in order, and desist at once from any more building, and give away some of your riches in charity with your own hands, and value these riches at their true worth, that is, own them as if they were not yours. . . . I ask you not to become a priest or a monk, but I say unto you: put some order in your life.*

To Ser Lapo's candid soul, it seemed almost incredible that any man capable, as Francesco was, of apprehending and, indeed, liking the *idea* of goodness should not then order his life accordingly. "Any good idea," he wrote, "is easily implanted in your mind, and causes your soul to flower. But the winds of the labours which you yourself have sought, dash these flowers to the ground, and they cannot bear fruit."

Fifteen years later his opinion had not changed. "Save for certain attacks of wrath, which arise from your nature or a bad habit, I have ever found in you great intelligence and a subtle awareness, and what is good has seemed sweet to you, as indeed it is." *

Why, then, was Francesco not a better man? Two causes, to Ser Lapo's mind, were at the root of all his failings: a cold heart, and spiritual pride. It was against these—far more than against covetousness or lust or sharp practice—that he warned Francesco in a letter which he himself called, in the superscription, "a simple answer to the subtle questions of Francesco di Marco."

Francesco, it appears, had had a bad dream: he had dreamed that a vulture (from which he had apparently demanded, like the ancient Romans, some omen to resolve his doubts about divine justice) had scorned the gold he had offered it, but, seizing some pieces of rotting flesh in its claws, had beaten its wings and flown away. In reply to this story, Ser Lapo wrote to Francesco "in deepest silence, in the peace of the night when the mind is at rest," to tell him what he must do. "First, my father, you must warm your heart with love of Him who created us, that his blazing love and charity may shine for you." Next, he must refrain from setting up his poor human judgement against that of such great teachers as St. Augustine:

> Seldom have I seen a man who could savour the truth better than you, when you set your mind to it. Now say: you well wot of the partridges which your friend [Francesco himself, of course] ate every day with that female in Avignon, and how much time he wasted in that and other worldly matters. Think you verily that your friend—entering at his present age in God's school—should marvel not to hold the first place there, and not to solve, on entering, all the problems of God's justice?

Closely akin to this form of spiritual pride was Francesco's other great failing, one almost incomprehensible to Ser Lapo— an ineradicable wilfulness, a belief that it was in his power to shape the whole of life to his own desires. "I beseech you, in God's name, rule yourself a little, and let the world go as it will."

To Ser Lapo himself such detachment came easily. "I am for going slowly, and I trim my sails—but the wind must be sent by *Messer Domeneddio*." *

Here is shown the fundamental, unchangeable difference of temperament that divided the two friends. Always the world will hold some men who, like Francesco, believe they can shape their own destiny, and a few who prefer to leave it in the hands of God. It says a great deal for the genuine liking between the two men that, in spite of such differences, the friendship still held.

But as the years passed and Francesco's irascibility increased, his patience with Ser Lapo's sermons began to wear a little thin— while, on his side, his friend was spurred on by an ever greater sense of urgency. It was then that he decided to write a long letter, not to Francesco, but to Margherita, asking her to show it to her husband at a propitious moment, "when he is at peace with a quiet mind."

> Tell Francesco [he began] how greatly a man would be mocked, who, already on the high seas with his ships, and the wind blowing in his sails, steered not towards some port. Our port is God. He made us; He calls for us; He returns our gifts to us a hundredfold. . . . Every man is evil, avaricious, proud, faithless, self-loving, envious; and if he shows some love, it is but a merchant's: "You did good to me, and so will I to you." But beseech your husband, who is your master, to have little to do with such evil folk. Let him put an end, if he can, to his vile and worldly dealings; all things are possible in God. Let him use the little time left to us, at the end, for God; let us strive at least to die in peace. For it would be too late to enter your horse, when the race is already run.*

This letter—Ser Lapo's last attempt to steer Francesco towards Paradise—was written only three years before the merchant's death, and five years before his own. He was only sixty years old, but he had already been suffering for some time from gravel and stone, for which the waters of Porretta had proved unavailing—and perhaps, too, after Francesco's death he found that life without him had lost some of its savour. In the same year as Francesco, Lapo's wife, Tessa, had also died, and—tiresome and complaining as she had always been—he found that, after all, he missed her. He wrote of "my fearful solitude . . . greater than I dreamed." In the spring of 1412 he fell ill, and on October 12 he drew up, in a hand that was no longer quite steady, his last deed— fitly enough, the will of another rich merchant, Lazzaro Fei of

239

Arezzo, who also (whether owing to his notary's influence or Datini's example) left his whole fortune to charity. He died twelve
days later, and was buried in the little church of S. Egidio, beside
the hospital which he had served for so many years. No tombstone
marks the spot, and the only record that remains of him in
Santa Maria Nuova is as unostentatious as he himself would have
desired. It is a line in one of the hospital's ledgers: "Ser Lapo
died on October 30, 1412, having been sick for seven months.
May God grant him His pardon." *

CHAPTER FOUR

THE HOUSE

"Maestri, manovali, opere, galcine, rena, pietre, grida e disperamenti." [1]—SER LAPO MAZZEI

 HE HOUSE STILL STANDS IN PRATO, ON THE corner of Via del Porcellatico and Via Mazzei. Over the door an inscription, carved after Datini's death by his fellow citizens, bears witness to his generosity and their gratitude.

Ceppo di Francesco di Marcho
Mercatante dei Poveri di X[to]
del quale il Chomune di Prato
        è dispensatore
lasciato nell' anno MCCCCX [2]

On the walls some faint traces still remain of the frescoes which the Pratesi painted in Francesco's honour after his death to tell, in sixteen pictures, the story of his life. That such a distinction— usually reserved for princes, saints, and Popes—should have been

---

[1] "Masters, workmen, labour, lime, sand, stones, shouts and despair."
[2] "The *Ceppo* of Francesco di Marco—Merchant of Christ's Poor—of which the Commune of Prato is the Dispenser—Left in the year 1410." The word *ceppo*—literally, log—came from a hollow log into which the members of a Franciscan fraternity, in the thirteenth century, dropped their alms for the poor.

241

awarded to the taverner's son of Prato shows, more clearly than any document, the position then held by a successful business-man. Each age has its heroes: the men who do what their contemporaries think important. It was fitting that the members of a merchant-city should choose to depict neither a saint's pil-grimage nor a ruler's progress, but a saga of trade, with a mer-chant for a hero.[3]

Lapo Mazzei described the new house, soon after it was built, as "the finest castle in the world." * This it certainly was not. As we see it today, it is a plain, uncompromising square house of no especial character on the corner of a narrow street, with no orna-ment but, on the upper floor, an open loggia. But in Datini's life-time it was the grandest house in Prato—and to the man who had set out to Avignon as a penniless boy it must have represented the seal of his success. "I know what delight you take in that garden of yours," wrote Domenico di Cambio, and he admon-ished him, when the plague was threatening: "Be not so much bound by the love of your fine house and garden, that you leave your skin there!" When one of the new rooms was finished, it was considered an honour to be asked to see it. "It will please me to see that fine room," wrote Domenico, "but I would have it be dry and the bed made up, that I can sleep there when I come to you. For though I myself have but a poor man's room, yet it comforts me to see such fine things." *

Francesco had begun to plan his house long before coming home. As early as 1358 his tutor, Piero di Giunta, had been in-structed to buy for him a piece of land on the corner of Via del Porcellatico, and it was here that—very slowly, brick by brick—the new house began to rise.

The work was supervised by a neighbour, Niccolozzo di Ser

---

[3] The frescoes, some of which we now know to be the work of Niccolò di Piero Gerini, are mentioned by Vasari, who attributed them to Antonio Viti da Pistoia. At the end of the sixteenth century they were mentioned by Miniati, and apparently even 50 years ago enough of them was still left for a plan to be made for their restoration, of which the drawings (with a list of the subjects) may be seen in the Cassa di Risparmio of Prato.

Naldo, but with exasperating slowness. Niccolozzo was a prudent man, and dared not take any decision without Francesco's approval. "We have left the scaffolding of your house as it is," he wrote in 1375, "not for the trouble or expense, but because we hope you will come yourself. For you could judge better with your eyes than your memory."

Four years later, in 1379, Francesco sent 50 florins to hasten the work, but Niccolozzo still held it up. "I would not see your florins cast away," he wrote. "You know your own intent touching the work and the stairs and every matter. But men have diverse tastes and desires, and when the work is done and the money spent, it is too late."

He pointed out, moreover, that Francesco could come and stay with him while the walls of his own house were rising.

> Remember I have kept for you a house with a hall, kitchen and bedchamber, and half a cellar, full of wine. . . . Thus you have a place wherein you could live at ease, even though it is not a palace, and then we could do your work in order and without haste. . . . And thus you would see with your own eyes how your work should be done.

The building was held up still further by delays in the post, but in the following summer Francesco received an answer to at least one of his questions.

> I have sent you in several letters the measurements of your house and the big house and the orchard . . . and now I send them again. The house is 14 *braccia* by 15; the big house 20 *braccia* by 15; the orchard 31 by 20.*

Already the question of planting the orchard had come up, and Francesco told Stoldo di Lorenzo, in Pisa, to buy "an orange tree, the greatest you can find," but when it arrived Niccolozzo did not know where to plant it. "I might hap to place it in the wrong place, wherefrom it must be moved again. And I know not what to do, touching the fig tree by the stairs. When you are here, we shall plant as seems meet to you and Monna Margherita."

In spite, however, of all these delays, the house was slowly rising, and when Francesco came home, his first wish was to get the roof on. So great was his haste, so anxious his supervision of the laying of every brick, that he would hardly take an hour off for meals or for going to Mass. His friends in Florence did not approve. His house, they wrote, was already the wonder of Prato; why go on striving to make it finer still? "I say not you should give up building; but I beseech you, spare yourself. Let your dinner and supper be at the set hour, and the food good." And, in another letter: "I beseech you, destroy not yourself! Watch over other men's toil for part of the day, at ease—and in the morn, go to Mass. The man who is a stranger in church will be a stranger to God." *

When Francesco had to be in Florence on business, he insisted on long daily reports about the work's progress, and was much annoyed when any detail was omitted. "I rejoice that you have begun to quench the lime," he replied, "with water from the well. But you tell me not if any men have been to the kiln, nor what sort of lime it is: this you should have told me!" *

Early in 1388 the upstairs loggia was almost finished: "Zaccheri [the mason] says that, when it is plastered he will distemper it while the walls are still fresh, for that is best." By the summer all the inner walls were plastered—("I damp the walls with my own hands every day," * wrote Piero di Giunta)—and the brick floors were being laid. In September the stones for the fire-places were being ordered—"12 blocks of stone as long as this string."

Finally, at the other end of the plot of land on which the house was built, Francesco erected a warehouse, with a flower-garden between the two buildings "and a cistern and a cellar underground and above-ground, and a narrow passage." * The walls around it were "painted" (i.e., plastered and distempered) and had stone corners, and on one of them he placed a little shrine to Our Lady, which stands there still.

Then at last—after ten years given up to building—Francesco

declared himself satisfied. "You say you are done with building," wrote a Florentine friend to him, "and now would attend to your trade and your soul. As to the building, it is high time." *

Let us see what, at the end of all this toil, the house was like. An inventory drawn up in 1407 described it as "a large and handsome house, situated in Porta Fuia . . . with a great dwelling-place and a well and a court and a loggia and a cellar, all painted and fine," and set its value at 1,000 florins.* Its size alone marked it as a rich man's dwelling, for even in Florence the finest private houses seldom consisted of more than twelve or thirteen rooms,[4] while five or six was much more usual, and, moreover, the walls, instead of being of wood or bare brick, were plastered and distempered. "I painted," said the painter's bill, "the stones of the whole courtyard in fresco and plaster, from head to foot to the full height of the house, all with my own colours: and it came to 20 florins." *

The roof, as was customary, was tiled, and the only architectural ornament—a handsome pillared loggia (often also called a *verone*)—was immediately beneath it, on the top storey. It was used, not only as an additional living-room in hot weather, but for airing furs and wools, beating carpets and blankets, and drying linen.

The windows, rather small, had heavy wooden shutters, opening inwards on hinges. Most of them were what were then called *finestre impannate*—i.e., made of oiled linen or cotton on light wooden frames; they opened outwards or could be drawn up, like blinds.[5] One letter to Francesco, however, refers to an order for "one window with bars" (of which the iron cost 26 *denari* a

---

[4] The inventories of several houses of rich merchants in Florence at the end of the fourteenth century show that the largest of them only had fourteen rooms, but by the following century the great new palaces of the Strozzi and Medici were, of course, much larger. Schiaparelli, *La casa fiorentina e i suoi arredi.*

[5] Two of the *finestre impannate* in Francesco's house in Florence were "painted," probably with a formal pattern, and one was made of "*carta di bambagia*" (cotton paper).

pound), so it is possible that the windows on the ground floor were of this kind. There is also a bill for 50 florins from the Vallombrosan monk Don Lionardo di Simone, *maestro di vetri*, for an *occhio*—a small round glass window.* But as this bill is in a long list of glass supplied, at Francesco's expense, for various Florentine churches, it is doubtful whether or not this *occhio* was for his own house.[6]

The main door—according to the bill of Goro, the stone-mason who was hewing its stone in April 1383—was framed by 18 *braccia* of "hewn stone," and on the cornice above it the taverner's son placed his arms: three red bands on a white field. This door was the one that, by Francesco's orders, was never opened in the mornings until his wife was up and about. But now we may open it and go in.

On the entrance-wall a large, faded fresco of St. Christopher is still visible.[7] He was the house's guardian, for it was believed that before his martyrdom the Saint had prayed that, wherever his body lay, "no harm should come, either from hail or fire, hunger or pestilence." The shape of the rooms has now been completely altered; but in one of them a portrait of Francesco still grimly looks down upon us, and doggerel verses beneath it say:

> *Francesco io son di Marco che lasciai*
> *Di mie sustanze herede i miei Pratesi*
> *Perchè la patria mia più ch' altro amai.*[8]

According to an inventory dated 1405, the rooms on the ground floor included an office, a small cellar, a guest-room with two

---

[6] Glass was no longer precisely a rarity in Tuscany, but was still considered a luxury, and after the great flood of 1332 a Franciscan preacher had included glass windows in his list of the luxuries which had drawn God's wrath upon the city.

[7] The fresco was begun by Niccolò Gerini, but he did not finish it, and in 1394 Francesco wrote that he had promised to pay 10 gold florins to "two young painters, who have come here to finish the St. Christopher begun by Niccolò." (File 112. To Stoldo di Lorenzo, January 14, 1394.)

[8] "I am Francesco di Marco, who left my Pratesi as heirs of all my fortune, because I loved my city above all other things."

beds, and the loggia called, to distinguish it from the upstairs one, *la loggia della corte*, which was not frescoed, but painted green. Such loggias—built on beside a house, for the express purpose of entertaining—were then a novelty, but soon became a fashion which added greatly to the beauty and liveliness of Tuscan towns. Often decorated with gay frescoes, bestrewn with rushes, and hung with garlands, they were the places where rich men gave their banquets or entertained their friends with music and dancing, while—since the loggia often gave on to the open street—many uninvited guests shared in the party, too.

There were two kitchens—one upstairs and one down—but it was the upstairs one which was in use, a habit which probably survived from recent times when (either because houses were made of wood, or because there was no chimney) the kitchen was placed, for safety, either in a separate room behind the house, or else on the top storey, under the roof. Indeed, even though dwellings of brick and stone had now become common, the fear of fire was still so deeply ingrained that Francesco's contemporary Paolo da Certaldo advised prudent householders never to go to bed until they had seen the fire damped and extinguished every night, and, moreover, always to have ready twelve large sacks "to carry things away with," and a rope "long enough to reach from the roof to the ground, so that you may let yourself down from every window in your house, if it were needful, in case of fire." [9]

All Francesco's downstairs rooms had vaulted ceilings—some of them painted—and brick floors, carefully polished and waxed. Since the same word—"*tappeto*"—was used for both a carpet and a cover, it is uncertain whether he had any carpets. The only *tappeto* mentioned (which came from Genoa and cost 10 florins) lay on the footboard of a bed, and though some Catalan matting is listed, its purpose is not stated. Reed mattings, however, were already common in town houses, and in the country cut reeds were strewn upon the floor.

In the hall stood three shields (*palvesi*)—two of them painted

[9] Paolo da Certaldo, op. cit., paras. 95 and 90.

with Francesco's crest, and one with a lion. Domenico di Cambio, when he ordered them, wished to know (since he himself was an ardent Guelph) if they were to be painted with a rake on the top, "as is the custom for the Guelphs of Florence." * Each shield, he warned him, would cost 58 *soldi*, with an extra 8 *soldi* for the painting—but this was a price which Francesco gladly paid, for he could never tire of seeing his arms reproduced: he placed them not only on shields and over doorways, but on his dishes, forks, and bed-curtains, and even on the frescoes and chalices he presented to the Church. To own arms was not, in the fluctuating society of the time, necessarily a sign of nobility, but it was a mark of *standing*. As a man rose in the world, he got himself arms; and this was why the taverner's son valued them and later on rejoiced when, after a visit from Louis II of Anjou, he received the right to add to them the fleur-de-lis of France.

It is not possible to make out the original shape of the rooms upstairs; but we know that there was a *sala grande*—probably in the centre, with the other rooms leading out of it. The other rooms on this floor were the master bedroom (Francesco's and Margherita's), two guest-rooms, the upstairs kitchen, the upstairs *loggia*, and a small room called "Francesco's office," but which appears to have been used as a store-room. His real office was the one in the warehouse opposite, which—according to the inventory of 1394—had four writing-desks—one "with a cover" and one "with a little chest, in which Francesco keeps his writings," two baskets for letters, and a money-bowl—as well as several chests and a cupboard. And it, too, was painted grass-green.

It will be observed that, though there were many servants, there were no servants' rooms—the explanation being that they slept wherever was most convenient—in the kitchen, on the landing, or on truckle beds in the room of their master or mistress.

The greatest luxuries in the house were two stone fire-places—one carved with Datini's crest, the other, in the guest-room, "in the French style" (*alla francesca*), by which was meant a fire-place possessing a chimney built into the wall, instead of (as was

248

still more usual) an open fire-place in the middle of the room with no exit for smoke.[1]

Datini's two fire-places were fully provided with fire-dogs,[2] tongs, shovel, and even bellows—*un ingegno da far vento*—but the only other warmth available to his family was that given by their warming-pans at night—called by the ribald name of *il prete* —or by the little earthenware jars containing red-hot charcoal, *scaldini*, which Italian peasant women still hold upon their knees. (No doubt this is why both men and women wore, in winter, fur linings to their gowns.)

For light they had "horn lanterns," wax torches on long poles, tallow candles, and little brass oil-lamps, almost identical to those used in Roman days, in which they burned the dregs of the olive oil.

There is no mention of any latrines (though they already existed in some Florentine houses of the period), but both in the chief guest-room and in the hall there was an *iscranna forata*, or commode. And for washing there were "two basins for washing feet and one round barber's basin" in the kitchen, and some towels "to wear when others [*sic*] are washing the head." *

The walls and vaulted ceilings of many of the rooms were decorated—some of the ceilings with a pattern of gold stars on a blue ground which is still faintly visible, and the walls in either plain colours or a geometrical pattern. From the bill of Arrigo di Niccolò *dipintore* we learn that he painted, at a cost of 10 florins,

---

[1] In 1368, when Francesco, Duke of Carrara, visited Rome, he found no chimney in the *Albergo della Luna*, "for fire-places were not then in use, but people made a fire on the floor in the midst of the house, or some made fires in earthenware boxes." The Duke therefore, "not deeming himself at ease in this fashion," took with him his own bricklayers "and caused two fire-places to be built with little vaulted arches, according to the fashion of Padua." Andrea Gataro in Muratori, XXVI, p. 582. In England, of course, fire-places arrived still later and as late as 1577 Harrison was writing of them as luxuries for "uplandish houses," saying that an ordinary man "made his fire against a reredos in the hall, where he dined and dressed his meat." W. Harrison, *Elizabethan England*, p. 119.

[2] "The fire-dogs must be handsome," wrote Domenico di Cambio, "for methinks you would place them in the fine guest-chamber." (File 1092, January 28, 1390.)

the walls of the passage (which he calls a *"viale"*) between the main bedroom and the kitchen with a marbled pattern, and its ceiling with gold fleur-de-lis on a blue ground. (This must have been after the visit of Louis of Anjou.) He also painted for 15 florins, in the guest-room on the ground floor, a "ceiling" and bed-curtains—as a substitute for a canopy and curtains made of cloth.

II

The list of furniture, as in most houses of the time, is to our eyes rather meagre. Moreover, it is surprising—in view of the fact that Francesco was both a draper and an importer of French cloth —not to find some of the rooms, at least, adorned by fine hangings. It must, however, be remembered that in the *trecento* such wall-coverings (except the actual bed-curtains and canopy) were not in daily use, but were carefully folded away in chests and brought out on grand occasions such as weddings and feast-days. It was only then that men hung out all their brocades and carpets, and adorned with them the walls of their houses, as well as their outer walls, window-sills and loggias, and even benches set up in the open street.

The hanging most often seen in the *trecento* was the *capoletto* or tester—originally, as its name implies, a piece of stuff hung at the head of a bed, but subsequently often used to decorate almost any wall or to form the back of a bench. Most often these *capoletti* were made of a fine French woollen cloth, *sargia* (serge); but sometimes, in summer, linen was preferred, often painted in bright colours or designs. In Francesco's house we find these materials used both for the bed and for a canopy and curtains. In his room in Prato he had "a canopy and curtains of painted linen," and in Florence others of blue linen painted with his arms and Monna Margherita's. The double guest-room in Prato also had "four painted bed-curtains," and one of its beds had "a large cover"—while the single guest-room had both bed-curtains and a canopy. The whole enclosure formed by the canopy and curtains made a little room within the big one, and indeed was called, as in France, the "*camera*."

By far the most important piece of furniture was the bed. In Francesco's and Margherita's room it was 6 *braccia* wide (about 4 yards), with a low footboard all round it which fulfilled the double purpose of bench and chest. In addition to its curtains and canopy, it had a striped mattress ("the cloth made in Paris"), two pillows of cloth-of-gold, and six pillows with cases of fine-drawn threadwork (*a reticella*). Its bed-cover was "lined with old sheets and stuffed with fine feathers," and it had also another "striped double cover, lined with azure cloth, and filled with fine wool," as well.as two feather quilts with striped covers. Thus, in bed, at least, Francesco and Margherita—even though they probably slept naked—cannot have suffered from the cold!

The other chief pieces of bedroom furniture were coffers and chests, in which not only clothes and linen but even furs and jewels were stored. These were often part of a bride's dowry, and were sometimes very beautiful, decorated with elaborate scenes of wedding-banquets or processions, or fine designs. Datini's, however, are unfortunately not described in any detail; the inventory merely lists one "painted coffer" and three chests with locks. In addition, Margherita had two little coffers, one "of black and white bone, made in Florence," and one "carved all round in ivory, which came from Avignon"; a leather box, in which she kept her rings; and a wooden one "covered with leather and painted with gold letters and designs."

The only other pieces of furniture in the bedroom were a *cappellinaio*, or hatstand,[3] a cupboard, a single chair,[4] and, finally,

[3] Sometimes these *cappellinai* seem to have been part of the bed itself, for another inventory mentions "a little bed with *cappellinaio*, and hung on it 1 pair of spurs, 1 pair of gloves, 1 pair of spectacles, and 2 keys." (Inventory, July 16, 1397.)

[4] This was called a *sedia regolata*, or chair strengthened by strips of wood nailed on with round nails—a practice forbidden by law, since it enabled a carpenter to conceal the quality of the wood underneath.

both in this room and in the best guest-room, a *desco da parto dipinto*, or painted "tray for childbirth." Such trays (so called because they were often presented to women after childbirth) were often elegant works of art, adorned with scenes of weddings or banquets.

No mirror is mentioned in these lists, but we know that there must have been at least one, given to Margherita in 1391 by Lapo Mazzei because he did not think his own house worthy of so fine an ornament.

> Having hung it in my hall [he wrote to Francesco] and then in my bedroom and at last in my study, I thought it looked not well in any place—indeed meseemed it complained of the rough home I had given it. And therefore I thought it would rejoice to find itself, instead, beside your loggia, among the arras cloths and the shining candour of the delicate walls, in the finest castle of the world, and the most noble part of it.*

Another mirror—"new and fine and good and clear"—was sent by Domenico di Cambio for Francesco's office. This was probably a concave one, as these were then often used to reflect the light on to a desk and thus "preserve the sight and comfort it, during constant writing."

Other ornaments were three "vases from Damascus"—a vase for rose-water, a bowl of white glass, and "a glass bowl, very well worked in gold"—and three pictures, all of sacred subjects.

The best-furnished of the guest-rooms was the one downstairs, which on one occasion entertained Francesco Gonzaga, and on another, Louis II of Anjou: it contained, in addition to "two beds with *predelle*, with their curtains, mattresses and quilts" and "another small bed of 3 *braccia*," a walnut trestle-table, a *cassapanca*, a commode, and "two small tables of walnut intarsia."

It is interesting to note that, instead of one double bed, there were two, but with a single curtain round them both. They both had white covers and bedspreads of vermilion French cloth, and the smaller bed had a "carpet." (This was the room with the French fire-place.)

The smaller guest-room downstairs contained, besides the bed with its chests, curtains, and canopy, a walnut trestle-table, a picture of Our Lady in a little shrine, and no less than six chests; the upstairs guest-room (decorated with a painted design simulating fur hangings) had a bed 4 *braccia* wide, with a footboard and a cushion, a chest, two painted coffers, and a stool. Every bedroom, in addition to its big bed, had also a small truckle-bed for a servant.

As to the living-rooms, the main hall seems to have been furnished very barely, and chiefly with tables: one large dining-table 8 *braccia* long, one long walnut trestle-table, and two small round tables. There were also two reed chairs and one bench and five pine poles for hanging up the washing; in the loggia a wooden press, a pail, and some jugs and glasses. Datini's office, too, had a small bed in it; and the rest of its furniture was a big trestle-table with a little stool, a long bench (no doubt for clients and peasants), three *cassapanche*, and two shields with Francesco's crest.

Perhaps the most sparsely furnished rooms were the kitchens. The downstairs kitchen contained only a dining-table, a *madia* (the flour-chest which is still to be found in every Tuscan kitchen), a wooden sink, a safe for dried meat, and the usual truckle-bed: the upstairs kitchen, only two wooden tables and a chest. But it is probable that the cooking-utensils hung on hooks on the wall, and we also find some scattered in the other rooms of the house. They included two enormous cauldrons (one of them, in the downstairs kitchen, could hold 3 barrels of water), as well as—

1 great brass pot,
2 copper bowls,
2 great copper jars for water,
2 iron pots, that hung on a chain above the fire,

1 copper frying-pan,
4 other frying-pans, 2 spits and a grill,
an unspecified number of other pans and frying-pans,
20 oil-jars (of which one was for cooking-oil),
2 barrels of vinegar,
1 pair of scales weighing 90 lbs.,
2 mortars and pestles (one in each kitchen),
1 salt-box,
1 sugar-barrel,
1 copper pan "for making black puddings,"
1 big pan for melting lard,
1 sieve and an iron shovel "for making pills,"
3 trestles and a great many fire-irons,
1 bowl "for making comfits."

There were also some tables and chairs in the upstairs loggia, which suggests that it was sometimes used as a living-room.

The list of cutlery and plates is not very lavish. Forks were still a rarity,[5] and the 12 silver ones were locked away in Francesco's own room; there were also only 7 silver spoons belonging to Niccolò dell'Ammannato (these were in pawn), a few silver knives, and two silver cups. Of pewter there are 12 soup-plates, 7 other plates, and 12 bowls. But there are some majolica bowls, decorated with Francesco's own crest, which he had ordered from Valencia, and also some decorated pottery jars of the type called *alberelli* (which may still be seen in old-fashioned chemists' shops) for preserves and drugs: ginger, saffron, cinnamon, theriac. And in the Florentine inventory there is some more earthenware: 6 small fish-plates, 18 soup-plates, 3 sauce-bowls, a ewer "for pouring water over one's hands," and 3 *rinfrescatoi*—literally "refreshers"—which are explained as bowls for cooling fruit.

Next we come to the contents of the linen-chests, which were

[5] Even the Pope, when Francesco was in Avignon, possessed only a couple of forks, though he had little golden skewers on which to spear his roast meat and his figs, and crystal ones for his strawberries.

very well stocked. Then, as now, a good Tuscan housewife's chief pride was in her linen-chests, and, moreover, Datini, as a draper, was able to get his linen cheap. Sine the inventories overlap and repeat each other and linen was kept in both Prato and Florence, it is impossible to make out a full list, but it is clear that Margherita always kept a stock of new linen, as well as that in daily use. Probably, too, some of the finer things were used only on great occasions—for instance, the "three great tablecloths worked in Avignon," the "four pillows of old scarlet taffeta, with pillow-cases worked in drawn-thread work and cross-stitch, and three of them in herringbone stitch, with four tassels each," and four pillows in cloth-of-gold, two on a rose ground and two on a blue.

The bed-linen (if some lists are not missing) appears to have been much less abundant than the table-linen. According to the list dated 1397, Margherita's chest then contained 5½ pairs of big double sheets, "for the bed of *Messere* and *Madonna*," with drawn-thread work, and 9 pairs of large sheets and 2½ small for the household—and that is all. On the other hand, there were 10 large tablecloths, and four smaller ones for the household—adorned by 6 stripes of cotton, generally in bright colours, at the head and foot—7 worn surnapes, and several rolls of linen, for making "70 handkerchiefs and two wimples."

A second chest contained only one large sheet—very worn—and one bed-cover, but there was a roll of linen for making 17 new table-napkins, "with open-work stripes," 3 "very fine new table-napkins, and a new surnape with six stripes," as well as 20 *braccia* of unbleached linen, and a canopy of linen "embroidered in silk, for a bed." In addition, there was an assortment of different kinds of towels—12 of one kind, "wrapped in a shift," 10 other "fine new ones," and 5 thick ones, "for rubbing the head." (It must be remembered that rubbing—"*frugacion*"—was much used as a substitute for washing, and was thought good for the health.) This chest also contained two table-cloths left in pawn—one "by Monna Lucia the taverner, for the tax she had to pay" and another by the baker, "for the money he owes us." (It was apparently not unusual for a rich man—even if not a usurer—to give small loans in return for such sureties as these.)

A third chest contained some more towels—15 "for the head," with cotton stripes, 2 large wide ones with four stripes, also for the head, and 7 fine worn ones with a cotton stripe. The towels "for the head," which were generally decorated with either a coloured stripe or drawn-thread work, formed a charming, simple headdress: they were worn folded square on the head and falling down over the neck and shoulders. This chest also contained more table-linen:

13 large worn table-cloths, with open-work stripes,
4 small ones of the same kind,
4 other small ones, torn,
12 large surnapes with cotton stripes,
7 old surnapes with open-work stripes for every day,
5 little old surnapes, for drying the hands, with faded cotton stripes,
4 hand-towels, new,
3 very fine napkins, with three wide and two narrow bands,
6 old napkins,
17 old napkins with two open-work bands,
12 old napkins "to keep before one when eating,"
9 *mantelluzzi* "to keep before one when others eat" [i.e., aprons for waiting at table?]

On the whole, Monna Margherita, when she surveyed her linen-chests, could feel well satisfied.

The general impression left by these lists, and by looking at the house itself, is neither one of luxury nor of much taste: the houses of Datini's contemporaries had not yet got the great carved fire-places, the floors or marble or mosaic, and the fine tapestries and sculptures that adorned the dwellings of the great merchants of the next generation. The pleasantest thing about *casa Datini* was its proportions—the height of its great bare rooms, the breadth of its well-built walls, the spaciousness of the loggias. The furniture was probably solid and well made, but otherwise one receives a strong impression that Francesco distinguished one object from another only by its cost: he bought himself fine linen, silver forks, and crested pottery, like his scarlet gowns, because such things were due to a man of his standing, rather than because he really liked them. In a similar manner, he placed pictures of sacred subjects in his house not so much because they pleased him as because everyone told him that to look at them would be good for his soul. Fra Giovanni Dominici, the preacher whose sermons he most admired, even maintained that such pictures should be shown to children "while still in swaddling-bands" —especially those depicting the Holy Child or virgins, "since like calls to like."

> The Virgin Mary is meet, with the Child on Her arm and a little bird or pomegranate in its hand. Other good figures are Jesus sucking milk, or Jesus asleep in His Mother's lap. . . . So let the child look upon his own image in the Holy Baptist, a little boy dressed in a gown of camel's hair, playing with the birds, sucking leaves and sleeping on the ground. It would not harm him to see . . . the Massacre of the Innocents, that he should fear arms and armed men. And thus it were well to nurture little girls on the sight of the eleven thousand virgins, talking and playing.[6]

Thus a man—so the good friar maintained—might turn his house "almost into a temple."

Francesco did his best. In addition to the fresco of St. Christopher over his threshold, he had three sacred pictures in his bedroom, one in each of his guest-rooms, and one in his office. But the business of ordering them he left entirely to Domenico di Cambio.

[6] Beato Giovanni Dominici, *Regola del governo di cura familiare*, pp. 131-2.

You say [Domenico wrote] you would have a picture painted for you on one of those panels, of our Lord, but you say not if you would have Him on the Cross, or how you would have Him. . . . I have two pairs [of pictures] made for Boninsegna. In one, each picture is the size of a folio, and on one Our Lord is portrayed, with Our Lady and St. John beside Him, and the other side shows Our Lady seated with the Child on Her lap—all in fine gold.

A few days later Domenico was suggesting "a *Pietà*—that is, Our Lord rising from the tomb [*quand' esce dal munimento*], with Our Lady beside Him, and the whole background in fine gold." [7] Plainly, in the writer's opinion, the artistic merit of these pictures was entirely secondary to their prime object—"to move a man's spirit to devotion." "Verily, men who are hard of heart and caught up in this world's toils, need these pious stories—and since I deem you are one of them, I will be solicitous that you are well served." *

These pictures were not the only works of art bought by Francesco: the same painters who supplied them and who decorated the walls of his house also adorned—at his expense—the walls and altars of several churches: in particular, the church of San Piero Forelli and the one dedicated to his patron saint, San Francesco. Here, while the walls of his house were still rising, he sent his bricklayers to build a little tabernacle, in which his stonemason, Goro, erected a pedestal of *pietra serena* from Fiesole for a Crucifix, and the painter Tommaso del Mazza painted frescoes of St. Catherine and other saints, and of the donors, Francesco and Margherita. In 1395 two other painters, Lorenzo di Niccolò and Niccolò Gerini, adorned the wall over one of the church doors with frescoes of the Annunciation, the Flagellation, and the Ascension, and a figure of God the Father, and Niccolò (who was then painting Datini's St. Christopher) also painted another

---

[7] Presumably Domenico meant a *Pietà* like the one by Lorenzo Monaco in the Accademia of Florence—in which Christ is represented as rising out of a sarcophagus.

Crucifix, a panel of the Madonna, a fresco representing "St. Francis with the stigmata and Francesco di Marco at his feet, with foliage and compasses in fine gold and ultramarine blue," and, finally, above the door leading to the cloister, another fresco of San Francesco between two saints, with portraits of Francesco and Margherita and the Datini arms. Well might Niccolò write to his patron, when the work was done, that "the monks commend you greatly, forasmuch as you have set in order and adorned all this side of the door, which was only fit for yokels before." *

Perhaps, however, the most valuable of all Datini's gifts to the Church were the coloured glass windows—"with stories thereon" —which he presented, not only to Prato, but to each of the principal churches of Florence: the Certosa, Ognissanti, Santa Maria Novella, San Gallo, San Miniato, and Santa Croce. These windows were the work of a Vallombrosan monk, Fra Lionardo di Simone, and their cost was estimated at 3 florins a *braccio*, as well as the monk's expenses "for wire, iron, stone-hewing, and food and wine for himself and his workmen." *

The number of these works of art suggests that Francesco was a generous patron of the arts. It must, however, be admitted that his letters to the artists he employed do not show him in a very agreeable light: he was impatient and exacting while the work was being done, and miserly when the time came to pay for it. One man who had tried working in his house for six months wrote to Luca del Sera that he had been obliged to leave merely on account of Francesco's capricious moods. "In good faith, had he been another man, I should still be there; but methought his strangeness of nature was so great, that one day I should be compelled to break with him." He added that Francesco would fly into a rage "if even a blade of straw gets caught in his feet," and that, night after night, "we sat up until past midnight, while he complained of all the injuries that had been done to him." * Even the most faithful of his workmen, the stone-mason Goro, lamented that he often had been reproved by him unjustly. "And yet I know not whether any other man would serve you as well and faithfully as I, and I am willing to bear with you now and always." * For twenty-four whole years, as his bill shows, Goro went on working for Francesco without payment [8]—and when he then at last asked for what was due to him, his patron was apparently overcome with surprise and indignation, for a letter from a friend in Bologna comments: "I marvel at Goro treating you so ill, for I thought him a good man." Even then, six months more passed before the bill was paid—an incredibly long list of hewn stone, cornices, columns, window-frames, thresholds, doors, doorsteps, etc., supplied between 1383 and 1407, and coming to 280 gold florins.

The chief point which emerges from the bills of Datini's painters is the contrast between the small amount paid for an artist's or craftsman's skill and the high cost of his materials. Sometimes, in consequence, a patron supplied the materials himself—for instance, when Francesco wanted a new pair of curtains for his bed, he first had the cloth woven in Florence, then mangled, clipped, and dyed, after which he himself bought the paints—and only then sent for the painter who was to decorate the curtains with his arms.

The most expensive colour was the fine *azzurro transmarino*, made of powdered lapis-lazuli, which Oriental alchemists called "the painter's flower." This (sometimes also referred to in the account-books as *"azzurro fino"*) came to as much as 1 florin an ounce, so that painters often used instead the cheaper *azzurro d'Alemagna,* extracted from copper. Gold, too, was very expensive —and very lavishly laid on. In 1395 we find the painter Niccolò Gerini demanding 5 florins from Francesco "for the great cost of the gold" for a single Crucifix. Consequently, the price of a picture largely depended on its actual size, and on the quality of the colours. Almost all the orders for pictures from Francesco's branch in Avignon specify the precise measurement required,

---

[8] On one occasion Goro excused himself for some delay in finishing Francesco's sink by telling him: "The *Signoria* have constrained most of the workmen of Fiesole and Settignano to work in S. Liberata"—an interesting sidelight on the methods by which the fine new churches of Florence were swiftly rising.

estimating the cost on that basis, and there is a letter, too, from Agnolo Gaddi to Francesco, telling him that two figures of the Madonna and S. Giovanni, if 3 *braccia* high, would come to 25 florins.* But it is amusing to note that a panel of Our Lady which Datini presented to a poor Franciscan monastery in Corsica was considerably cheaper. "It would have cost more, had it been painted with gold; they did it with silver-gilt, that it should be less costly." *

In a dispute that arose between Datini and the guild of doctors and apothecaries—in which the painters' guild was incorporated, and which also included the mercers, barbers, illuminators, leather-workers, saddlers, purse-makers, and even a few armourers and blacksmiths—the guild's consuls suggested that, since Datini still dealt in a mercer's goods, he ought to join their guild. This (since he already belonged to the wool and silk guilds) he refused to do; but undoubtedly his close association with them enabled him to get his materials at a favourable price. All these different crafts, indeed, were very closely interdependent. A mercer like Datini would import from Lyons or Provence the ox-guts which the Florentine goldsmiths used for hammering their metals into gold cords, or into gold and silver leaf. The painters bought their colours and varnishes from the apothecaries, their brushes and canvases from the mercers, their panels from the carpenters, and their leather from the saddlers. Sometimes the same man was both apothecary and painter, and Agnolo Gaddi, in recommending two artists to Francesco, mentioned that one of them was a saddler by trade, the other "a painter who carves figures." No hard and fast line divided the craftsman from the artist; a *dipintore* would not disdain to pass from painting a sacred altar-piece to distempering the walls of a house, or to the decoration of chests, curtains, shields, and banners, or saddle-cloths and harness, of waxen figures or earthenware bowls. Arrigo di Niccolò *dipintore*, who painted one of the panels which Francesco presented to the Church, also distempered and decorated the walls of his court-yard and of his warehouse—and was paid at much the same rate for both services. He earned rather less than a florin a day, as did Agnolo Gaddi, while a *dipintore di cortina*, Maestro Maso di Venezia, received 30 *soldi* (just over a florin) a day.* Moreover, these painters, and any workmen they brought with them, also received board and lodging, and there was a pleasant custom—which survives in the country in Tuscany to this day—of celebrating the completion of any stage of the work with a dinner for the workmen. Thus, on one occasion we find Francesco standing a dinner, "to do honour to the carpenters," at which the food served was a quarter of a kid, some eels (brought all the way from the lagoons of Comacchio), some broad beans (*bacelli*), and 91 oranges—the whole dinner coming to *lire* 23.11.4.*

Sometimes, however, a skilled painter would demand to be paid not by the day, but for each finished piece of work—the price, if it had not been settled beforehand, being estimated by impartial "arbitrators"—and this is apparently what happened when Agnolo Gaddi, with Niccolò Gerini and another painter, decorated the walls and loggia of *casa Datini*. Their patron considered their demands grossly exorbitant. "Methinks," he exclaimed, "when Giotto was alive he was cheaper! . . . Having found some soft soil, they mean to dig their spades therein, up to the hilt. God preserve me from others of their sort." *

What Francesco, however, did not mention was that he had turned all three painters—unpaid—out of the house, and that they had gone back to Florence, leaving their work in San Francesco half done. They spent the next few months in besieging him with alternate prayers and threats, but Datini not only refused to pay, but was amazed at their daring to complain:

> You marvel [Niccolò Gerini replied to his reproaches] that I go about complaining of you. . . . Verily, I complained of you to Goro the stone-mason, and I trow I was right: you well know how long a time has passed since I served you well and speedily, leaving my shop and family to serve you, and you have not paid me a single penny. And even now I would

gladly serve you well, if you would first pay me for the work
I have done.*

After several months the painters' patience gave out, and they
appealed to the court of their own guild. Experts were called in,
who visited Datini's house, said "they had never seen so fine a
piece of work," and valued it at 60 florins; Datini protested that
he would rather lose this sum at sea than pay it; Ser Lapo intervened; and at last, most reluctantly, the merchant disbursed 55
gold florins. And Ser Lapo commented that if he had been able
to spend in prayer all the time he had wasted on this business, "he
would have found the road to Paradise." *

CHAPTER FIVE

THE FARM

"The country makes good beasts and evil men."
—Paolo da Certaldo

N 1392, AT LAST, FRANCESCO'S HOUSE WAS FINISHED
—but he was not yet content. He gradually
bought up twenty other houses in Prato, some
with small plots of land, others with a threshing-
floor or an enclosed court, and one with "two
canals and a court for making wine." * These he
then let to artisans or shop-keepers,[1] and he also bought or rented
—as well as his Florentine warehouses in Via Porta Rossa, Via
Parione, and Por S. Maria—several houses in Florence, Pistoia, and
Pisa. And, finally, he fulfilled the desire which sooner or later
comes to every Tuscan: to own a plot of land. Though himself
a townsman, the society to which he belonged was not—nor has
it ever become—wholly urban. Always the Tuscan cities have
held their arms wide open to the country, and in the *trecento* it
was often difficult to tell where the one ended and the other
began. Not only did orchards and gardens encroach within the

---

[1] The estimated value of these houses was between 15 and 150 florins,
and the list of tenants includes a baker, two cobblers, a barber, a tailor, the
town messenger, etc. The rents varied between 2½ and 8 florins a year.

264

The Merchant on His Horse
CODEX CASANATENSE 4182

Tuscan Farm

BY AMBROGIO LORENZETTI

city walls, but a large part of the population was of peasant stock.
First, in the course of the eleventh and twelfth centuries, the
cities had opened their doors to starving serfs who had fled to the
towns in search of bread, work, and freedom; then, as the great
feudal properties began to break up, it was these men's former
masters who exchanged their country castles for a single grim
tower in a narrow street. And more recently the desolation
wrought by the Free Companies had driven some of the remaining country folk to seek the comparative security and plenty of
the towns. Most of them became the humblest workers of the
guilds—the men who might form no associations of their own,
the *popolo minuto*—but some turned into skilled craftsmen or set
up a little shop. In a couple of generations they had saved a small
hoard—and then their first instinct was to put it back into the
land again.

Thus it was that in the second half of the *trecento* the country
ceased to be the abode only of rich seigneurs in their castles or
poor peasants in their huts: the *petite bourgeoisie*, too, began to
buy a few acres and build little farms. The wheel had come full
circle: the descendants of the same men who had left the land
two or three generations before had come back there again. The
farms were mostly small, like the fortunes of the men who bought
them, and to extract a livelihood from them every square inch of
soil had to be tilled, every stony hillside terraced and planted.
And so the villages and the towns soon came to be green with
orchards, and the hills "crowned with olives and garlanded with
vines."

The first piece of land that came into Francesco's possession
was on a very pleasant site. A few miles from Prato, on a hill
above the River Bisenzio, there was a little spring—"situated in the
place called *Il Palco*"—which provides an admirable example of
the manner in which legends are created. Apparently its waters
had some healing properties, and on June 8, 1308, the Council of
Prato decided to buy the land around it and to compensate the
owner for the damage which his trees and vines had suffered

"from the multitude of persons going to bathe in the spring." [2]
The land was bought for 638 *lire*, 15 *soldi*, and within thirty
years a legend had already sprung up, and a little shrine was
built. The spring, it was said, possessed its healing powers because "the martyr Proculus, as he was passing through the territory of Prato during his flight from the cruelty of the heathen,
by his prayers miraculously produced out of the earth a living
spring, which from that day forth has been called the *fontana
procula*. And many sick men drink of this water, and are healed
of their fever." [3]

Close to the spring there was a farm which had belonged for a
hundred years to Monna Margherita's family, and which came
into Francesco's hands soon after his return.[4] "*Messer lo Conte del
Palco*"—so Ser Lapo Mazzei jocosely addressed him, and on many
a day he ambled over from his own farm at Grignano to share a
partridge and some good wine with his friend. Before Francesco's
first Christmas in the new house he wrote to ask, in a mock formal
style, if he might bring his wife and children, too. "If it haps
that your Lordship, without inconvenience, could send us your
charger—better known as the little nag—before Christmas . . .
I would come up on my mare, and would put my two boys on
your palfrey, one on the saddle and one bareback." *

In the course of the next few years Francesco went on buying
little plots of land until, in 1407, he owned some 660 *staiora* (about
300 acres)—partly in small orchard plots of 5 or 10 *staiora* (between a quarter of an acre and an acre) close to the city gates,
and partly in little farms of 10 or 20 acres in the hills above the
town. The average price of Datini's land was between 8 and 10

[2] G. Giani, "*La Fonte Procula*," in *Archivio Storico Pratese*, July 1927.
[3] From a hagiography of S. Proculo in the Cathedral of Prato. Quoted by
Guasti in Mazzei, I, p. 130.
[4] Mons. Giovacchino Limberti, *Il Convento di S. Francesco al Palco*,
p. 50. The writer gathered this information from a deed in the Biblioteca
Roncioniana, which stated that this property was part of Margherita's
dowry. In his will, however, Francesco explicitly stated that his wife
brought him no dowry.

florins a *staioro*, except for the woodland, which was worth only 4 florins, and the total value of all his land in 1407 (excluding the house at Il Palco) came to just over 6,000 florins—a small amount compared to what he invested every year in trade. But deep in the heart of every Tuscan lies the conviction that the only real riches, the only true security, is in land. Datini, too, shared it, and Ser Lapo—who so greatly disapproved of many of his friend's trading-ventures—undoubtedly felt that to use money in farming was on an entirely different plane from placing it in trade. In 1406 he was urging Datini to buy a small property which marched with his own land, because he wanted "a good neighbour" there, and not "a grand or proud person." "I will say it is for me, for I could thus save you 25 florins; and in all, with the house and the walls and shed in front of it, methinks it will be less than 300 florins. And these 300 would be in harbour, instead of sailing across the seas." *

If we wish to know what Datini's farms and his peasants looked like, we have only to look at Lorenzetti's picture (facing page 265) of a countryside under "The Good Rule"—i.e., in peacetime. The Pistoiese hills, then as now, were greener than Lorenzetti's *crete senesi*, but the crops were the same: wheat, oil, and wine—the Biblical products, the food of all men of Mediterranean stock. The land, in Datini's deed of purchase, was divided into olive groves, vineyards, ploughland, and wood—the latter being generally ilex or scrub oak. Datini's peasants—like those in the picture—threshed their wheat with heavy wooden flails (such as may still be seen in some remote Tuscan farms); their garments were short grey tunics of coarse homespun wool— *bigella*—and their chief beast of burden was a donkey. They did, however, also possess small brown oxen, considerably smaller than their modern counterparts, and rough wooden ploughs and harrows which did little more than scratch the surface of the soil. Vines and olive trees, which do best in stony land, grew on the hillsides, as they do today, on terraces labori-

267

ously built and supported by rough stone walls, and there were also some fruit trees—in particular, almonds, figs, and nuts. But even these acres were sparsely and thinly cultivated, by too few labourers—as is shown by a letter of Ser Lapo's which speaks of handing over a farm of as much as 60 *staiora* (about 20 acres) to a single man without a family—"and you will see it well-kept." *
Moreover, between these fields stretched wide areas of untilled land: the greater part of most valley bottoms still consisted of undrained swamps or lakes (from which came the eels that formed an important item of Datini's diet), and the forests which covered most of the hills often extended to the very gates of the cities.

The farm-houses, too, were few and poor. Datini's own villa, indeed, was enlarged and embellished by him until it came to be worth as much as his town house—1,000 florins—but it is safe to surmise that its furniture was very scanty. "I remember," wrote Leon Battista Alberti some fifty years later, "when our most important citizens went to the country, they took with them only a few loads of beds, pots and pans and food for the summer—and brought all these things back with them, when they returned to town." [5] Apart from this villa, the list of Datini's real estate only mentions, in the country, a couple of "labourers' houses," one house "with an oven and a stable and dogs and a shed," and "one tower with a dove-cot and a walled court, enclosing a labourer's house and oven." But we know that later on—in this more progressive than Ser Lapo—Datini built some better houses for his peasants, for the notary reproached him for this extravagance: "If you put them into houses fit for craftsmen, they will die of heat!"

Most farms, indeed, were poor for a very simple reason: their owners were also poor. We may read, for instance, in the *Ricordanze* of Odorigo di Credi, that in order to buy next year's grain

---

[5] L. B. Alberti, *De iciarchia*, Book I. In Francesco's will, Il Palco was left, like all his other possessions, to the poor, and later on it became a monastery—il Convento di S. Francesco al Palco.

for his peasant, he had to pawn his own gown.[6] Certainly few of these small holders could afford to build or repair farms, buy cattle, or pay *fattori* or overseers—and many of them, being themselves craftsmen or shopkeepers, could get to their farms only once or twice a week. This state of affairs may well have contributed to the rapid development of the *mezzadria* system of farming—which, although of much older origin, spread all over Tuscany during the second half of the *trecento*.[7] By this profit-sharing system, in accordance with detailed contracts drawn up between landowner and peasant (which have changed remarkably little to this day) the landowner supplied a house, tools, seed, and cattle, and the peasant the labour—both sharing the profits in equal parts. It is easy to see that this system would appeal to the new small holders, since it eliminated the need for constant supervision by *fattori* or foremen or the regular payment of salaries. Only four of Datini's farms are specifically described as being farmed in this manner—i.e., "*a mezzo*"; the others were rented to the men who worked them—the rent being paid, not in money, but in kind: "A plot of land of about 3½ *staiora* . . . with vines, olives and trees, which cost us 28 florins, and is let to Cambino d'Andrea, labourer, for 7 *staia* [bushels] of grain in a year." *

The great point of the *mezzadria* system, at least in theory, was the identity of interests of owner and husbandman. Yet it can hardly be said that the memoirs of Datini's contemporaries reveal a harmonious relationship between the two. The old feudal lord had often been cruel and overbearing; he had made

[6] "Item, on the 11th of November, I put in pawn my green *cioppa* lined with green taffeta, with the money-lenders of Ponte alla Carraia for 20 *lire di piccioli*, of which I must pay 16 to Francesco, our labourer, to pay for the grain he had from Maso." Odorigo di Credi, *Ricordanze* (1405–25) in *Arch. Stor. Italiano*, vol. IV.

[7] The first known *mezzadria* contract, between the Abbot of S. Fiora on Monte Amiata and one of his serfs, dates back to the eighth century, but it was not until the *trecento* that this system of farming really took hold in Tuscany, superseding the long-term contracts (leases in emphyteusis, *ad pastinandum, a livello, parziaria*, etc.) which had been more suited to the conditions of the great feudal estates.

intolerable demands upon his serfs. But, for all that, he had been closer to them in mind and habits than these new men from the towns: he had thought the same things important. To the shop-keeper or lawyer turned landowner the peasant was merely a dense brute—and the countrymen often retorted with the under-dog's weapons: sullen resentment and craft. Many books of precepts and diaries testify to this mutual distrust—though the voice that speaks is always the landowner's, since he alone was able to set down what he felt. Paolo da Certaldo, for instance, went so far as to warn a townsman to visit his lands as seldom as possible, and never on feast-days, when his peasants were gathered together on the threshing-floor—"for they all drink and are heated with wine and have their own arms, and there is no reasoning with them. Each one thinks himself a king and wants to talk, for they spend all the week with no one to speak to but their beasts. Go rather to their fields when they are at work—and thanks to the plough, hoe or spade, you will find them humble and meek." [8]

The wise townsman was advised, as soon as he reached his farm, to lose no time in seeing in what ways his labourer was cheating him. "Go round the farm field by field with your peasant," wrote Giovanni Morelli, "reprove him for work ill done, estimate the harvest of wheat, wine, oil, oats and fruit, and compare everything with last year's crops. . . . Find out about his condition and reputation, see if he talks too much or boasts or tells lies or praises himself for being faithful. Trust him not, keep your eyes ever upon him, and examine the crops everywhere—in the fields, on the threshing-floor and on the scales. Yield not to him in any matter, for he will only deem you are bound to do so. . . . See none of them, save it be needful; ask no service of

[8] Paolo da Certaldo, op. cit., paras. 102–3. A similar warning had been given by the jurist Odofredo more than two centuries before. "If a knight be alone with a rustic and even threaten him with taking out one of his eyes, the rustic replies not; but if divers rustics be together, they shout against him and would even pull him off his horse!" In short, Odofredo concluded, "when they are together, they will do any evil thing . . . but when alone, they are nought but hens!" Tamassia, *Odofredo*, pp. 165–6.

them, without pay, unless you wish to pay three times the cost;
look not kindly upon them, and speak few words. . . . And
above all, trust none of them. And if you do thus, you will be
the more loved and respected by them and will obtain whatsoever
good there is in them." [9]

Such advice rang very pleasantly in Francesco's ears. From
his letters it would seem that his visits to his farms were spent
very much as Morelli thought advisable. The following one was
written in November, when he had gone to Il Palco "to get the
sowing done and the olives picked."

> I stayed there until nightfall, without food or drink—for
> I was constrained to shout at the men touching many mat-
> ters. . . . Since Meo the foreman is not there, methinks
> naught will be done, except I be there myself; and the sow-
> ing season slips past, and the olives fall into the ditches and
> the water carries them away. . . .[*]

It is, however, but fair to admit that the landowner's duties
were also recognized—if somewhat grudgingly. "Aid and counsel them [the peasants]," Morelli advised, "whenever any injury
or insult is done to them, and be not tardy or slothful in this matter." [1] And how a kindly man like Ser Lapo interpreted this advice is shown in a letter asking Francesco to find a place for a
peasant whom he was obliged to dismiss from one of his farms.

> I have kept Moco my labourer for many a year, though,
> when his sons were old enough to be of use, God took them
> from him, so that I have always had him alone. And he is so
> solicitous at the plough, and such a fine vine-pruner and so
> ingenious, that I know not how to make a change.

He had now found, he said, a large family, which he wished
to place on his farm.

[9] Morelli, *Cronica*, pp. 263–4.
[1] Morelli: op. cit., p. 264.

But my cowardly or compassionate soul (I know not which) knows not how to say to Moco: "Look for another farm.". . . And therefore I pray you, tell me within eight or ten days if you have aught for him.*

The produce from these farms served, of course, first of all to feed their owner and his household. It was Datini's farms which produced the wheat, oil, and wine, as well as the capons, ducks, pigeons, eggs, and vegetables, which Margherita sent to Florence or Pisa two or three times a week for her husband's table. And when the whole family was in Bologna in 1401, Datini sent for 1,138 pounds of olive oil—of which he kept enough for his family's use, and sold the rest, at a *soldo* the pound.* In those times, when a single bad harvest or the passage of troops was enough to cause a local famine, a prudent householder always stored in his town house at least a year's provision of the two basic foodstuffs —grain and oil. But equally it was undesirable to store too much, for fear that envious talk might arise which would lead to an increase of one's taxes, or would cause the hungry mob to pillage the store-rooms and burn the house.[2] A rich man's life—as Francesco so often complained—was not an easy one!

Finally, at least a tithe of a farm's produce was set aside for religious communities or for the poor: "For if you give it not, you offend our Lord, and He will send storms and droughts, and all the other plagues that He bestows on the fruits of the earth and its creatures." [3] Many passages in Francesco's account-books record donations of wheat, oil, or wine to monasteries and convents—and even of oranges from his own garden. And in addition—to propitiate those in authority in this world,

---

[2] "Bring home only what is needful, and a little each time . . . lest the neighbours become envious and say you have a thousand farms . . . for thus you will be called a rich man and be hit by a great *prestanza*. If the poor see you have wheat to sell and would keep it to increase its cost, they will rail and swear at you, and rob you and burn your house, and you will be hated—which is most dangerous—by all the *popolo minuto*. And God preserve our city from their rule!" Morelli, op. cit., p. 270.

[3] Paolo da Certaldo, op. cit., para 338.

too—he sent generous gifts of food to prominent citizens, and more disinterested gifts to old friends like Piero di Giunta and Lapo Mazzei: a brace of partridges, some flasks of wine, a basket of oranges, or an eel from one of his ponds.

As Datini's crops increased, he required more granaries and cellars, and some of his farms, too, were provided with a threshing-floor and stable, sheep-byre and pig-stall, and square, towered dove-cot. The frenzied energy with which he embarked upon this work is called in Tuscany, to this day, "rubble disease" —*la malattia del calcinaccio.* Whole days were spent by him "among masons, workmen, mortar, sand, stones, cries and despair," while again he neglected his mealtimes and his health and Monna Margherita waited in vain for him at home. "You say you have a little fever," wrote his brother-in-law; "I marvel not, in view of your disordered manner of toiling out of doors in the heat and the cold, never eating at the appointed hour, and living with so much rancour and vexation and tribulation. . . ." *
Ser Lapo was no less concerned.

Other wise and virtuous citizens do some building, but all, save you, in moderation! One man has a bailiff, another a friend or a paid overseer. But you are so greedy, you will allow no single groat to be misused, nor a single brick to be laid lengthways, when it would look better upright—as if your little house were to be the dwelling-place of your immortal soul! And no cart is filled, without your lending a hand, and no stone or brick is wetted without your changing its place, with shouting and tribulation.

And what, he asked, was the purpose of all this toil? "To make ourselves, like crabs, a fit little hole, wherefrom we shall be banished. And in doing this we spend the whole of our life." *
But meanwhile the walls of Il Palco were rising, and, wet or shine, whenever Francesco could snatch an hour from his business cares, he hurried off there to harry his workmen and lend a hand himself. There is something very pleasant about the picture

273

of the prosperous, elderly man—for he was over sixty—laying aside his dignity and his fine robes for a few hours of hard work among bricks and mortar. "You well know," wrote Ser Lapo, "that the burdens you carry at Il Palco when you build rejoice your heart," but he added: "Methinks God meant your labours to extend further than a wheelbarrow." * Domenico di Cambio was no less disapproving. "I send you a new pair of gloves," he wrote. "They are gentleman's gloves, so let me remember you not to wear them to wheel barrows!"

One day a tile fell from a roof, and hurt Francesco's head; another day he stumbled over a heap of stones and injured his leg—and, of course, Domenico did not fail to point a moral. "I am grieved. . . . But I must recall to you, these are the warnings God sends to a man." *

And, indeed, Francesco himself was growing a little weary. "I might say with Dante," he wrote, " 'What pleased me once, now pleases me no longer,' and naught grieves me more than the time I have wasted on such matters." *

Mazzei's admonishments were partly inspired by a feeling that it was most undesirable for Francesco, who had only just succeeded in being exempted from surtaxes as a Florentine citizen, to make himself conspicuous by building another fine house. Margherita, too, fully realized this danger. "It were wiser to give it up," she wrote to her husband, "and also all else that may tell men about your riches. And it is well, when there is tribulation in the land, to stay quiet." *

II

The tribulation to which Margherita referred was one which had recently fallen upon Tuscany, and which was particularly grave for landowners and country folk. For the last ten years the Duke of Milan, Gian Galeazzo Visconti, who had already seized the greater part of northern Italy and whose ambition it was to place the whole of central Italy under his rule, had been a men-

ace to the peace and independence of Tuscany. After several
years of sporadic warfare, in which Sir John Hawkwood's
"White Company" had destroyed a large portion of the Tuscan
countryside, Visconti had allied himself with Florence's traditional enemy, Pisa, and in the spring of 1397 he sent one of his
condottieri, Alberico da Barbiano, to harass the·territory between Siena and Florence.[4] This particular band of free lances,
the *Compagnia di S. Giorgio*, was distinguished by the boast of
its captain that it consisted only of Italians, without a single
foreigner, and that it observed strict military discipline. But how
little truth there was in his boast may be seen in the records of a
contemporary chronicler, Ser Naddo da Montecatini. "The
cursed Duke of Milan, to avenge the Pisans, sent more than 6,000
horses to Pisa in December and January and again in March,
with fine troops and good captains, among whom the chief is
Conte Alberico da Barbiano. . . . And after staying there two
months, they increased their numbers and moved towards Siena.
. . . And on March 23 they were at Mercatale di Greve and
stole horses and a great deal of wheat and cattle and took many
prisoners, both male and female. . . ."[5]

This company, in short, like every other band of free lances,
lived on the land through which it passed, sometimes settling
down, like a flock of locusts, in some prosperous district for several months, and leaving it a waste desert when it moved on.
Wherever the soldiery had been, fields and vineyards were laid
bare, farms looted and burned down, cattle slaughtered, and the
peasants killed or taken prisoner. Even monastery walls were not
respected by the marauders, as may be seen from a reference in
Fra Filippo degli Agazzari's *Parables* to a prior "who had a great
deal of trouble from the many companies which came to molest
the territory of Siena—so that once or twice a year, or even

[4] Alberico da Barbiano, an adventurer of noble birth, had had a varied
and successful career, having served his apprenticeship in arms in the famous
"White Company" of Sir John Hawkwood.
[5] "*Cronica di Ser Naddo da Montecatini (1374-98)*" in *Delizie degli eruditi toscani*, vol. 18, Florence, 1784.

thrice, he was obliged to move all his possessions into a walled town, for fear of these companies." [6] As soon as the rumour spread that one of these bands was approaching, each little city on the way threw open its doors to the inhabitants of the surrounding territory, and men, women, and children came pouring in to take refuge behind the walls, driving their herds before them and bringing with them all that they could carry of food, fodder, and furniture. Then, when the troops had passed on, they gathered up what they had saved, and returned to their devastated farms.

On this occasion the dread of the approaching company was so great that the Florentine *Signoria* proposed—in order to defend its territory—to raise a loan which included both the peasants and the priests (who generally were exempt) and also to levy another forced loan, called a *prestanzone*, of which Francesco's share was 250 florins. "War has broken out among the Pisans," he wrote to his wife on March 19, "and I and the other merchants are all undone. May God provide what is needful."

He seems to have regarded the approaching danger much as he would have taken a storm of locusts or any other natural calamity—distressing, but part of the ordinary hazards of human life. He himself did not dare to leave his business in Florence, but he sent instructions to his wife to bring into safety, within the walls of Prato, all that could be removed from their scattered farms.

> See to it with Barzalone and Niccolò that all things in Il Palco are brought to Prato, and naught remains there, not even pieces of iron, for all is in danger. For this eve they came within twelve miles from here. And also bring in the straw at Chiusure, and put it wheresoever you think best, for if the beasts cannot have oats, they must do with straw.

Margherita assured him that it would all be done, but now Francesco began to wonder whether he ought not to go to Prato

[6] Fra Filippo degli Agazzari, *Assempri*, XLI.

himself, and sent a man to meet some goods which were coming
from Pisa by the Arno, and to spy out the land. "No man here
knows what to do, or puts his trust in any measure. I stay in the
house and dare not venture forth; and I know not what to do,
whether to stay here or to go home to Prato. There would be
some jeopardy in going, for one of my standing."

Perhaps the seriousness of the situation may be gauged by the
fact that for once Francesco himself urged his wife to be charitable without stint: she was to distribute bread and wheat to all
who asked for it. "This is a time to gain Paradise for our souls,
and I am glad to spend without stint. . . . For God will pay us
in full."

Three days later he told his wife also to bring all the oil-jars
into town, and to let the peasant and his wife come down to live
in her house: "For remember that those men go about burning
all that they find."

At last, however, the danger moved on.

> I believe that for the nonce we are secure, for the enemy
> moves towards San Casciano, and our men are at his heels.
> Methinks they will go back to Siena to restore themselves.
> . . . I marvel not [he added] that you have been afraid; for
> here, when a hunted fox ran inside the walls, the gates were
> shut in the face of the men and dogs pursuing her, and the
> sentries ran away.

This last sentence brings a vivid realization of how close untilled land still was to the city gates.

Hardly, however, had the astute old merchant ceased quaking
when he was considering how he could extract some profit from
the situation. While the danger lasted, the *Signoria* had lifted all
duties on food entering the city, and this was an opportunity
that could not be lost. He told his wife to have a bushel of wheat
ground at once; "And send the flour speedily before Saturday,
that I may make some money out of the Commune, which has
made so much out of me!"

The letter ended with a most unusual word of praise for his wife's behaviour during the emergency. "That you have ordered the house in a fashion to do you honour, pleases me. The wise may be known in times of need." *

The danger passed by—the peasants returned to their farms—the fields were ploughed and sown again—and Francesco went on with his building. Ten years later he was still at it, and Ser Lapo was begging him at least to make use of a supervisor. "May it please you to place a faithful overseer in charge of your building, so that you only give orders and then look on, as a Cardinal would, or a Seigneur—such as indeed you are."

The only kind of building that Ser Lapo thought justifiable was that done to the glory of God, and his soft, persuasive voice suggested that at the crossroads between Prato and Poggio a Caiano, where Francesco had just purchased a plot of land, he should erect a shrine to Our Lady. No one, he pointed out, would be moved to pray for Francesco, after his death, on account of his fine house: "But if you build that blessed shrine at the crossroads, for all centuries to come someone will kneel there daily, and no day will pass but someone will pray for you."

The shrine was built, and next Ser Lapo suggested that a church should be erected beside it, "like S. Maria delle Grazie or S. Annunziata in Florence or the new S. Brigida. . . . And so you would hear Mass with but little cost." Apparently Ser Lapo himself, too, hoped to hear Mass conveniently in this manner, for he added that the site was only a stone's throw from his own village, Grignano, which had no church.

And those poor little families of Grignano, which number some fifteen hearts, wander to other churches like lost sheep; and often they hear not Mass at all, which is shameful. . . . Now here is my counsel. Buy land for about a hundred florins, and give it to the said church . . . and the priest will pledge himself to say Mass perpetually.

5. THE FARM

But all these counsels fell on deaf ears: Francesco went on building, and for himself alone. And Ser Lapo went on quaking at the sight of his friend's "terrible walls . . . which it affrights me even to think of." "Pray beware of being buried under them. . . . And fetter not your soul in such tight bonds, that if in the next life you are asked for tidings of the world wherefrom you came, you can only answer, in shame: 'So busied was I with building, I could not see life itself!' " *

CHAPTER SIX

THE PRIVATE
ACCOUNT-BOOKS

"Sei tu ricco, si? Or sappi che tu sei spenditore di Dio." [1]
—SAN BERNARDINO DA SIENA

FEW THINGS ABOUT A MAN ARE MORE SIGNIFICANT than the way he chooses to spend his money. "It is a fine and great thing," wrote Datini's contemporary Messer Paolo da Certaldo in his *Libro di buoni costumi*, "to know how to earn money, but a finer and greater one, to know how to spend it with moderation, and where it is seemly." [2] Datini, as we have seen, took great pleasure in building and in furnishing. What were his other personal expenses? And was he lavish or miserly?

The answers lie in his private account-books and note-books, which are among the most informative documents in this collection.* Most careful householders of the time kept records of this kind, in which they set down those items which, for one reason or another, they wished to keep private, and indeed sometimes

---

[1] "Are you rich, indeed? Know then, you are God's almoner."
[2] Paolo da Certaldo, *Libro di buoni costumi*, para. 81.

these records—generally called *Quadernacci, Ricordanze,* or *Libri Segreti*—developed into veritable diaries or family chronicles. A man would pass from setting down his family expenditure to recording the birth and death of his children and the history of his ancestors, and go on to describe all the principal happenings of his daily life, or even of events of wider scope. Thus we sometimes catch glimpses of the life of the time as in a convex mirror: a miniature world, in the frame of the family circle.

Francesco's note-books are unfortunately less informative. They are incomplete—overlapping each other, but covering only the years 1386-8, 1394-8, and 1401-8—and only the few longer notes entitled *Ricordanze* provide detailed records of some event: his journey back from Avignon to Prato, his pilgrimage to Arezzo with the Bianchi, his flight from Florence to Bologna during the plague—and sometimes a more private matter, such as the process of marrying off and dowering a servant-girl he had got with child. His other *quadernacci* are merely account-books in which he set down his expenditure of petty cash —but this, too, is not without interest. The records of what he spent on the overdue salary of an old servant—or on a new bridle for his mule, a good dinner, a slave, a dog, a prayer-book for Margherita, a cymbal for Ginevra, or new spectacles for himself—tell us a great deal, too, about the daily life of any prosperous bourgeois family of the time. Some of the entries are rather odd: here, for instance, in 1397, is a payment of 10 florins, 17 *soldi* to Francesco's agents in Genoa for a shipment of "dried raisins, almonds, peacocks, marmosets and porcupines." * Alive or dead, one wonders—especially the porcupines. That he kept peacocks, however, we already know from another source, for in 1393 he was writing to his agent in Genoa to get him a pair, and asking him "how they should be kept, from their birth until they are great, and what food it is meet to give them." * Evidently these birds were still a rarity in Prato.

It is not easy to make out whether Francesco was generous or stingy. Some of his friends accused him of meanness. "To save 12 *soldi*," wrote his partner in Florence, "you will pass this Lent without comfits. You are one of those who would keep money in their purse, and hunger in their belly." And a later letter, enclosing a list of prices, repeated the same complaint.

> I fear me you will demean yourself like the Pratese who came to Florence and asked an apothecary the price of a pound of saffron, and then asked again: "And what is the price of a half a pound?" and then: "And of an ounce?" And so he went on enquiring, and when he had been told all, he said: "Give me half of an eighth of an ounce." And thus are you, who ask about many things, and then buy naught.*

Francesco's account-books, however, do not confirm this accusation; they reveal inconsistency rather than avarice. He would turn his *cioppa* and set down such minute expenses as 2 *denari* (pence) "for two leeks for Lucia, who has been on bread and water all day." * But he ordered the finest silks and velvets for his wife's gowns, gave princely gifts, demanded good and costly food, and entertained without stint. Monna Margherita, if she had known the expression, would have called him penny-wise, pound-foolish. "At one time you count the wicks," she protested, "and at another you let a whole torch blaze without need!" *

It is almost impossible to translate the items in these account-books into terms of modern currency, but it is easy to discover the relative purchasing values of the *fiorino*, *lira*, *soldo*, and *denaro*, and to see which things were cheap or dear. Roughly speaking, the things that were produced locally were cheap, and anything that had to be imported was dear. Eggs, vegetables, fruit, game, and fresh-water fish (mostly tench and pike) were all comparatively cheap;[3] salt, sugar, and all kinds of spices, expensive but nevertheless freely used.[4] Local red wine cost less than 1 *lira* a barrel, but a jar of Tyrian wine cost 28 ducats.* The coarse undyed stuff of which maid-servants' and children's clothes were made cost only 9 *soldi* a *braccio*, but the crimson samite of Ginevra's wedding-gown, 3½ florins a *braccio*, and white damask, 2½ florins.* In general, labour was cheap, but materials dear: a painter was paid one florin a day, but the same sum was required to buy a single ounce of the ultramarine blue he worked with; a tailor asked only about one florin to make a gown, but the finished garment, if made of fine silk or velvets, and fur-trimmed or embroidered, might come to more than a hundred.*

There is also sometimes a curious disproportion in fees: an average doctor's fee was one florin (though a visit to the astrologer cost only 11 *soldi*), but Datini paid the same sum for a single day's work to the expert cook whom he engaged for his daughter's wedding-banquet. A maid's yearly wages came to 10 florins, a poor girl's dowry to 14 or 15 (though Datini gave his own slave "Andrea, who is wedded to a young barber," the more generous sum of 25 florins).* Land in the neighbourhood of Prato was 8–10 florins the *staioro* (rather less than half an acre).* A pig cost 3 florins, a good riding-horse between 16 and 20 florins, and an adult female slave between 50 and 60 florins.*

---

[3] For 3 *denari* Francesco could buy an egg, and for 1 *soldo* a pound of oil or a pound of beef; veal (the best meat) was 1½ *soldi* the pound and tench 2½ *soldi*. Pigeons cost 4–5 *soldi*, while a pheasant cost 1 *lira* (20 *soldi*), a hare 2 *lire*, a couple of peacocks between 5 and 6 *lire*, and a wild boar (weighing 384 pounds) 26 *lire*, 17 *soldi*. (File 212. M. 29. *Spese di casa* and File 603. F. VII. *Fondaco di Firenze, Memoriale B.*)

[4] In the apothecary's bill, powdered sugar and the small round comfits called *tregea trita* came to 36 *soldi* the pound; the sweet called *pinocchiato* (made with pine-kernels) cost 4 *lire* the pound, and a "tart of marzipan, made with sugar" of 3 pounds, the considerable some of 6 *lire*, 15 *soldi*. The same bill lists pounded cloves at 6 *soldi* an ounce, pounded ginger at 3 *soldi*, pounded pepper at 2 *soldi*, and 2 ounces of "strong fine spices," mixed, at 7 *soldi*. (File 603. *Fondaco di Firenze, Memoriale B*. Bill of Filippo di Lapo & Co. *speziali*, November 13, 1421.)

In short, the general impression left by these account-books is that while daily necessities, such as food and coarse woollen cloth, were cheap, any luxury article—such as fine imported cloth or spices—was exceedingly dear; and that everyday life was conducted with a cheese-paring frugality alternating with sudden splashes of extravagance. The latter was generally bestowed, as one would expect, on objects which made a fine outer show: handsome garments, lavish banquets on such occasions as Louis of Anjou's visit or Ginevra's wedding, and gifts to the Church or to men of rank.

Francesco's house and household have already been described. But one further item must be mentioned: the stable. He always kept several horses in Prato, as well as two mules for himself and Margherita, and, of course, several pack-animals to travel between Florence and Prato. One horse, which Ser Lapo bought for him in 1401, cost 16 florins, but in the following year he gave 22 florins for another, of which Mazzei wrote that "no Catalan ship could fly faster," and in 1401 he paid 28 gold ducats for a bay palfrey four years old.* It must be remembered, however, that a fine mule was then considered much more valuable than a horse, being the mount of great princes and prelates, and in 1397 Francesco committed perhaps the greatest extravagance of his life to obtain such an animal—paying no less than 122 florins, 16 *soldi*, for a Spanish mule from Valencia.*

This animal, indeed—referred to by Francesco as "that blessed mule"—is the subject of a prolonged and heated correspondence between Datini in Florence and his partner in Valencia, Luca del Sera. "I crave it so greatly," Francesco wrote, "that methinks I shall never see it arrive." He added that it should be "neither too large nor too small, with a good coat and all the virtues that a mule can have; and let it be as mild as a lamb and without vice."

Seventeen months later the mule had not been found.

Francesco will never write to you with his own hand [his clerk wrote at his dictation] until he has the mule, for never has aught seemed to him as shameful as this. If you could have turned yourself into a mule, you should have done so, to satisfy me, who could never have any greater pleasure! *

But at last, in November, the mule was found and sent off by sea to Pisa.

A few years later there is the record of the purchase of another young bay mule (this one cost only 49 florins), as well as of a "hawk from Barbary," whose voyage alone cost 1 florin, 10 *soldi*.* But there is no record that Datini ever went out hawking, and probably he merely regarded the bird as one of the fit appurtenances of a rich man. Nor did he apparently ever learn much about the care of his horses. His wife, as we have seen, reproached him for overfeeding his mule so grossly that it had to be bled, and Domenico di Cambio—who prided himself on having been "a master in keeping horses, even when I was in my mother's belly"—told him that a nag sent out to grass at his farm had come back thinner than before. "You know little about feeding up a horse. In the time you have had him, he should have been as broad as he is long!" *

II

By far the largest sums spent by Francesco were on clothes, and these he never seems to have grudged. In this there was an element of calculation as well as vanity. A prosperous merchant's prestige required that his appearance should convey his prosperity: then, as at all other times, money drew money. But in addition it is probable that Francesco's years in Avignon had confirmed in him a natural taste for the best, and that he took real pleasure in having everything fine about him. "*I mercatanti*," as Boccaccio remarked, "*son netti e dilicati uomini*" ("Merchants are cleanly and refined men"—*Decameron*, X, 9).

The inventories of the house in Prato in 1394 and 1397, and of the Florentine house in 1400, fortunately include all the clothes in Francesco's and Margherita's chests.* Francesco's account-books set down every item of Ginevra's trousseau; and both Francesco's and Margherita's letters contain frequent references to their clothes, many of which were made—with materials sent by Francesco from Florence—under Margherita's watchful eye in Prato. We are therefore able to form a pretty accurate estimate of the family wardrobe—as well as knowing, from contemporary pictures, what these garments looked like.

Let us follow, first, the course of Francesco's dressing. Next to his skin he wore a linen shirt (*camicia*), of which six are listed in the inventory of 1397. It is certainly a mistake to believe that shirts were not in habitual use in the later Middle Ages, or that clean fine linen was not appreciated. The first act of hospitality of a lady in the *Decameron*, when some foreign merchants arrived in her house, was to offer them not only fine gowns, but *panni lini* (linen)—because, she said, she knew they were far away from their wives and had travelled far.[5] It should be remembered, however, that the name *camicia* had a double meaning: it was sometimes applied to the linen garment worn next to the skin, but sometimes also to a tunic, rather like a Russian blouse, split at the sides and belted at the waist. The illustrated *Cronaca* of Giovanni Sercambi of Lucca, a contemporary of Francesco's, shows many working-men (bricklayers, grooms, servants, and sailors) wearing shirts of this kind; and it was probably this garment that was worn by men who vowed to go on a pilgrimage dressed only in their shirt.[6]

More often, however, the *camicia* was, as it is today, an undergarment. It is possible that Francesco slept in one, but much more probable that both he and his wife slept naked, like most of their contemporaries.[7] Both husband and wife, however, wore

[5] *Decamerone*, giorno X, Novella 9.
[6] C. Mazzi, *La Camicia*.
[7] Many contemporary pictures, besides the fresco in San Gimignano (facing page 168), show couples in bed naked, while medical treatises of the period show naked patients in bed in hospital. And although pictures of

nightcaps—called *cuffie* ("coiffe") or *capelline*, or sometimes *benducci* or *bendoni*, but all of much the same shape—close-fitting, with a strap under the chin, and generally made of linen. In 1396 we find Francesco ordering three good *capelline*, "to wear at night, lined with a black lining"; they were to be "the best and finest that can be found." And in 1408 a barrel of goods sent to Datini from London contained, as well as 12 brass candlesticks, "4 large white double caps" and "4 white double nightcaps." *

The inventory of 1396 also mentions six pairs of breeches (*brache*) which were also called *panni di gamba*. These must sometimes have been very wide, for Datini's contemporary Sacchetti has a tale to tell of a mouse running up the leg of a merchant's *brache* as he sat in the market-place, and another of a miser who, in order not to pay duty on his eggs as he entered the city, concealed them in his *brache*.[8] Fashionable breeches, however, in Datini's time were already tight and narrow—to the great scandal of old-fashioned moralists.[9]

As to hose, the same list mentions three pairs of long *calze*, blue, with leather soles, as well as "two pairs of black hose to wear with slippers" (*scarpette*), and Francesco also possessed, according to a letter of Margherita's, at least eight or ten pairs of white linen undersocks (*calcetti*). The long hose, which were made of either woollen cloth or linen, were apparently difficult to fit, for a letter to Domenico di Cambio states that Francesco was returning a pair which were too loose at the calf. "You must blame yourself," Domenico firmly replied, "for sending me no pattern." * The only shoes mentioned in these lists are "two pairs of white slippers" (made of cloth, not leather), but the Florentine inventory in 1400 also includes "a pair of boots, to the knee."

---

sacred subjects invariably show the Virgin, St. Elizabeth, or St. Anne in bed fully clothed, this must be considered merely a sign of respect toward a holy person—just as Giotto represented the Pope in bed in all his vestments and wearing a mitre.

[8] Sacchetti *Novelle*, XXXVI and XLVII.

[9] "*Egli hanno messo il culo in un calcetto!*" Sacchetti complained. *Novelle*, CLXXVIII.

Over his shirt Francesco wore a doublet (*farsetto*)—of which at one time he had four, one of vermilion *saio* (a word generally used for a heavy silk, but sometimes for a very fine cloth) and three of fine linen. Generally such doublets, which were short and tight and fastened by laces, were made of fine cloth or linen, and lined with cotton wool and quilted.

However, Francesco's gowns and cloaks were the handsomest part of his wardrobe. While quite young men or working-men would not hesitate to appear dressed only in doublet and hose, a man of standing usually wore over them a long gown—generally called a *gonnella* in Tuscany, but referred to in all the Datini lists as a *cioppa*. At this time the short, tunic-like *gonnella* of France, which Villani deplored, was the fashion among the young,[1] but Francesco, like most older men, preferred the long *gonnellone*, like a lawyer's or a doctor's, in which he may be seen in his portraits. In 1397 he had as many as nine of these, of which five were old ones for everyday wear, two had fur linings, one was of dark cloth lined with vermilion, one of cloth lined with green taffeta, and one "old undyed one, for writing." He also had a gown of dark camlet—a cloth made of goat's or camel's hair—lined with pale-blue taffeta, and one "for riding" of grey cloth lined with Sardinian sheepskins. And, finally, there were two very grand gowns for great occasions—one of *rosato*, the aristocratic colour, with a fur lining of squirrel, and one dyed "in grain," lined with scarlet taffeta. The latter must have been Francesco's best, for he sent for it when he was to appear before the *Signoria*.

Above the *cioppa* came a full, round cloak, generally of a dark colour, fastened at the neck and reaching to the wearer's feet. This almost constituted the outdoor uniform of Florentine citizens, being worn by men of every class except soldiers, knights, and the very poor. In 1397 Francesco possessed five such cloaks

[1] Villani complained that, since the rule in Florence of the French Duke of Athens, all the Florentine young men insisted on wearing "a short and narrow gown, so that none could apparel himself, without another's help." Villani, *Cronaca*, XII.

—one "grey with a shepherd's hood," two old blue ones, one scarlet, and one of brown cloth; and in addition he had two shorter riding-capes, one pale blue and one grey. Finally, he possessed *"una roba da andare coi Bianchi"*—a long white pilgrim's cloak or *schiavina*.

As to his headdresses, Francesco's lists include nine hoods—two of them of the same stuff as his riding-cloaks. These hoods, in Tuscany, were never worn by nobles, soldiers, or working-men, but were the distinctive headgear of the prosperous bourgeoisie—lawyers, merchants, and doctors. They were not taken off in greeting, like a hat, but, according to Benedetto Varchi, were "raised to a height of two fingers, while bending the head," before a bishop, magistrate, or other superior. (This was called *"far riverenza di cappuccio."*) [2] These hoods varied greatly in shape. Villani complained that since the arrival in Florence of Walter de Brienne, young men wore them with such long points that they nearly reached the ground and could be wound round the head against the cold like a scarf,[3] and Sacchetti described a doctor, Gabbadeo of Prato, who thought himself elegant because he wore his cowl with "a short point on one side, so wide that it could hold half a bushel of wheat." [4] But Francesco, according to his portraits, seems to have preferred the plain monkish fashion of his ancestors. He also owned five round *berrette*, of which it is specified that two (both vermilion in colour) were "to be worn over the cowl," and three smaller ones "under the cowl." In the Filippo Lippi portrait he is wearing a large *berretta* over his cowl.

No gloves are mentioned in the list (they were still a luxury), but in one portrait Francesco is holding a pair, and Domenico di Cambio mentions several other pairs in his letters—including some of kid, and others, which he said, were more fashionable, "covered with English cloth, both white and red." *

Margherita and Ginevra owned only one pair of gloves each—

[2] Varchi, *Storia Fiorentina*, IX.

[3] Villani, *Cronaca*, XII.

[4] Sacchetti, *Novelle*, CLV.

Margherita's being made "of double kid, bordered with gold thread"—but it seems that for a woman to wear gloves was not considered very respectable, ever since a law passed in Florence in 1388 had decreed that all prostitutes, whenever they went out, should wear gloves on their hands and a little bell on their heads, "so that the token of their shame should enter into eye and ear."

Other chests contained the clothes of the ladies of the household. Both Margherita and Ginevra were very well provided—indeed, better than Francesco himself. The pictures of the day plainly showed how little attention the Tuscan ladies paid to the constant efforts of the sumptuary laws to restrict both the number and the cost of their gowns. The materials forbidden were *panni divisati* (of more than one colour) or striped and checked, as well as embossed velvet, brocade, samite, and rich embroideries in silver or gold. But when, in 1343, the Florentine *Signoria* ordered their officials to enter private houses and examine the citizens' cupboards, the lists of what they found there plainly show that most ladies possessed gowns made of the forbidden materials—and very lovely some of them must have been! The lists describe "white marbled silk, with vine leaves and red grapes, lined with striped white cloth—a cote with red and white roses on a pale yellow ground—a gown of blue cloth with white lilies and white and red stars and compasses, and white and yellow silken stripes across it, lined with striped red cloth"—and so forth.[5]

Monna Margherita's gowns were not quite so elaborate as this, but several of them were of expensive silk, velvet, and damask. Her underclothes, on the other hand, were somewhat scanty. Next to the skin she wore a shift of fine linen, of which four are mentioned in the inventory of 1394, and eight in a washing-list in 1397, as well as four belonging to Ginevra and five to Margherita's niece, Caterina. But these shifts were apparently Margherita's only undergarments: there is no mention of drawers or

[5] Paolo d'Ancona, *Le vesti della donna fiorentina nel secolo XIV*.

nightgowns—though, like her husband, she had nightcaps to wear in bed.

Above the shift, in winter, came a lining either of fur or of warm woollen cloth, worn immediately over the shift and under the gown. Margherita had four of these—one of cloth and three of fur—respectively, of otter, cat, and miniver. (In summer, of course, the gown was worn immediately over the shift.)

Then came a long-sleeved gown, the basis of Margherita's wardrobe. Generally this garment was called a *gamurra*, and was often worn under another rather more elaborate "sur-cote" called a *cioppa* or *giornea*;[6] but sometimes a married woman wore only one full long-sleeved gown, and this was plainly Margherita's habit, since she possessed only one under-gown but a great many *cioppe*. The list dated 1394 mentions seven, and the one dated 1397, eleven, of which only two are the same as in the previous list, and these—after barely three years' wear—are already scornfully called old. This is the more remarkable in that the material was much too good to wear out quickly: Margherita, like any woman of later times, was merely tired of it. Her gowns (although she was already over thirty-five years old, which was considered middle-aged) were of fine stuffs and gay colours: "purple (*paonazzo*), lined with green cloth," "blue damask, trimmed with ermine," "camlet, lined with pale-blue taffeta," "ash-colour, with a border of miniver at the hem," "Oriental damask," and "*rosato*"—the old rose which, like the Roman purple, was considered the aristocratic colour. In addition she had another gown of cloth lined with miniver, and one (perhaps for bad weather) of *monachino*—a rough woollen stuff, of a reddish-brown colour, such as was worn by monks and shepherds. And,

[6] The *gamurra* was generally made of a woollen material and in a plain colour; the *cotta* (cote) of a richer material, such as damask or brocade. The *cioppa* always had sleeves, and the *giornea* was sleeveless. In general, girls wore, on festive occasions, a *cotta* and a *giornea*, and married women a *gamurra* and a *cioppa*. But, as in all other periods, individual taste and caprice modified the laws of fashion—and complicated the chronicler's task. Cf. Calamandrei, *Le vesti delle donne fiorentine nel quattrocento.*

finally, we know that she possessed a rich over-gown called a *roba* or *sacco* of the heavy silk called *zetani*, which her husband ordered for her in 1392 from his agent in Genoa.

> I would have, to make a gown, a piece of blue *zetani* [7] from Roumania, the best and finest that can be found; so tell me if aught perfect can be found there, and if no *zetani* can be found, tell me of any piece of damask, of the same colour, as good and fine as may be. . . . If it be not an excellent and most beautiful thing, I will not spend the money. I advise you, it is for a sacque for Margherita." *

All these gowns reached to the ground, but they must have varied greatly in cut, for whereas some of them (as listed in Ginevra's trousseau) required 30 or 32 *braccia* of stuff, others needed only 14 or 16 *braccia*. The explanation is that the fine gowns worn on feast-days often had elaborate sleeves and, above all, very long trains—a fashion condemned by the Tuscan sumptuary laws on the score of expense, and by San Bernardino on the grounds of both cleanliness and morals. "What doth a woman's train stir up," he cried, "when she walks in the road? Dust—and in the winter it wallows in the mud. And the person who walks behind her in summer breathes the incense she has stirred up, and that is called the devil's incense. And lo! in winter she muddies herself and spoils her garments at the hem. . . . And if she sets the maid to clean it, how loudly she swears, wishing at the devil the sow, her lady!" [8]

Above the *cioppa* Margherita wore a full draped *mantella* or cloak—the indispensable outdoor garb, whatever the weather, of a respectable married woman. The Florentine moralists would have liked young girls to wear them, too, for they objected to the new-fangled French fashions of short and tight gowns, main-

---

[7] *Zetani vellutato*, a heavy silk embossed with velvet, was the most highly prized of all the stuffs of the period. Calamandrei, op. cit., p. 132.

[8] S. Bernardino, *Prediche Volgari*, ed. Pacetti, pp. 424-5.

taining that they were "neither beautiful nor decent." [9] Certainly they showed off a girl's figure, instead of concealing it; but the pictures of the period plainly show that, in spite of the moralists, it was only older or married women who still shrouded themselves in the "decent" cloaks.[1] These cloaks varied in length, being sometimes long, like a man's, and sometimes short capes worn especially for riding. Margherita had four long cloaks in 1394—one of *monachino*, presumably for everyday wear, one of fine scarlet lined with woolen cloth, one old one of *zadelanda*(?), and a best one of rose colour. In 1397 she had six: the same scarlet one, a riding-cape of *monachino*, a cloak of "purple" lined with "vermilion taffeta," and three others—one black, one blue, and one "of dark cloth with a hood, to wear as a widow" (though her husband was by no means dead at the time).

In addition, Margherita possessed a *cotta*, or sur-cote, of Oriental cloth of silk lined with vermilion linen, three jackets and two plain woollen indoor gowns (*guarnelle*).[2] And, finally, she had three pairs of sleeves—one of vermilion velvet ("which was left over from the cope made for S. Francesco"), one of white vair, and one of white rabbit lined with fur. These separate sleeves, which could be drawn over any gown, were often the most elaborate part of a woman's dress. Sometimes they were tight and narrow, to the wrist, but sometimes also so wide that they awakened the derision of the novelist Sacchetti, who called them "sleeves or rather sacks." "What more foolish, inconvenient and useless fashion," he cried, "has there ever been? For none can take up a glass or a mouthful from the table, without soiling her sleeve or the cloth, with the glasses she has turned over." [3]

[9] That girls, in practice, did not wear cloaks was recognized even by the sumptuary laws of Lucca, which made special concessions for *damoselle* "until they have found a husband, or are cloaked."

[1] Villani, *Cronaca*, IV, p. 12.

[2] The *guarnella* took its name from the coarse unbleached stuff of which it was generally made. It was a plain dress, often sleeveless—like a schoolgirl's tunic—and was mostly worn by maid-servants and little girls.

[3] Sacchetti, *Novelle*, CLXXVIII.

Most of Margherita's gowns had headdresses to match them. She called them all *cappucci*—wimples—but the translation is misleading, since a Tuscan lady's headdresses were of very various shapes. Originally high at the neck and framing the face, they gradually came to be worn more open at the neck, and sometimes had a lapel of cloth hanging down at one side of the face or even draped round the head; it was only older women who wore the old-fashioned wimple, tightly framing the face, like a nun. Margherita was extremely fussy about having a headdress to match each of her gowns, and in one letter to her husband she complained that, when she had soaked in water some cloth he had sent her before cutting it out, the shrinkage was so great that only 20 *braccia* were left—enough for her cloak and gown, but not for a hood. "So see to it, if there is no way of getting me a little more for the *cappuccio*, for I should not like to have a new cloak with an old *cappuccio!*" *

Above her wimples Margherita also sometimes wore a hat of beaver (*bevero*) in winter, or of samite (*sciamito*)—though this was one of the precious materials forbidden by the sumptuary laws—or, in summer, of straw—one black and one white. The possession of *two* straw hats was rather unusual, for they were seldom worn except for travelling, but Ginevra had one, too, costing 14 *soldi*. The girl also appears to have worn, at least indoors, the white *bende*, which were generally worn only by older women or widows.

Another very important part of the dress was the belt, which was generally worn over the *cioppa* or *giornea* rather than on the under-dress—the latter being usually drawn together at the waist by fine side-laces. Margherita had two belts—one with a blue band and one with a black, and both with silver-gilt buckles. The amount of silver was regulated by the sumptuary laws, which in 1330 forbade any silver belts at all; later on they merely specified that none must weigh more than 5 ounces. Apparently, however, Margherita liked rather heavy belts, for when she received one weighing only 3 ounces she returned it to Domenico di Cambio. "I had it made," he replied somewhat huffily, "as is the fashion here for the noble ladies of Florence, and could not guess that she wanted one like a peasant woman's." *

There is, curiously enough, no list of Margherita's shoes, but her letters show that she sometimes wore heavy wooden pattens held up by leather laces, like sandals, and sometimes *pianelle*—the leather shoes without a back, whose high, flat soles were formed by several layers of leather.[4] Francesco's private account-book also contains a record of slippers bought for Ginevra and for his niece, Tina.

Stockings, in our sense, were of course still unknown, but Margherita wore fine white linen under-socks, made at home (*calcetti*), and above them long hose made of silk or cloth, sometimes red or blue but mostly white. Sometimes, too, the foot of these hose had a leather sole—but this was considered so great a luxury that for a time it was forbidden by the sumptuary laws.

In addition Monna Margherita possessed a few minor treasures which she kept carefully in one of the chests in her bedroom: two painted ivory combs, three rosaries—one of coral with a gold cross and pearl beads, one gilt, and one of black bone with a silver-gilt cross—two purses of fine embroidered wool, a silken veil "made in Venice," a silk embroidered handkerchief "made in Sicily, to wear at one's side," and two fans of peacock feathers.

As for Ginevra, her clothes were as numerous as her mother's. The sumptuary laws permitted little girls under twelve to wear fine stuffs forbidden to their elders (no doubt because so little material was required) as well as jewels and gilt and silver buttons. And though most pictures of the time show little girls dressed only in straight, tight little cotton or woollen gowns—*guarnelle* —such as maid-servants wore, Ginevra at the age of six already possessed a handsome wardrobe.

Bid Monna Ghita [wrote Margherita when the child first came to Prato] to put on her new gown and her sur-cote and

[4] These were worn, of course, to increase a woman's height, and in Venice were sometimes as much as one foot high.

to send me her grey and her striped gowns and the cloth I left with Andrea, and to put on her best hose which I left with her, and the new slippers. And send me her clogs and her little cap and bonnet and striped pelisse, and her samite garlands, both the black and the pink. . . .*

In the same year Margherita cut down her own purple gown to make the child another gown. As she grew older, Margherita's letters and Francesco's account-books frequently mentioned articles for her wardrobe: cloth for her gowns and gilt buttons for her sleeves, as well as "garlands" for her head. In 1403, when she was twelve years old, she had "a purple sacque with slashed sleeves" and "a little quilted doublet"; in the following year a rose-coloured gown; in 1405 a sacque of *sbiadato* (a greyish-blue cloth), also with slashed sleeves, and another doublet; and in 1406 "a scarlet sacque lined with cat" and another new gown, while her last year's gown was given "a crimson collar and sleeves refurbished." *

As for her trousseau, we have described elsewhere the fine clothes that she wore on her wedding-day, but must add that the 32 *braccia* of crimson samite of her long-trained wedding-gown cost no less than *116* florins, her gilt and enamelled belt 17 florins, and her jewelled headdress over 20 florins. Her trousseau also included a second robe with a train of white damask, costing 68 florins, and four *cioppe* or gowns without trains: one of rose-coloured cloth (*rosato*), one of purple cloth with a printed design, another lined with scarlet taffeta, and yet another of *panno marmoreo* (marbled). She also had two rather less expensive cloth dresses, one of the pale greyish-blue cloth called *sbiadato* and one of dark-green cloth—the latter relieved by slashed sleeves of green and white velvet. Finally, she owned an expensive cote, worth over 36 florins, of the fine crimson cloth called *baldacchino* (from Baldaccho=Baghdad), a short, tight *gamurra* (a simpler gown) made with only 7 *braccia* of scarlet cloth, and several white *guarnelle*. The only underclothes mentioned are 13 shifts at 26

Works of Mercy: ABOVE, *Clothing the Naked*
BELOW, *Comforting Prisoners*
SER ZUCCHERO BENCIVENNI'S *Pater Noster*

The Apothecary's Shop

soldi each, but presumably others were made at home and included with the rest of the linen, of which the list is missing.

Ginevra also had two fur linings made of dormice (which cost 35 florins between them) and one of cat, and two ermine collars, though the latter were, in theory, strictly forbidden by the sumptuary laws to any ladies but the wives of knights.

Finally, Ginevra also possessed, as well as the ornate headdress worn on her wedding-day, at least five others, for which a bill of over 8 florins was paid to an embroidress, Monna Agnoletta. They were a hood of white cloth and another of striped samite, another taller headdress on a frame, a hat of cloth, and a little round cap embroidered with sequins.*

What San Bernardino thought of these varied headdresses he said very plainly: "I know some women who have more heads than the devil: each day they don a new one. . . . I see some who wear them in the shape of tripe, and some like a pancake, some like a trencher, and some like a flap, some folded up and some turned down. Oh, women, I bid you, take them off! . . . You have made a God of your head!" [5]

Ginevra's jewellery was much less valuable than her gowns. Her most valuable ring, a sapphire, cost only 20 florins, but—since rings were worn on every finger, and even on the upper joints— she also had several other rings made with an emerald worth 15 florins, a pearl and a sapphire worth 15 florins each, and two smaller diamonds. Her other ornaments, moreover, came to as much as 136 florins, and included silver belts, necklaces, garlands, buckles, beads, and buttons—all of which were considered the most important part of a woman's dress, since they could be transferred from one garment to another and last a lifetime. The belts, in addition to the fine one which Ginevra wore on her wedding-day, were four, one being gilt, "in the fashion of Perugia," mounted on a multi-coloured band and worth nearly 7 florins. She had one set of 240 gilt buttons (at 28 *soldi* the ounce) worth 14 florins, 3 *soldi*, another of 67 buttons, and two

[5] San Bernardino, *Prediche Volgari*, ed. Pacetti, p. 421.

297

smaller sets worth respectively 4 florins, 16 *soldi*, and 1½ florins. According to the Florentine sumptuary laws of 1356, these buttons (in order to restrict their numbers) might be placed only between the wrist and the elbow, but it is plain that Ginevra must have disregarded this rule. The goldsmith's bill also included a necklace "worked in the manner of Perugia, with a hanging pendant" worth nearly 14 florins, a pair of clasps and a silk cover for her prayerbook, nearly 17 florins' worth of "gilt leaves for dresses," a little knife with an ivory handle, and a thimble.*

The high cost of trousseaux such as these was a matter of great concern—according to the writers of the time—to both lawgivers and moralists, fathers and bridegrooms. Fathers dreaded the birth of a girl, in view of the large sums they would have to spend to get rid of her; and young men felt equally reluctant to take on the burden of a wife. "Nothing in the world," wrote Giovanni della Casa in his cynical little pamphlet *Whether It Is Good To Take a Wife*—"nothing leads a man to poverty so speedily as taking a wife: one must feed her and clothe her and give her money to adorn herself—one expense after another, without end." [6]

The number of marriages diminished, and the lawgivers took fright. Sumptuary laws attempted to restrict not only the cost of a wedding, but every detail of the trousseau, from the bride's gowns to her jewellery, ornaments, and shoes, and even to the value of the coffers in which her trousseau was packed, and the amount of her linen.[7] And—on somewhat different grounds—moralists and preachers uttered impassioned protests. "You give your daughter," cried San Bernardino, "to a man as his wife. But

---

[6] Giovanni della Casa, *Se s'abbia da prender moglie*. The author concluded that it was entirely unnecessary to take "a permanent wife," since she was so much more expensive than a concubine.

[7] The value of a bride's jewels, according to the sumptuary laws, was limited to 50 florins and that of her coffers to 3 florins, and the coffers might be "neither gilded nor silvered nor covered with enamel or azure paint," but merely decorated with the arms of the bridal pair. "Sumptuary Laws of Florence, 1355," ed. P. Fanfani in *L'Etruria*, Florence, 1852, pp. 366 ff.

neither he, nor his father and mother, think whence her chattels came. Were they wise they would ask: 'Whence come all these things? Whereof is this dowry made?' Often, most often, it is the fruit of robbery and usury, of peasants' sweat and widows' blood, and the marrow of unprotected orphans. If a man took one of these gowns and pressed it and wrung it out, you would see, flowing out of it, a human being's blood!" [8]

Datini's meticulous account-books mention not only the total price of each gown and the amount of material used (down to a fraction of a *braccio*) but also the price per rod or per *braccio*, so that it is possible to discover the relative value of these materials on the Tuscan market. Of the silks mentioned in Ginevra's trousseau, samite was the most expensive at 3½ florins a *braccio*, and next came white damask at 2½ florins. The cloth called *rosato* or *paonazzo* (1½ florins a *braccio*) came next in cost, and then velvet and fine scarlet cloth at about 1 florin a *braccio*. Some rather cheaper cloths are quoted by the rod (about 4 *braccia*)— for instance, the cloth called *sbiadato* (6 *lire*, 3 *soldi* per rod), green cloth (7 *lire*, 9 *soldi* per rod), and *perpignan* (4 *lire*, 16 *soldi*), while the cotton stuff called *guarnella* cost only 8 or 9 *soldi* a *braccio*. Fine silks, such as were used for linings, were very expensive and were generally sold by weight, and so were sewing-silk and fringe: the scarlet taffeta for lining Ginevra's *cioppa* cost 24 florins, 10 *soldi* for 31 ounces of taffeta. Scarlet sewing-silk was 18 *soldi* the ounce, and two ounces of fringe cost 1 florin, 14 *soldi*.*

In addition, of course, there were the tailor's bills—but these were relatively small, since all forms of labour were cheap. Apparently it was not unusual for a tailor to spend a few days or weeks in a rich man's house, bringing one or two of his workmen with him, and then to settle down to make the whole family's clothes, and there is a letter from Francesco to Stoldo di Lorenzo in 1393, telling him to send a Florentine tailor, Antonio *sarto*, and two of his men, to his house in Prato. "I will send the nag, or

[8] San Bernardino, *Prediche Volgari*, ed. Pacetti, p. 410.

the mule if he would lever." Francesco specified that he wanted the man to come only if he was prepared to finish the work completely, "not to cut the clothes and take them back to Florence, for we should be ill-served," and he added that the garments to be made were worth more than 150 florins.

> . . . That is, Monna Margherita's gown, which is of damask, and the lined cloak of the cloth that Nofri made, and for me a gown and cloak of the same cloth and a few other little things. . . . It is true that I have not yet quite resolved to line my *cioppa* with taffeta, but perchance shall line it with squirrel; and it may be, I shall make two *cioppe* of the said cloth, and line one with squirrel and one with taffeta.*

Apparently Antonio gave satisfaction, for there is a bill of his dated fourteen years later which includes clothes for Francesco, his wife, his daughter, and his niece over a period of eight years and comes to 41 florins. The average cost of making a *cioppa* with a cloth lining was 4 to 5 *lire,* and of a cloak 3 *lire,* while even an elaborate *sacco* for Margherita came to only 8 *lire,* and a doublet to 1½ *lire.* It also appears that Francesco sometimes thriftily had his *cioppe* turned, which cost him 3 *lire.*

Fur seems to have been much less expensive than cloth. The pelts mentioned in these lists are ermine, miniver, squirrel (*scheriuolo*), dormouse (*ghiro*), cat (*soriano*), and *pelli sardesche* (probably Sardinian sheepskins), but Francesco also seems to have had one more expensive lining of marten or fox, for in 1396 Domenico del Cambio was writing to him about it. "A lining of fox would cost 4 florins and one of marten 10 florins." And Margherita had three fur linings: one of Sardinian sheepskins, one of cat, and a grander one of *vaio,*[9] miniver.

The latter (miniver = "*menu vair*") was by far the most fashionable fur, both for men and for women. Ermine had been forbidden in Florence to all but knights and their ladies, and in

---

[9] A little squirrel-like animal with a grey back and white belly. The cloak given to the poor man in the illustration facing page 296 is made of this fur.

Datini's time miniver, too, was permitted only to knights, magistrates, and doctors.[1] But, like most other sumptuary laws, this one was observed very loosely, and in practice both miniver and ermine were worn by anyone who could afford to buy them. Indeed, a sonnet of the time purports to be the vair's lament for the low estate to which it had fallen—so low that it was now held cheaper than any mouse.

> Io mi lamento e dolgo e sono il vaio
> che solea esser per ogni reame
> di chavalier hornamento e di dame
> nè portavami in testa ogni somaio.
> E oggi al filatoio e al telaio
> i' veggio far di me letame
> e tal mi pone pegno per la fame,
> ch'io torno senza pel dall' usuraio. . . .
> Dov'io ero tenuto il più gentile,
> oggi più che lo topo son tenuto vile.[2]

And, finally, there were, of course, clothes for the household. The scarlet cloth and new hose which Francesco ordered for the six extra men-servants to wait at table at Ginevra's wedding-banquet cost him florins 6.4.2, but usually his maids wore the plain straight gowns (of cotton in summer, and in winter of the coarse, undyed woollen cloth called romagnolo or bigello) which the sumptuary laws assigned to them. Headdresses or hats, whether of cloth or silk, were forbidden to all maid-servants,

---

[1] Sacchetti tells the tale of a poor country doctor, Maestro Gabbadeo da Prato, who was advised to set up practice in Florence but feared to do so because his miniver, though "honorable" in Prato, was so moth-eaten that no furrier could recognize the skins. Whereupon his wife generously gave up to him the fur of her own gown. Novelle, CLV.

[2] "I who weep and lament am a vair, who once in every realm was the ornament of ladies and knights—nor did any ass wear me on his head. But now I am treated like dirt by the spinner and the weaver and perchance, owing to hunger, am put in pawn, so that I come back hairless from the usurer's. . . . Where once I was thought the finest, now I am held cheaper than a mouse." From a Codex in the Laurentian Library in Florence, Conventi soppressi, 122.

and so were the high shoes called *pianelle* or gilt or silver buttons; they were told to wear plain linen kerchiefs on their heads and clogs on their feet—on penalty of being fined 50 *lire* or birched naked through the streets.[3] Nevertheless, Francesco's account-book shows an entry of 9 florins, 3 *soldi* "for 10 *braccia* of pale-blue cloth a *tre licci* [woven on a loom with three shaft-needles] for Giovanna our slave," and, a little later on, a lining for the same woman, costing 2 florins, 1 *soldo*.[*] There is even an entry for two sheepskin linings for the maids' winter wear. Moreover, the fine trousseau which Francesco gave to Ghirigora—the little maid-servant whom he married off before she bore his child—included not only a pale-blue *cioppa* with a hood of the same cloth (costing 10 florins) and a cote of green cloth edged with fur, but a good supply of underlinen and house-linen, a mirror, a spindle and an ivory comb, and—to hold all her belongings—"a pair of painted lady's chests." [4]

It would seem, indeed, that on her wedding-day even a maid-servant's attire was, as was natural, as close as possible a replica of her mistress's, for when in 1398 one of Francesco's men-servants was about to get married, his bride was provided with a belt and garland like Ginevra's, only of cheaper metal, and it was Margherita herself who sent Francesco a list of the gifts to be bought: two metal rings "which look seemly and cost little," a *cintoletta* (little belt) worth 4 *lire,* and "a garland that makes a fine show," as well as "a counterfeit belt to give to his sister, who is fourteen years old." "And the price he wants to pay for all of

[3] Sumptuary laws of Florence, 1355.
[4] Here is the complete list of Ghirigora's trousseau: "6 napkins, new, 1 pair of painted lady's chests, 1 tablecloth of 8 *braccia*, very wide, 9 new towels, 6 new shifts, 6 handkerchiefs, 6 net caps, new, 1 pillow covered with striped taffeta, 2 velvet caps, 1 old and 1 new, 1 bowl, and 1 mixing-bowl of brass, 1 mirror, new, 1 boxwood comb, 1 ivory comb, tape, black and white thread, scissors and needle and spindle and an embroidered pincushion, 1 pair black hose, new, 1 pale blue gown, new, with a hood of the same cloth, 1 cote of green cloth, edged with fur, 1 winter fur lining, white, 1 old gown and hood, one old under-gown, 1 rosary and 2 gold rings, 1 pair of cotton veils, medium size." (*Quadernaccio A di Ricordanze di Francesco di Marco.*)

them is 10 *lire* and no more. Methinks it is best you should first buy the things made of brass, and then spend all that is left on the belt." *

A funeral, too, entailed the purchase of expensive clothing. At the death of his brother-in-law, Bartolomeo Bandini (who had been sponging on him for many years), Francesco was obliged to disburse no less than 292 gold florins for mourning cloaks (at 26 florins each) for the whole household. These "great cloaks" were worn over the head and hung down to the ground, but were used only by a dead man's close relations or servants. For a friend a smaller cloak was enough, as is shown by a letter to Margherita from her sister, about an old friend's funeral:

> Francesco will have told you how to go, that is with an unlined cloak and decently veiled under the hood. Some of the women thought we ought to go with the "great cloak," but I have asked for counsel and all tell me it will suffice to go in this manner—so do this, and pray God for him.*

Finally, in the list of personal possessions of the Datini family we must include their jewels, which Francesco kept in one of the chests in his bedroom, according to the best Tuscan tradition, but which were very much less valuable than his clothes.

Apart from Margherita's silver belts, this jewellery consisted only of rings, which were worn by both men and women on every finger, and also sometimes on the upper joints of the fingers. It is not plain which were Francesco's and which Margherita's. This is the list:

> 1 silver ring, and therein I know not what medicinal stone.
> 1 big pearl on a plain gold ring, costing 40 florins.
> 2 sapphires, one red [a ruby], one blue, on a gold ring, costing 50 florins.
> 1 green emerald with a chiselled gold ring, costing 10 florins.
> 1 blue sapphire with a gold ring, given by Niccolò di Buonaccorso, costs 10 florins.

2 pearls, one better than the other, on a gold ring—one costs
15 florins and the other 7.

1 small blue sapphire in a gold ring, costs 2 florins.

2 plain gold bands, with which she [Margherita] was married, cost 8 florins for the two.

1 red cornelian, engraved, on a gold ring, which belongs to
Francesco, costs 1 florin.*

All these rings put together came to only 143 florins—less than
the cost of two gowns.

III

The chests in Francesco's bedroom, which contained his rings
and Margherita's few treasures, also held some other valuable
possessions: his books. The inventory of the Florentine house
describes the following volumes, all "in the second chest":

1 big book of the *Life of the Saints*, bound in red leather.

1 *Chronicles* of Matteo Villani, which belonged to Messer
Antonio di Jacopo di Filippaccio and which we bought for
6 florins, bound in leather (worn on top).

1 book of the *Gospels*, bound in parchment, given me by
Baldo Villanuzzi.

1 little book of the *Epistles* of Saint James, bound in boards
with red leather.

1 similar book by Boethius and a little book by Fra Jacopo da
Todi.

1 similar book, bound in white, which are the *Letters* of Don
Giovanni dalle Celle,[5] which he wrote to Guido of Messer
Tommaso [del Palagio] and Guido's answers.

1 Children's *Psalter*, old and falling to pieces.

3 quires of new parchment, containing a work copied from
the book of Guido da Mercatale Guiducci.*

[5] Beato Giovanni dalle Celle was a noble of Volterra who joined the
Vallombrosan order, lived in a hermitage near Le Celle in Tuscany, and
preached against the heresies of *I Fraticelli*.

This was not, however, the whole extent of Francesco's library. We know that he also had a *Divina Commedia*, from which he sometimes quoted, a quire containing a *Life of Christ*, a translation into the vulgar of St. Jerome's and St. Gregory's *Letters* and also of St. Paul's *Epistles*—all books bought for him by Ser Lapo—and also the *Fioretti* of San Francesco. All these books, of course, were in manuscript, and it was considered a charitable deed to employ as copyists the men in the debtors' prison, *Le Stinche*. Generally, too, these books were handsomely bound, as may be inferred from Ser Lapo's letter of reproach to Margherita when she had failed to provide a cover for her prayerbook.

> At one thing I marvel: that you should have, like others of your standing, many gowns and adornments for your person, and yet should not have cared to adorn a little your Book of Our Lady—for you know what a binding it has. You know that men are ashamed to keep even their worldly books in worn-out bindings—and if this be so, what should we not do for a thing belonging to the Mother of God? . . . Send it me, and I will have a fine one made for you: let it at least be honourably bound before this Holy Nativity.*

Since his books were valuable, Francesco was inclined to treat them like his other treasures—to keep them safely locked up—but gradually Ser Lapo persuaded him that the purpose of books was to be read. "Remember you," he wrote, in asking for the loan of the *Life of the Saints*, "we said together that even if you never read that book yourself, it would bear fruit, for it would be of profit to those to whom you lent it." On another occasion he wrote asking for a loan of the *Fioretti* to read aloud to his sons. "If Monna Margherita keeps my book of San Francesco locked in her chest, I beseech her to send it back; the little boys would take delight in it on winter evenings, for it is, as you know, very easy reading [*apertissima lettera*]." And that Francesco followed his friend's advice is shown by several entries in his memorandum-books: in 1399, a loan of "a fine new book of the *Life of the*

Saints to Frate Piero de' Frati degli Agnoli," and in 1401, the same book to Matteo Villani, and the Jacopone da Todi to Lionardo Mazzei (Ser Lapo's brother). Each entry ends with the words: "We would have it back"—and later on, in a different ink: "We have had it." *

Francesco also possessed—or bought to give to the Church—several illuminated Missals and prayerbooks. The finest of these was a Missal which he presented to the church of S. Francesco in Prato, illuminated by "Matteo di Filippo *miniatore*, a friend of the monks of the Angels," and costing 15 florins, 1 *soldo*.[6] And both Margherita and Ginevra had illuminated prayerbooks.

IV

Finally, these account-books record the sums spent by Francesco on gifts—to friends, to the Church, in alms, or to persons of high rank. To his friends—as was natural, in view of his trade—the most frequent gift was a length of good cloth; to the Church—in addition to all the glass windows and paintings already described—vestments adorned with costly embroidery,* silver candlesticks, a fine enamelled chalice "engraved with Saints and with Francesco's arms," and a silver lamp from Avignon worth 50 florins, "of the finest fashion that can be found." *

Of all his gifts, however, the most extravagant was the one he sent in 1406 to the Cardinal of Bologna, whom he hoped to persuade to officiate at Ginevra's wedding. This was "a very fine mastiff" from Catalonia, equipped with the following luxurious appurtenances: "a collar of gilded silver engraved in enamel with the Cardinal's arms, and a chain of gilded copper with a tassel," a coat of scarlet cloth, "like a race-horse's, to wear upon

[6] This missal contained "2 miniatures with figures, 17 miniatures without figures, 116 letters in colour, 66 full letters, at 1 *soldo* each, and 2,000 common letters, at 14 *soldi* a hundred." The "letters in colour" were called *lettere rifesse*, as in Lucca garments of two colours were called *panni rifessi*, and in Florence *panni divisati*. (Mazzei, II, p. 421, n. 1.)

the mountains," and a breast-strap lined with chamois-leather and covered with red velvet "to defend him against wild boars." "And this equipment," Francesco proudly noted, "cost more than 50 florins." *

To make sure that the dog would really reach the Cardinal, he sent it by one of his own servants to Luigi di Ricovero, the Cardinal's chancellor, together with a sapphire ring worth 52 florins to Luigi's wife. And indeed a warm letter of thanks came back from the Cardinal addressed to "the noble and illustrious Francesco di Marco di Prato, our good friend."

> We have received your mastiff, which your courtesy has bestowed on us. And verily he is one of the finest dogs we have ever seen, considering besides the fine equipment you have sent with him; so that we hold him as dear as any gift can be held.*

The son of Marco di Datino the taverner had risen far! In spite of the fair gifts, the Cardinal did not himself officiate at Ginevra's wedding; but when, in the following year, she gave birth to her first child, he sent her a personal letter of congratulation, and appointed the rector of the Cathedral of Prato as his proxy at the christening.

Finally, Francesco's account-books set down, with great frequency, his gifts in alms, both in money and in kind, to "Christ's Poor." Such gifts did not necessarily spring from a warm heart; they were, to rich men of his time, a matter of course, for the medieval concept of all-embracing charity was based on the belief that the true benefits of alms-giving are to the *giver*. The idea of merit in the receiver—"the deserving poor"—is a Puritan one, fostered by the smugness of the industrial age; but to the medieval man, to give was good in itself. The beggar at the church-door, the leper with his bell, the blind, the lame, the feeble-minded—as well as those who only feigned these afflictions—all received the groat of every passer-by. They were "God's Poor"; the alms were begged and granted "for the Love of God";

and the Saint who kissed the leper was embracing the Son of God Himself.

The rich supported hospices for orphans, pilgrims, widows, old people, and the sick; they supplied dowries for poor girls, gave vast donations to monasteries and convents, built churches and chapels. Many trading-companies kept a special account in their ledgers for the portion of the company's profits to be allotted to charity, and this was called "God's account"—*il conto di Messer Domeneddio*. In some companies, such as that of the Peruzzi, a specified proportion of the original capital was assigned, at the company's foundation, to charity. And in the books of the Compagnia dei Bardi the accounts of "the share of Messer Domeneddio" were kept in precisely the same manner as those of "the share of Messer Ridolfo" or any other member—sharing in the general profits and losses. At the end of the year, when the dividends were paid, God's account received an amount equivalent to two shares.[7]

In this, too, Francesco was completely a man of his time. Though none of his companies appear to have followed the practice of laying aside a specified portion of their profits for charity, his bank's ledgers show a regular monthly payment for alms, and Ser Lapo, whose standard in the matter of charity was an exacting one, wrote to him: "Methinks more than twenty-five families are now alive, first thanks to God, and then to you—and you give succour to more than a hundred a year." * Both Francesco and his wife took it for granted, too, that any delicacy sent to Prato must be shared with the Church and with the poor.

> I hope to send you [Francesco wrote to Margherita] a bale of herrings and about a thousand oranges. You must sell half the oranges and bestow the other half on whomsoever you please. And do the same with the herrings, or, if you please, you may give away all the herrings and oranges—the greater

[7] Sapori, *"La beneficienza delle compagnie mercantili del trecento"* in *Studi di storia economica medievale*, pp. 5–6.

part to God [in alms] and the rest to friends and kinsfolk, both rich and poor.*

And the list which followed apportioned 50 oranges to each of the city's convents, for the nuns.

Sometimes Francesco's alms would take the form of clothing— a warm lining, for instance, to a monk or a poor woman, or "to the boy who broke his head"—but most often they would consist of food or wine to a monastery or hospital—"10 barrels of red wine from Piemonte to the monks of the Angels" or "3 barrels of wine to Fra Giovanni Dominici" or "80 lbs. of tench to the monks of the Angels" or "a barrel of oranges, figs and raisins to the Hospital." * And there were also, of course, the regular tithes to the Church, both in money and produce, which Francesco's spiritual adviser, Fra Giovanni Dominici, exacted with great firmness. "Remember you," he wrote, "the time appointed for your debt with God, for you paid it not at Easter. And fail not, for the Creditor would demand of you an interest too heavy to bear." *

Here are a few typical examples of small sums given in alms and recorded in Datini's account-books:

Item, March 27, 1395. 1 *lira* for Monna Margherita to give, for the love of God, to a poor woman whose son is in prison and will speedily have his leg cut off.

Item, January 15, 1399. 5 gold florins, to give to Domenico d'Antonio, mace-bearer of the *Signoria,* for the love of God, to give one of his daughters in marriage.

Item, April 11, 1401. 7 gold florins, given for Fra Bonifazio Ruspi of the Franciscan Order in Corsica, and we gave them on his behalf to Nanni di Tasso, painter, in part payment of the 10 florins we gave him for the love of God.

Item, August 15, 1402. 20 *soldi* for the love of God, for a pair of spectacles for Fra Bonifazio.

Item, January 16, 1403, in Prato, 10 *lire* of *piccioli* to

Schiavo, our labourer, to give for the love of God to his niece, the daughter of Ceccherello his brother, who has been married in Prato. May they go to our Soul's profit.

Item, May 2, 1405. 2 golden florins, taken by Ser Nisi to Tommaso di Giovacchino for Giovanni—which we gave for the love of God for a girl's dowry.

Yet even in this distribution of petty cash Francesco did not entirely discard his customary prudence, and when "a hermit" came to beg of him, bearing a letter from Ser Lapo Mazzei, he told his *fattore* "to mark well what he does and what sort of life he leads" and only then, "if it is a good charity," to give him some bread and wine.*

It is plain, too, that though Francesco conformed in alms-giving to the general custom, Ser Lapo would have liked his gifts to be still more lavish—and never to be entrusted, as they sometimes were, to one of his *fattori*. "You charge Barzalone to give clothes and money on your behalf, but he is more timorous than a hare." He complained, too, of another member of Francesco's household, who had been sent to look for a poor family to which to give two sacks of wheat, but who, "after searching from house to house, came home . . . saying he had found no one in need." *

Some of the notary's most eloquent pleas were for dowries for poor girls—a very favourite form of charity, since no young woman could hope to get married without one. Sixty *lire* was enough to get a husband, and eighty generous. On one occasion we find Ser Lapo pleading for "the daughter of Sandro Mazzetti, who only a couple of days ago was one of the richest merchants of Oltrarno, and now is a beggar in S. Spirito," on another for the daughters of a man inappropriately named Quattrino (coin), "but who has neither hose nor shirt, but only a short tunic on his bare skin and a torn old cape. And he has several great daughters, and one of them is eighteen, and handsome; no wine at home, and little bread. And he has not a penny to spend on her dowry."

On yet another occasion Francesco's charity was besought for "that desolate widow of *Il Serraglio*, who sells oil, and who has all those great girls to find a husband for. . . . Lo, put into this what it would cost you to build with two or three *moggi* [1 *moggio* = 24 bushels in Florence] of lime!"

This time, however, Francesco's ears were "stopped with wax," and Ser Lapo had to turn to Margherita before he could get the desired aid.

> I beg and beseech you, in the name of God and of the love between us all, that if verily there be want there, as I believe, you will persuade Francesco to help me with these girls; and I vow he himself will have greater gladness therefrom than from all the walls he has built. Churches are good and so are holy pictures; but for the once that God mentioned them he spoke a hundred times of the poor.*

Another "very good charity," to use Ser Lapo's favourite expression, was to give alms to men in prison—and certainly their need, too, was very great. Not only common criminals but political prisoners and heretics or men imprisoned for trifling debts might pass some fifteen or twenty years of their lives within prison walls, dependent for anything beyond the meagre prison fare on what they could pay to the chief jailer, who, having himself paid a high premium for the privilege of "managing" the establishment, extorted from its inmates all he could get out of them. Some of them earned a little money as copyists, but most depended entirely on the alms or food brought to them by the charitable.

Among the prisoners who benefited from Francesco's charity there was a knight of Montepulciano, Ser Jacopo del Pecora, who—at the time of his first begging letter to Francesco—had already languished in *Le Stinche* for over fifteen years. In 1390, when his city had been captured by the Florentines, he had borne arms against them, and subsequently had been arrested on a charge (which was never proved) of conspiring against the city's new rulers. Since then he had spent his time in prison in writing love-songs and hymns and a long poem in imitation of the *Divina Commedia*—and, when he was not included in an amnesty to prisoners granted in honour of the Madonna, another long soliloquy in *terza rima* entitled "Soliloquy of the most unhappy Jacopo of Montepulciano to the Virgin Mary." "The whole world," he wrote, "opened its prison-doors, but to the innocent Jacopo this mercy was denied."

Like other prisoners, he asked rich men for alms; and his letters to Francesco, in their self-assurance and dignity, afford a curious glimpse of the prison life of the time.

You know how, though innocent (God be my witness), I have been kept in prison on suspicion for fifteen years, and know not whether this long torment will ever have an end. . . . I would be patient, but it weighs heavily upon me, now that old age is approaching. . . . I live, and know not how; God alone knows. I have no income . . . the pen with which I write is my land and my harvest, and I keep alive with grievous toil. I receive alms from several citizens, and there are some who, beside giving alms, meet my greatest needs. . . .

Now I have had your gracious offer, yestereve, by your messenger. . . . And take note: when I need alms from you, I will say so plainly. For naught causes me less shame than being poor. And when I would have aught from you in loan, pray set this request apart from the other for alms. Alms should come from you, of your own free will. . . . But I beseech you, in case be I beg aught of you as a loan, set it down in your book, saying: "Due from Jacopo da Montepulciano." . . .

And in short: Francesco, I have some few clothes and books of mine in pawn, and they are of but little worth, methinks thirteen *lire* would get them back. And I have lost them. And by God, as I said before, I feel no shame for being poor. I have there, among other things, a pair of sheets, and have no others, and have already for the last two weeks slept without them, on a poor bed. If you get back those little things for me, it would please me greatly; and I would wipe out the debt with you, a little at a time.

Francesco, I know your gains and losses in the past year, and I know how the Commune treated you, and what a man's position is, when he has no standing, and yet is believed to be rich. [Francesco was neither a Florentine citizen by birth, nor an official, and thus had no means of defending himself from severe taxation.] I know all this, and therefore ask for no more; and this is a time when I would have not alms, but a loan. . . . Furthermore, you will do me the honour, one day, to see you and speak with you. Christ keep you. Your friend Jacopo da Montepulciano, in prison.*

Apparently this letter pleased Francesco, and Jacopo got back his sheets. They were, however, only a single pair, and after a while he wished to wash them—so another letter was sent off, this time addressed to Monna Margherita.

Dear to me as a Mother. With great trust I turn to you, beseeching you to lend me for four to six days a pair of sheets for my poor little bed, which is 3 *braccia* long and 2 wide— a pair of servants' sheets, that I can get mine washed, since fate has brought me to such a pass that I have no more than one pair. And as soon as I get mine back from my washerwoman, I will send back those you lent me.

Commend me to Francesco and beseech him to forgive the many burdens I lay upon you every day. God knows how unwillingly I do it, and how unseemly it is. I say no more. Christ guard you.*

The acquaintance ripened. On the following New Year's Day Francesco's account-book records the gift, "from Francesco's own purse," of two gold florins "to a friend of Jacopo da

Montepulciano, to get him out of prison." * And finally, two years later, the story came to a happy end: Francesco paid Jacopo's fine or gave bail for him, and when next he wrote, he was a free man.

> Dear to me as a Father [he wrote]. By God's grace and mercy and your good and great aid, I am out of prison. I tell you this for your pleasure, since I know it will rejoice your heart.*

It is this incident that was depicted, after Francesco's death, in one of the frescoes on the walls of his house: the great merchant performing one of the most approved *opere di misericordia*—setting a prisoner free.

CHAPTER SEVEN

FOOD, DRINK, AND PHYSIC

I. FOOD

F WE MAY LEARN A GOOD DEAL ABOUT A MAN from what he chooses to spend on his house and his clothes, on works of art and on alms, his taste in food and drink is no less revealing. In this respect the Datini papers are very informative. Both Francesco and Margherita liked food, and wrote about it often; Ser Lapo had much to say about good wine; and the account-books also contain some poulterers' and apothecaries' bills, and an occasional marketing-list. Finally, as we shall see, Francesco received some very full instructions from his doctors. From all these sources a pretty clear account emerges of what both husband and wife ate and drank, and the physic they took.

Was Francesco as well fed as he was clothed and lodged? By the standards of his own time—or, at any rate, by those of his poorer partners—he undoubtedly was. Stoldo di Lorenzo, for instance, found the "delicate viands" at his table so rich that his stomach could not bear them, and Domenico di Cambio, in writing to thank him for a week's hospitality to his wife and daughter, wrote that he would now be obliged "to bring them back to the little cooking-pot . . . for they have spent eight days as at a wedding-banquet." *

By the standards, on the other hand, of later centuries (even of the next one) Francesco's food, though abundant, was neither delicate nor well prepared, and—like other men of his time—he restricted his meals to two a day. Breakfast, in the Middle Ages, was unknown, and even a piece of dry bread and a glass of wine before going out to the day's work were considered something of a luxury. When Domenico di Cambio boasted to Francesco that his wife gave him "some roasted chestnuts every day before going out," he explained that this was only "because she pampers me, as I do her." * And that this was indeed an unusual luxury is shown by the prescription given by some doctors as a prophylactic against the plague: to "take a piece of toasted bread and half a glass of wine" before leaving the house in the morning.*

The two meals of the day were *desinare* and *cena*—dinner and supper—the first being taken at terce (nine or ten in the morning) and the second at sundown. Sometimes in the summer, when the sun set very late, a snack—*merenda*—was allowed between these meals, but this was disapproved of by the austere. "If it be possible," wrote Paolo da Certaldo, "order your day so that you eat not more than twice, dinner in the morn and supper at night, and drink not save at meals, and you will be much more healthy. And also this is living like a man, while to eat all the time is like a beast." He even advised that the only hot meal in the day should be the first one: "Cook once a day in the morning and keep part for the night; and eat little at supper, and you will keep well." [1] As for Ser Lapo, he wrote to Francesco that he often went to bed having eaten only a few olives and some bread. "For oft at night I sup soberly, and naught is better than a handful of olives: so the doctors will tell you." *

From Francesco's letters it is plain, however, that such an austere régime did not satisfy him: he liked plenty of good food,

[1] Paolo da Certaldo, op. cit., paras. 143 and 149.

316

and saw to it that it was well cooked. We have seen how many of his early letters from Avignon were concerned with the food he hoped to find when he came home: the capons that were to be fattened, and the vegetables to be sown. "I would have the great cooking-pot." And when at last he did return, his tastes had not changed. A letter to his household, ordering his dinner for a day on which he was going to ride to Prato from Florence, stated that he would expect to find "a good broth with fat cheese of one kind or another to eat therein," some fresh eggs, several fine fish from the Bisenzio, "and if there are some in the market that are still alive and are fresh and good, take several pounds . . . and many good figs and peaches and nuts . . . and look to it that the table be well laid and the room well cleaned." *

The basic material of his meals appears to have been both good and abundant. When he was in Florence his wife sent him country eggs, fowls, game, cheese, vegetables, and fruit, and to these he added the spices, comfits, salted fish, and other delicacies available in town, which were also sent after him when he moved back to Prato. His cheese came from Parma and his eels from the lagoons of Comacchio. His bread was good country bread, made with the flour from his own wheat and baked at home, and if it was too heavy, he complained to his wife that it must have been made with the coarser flour meant only for the servants' loaves. "Bid Nanni take a sack to the miller and say that it serves for making bread for *me*—wherefore he must grind it as fine as he can." *

After bread, the most important part of Francesco's meal was the first course—*la minestra*. Sometimes this was broth—(generally made with chickens, capons, or partridges) into which was poured a sauce made with pounded almonds, a little cinnamon, clove, and ginger—the whole liberally besprinkled with cheese, or sometimes with sugar. The quality of the broth may be inferred from the fact that in a Tuscan recipe of the time a chicken broth for twelve persons required "six fat capons"! [2]

[2] Here is a recipe: "If you would make chicken broth, take young fowls and boil them, take shelled almonds and grind them and mix them with

Often, too, the first course consisted instead of what is still called *minestra asciutta*—i.e., a dish of *lasagne, ravioli*,[3] or rice, or (though this was more of a delicacy for banquets than for daily use) of the dish called *bramagere* (*blanc-manger*), whose name— though, alas, not its ingredients—still survives in the English blancmange. The stuffing of the *ravioli* consisted of pounded pork, eggs, cheese, and a little sugar and parsley, after which the *ravioli* were fried in lard and powdered with sugar. Rice, too— which Francesco mentions in several letters—was served sweet —like an English rice-pudding, only cooked in milk of almonds with a great deal of sugar or honey. Rice was also one of the chief ingredients of the *bramagere*, which included, in a recipe for twelve people, "4 fowls, 4 pounds of almonds, 2 pounds of lard, 1½ pounds of sugar, and an eighth of a pound of cloves. And when it is cooked and you serve it, sprinkle rose-water over the bowls, and sugar and white fried almonds and cloves. This dish must be white as snow, and thick, and potent in spices." [4]

As to meat, Francesco's account-books mention veal, pork, kid, and mutton. Beef appears very seldom, and was, indeed, not often used, for even at the Priors' table in Florence it was served only occasionally, and then always boiled.[5] Veal, on the other hand, was considered the best and most wholesome meat. "Place it in your belly," advised Francesco's doctor, "in every way you can, for you could have no more wholesome victuals." [*] Good meat,

---

the chicken broth and rose-water and verjuice. And take cinnamon and ginger and clove—half of them ground and half cut up very small, and put them in the broth and boil all these things together. And when they sit down at table, put the fowls in the broth and see that they are very hot. And when you serve it, place some sugar over the bowls. And it will be a good dish." *Libro di cucina del secolo XIV*, ed. by Lodovico Frati, Recipe VI.

[3] *Lasagne*—long, undulating strips of macaroni paste, cooked like macaroni. *Ravioli*—small paste envelopes of wheat-meal paste, often cut into the shape of crescents, and filled with stuffing.

[4] *Libro di cucina*, ed. Frati, Recipes LXII, LXIV, and IV.

[5] C. Mazzi, *"La Mensa dei Priori di Firenze nel secolo XIV"* in *Archivio Storico Italiano*, Serie V, vol. XX, 1897.

however, was expensive—"I have some veal from Prato which cost 9 florins," wrote Ser Lapo to Francesco, in inviting him to dinner, and Francesco took good care to see that his own meat did not come from the coarse grey cattle of the Maremma, but from the smaller, more tender calves of his own region.

> Purvey me a good piece of veal [he wrote to his carrier] like the one we had on Sunday . . . and bid Belozzo not to take the *maremmano*, and bid him, if he knows it not, to go where there are most people and say: "Give me some fine veal for that gentleman from Prato," and they will give you some that is good. And bid Margherita to put it on the fire in the saucepan wherein I cooked it last time, and to take off the scum . . . and purvey some melon and other fruit.*

On one occasion, however, it appears that one of his agents sent him a piece of *maremmano* veal "such as has never been eaten in my house, neither in Pisa nor Avignon nor elsewhere"— and he was extremely indignant. "You should feel shame to send such meat to as great a merchant as I am! I will not forgive you, save you make amends, and I will come and eat it in your house, and only then shall we be friends again!" *

The best viands to be procured in Florence were those reserved for the Priors' High Table, and it was therefore with great satisfaction that Francesco was able to tell his wife one day that he was sending her "3 pieces of the veal which the *Signori* have had." "Send one piece, the best, to the *Podestà*'s wife, and tell her I could not have another, for the *Signori* would have as much as they pleased. . . . And with the last piece do what you will: methinks you would do well to invite Messer Piero [di Giunta] and Monna Simona, Barzalone and Niccolò—and make a fine dish of herbs and eat in company." *

Pork, too, was eaten in great quantities—young suckling pig roasted on the spit, with a spray of rosemary in the mouth (such as may still be seen in Italian country fairs), pounded pork in pies, hams and sausages and *mortadella*.[6] People who had their own pigs cured them, of course, themselves, smoked their own hams, and made their own sausages—but, in addition, we find Francesco sending some sausages to his wife from Florence. Pork was also much used—together with veal, capons, fish, and spices —for making jelly, which was made very strong and stiff, and was considered a great delicacy. Thus, when the wife and daughters of Guido del Palagio were about to spend a day with the Datinis in Prato, pork jelly was to be one of the main dishes, "to do honour to all these folk without too much trouble." "You should prepare tomorrow," Francesco wrote to his wife, "a great basin of pork jelly, and I will give orders for a man to bear it on his head. And if it be well made and stiff, it will travel well, for the weather is not hot."

Francesco added that he himself would order, in addition, "a roast of 12 capons and 2 kids. Or if you would lever do without the jelly, we will eat roast pork and salad. But since they have never been here ere now, I would do them honour." *

Francesco was particularly fond of both capons and guinea-fowl, which were also considered good for the sick. "I sent you three couple of guinea-fowl yesterday," he wrote to a sick servant, "and look to it, that you eat them, for you could eat naught better or more wholesome, and I will go on purveying them for you." *

Francesco's poulterers' bills also included peacocks—a great delicacy—geese, pigeons, ducks, and turtle-doves, and the doves were supposed to have "the singular virtue of strengthening the memory and the emotions."

As to game, Francesco mentions venison, wild boar, hares, pheasants, and partridges—sometimes from his own land, and

---

[6] A recipe of the time for "good and perfect *mortadelle*": "Take a pig's liver and boil it, and take good herbs and pepper and eggs and cheese and as much salt as is needful, and beat them together in a pestle, and make paste and mix them with some of the liver. And then take away the membrane and make the *mortadelle*, and when they are made, fry them in good dripping and serve them hot." *Libro di cucina*, Recipe XLVI.

sometimes bought in the market or presented by noble friends. We find Margherita, indeed, writing in some anxiety about a "very fine and big deer" presented to her husband while he was away in Florence—"and since the weather is warm, you must resolve speedily." *

Partridges were very popular, and were eaten at any season of the year. We often find Francesco sending them as gifts—though Ser Lapo protested, as usual, when he had been too lavish.

> You will not leave me alone with your partridges and God knows I am not fain to see such great destruction all at once, and I would not give them to the gluttons, and it grieves me to sell them. . . . When you have coarser things, fit for labourers, I will accept them; but, by God, wipe me from the page on which you have writ down the friends on whom these birds must be bestowed.

And he added that his wife said she would not eat them "because of the odour they give out, when they are cooked." *

This diet—in so far as meat was concerned—was only partially approved of by Francesco's doctor, as he grew older.

> I will concede you fowls and partridges, pigeons, veal, mutton and kid; and with each of these you can make use of the things that promote urination, such as parsley, capers, asparagus, and other things with which vinegar is mixed; for vinegar, in small quantities, encourages urination. The meats which displease me for you are goose, duck, young mutton and pork—in especial fresh; and I not only disapprove of these viands, but bid you beware of pies of any meat whatsoever, and of every other dish that coarsens and clogs the blood—such as mixed herbs, fritters and pastry.*

Finally, like most men of his time, Francesco ate a great deal of fish—for fast-days were not merely a matter of personal piety, but imposed by the statutes of the Commune, which forbade any sale of meat on Fridays and Saturdays. The fish mentioned most often are tench and pike (from the Bisenzio or the Arno), but he was also very fond of eels—sometimes brought all the way from the lagoons of Comacchio—and there is at least one mention of salted trout, and many of tunny and herrings, which were apparently considered strengthening, since Ser Lapo Mazzei begged for a small barrel of them from Pisa—"because I delight in strong viands, and they strengthen me for the burdens I bear in ruling my family." Sometimes, too, when Francesco was in Prato and required larger fish than the Bisenzio could produce, he sent for a large pike or some eels from Florence—though the best of these, too, were often commandeered for the Priors' table.[7]

It must not be thought, however, that Francesco's diet, even on fast-days, was monotonous. In addition to pike and eels, he did not despise frogs, and we find him asking Margherita for a basket of them "caught fresh this eve, but I bid the woman cook them, to save you toil." *

Small pike, we are told, were best eaten fried, but big ones were boiled and served with white sauce, or roasted and stuffed with raisins. Eels were eaten pickled in their own fat, with strong spices and wine, or in a pie, with spices, olive oil, and orange and lemon juice; and fish in a broth made with a paste of flour, bread, parsley, nutmegs, and "strong and sweet spices," or in jelly, with spices and saffron and powdered laurel leaves—the best fish for this purpose being tench and pike. And there was also a very elaborate fish-pie made with three large tench or a big eel, dates, raisins, pine-seeds, and spices, pounded with parsley and marjoram and fried in oil.[8]

Moreover, there were a large number of elaborate recipes for other "Lenten dishes," mostly made of vegetables, eggs, cheese,

---

[7] "I have sought the biggest fish that could be found, but because the old *Signori* and the new are dining together [the Priors going out of office, and those coming in] they have taken all the best fish for themselves. I send you 60 lbs. of tench and 12 lbs. of pike, but no large pike have come today, and no eels." (File 1092. Domenico di Cambio to Francesco, October 31, 1398.)

[8] *Libro di cucina*, etc. Recipes LXXVIII, XIII, XCIV, LXXXVIII, LXIII and XXXVI.

and spices—though Maestro Lorenzo warned Francesco against the use of eggs and cheese together. There were special "Lenten *lasagne*," stuffed with powdered nuts and sprinkled with sugar, and *ravioli* stuffed with herbs and cheese and sprinkled with spices. A dish called *herbetelle di quaresima* (Lenten herbs) consisted of spinach, beetroot, parsley, and marjoram boiled together, fried in oil, and then sprinkled with spices. Among other vegetable and cheese pies there is an especially elaborate recipe for leeks, entitled "a white dish of leeks [*porrata*] for twelve greedy men": "Take 4 lbs. of almonds, 5 ounces of pounded ginger, 4 bunches of white leeks, boil them and pound them, then take scalded almonds, boil them with the leeks, and throw spices on top of the bowl." Vegetable jams, too—especially of turnips and carrots—were a favourite Lenten dish, and we find Francesco telling Margherita to make plenty of them, for he remembered enjoying them as a boy. "Monna Piera was wont to make good ones of turnips—or perchance I had a great hunger then, whereas now I have a small one." *

In his own kitchen-garden Francesco grew broad beans so tender that, according to Ser Lapo, who begged for a sack of them, "they melt before they even touch the fire." And he also grew his own chick-peas, and warned his wife to soak them all night before cooking. "They should be boiled in a little water and often stirred, that they cling not to each other as they swell. And after a while, take a greater pan, well scoured, and pour them therein, with their water and oil and salt and let them boil gently, and when needful, fill up with a little more water." *

Onions, too, and garlic gave savour to almost every dish—the latter forming the basis of a sauce called *agliata*—and Margherita's garden, like that of every other careful housewife, was also rich in mint, stonewart, thyme, marjoram, and rosemary. The latter, indeed, with which the delicious *pan di ramerino*, still beloved by Tuscan children, was made, was considered almost miraculous in its efficacy, since it possessed no less than twenty-six "noble and admirable properties" including those of

323

curing colds, toothache, aching feet, bad breath, sweat, lack of appetite, gout, consumption, and madness! In addition, "if you would keep your face beautiful and clear, take rosemary and boil its leaves in pure white wine and wash in it." And "if you put rosemary leaves under your bed, it will keep you from evil dreams." And, finally, "if you plant rosemary in your garden or vineyard or orchard, your vines and fruit will grow in great abundance, and it will delight your eyes when they fall upon it." [9]

Mushrooms, too, were much favoured by Francesco—in particular, the delicious small *prugnoli*—and so were the highly flavoured peppery white truffles, which, then as now, were rooted up in the oak-woods by long-snouted black truffle-pigs. As to cheese—in spite of the doctor's warnings—he delighted in the fresh round sheep-cheeses made at lambing-time and called *marzolini*—telling Margherita to send him two at a time, and to store the others in a clean oil-jar, "that they become not dry." And he also used, for sprinkling on his food (as we still do now), the best Parmesan—procuring it direct from Parma.

Both meat and fish were almost always served with rich sauces and well stuffed; indeed, it is perhaps the contemplation of these sauces and spices which—more than anything else in these papers—opens an alarming gulf between the Datinis and ourselves. What appetites they must have had—and what digestions! Three of the most popular sauces for everyday use were a red one called *savore sanguigno*, made of raisins, cinnamon, sandal, and sumach (a substance now used only for tanning) pounded together and mixed with meat and wine; [1] a sauce called *peverata*, made of meat, fish, pepper, cinnamon, ginger, and nutmeg and

[9] "Properties and virtues of certain spices," according to a French medical treatise, translated into Italian in 1310 by a Tuscan notary in Avignon, Ser Zucchero di Bencivenni. Codex 47, LXXIII, Biblioteca Laurenziana, Florence. Printed by Ciasca, *L'Arte dei medici e speziali nella storia e nel commercio fiorentino dal Secolo XII al XV*, pp. 748–58.

[1] Biblioteca Marucelliana, Florence, *Manoscritti*, C. 226 (a miscellaneous codex of the fifteenth century), p. 128.

coloured with saffron;[2] and a white sauce called *camellina*, made of sugar, cinnamon, cloves, bread, and vinegar. And at banquets there were sauces containing not only many other spices, but also precious stones or gold and pearls.[3] As for the stuffing—the more varied the ingredients, the finer the dish! Not only chickens and partridges and peacocks but even veal, mutton, and wild boar were stuffed with a mixture of sugar, fats, spices, onion, garlic, and pounded almonds.[4] Above all, no banquet was complete without a *torta*—the "grete pie" of English medieval cooking—a dish which ingeniously evaded the sumptuary law against the serving of more than three courses by putting both meats and sweets in the same dish. One of these *torte* —whose recipe is given in the *Libro della cucina del secolo XIV* —contained pork, chickens, ham, sausages, onions, parsley, dates, almonds, flour, cheese, eggs, sugar, salt, saffron, and several other spices. First the chickens were fried in oil, then the ham was made into *ravioli*, and then the chicken, sausages, and *ravioli* were laid on layers of pastry, alternating with layers of dates and almonds. The pie was then covered with pastry and cooked in hot embers. And there is also, in the same book, a fascinating recipe for "a pie with live birds," in which live song-birds were put into a pie of which the roof had little windows—the whole pie being then hung on a tree of pastry.[5] "Wasn't that a dainty dish to set before a king?"

[2] *Libro di cucina*, Recipe LIX.

[3] The *Libro di cucina* advises to "place in every sauce, savour or broth, some precious things, such as gold, precious stones and fine spices."

[4] At banquets the *plat de résistance* was sometimes a peacock, stuffed with pounded pork and capon and cinnamon and nutmeg beaten up in white of egg. The bird was first boiled, and then roasted on a spit; then the skin and feathers were put on again and he was placed on a great wooden platter with an iron skewer through his head to hold it up, "so that he seems alive." And finally—if the occasion was a great one—some cotton-wool soaked in acquavitæ was put in his mouth and set fire to, "so that he casts fire out of his mouth." "And for greater magnificence, when the peacock is cooked, you may adorn him with leaves of beaten gold." Codex 158, Biblioteca Universitaria, Bologna.

[5] *Il libro della cucina del secolo XIV*, ed. Zambrini.

Above all, every dish was rich in spices—partly, no doubt, to disguise the taste of imperfectly cured fish and meat, but chiefly because most spices were considered wholesome, as well as good. Moreover, we must remember that, except for wine, Francesco and Margherita had no other stimulants, coffee and tea being as yet unknown.

Although the importation of spices was among the most lucrative branches of Francesco's trade, he also bought them in small quantities for household use from his apothecaries in Florence—tradesmen who belonged to the same guild as the doctors, and whose wares must have been quite as varied and diverting as those of a big American drug-store today. In addition to spices and drugs, stored in great jars of pewter or majolica, the apothecary sold sugar, herbs, fruits, comfits and orangeade, conserves and honey and ready-made sauces (it was here that Francesco bought his *savore sanguigno*), scents and cosmetics and wax, parchment for letter-writing and for painting, and also paint-brushes and paints. In a corner of the shop stood a great mortar, with the heavy pestle suspended to the ceiling, while in the back there were the furnaces and ovens in which the apothecary prepared his brews and did his cooking—since he was often also a distiller of alcohol and a pastry-cook, and sometimes even an embalmer and undertaker.[6]

Among the items listed in two bills sent to Francesco in 1406 by his apothecaries in Florence, Filippo di Lapo e Compagni *speziali*, we find several orders for sugar—which was used more for medicinal purposes than for sweetening (in cooking, honey was preferred) and was thought especially good for affections of the chest—as well as pounded almonds, rose-water, camomile, mustard, electuaries (referred to as both cordials and clysters), ready-made sauces, oil of wormwood, orange and citron juice,

[6] In 1378 the Florentine painters were officially included in the same guild as the doctors and apothecaries, and in Bologna the *Arte degli Speziali* also included distillers, wax-makers, and sellers of acquavitæ, rose-water, liquorice, honey and dried fruit, comfits, paints, rat-poison, and Church wafers! Ciasca, *L'arte dei medici e speziali*, pp. 75 and 347.

dried raisins, candles, "small torches," and "a tart of marzipan." But by far the larger part of the bill was for various kinds of spices: saffron, pepper, ginger, cinnamon, clove, nutmeg, cassia, and *galinga*.*

Saffron and pepper were ordered most often, and were also the most costly. Saffron (which was also the best yellow dye) was thought so wholesome that Francesco's doctor urged him to put some in every dish, and it was included by Ser Lapo in some pills against the plague. But, indeed, it was to be found almost everywhere—in no less than seventy recipes of the *Libro della cucina*, in the preparation of painters' colours, in the curing of fish and meat, in many medicinal drugs, "especially for those of cold complexion," and in recipes for cosmetics "to cause hair to shine and not to break." It was even included, in one of the Datini papers, in a list of "things that are needful for men travelling by sea." [7]

Pepper, too, was used not only for cooking and for the curing of fish and meat, but for many medicinal purposes. Cassia was ordered by Francesco's doctor as a purge, and *galinga* (ganingal) —a bitter Chinese root brought to Europe by the Arabs—was used both in comfits and in medicines, for its stimulating and heating properties.[8] Ginger, which was bought in Alexandria, was used in cooking with fish and meat, was made into jam, and was put into aromatic wines.[9] Cinnamon—originally brought back from China by Marco Polo, and also grown in Ceylon— was valued for its aroma and for its medicinal properties, since

[7] Saffron was so valuable that in the preceding century it had been easier to raise a loan, at San Gimignano, on its security than on that of lands or serfs, and even in Francesco's time both saffron and pepper were sometimes paid to officials of the Commune in lieu of money. Datini used both the local Tuscan saffron and the imported Catalonian. In addition to its properties for cooking and dyeing, it was believed to have the virtue of "comforting the heart and the stomach," and "curing red and bloodshot eyes."

[8] There were two kinds of *galinga*, one from China, and one from southern Asia. It was one of the spices with which the Florentine apothecaries were obliged, by their statutes, to be provided—and, according to Bencivenni, "its mere odour warms and comforts the brain."

[9] Ciasca: op. cit., pp. 390-1.

"it greatly comforts both a cold and humid stomach and a cold liver, encourages menstruation and urine, expels the humours of the stomach . . . and is valuable in windy colic." * Nutmeg (*noce moscata*) and nutmeg-peel (*mace*) were also much used both in wine and in cooking, and cloves were indispensable in every household both for food and aromatic drinks, and for relieving coughs and asthma.[1] There was, in short, hardly any Eastern spice so rich and rare that it did not reach the cooking-pots or medicine jars of the merchant of Prato.

In addition, the bills of Francesco's apothecaries included several kinds of comfits—for Francesco, like many other Italian merchants, had acquired the Oriental habit of offering his guests both comfits and very sweet jams—in particular, the thick and delicious home-made quince-jelly, *codognato*, which can be cut with a knife, like a cake, and a sweet made of pine-kernels, called *pinocchiato*. Comfits were most often prepared by the apothecary, and we have the recipe supplied to Margherita by her doctor for the small round comfits called *tregea* (*dragées*)—of which the chief ingredients were cinnamon, nutmeg and nutmeg-peel, ginger, aniseed, sugar, and ganingal.*

Another very popular comfit—of which Francesco once sent a ten-pound box to a friend—was *zuccata*,[2] and this was apparently considered an especially manly dish, for Domenico di Cambio wrote, as he sent it off: "There is no finer gift today than a box of *zuccata*, for a sponge-cake is fit for women after childbirth, but a *zuccata* is for gentlemen." *

Finally, Francesco had, it appears, so great a liking for fruit that his doctor feared he would exceed in it.

> Touching the fruit to which you bear so sweet a love, I grant you almonds, both fresh and dried, as many as you

---

[1] Ser Zucchero di Bencivenni, in Ciasca, op. cit., p. 753.

[2] *Zuccata* was made with small pumpkins placed in a jar and scalded for ten days running, and then boiled in sugar and honey and left out of doors (but not in the sun) to "absorb the honey" and harden. *Libro di cucina*, Recipe CXXIX.

Tasting New Wine

BY TOMMASO DA MODENA

Mending Barrels

BY TOMMASO DA MODENA

The Sermon
BY SANO DI PIETRO

will; and nuts, both fresh and dry and well cleaned . . .
and fresh and dried figs before a meal, and also grapes; but
after a meal, beware of them. Take melons, in season, before
a meal, and cast not away what is therein, for that is the best
and most medicinal part. And I will grant you many cherries, well ripe, before a meal; but by God, after a meal let
them be. And I beseech you, since I am so generous in con-
ceding fruit to you according to your mind, be so courteous
to me as to cast aside the others which are harmful, such as
baccelli,[3] apples, chestnuts and pears.

Apparently, however, Francesco would not deny himself even
these, for a month later Maestro Lorenzo was scolding him for
his greed.

It is, if you take thought, not only harmful for you but
very shameful—at the age you have reached—not to have
learned a little continence. And think not to excuse yourself saying: "The things I want are cheap"; for the theologians and moral philosophers think it a greater sin to be in-
continent in vulgar matters. . . . Now bethink you if it is
a fine crown for old age, that a man be called the slave of his
greed! *

II. DRINK

And now at last we come to the pleasant subject of wine. That
which grew in Francesco's and Ser Lapo's own farms, at the foot
of the Pistoiese hills, was as good as any in Tuscany. From here
came the "*vino di Filettole*," and the "sparkling *Carmignano*,"
which Redi said it was a sin ever to mix with water and which
Ser Lapo grew in his own little vineyard, staking and tying the
vines with his own hands. Francesco's vineyards also produced

[3] *Baccelli* are young broad beans in their pods, which are still often eaten
in Tuscany as fruit.

trebbiano—a sweet white wine which was then a speciality of the Marches.[4] But the most delicate wines were *vernaccia* and *greco*—the former being a sweet wine made from grapes which had originally come from Corniglia on the Ligurian coast, and which was especially grown in the Val d'Elsa;[5] while *greco*, which also grew in the Val d'Elsa, was a sweet white wine described by the cellarman of Pope Paul III as "a perfect drink for gentlemen. . . . It has perfection in it: colour, scent and taste." Finally, it is in the Datini papers that we find the earliest use of the term "Chianti" to designate a special type of wine.

Many were the evenings which Francesco and Ser Lapo spent together, with a flask of good Carmignano between them—and then even Francesco would forget his cares. "In tasting those good wines," wrote Ser Lapo reminiscently, "we did naught but laugh." Ser Lapo was a great connoisseur in wine—it was his only luxury. "For my part," he confessed to Francesco, "either because verily I require it, or because I am spoiled, I would spend money like dust to obtain it!"

When Francesco sent him some flasks of choice wine from his own vineyards, he at once invited some cronies to share it: "And I said it was wine that had come from Avignon, and it seemed to them so good, so sweet, that they believed me!" *

In general, however, Ser Lapo had but a poor opinion of Francesco's taste in wine. "Neither you nor Monna Margherita are expert in such matters," he wrote. "I would believe her touching any matter, save only white or fortified wine." And he went on to tell Francesco what he should do (since it was September and the vintage was in full swing) to make the heavy, sweet fortified

---

[4] *Trebbiano* is called by Crescenzi "a noble wine, which keeps well"; he adds that it is made of small round grapes. *Trattato dell' Agricoltura*, I, p. 193.

[5] According to one version, *vernaccia* was first imported into Tuscany by one of the Bardi, as early as the first half of the twelfth century. According to another, it was brought to San Gimignano in 1280. Certainly by 1286 the tolls of San Gimignano distinguished between ordinary wine, *vernaccia*, and *greco*. Paolo Guicciardini, *Cusona*, I, p. 129.

wine called *vin santo*, which is still the pride of Tuscan farms.

When Francesco had been ill, Ser Lapo saw to it that he had a really good flask of red wine to bring back his strength, "and you will need no other doctor. Take it before your meal, and during it and after—that is, as you rise from table." And sometimes, too, on one of his long journeys to inspect his hospital's lands in Mugello, Valdarno, and Casentino, Ser Lapo would find time (after a visit to La Verna, "in devotion and love") to buy some good wine. "I have not looked to the cost, so as to have something perfect, as Francesco told me; and verily it is among the best I have drunk this year, and will bear being transferred into other barrels."

It was at this time that Francesco was becoming a landowner himself, and each of his new farms had a vineyard. Thus he added wine-making to his other anxieties, and was often obliged to turn to Ser Lapo for advice.

> I have washed out those three little butts of mine [he wrote at vintage-time] where the wine of La Torre is to be put. Tell me if I should take a quart of white wine, and warm it as you tell me and rinse out the butt with it. . . . Tell me if it should be boiled, or warmed, or cold; and if I am to leave the butts as they are, or place them in the sun.

To which Ser Lapo replied, on the back of the same sheet, that the butts only needed washing and draining.*

Francesco, however, was as irritable and anxious about his wine-making as about all his other occupations. When he could not get to Il Palco himself, he pestered his *fattori* and labourers with long letters of instruction. Had the barrels been well aired and mended? Would it not have been wiser to put new hoops round them? Had the butts been well rinsed? Had the new wine been mixed with the old? It was apparently a common practice to mix two sorts of wine together, in the belief that the stronger of the two would transmit its virtues to the weaker—and here is Francesco storming at one of his servants because this has not been done:

> I am mad with rage over what Nanni told me, that you have placed the new wine in that big butt, without having mixed it in equal parts with the yokels' wine. Now, when you mix it, it will already be fermented. . . . Now you have spoiled both the old and the new, and it grieves me to the heart. . . . There is no child such a fool, he would not have known how to do it! *

It is hardly surprising that his peasants found him a trying master and that his partner in Prato told him he would do better to stick to trade. "In good faith, Francesco—with due respect—methinks you err in attending to such matters as wine and oil and wheat: they are not meet for you. . . . Lo, be content with the state unto which God has called you, and leave these matters to those who needs must do them!" *

Francesco also sometimes imported wine from other Italian regions, or even from abroad. One account-book records "10 barrels of red wine from Piemonte given to the monks of the Angels" and another contains a list of prices of foreign wines: 28 ducats for a jar of Tyrian wine, 20 for "wine from Roumania," and 27 for malmsey—the sweet white wine from Malaga and Cyprus which he bought from his agent in Genoa. We find him ordering from Venice a *caratellina* of malmsey and one of Tyrian wine (each holding a barrel and a half) to be sent to Ser Lapo Mazzei as gifts for Matteo Villani, and for Francesco Federici, the treasurer of the Florentine Commune.* The latter, evidently, was a man with whom it was desirable to be on good terms, and to whom gifts were not unwelcome. "He says you have bound him to you greatly by bearing him in mind, despite all your cares and labours, even in Bologna. And he said it to me so joyfully, it seemed as if roses were blooming in his face!" *

III. PHYSIC

It is hardly surprising, after reading about Francesco's diet, to discover that both he and his wife had frequent recourse to physic. They had a wide choice of doctors to consult. By the second half of the fourteenth century the *Arte dei medici e speziali* of Florence was one of the city's largest guilds, numbering over 1,000 members, and the medical faculty of the University provided courses not only in surgery and medicine, but in canon and civil law, philosophy, rhetoric, and *notaria*—thus continuing the tradition of an earlier age that a doctor in medicine should also be a grammarian and philosopher. Every doctor, before he was allowed to practise, was examined, in the presence of a notary, by a commission consisting of two consuls of his guild and four established practitioners, of whom one was a surgeon, and it was only after this examination that he was accorded the title of *Magister* and exempted from the payment of taxes. He undertook to lead a respectable and dignified life, without ever frequenting taverns or brothels, and—clothed in the fine red cloak and hood lined with vair, which was permitted only to magistrates, knights, and doctors—could set forth on his rounds accompanied by an attendant and riding on a horse provided by the Commune.

The registers of the Florentine guild show that in Francesco's time it included not only general practitioners, but surgeons, dentists, wound specialists, eye specialists, bone specialists, and specialists for stone and gravel. There were panel doctors, paid by the Commune to attend the poor, and yet others appointed for the care of prisoners and of men sentenced to flogging, amputation, or the loss of their eyes. There were even some women doctors—some of them relations of physicians, to whom the secrets of their profession had been imparted by their husband or father, but also some independent practitioners.[6] And, finally,

[6] Ciasca, op. cit., pp. 267, 287–8 and 300–1.

there were a great many people who lived—and very profitably —on the fringes of the medical profession, trading on the frailty of the human body and the infinite credulity of the human mind. Barbers applied plasters and leeches, practised blood-letting and dentistry, and set fractured bones; apothecaries administered enemas, practised massage, and prescribed elaborate nostrums which they themselves had brewed; witches and quacks prepared magic comfits, love-philtres and poisons and healing tisanes; herb-collectors and snake-charmers collected the ingredients for these potions; and astrologers and alchemists added to the chorus. Finally, as these letters show, a great many popular prescriptions were merely passed on from mouth to mouth or copied out of popular compendia (*ricettari*) in which a Pope's prescription for blindness lay beside "a prayer to stop the flow of blood," and an unguent for bruises invented by an English monk beside a nostrum to bring back lost youth—while the greater part of the book was given up to incantations and exorcisms, punctuated, as the patient recited them, by many signs of the Cross.

What Francesco's great contemporary Petrarca thought of even the most respectable practitioners of his time, he has plainly recorded in a letter describing a fever that had laid him low.

The physicians came running. Having disputed at length, as they are wont, they ordained that at midnight I would be dead; and the night had already begun. . . . They said that the only remedy by which I might prolong my life would be to draw some little cords tightly around me, to keep me from sleep, and thus I might perchance live to see the dawn. . . . Their orders were not carried out, for I have always besought my friends and bidden my servants to do naught of what physicians have commanded, but if indeed something must be done, to do just the opposite. Wherefore I spent the whole night in a deep sweet sleep. . . . I, who

334

was like to die at midnight, was discovered by the physicians, when they came back on the morrow, writing.[7]

Francesco and Margherita, however, were not of Petrarca's opinion. Like most of their contemporaries, they had an unbounded faith in physic and physicians and made full and indiscriminate use of any specifics that came their way. "You know not how to rule yourself," wrote Domenico di Cambio to Francesco, "and take so many medicines and syrups that it has destroyed your stomach." *

In Prato, as in Florence, there was a panel doctor for the poor, who received from the Commune a salary of 50 or 60 florins a year with an additional grant for his horse, but an established doctor might ask as much as 2 or 3 florins for a private consultation or for an opinion in a law-suit, and sometimes—especially during the Black Death—a doctor would exact payment or a pledge before even crossing his patient's threshold, after which his visit would often consist of no more than gingerly taking the sick man's pulse with an averted head, and examining his urine, while holding a little phial of scent to his nose.[8]

Among the local doctors in Prato, Monna Margherita apparently preferred the cheapest, for Ser Lapo remarked that, poor as he was, he did not take advice from minor doctors, "like Margherita, to save the cost." The names mentioned are Maestro Matteo di Giovanni, Maestro Lorenzo di Agnolo, and a Maestro Bettino—who appears, however, to have been more concerned with religion than medicine, for his only letter to Francesco deals exclusively with the penitential processions of the Bianchi, and with a book he was intending to write about "the greatest, most outstanding and most notable miracles." *

Even after their return to Prato, however, both Francesco and Margherita continued to consult the Pope's physician in Avignon, Maestro Naddino Bovattieri, who prescribed by letter—

[7] Petrarca, *Lettere Senili*, vol. II, Libro XIII, Lettera VIII.
[8] Marchionne di Coppo Stefani, *Cronaca fiorentina*, VIII, 634.

unsuccessfully—for Margherita's sterility; [9] and they also applied to Maestro Giovanni Banducci of Prato, and, later on, to his son Bandino, who went to Bologna with Francesco in 1400, and for whom, while he was studying medicine in the University, Francesco paid out various sums of money for clothes, books, and candles, "when he sits up at night."

All these rival practitioners apparently observed—as the statutes of their guild required—strict medical etiquette, for there is a letter from a Florentine consultant telling Francesco that he would prescribe for him only after his own doctor had examined him and sent in a report. "What you write yourself is as plain as would amply suffice, but I say this to you, in view of the physician's reputation." *

As to fees, Maestro Giovanni Banducci received a fee of one florin for each visit,* and Francesco's account-book also records a payment of 20 florins to Maestro Lorenzo Sassoli "for the toil he has had in our house," though the number of visits is not specified. A later entry records the gifts of various household goods presented to Maestro Lorenzo "because he has practised medicine in the house for some time, and has never received anything"; these objects included "a painted lectern, for his studies." * But apparently often, too, a country practitioner had to content himself (as, indeed, sometimes happens today) with being paid in kind, for we find Maestro Lorenzo Sassoli writing to Francesco, in the early days of his practice: "I am paid by my patients with cheese and fresh eggs and perchance a basket of cherries." *

What precisely was the matter with Monna Margherita we do not know, but she seems to have suffered from some internal complaint which not only prevented her from having any children, but caused a number of vaguely defined "pains" (*doglie*). In addition she had periodical acute attacks of malaria.

On one occasion Francesco wrote to Guido del Palagio that she was in bed with "a double tertian fever, of which one is with

[9] Cf. Part I, chap. 1.

The Doctor's Visit
CODEX AVICENNA

her all the time, and the other begins at 16 hours and lasts until 6 the next morning." * Several doctors were consulted, but Domenico di Cambio—who prided himself on having "some little skill in almost any matter"—declared that his own prescription was the best, for it had cured two hundred people.

> If she would be healed right speedily, let three sage-leaves be picked at morn before sunrise, and let the man who picks them, be on his bended knees, saying three Paternosters and three Hail Marys in honour of God and the Holy Trinity, then send the leaves here in a letter, and I will write divers words on each. And as the fever approacheth, let her say a Paternoster and a Hail Mary, and then eat a leaf, and so for each one of the three. And when she is done with eating them, she will be rid of the fever. But she must have faith, for if she hath not, they will be of no avail.[1]

In the following spring, however, Margherita's attacks came back with renewed violence.

> Marvel not [she wrote to Francesco] that I have not written these two days, for I have had a greater fever than I ever remember, with a chill. And when Guido brought me a letter from you, the fever seized me like a fit of trembling, so that I knew not what he was saying, and I told him to answer you, but not to tell you of my sickness.

In addition to malaria, Margherita suffered often from colds or "rheums," headaches, indigestion, and wind—which was

---

[1] The expression *doppia terzana* (double tertian fever) was used for a fever which recurred every day, with violent paroxysms on alternate days. It would be interesting to know whether Domenico di Cambio's charm was one in wide use in Florence. The patient repeated the following prayer three times, crossing himself as he prayed: "When Jesus went to be crucified and was trembling greatly, an old Jew asked Him what fever He had, that He trembled so? And He replied, He had no fever and never would have, nor would this man [who had questioned Him] or any other who would repeat and listen to these words with devotion, for love of Him. Amen. Amen. Amen." *Una curiosa raccolta di segreti e di pratiche superstiziose fatta da un popolano fiorentino del secolo XIV*, ed. G. Giannini, p. 45.

called "the mother's complaint" (*mal di madre*)—while Francesco also had colds, toothache, and indigestion. And for these ailments, too, Domenico di Cambio had some simple prescriptions.

For toothache—he wrote—"take two ounces of whole millet from the apothecary and place it in a small new pan and put therein two glassfuls of wine and boil it all together very well; then pour out the wine and keep it in your mouth as hot as possible." For the itch, from which both husband and wife suffered, they were to take a rough cloth and rub themselves down with it, "and doubtless it will disappear." * And for headaches Margherita had a prescription given her by a woman called *la Gherardesca*. She was to put some black pudding in a pan with the must of some good red wine and let it stew in the oven for a day and a night. Then she was to take the lye, pass it through a sieve, and wash her head with it. As for the "mother's complaint," her doctor gave her some comfits for it, but their recipe is not given. The popular remedy—since it was believed that St. Elizabeth had also suffered from this complaint—was to wear on one's person any small object inscribed with the following prayer, and to read it aloud, making the sign of the Cross.

> Elizabeth suffered from the mother's complaint in her youth ✠ and she always prayed God to keep it in her body, in retribution for her sins. And she always kept it in her body ✠ until ✠ the angel Gabriel ✠ announced to her ✠ the birth of St. John the Baptist ✠ and then she was freed ✠ of the said complaint ✠ and then she prayed God that whoever should wear her name with reverence upon her person, should be freed from every ill. ✠ And so mayest Thou deign to free this Thy servant.[2]

How little could be done to assuage even the most acute suffering in childbirth is shown in the following letter:

[2] *Una curiosa raccolta*, etc., p. 47.

Your maid has been about to give birth since Tuesday even, and it is the most pitiful sight ever seen, for never did a woman suffer so greatly; there is no heart so hard it would not weep at the sight of her. She must be held down, or she would kill herself; and there are six women who care for her in turn. This morn they think the child is dead in her belly.*

Purges of course were taken in great abundance, as was the custom of the time—generally based on cassia or rhubarb, and so violent that they produced complete prostration for several days. A purgative "syrup" ordered to Francesco by the celebrated Florentine consultant Niccolò Falcucci was to be taken hot for three days running, two hours before dawn—after which the patient was to sleep again. And on the fourth evening he was to take some pills, and after them a clyster. "And if the pills, after moving the bowels, make you vomit, help them and purge the stomach well, for it is useful to you. Your humours are so viscous, coarse and sticky that they cannot move at one time, without great trouble." *

The medicine, however, which was considered miraculously efficacious was *otriaca* or *theriaca* (theriac), an antidote compounded of many drugs which was believed to be a panacea for all ills. In some cities this brew—its mysterious ingredients stirred together in a great cauldron—was made in public by the physicians of the University. Mazzei recommended it as a prophylactic against the plague, and we also find it prescribed for the most various diseases, from constipation to a high fever.

Now and again, however, in this confused world of quackery and superstition we meet a real physician—a man who combined book knowledge, intuition, and natural good sense. Such a man was Francesco's own doctor, Maestro Lorenzo Sassoli of Prato. His father—an apothecary called Agnolo di Tura di Sassolo— died in the plague of 1400, and it was with Francesco's help that the young man was able to study medicine in Padua, Bologna, and Ferrara before setting up practice in his native city. His letters to Francesco, which began when he was still a medical student in Padua, vividly describe the struggle of a penniless young doctor and reveal good sense, affection, and gratitude. "I have resolved," he wrote in his first letter, "to consider myself your son and obey to your orders so long as I live, as if you were my father."

Very soon he had good news to send: he had been appointed a lecturer in the University of Padua, "the most famous in the whole of Italy . . . and you wot well how great an honour that is for me." Yet even with a lecturer's post, life at a university was hard. The cost of lodgings, of matriculation, of books, and of procuring even the most modest equipment was so great that generally only a rich young man or a physician's son (who had his father's books and instruments) dared enter the profession. Lorenzo Sassoli was fortunate indeed to have such a patron as Francesco, who opened an account for him with his agent in Venice, Bindo Piaciti. A few months later Lorenzo was writing "to render account, as to a father."

> I took 130 florins all at once for my expenses, but it was to pay some debts. . . . I had hoped, for my pleasures, to receive some salary for my lectures but owing to the great extravagance of the *Signore*, all of us who are lecturing fear we shall receive no salary. So that perforce I must be careful in my spending.*

In the following spring he told his patron that he had now been appointed lecturer in the University of Bologna, "and, according to the Statutes of Bologna, I must become a doctor in medicine before the opening of the University." But a few months later he was obliged to give up the plan—Bologna having fallen into the hands of the Duke of Milan—and took up a similar appointment in Ferrara instead. "For I would fain not leave a University if I may abide there, since it seems to me more pleasant to deal with scholars than with any other manner of men."

These university years were probably the happiest of Maestro Lorenzo's life; yet the time came when he had to return to Prato, and he found little there to please him. "Meseems I have come to the land of the Philistines," he wrote, and complained that his conversations with his fellow physicians in Ferrara, "to throw light on every uncertainty," had now given place "to disputations touching the sowing of lupins and sorb-apples." *

Nevertheless, since the Commune offered him a salary of 50 *lire* a month, he perforce settled down there for a while, and it was then that he became Francesco's regular doctor, speaking no longer in the humble tones of a penniless student, but with the authority of an established physician.

His patient by now was a man of over seventy, plainly possessed of a strong constitution, or he could never have reached what was then considered a great old age, but even more choleric and anxious than he had been in his youth and, moreover, afflicted, as appears in these letters, by the complaints of the sedentary and the self-indulgent: stone, gravel, and constipation.

Maestro Lorenzo believed in what is now called psychosomatic medicine; he treated, in his own words, *"l'animo e lo corpo"* (both soul and body). Already two years earlier, before leaving Ferrara, he had sent a short homily to his adopted father, warning him that he could no longer go on working and worrying as he had done in his prime. "Methinks the chill you have taken is through your own fault, for assuredly it came to you only because you take your tribulations and your labours as if you were a man of thirty, and this you must not do."

A few months later he wrote again.

You write to me touching the great unease which torments both your body and soul. I know not what I could say that would serve to make you take a little ease; but I will speak to God, and not to you, and beseech Him in His mercy to set your spirit at rest—as is needful for yourself most of all, and therefore for me and your other children.

And the letter ended with protestations of filial affection and a promise that, whatever his other occupations might be, he would always be able to hasten to Florence on Francesco's behalf.

> For were the whole of Prato on my hands, I would forsake them all, for your life is dearer to me than any friends or kinsfolk. . . . And every man knows that any little learning I may possess, I owe first to God, and then to you.

During the first year after Maestro Lorenzo had set up practice, few weeks went by without his sending Francesco some prescription. On one day it was some "pills for his hearing." On another, a warning "not to exceed in fruit, owing to these fluxes which abound this year" but to "use vinegar often, both cooked and raw." And since Francesco had apparently called in another doctor, a "Maestro Francesco," who allowed him to eat whatever he liked, Lorenzo wrote again with some irritation. "Whensoever I meet him [the doctor], methinks I shall explain *my* arguments to him; and when he has heard them, perchance he will tighten the reins even more than he loosened them. . . . For that any man ever died of not eating great bellyfuls of fruit, I never read in my books; I know not if you have found it in yours."

A month later he was again referring—in answer to a letter of Francesco's—to his patient's uneasiness of mind.

> Pray tell me how you feel, and that you now take the vexations of your trade more easily. For if you do not, ailments and bodily anguish will be your first profits. . . . In all your great tribulations and in the hard practice of trade, you bear the reputation among your fellows of conducting your affairs with great wisdom, and in a manner suited to the times. But your own person you cannot rule.

It was in this year, when Francesco was seventy-one years old, that Maestro Lorenzo wrote him a long letter which is a remarkable document. It is a complete rule of life—"in food and drink, sleeping and physic, and every other matter that appertains to wholesome living."

After a long paragraph about diet, which has already been quoted in the section on food, and of which the gist, in one word, is "moderation," Maestro Lorenzo turned to *"il viver medicinale"* ("the life of physic") and began with an instruction which, in those times of violent and constant physicking, is surprising: "Throw away all physic save cassia, and use that only when your bodily functions move not of their own accord; and then use it with ginger. . . . And also use theriaca both in winter and summer, especially when there is a new moon or when it rains." To encourage urination he advised some conserve of ginger before dinner. "And that is all you need observe in the way of physic."

With regard to sleep, he advised waiting for at least an hour after meals before going to bed: "But assuredly I may preach a long time, before you do it . . . and let your manner of lying be either face downwards, or on your right side." As to exercise, Francesco was to rub his head lightly on waking with a rough towel; then try to move his bowels, and then begin to walk about, "until you feel warm, especially your hands, and then take a little rest, before eating."

But, above all, Maestro Lorenzo was concerned with his patient's state of mind.

> Touching the accidents of the spirit, I would I were Maestro Domenico of Peccioli [a celebrated Dominican preacher] to preach to you as is needful; yet let me speak to you touching the things of which you must most beware. To get angry and shout at times pleases me, for this will keep up your natural heat; but what displeases me is your being grieved and taking all matters so much to heart. For it is this,

as the whole of physic teaches, which destroys our body, more than any other cause. Wherefore I beseech you to restrain yourself in this, above all things.

And the letter ends: "If you do all that I have written, from the first to the last, I am certain that, with God's grace, you will lead a happy life, in a healthy body. And so I pray God, through His grace, to inspire your mind.*

No doubt Maestro Lorenzo was right; had Francesco followed this advice, he would have spent his last years in better health. It is probable, however, that he would still have continued to suffer from two complaints which even a cheerful mind cannot heal—piles and gravel. For the former, Ser Lapo, who himself suffered from both complaints, advised "an onion well cooked and pounded with the pestle, and anoint the place well with it"; for the latter, half a bowlful daily of water in which black chickpeas had been brewed—to be taken in the morning, after a light supper the night before.

Some years before this, in 1387, Francesco had been considering taking, for his gravel, the waters of Montecatini—the celebrated spa near Pistoia whose waters were then a novelty—and had written to Maestro Giovanni Banducci to ask his opinion of them. "For I have so great a faith in you and in Maestro Niccolò that meseems aught I took for physic, lacking your counsel, would profit me but little."

> Many folk [he wrote] go to the baths of Montecatini and some fetch the waters here, wherefore I pray you tell me if I should fetch them here, and both Margherita and I drink it, as is the custom. There are also some who say the waters of the Porretta are better, but I believe none but you.*

Ser Lapo was one of those who preferred the Porretta waters, partly because they had recently been tested and approved by the whole faculty of medicine of Bologna: "They were all compelled to drink the waters of Porretta—I mean compelled by the Uni-

344

versity of Bologna; and they saw in them great efficacy in promoting urination and cleansing one of stone and gravel, for a period of three years." He added that the waters were also efficacious in "restoring hearing and appetite and a fair complexion . . . and not harmful even to a woman with child." It was, however, necessary to drink them on the spot, "for if they are sent in barrels, they are swiftly corrupted and lose their power." The report had been shown to Maestro Lorenzo, who had commented: "I would approve the waters for Francesco, did I not greatly fear that, after taking them, he would not observe the rule of abstinence from certain things for 15 days or even 30; and therefore I dare not advise them for him."

The rule for patients partaking of these waters was "not to touch water, to make merry without vexation, to eat neither fruit nor roast meat nor vegetables nor anything fried, and to abstain completely from women."

Still, however, Francesco hesitated, and so great was Ser Lapo's annoyance that he allowed himself an uncharitable wish: "Would to God, that whoever dissuades you from them [the waters] would himself urinate with pain for at least two or three days—and methinks his counsel would suffer a change." *

Ser Lapo's medical advice was not confined to the treatment of gravel: it extended, like Maestro Lorenzo's, to his friend's whole way of life. In this, as in everything else, his rule was moderation. "Verily I will show unto you that all our infirmities come from not ordering our gullet according to the needs of our body—not erring in either too little or too much. . . . And the same is true of matrimony."

When Francesco was in Bologna during the plague, Ser Lapo sent him a rule of health which is, in some respects, singularly modern.

Let not the sun go down behind the hill, without your having gone forth; or if indeed you cannot, take before meals a little exercise to tire you, without however causing you to sweat. You should have a block of wood and a saw, and give a few strokes, or go speedily upstairs divers times. For your food has no help from nature, and even as embers die out if they are not stirred, so the food in your stomach is frozen, for lack of exercising your person. And after supper, wait for at least two hours before sleep, that the food can take shape; for, in good faith, the physicians will approve this more than so many clysters—that is, that you should take food easy to digest, and helpful to your bowels' functions. And it would help you much to drink a quarter of an hour ere your repast, a full half-glass of good red wine, that be neither too dry nor too sweet.

So much for purely physical advice. But Ser Lapo never forgot that the body is, after all, but a servant. Swiftly he went on to say that the real reason for striving to keep well was one only—to be fit to give thanks to God: "For I note, Francesco, that in sickness I can scarce remember God and can scarce say a Paternoster." As he wrote, the Black Death was all around him and had taken two of his children, yet still he maintained that a man's first duty to God was thankfulness. "To this we should turn our hearts, and sometimes at Mass, and in our chamber, and as we walk along the street, lift up our eyes. Thus, if a fever cometh, we shall not be seized by so great a fear of death, but say: 'I am here, my Lord; I wait for your commands!' " *

CHAPTER EIGHT

PLAGUE
AND PENITENCE

"Pace volli con Dio in su lo stremo
Della mia vita. . . ." [1]

—DANTE, *Purgatorio*, XIII, 124

T THE TURN OF THE CENTURY FRANCESCO—WHO had reached his sixty-fifth year—appears to us in a new aspect: wearing the garb of a penitent and a pilgrim. Clad in a long robe of coarse white cloth, with a cowl on his head, a friar's cord about his waist, and a lighted candle in his hand, he set forth barefoot, in a company of several thousand men, for a nine-day pilgrimage.

To none of Francesco's contemporaries did it seem strange to see him thus: the performance, in calamitous times, of such acts of devotion and self-abasement was part of an accepted pattern of life. The Datini papers, indeed, bring fresh confirmation of the extent to which a life of Christian conformity was led even by men (like Francesco himself) whose natural temperament was far from pious. Just as many of the laws they obeyed were

[1] "I would make peace with God on my life's brink."

347

still largely founded upon usage—*consuetudo*—so their devotional life rested upon a series of unquestioned, familiar acts, from the cradle to the grave. Hard-headed merchants not only gave lip-service to Christian doctrine, but paid tribute to it in their daily practice: they led their whole lives within an intricate framework of pious observance. During his whole youth and prime Francesco was not, and did not consider himself, a virtuous man; but he never questioned the necessity or the efficacy of these devout customs. His business contracts, like his private letters, began and ended with a pious formula; the Ten Commandments stood at the head of his ledgers; a fresco of St. Christopher guarded his front door. In Lent and on other fast-days both he and his wife fasted so strictly that Domenico di Cambio said his health would not permit him to come and stay with them,[2] and if he sometimes worked on a Sunday, he blamed himself most severely in the year in which he had attended only *six* Lenten sermons! Though he often scoffed at priests and monks, he went regularly to confession, and, in sickness, called five Franciscans to his bedside; though ungenerous by nature, he gave alms freely, paid his tithes regularly, built shrines and chapels. There was hardly a rich man of his time who did not do the same, and the few who failed to fulfil these duties were considered wicked men.

Many of these acts, of course, had a strong propitiatory character; it was through them that men hoped to receive protection from the terrors and mysteries of life in this world, as well as God's mercy in the next. Man is at all times a fear-ridden animal; and certainly many Tuscans of the *trecento* had good reason to dread a sudden death. The persistence of the tradition of vengeance by bloodshed—still considered not only a sacred duty but a pleasure [3]—the permanent sense of insecurity produced by party

[2] "I trow I could never be aught but at ease in your house, but men tell me you fast every day, and therefore I will not come, for my stomach is not apt for fasting." (File 1092. Domenico di Cambio to Francesco, March 16, 1389.)

[3] Paolo da Certaldo, in enumerating the five chief pleasures and griefs of life, wrote: "The first grief is to receive an injury; the first pleasure, to wreak vengeance." *Libro di buoni costumi*, para. 270.

strife and civil war, the frequent recurrence of famine, and, above all, the constant, haunting menace of the Black Death—this was the dark background of their lives. In the years of Francesco's youth the Florentine *contado* had known, for various reasons, at least five years in which the harvest failed: at the root of the riots of the *popolo minuto* there was always the simplest, most compelling of human motives—hunger. As to the plague— by the time Francesco was sixty, he had already seen five outbreaks of the dread *"moría"*: the first in 1348, which had carried off both his parents, two others in Avignon, and two in Prato soon after his return. And, finally, in his old age, in 1399, another one was threatening.

It is this dread which pervades a great many of the Datini letters—for echoes of these epidemics reached Francesco not only from friends at home, but from distant correspondents abroad. These letters show how very little had been learned about the plague during the half-century that had passed since its first appearance. To Monna Margherita, as to Boccaccio, it still seemed a visitation as mysterious and uncontrollable as the Day of Judgement. Still everyone differed as to how best it could be averted. Some men sought protection in abstinence, and some in high living; some shut themselves up in their own houses, and others tried to run away—the town-dweller to the country, the countryman to the town. Some—like Ser Lapo Mazzei and Monna Margherita—had a faint belief in the efficacy of drugs and prophylactics; others, like Niccolò dell'Ammannato, thought that the disease hung in the air for several months, "like a corruption," before reaching its full fruition, and that the only hope lay in immediate flight.

There are few years in which Datini's correspondence does not contain some reference to this menace. The first epidemic after his return—a comparatively slight one—broke out in 1383. "The plague," wrote his brother-in-law in May, "waxes in divers places and spreads in this direction." A fortnight later it had reached Florence. "I find the people here much afraid, and the deaths are beginning . . . and in God's name we will send you our boy, Pippo." A few days later the panic had spread so widely that a decree of the *Signoria* attempted to prevent the general exodus by forbidding anyone to leave the city, but no one heeded it. Niccolò himself, with his other children, fled to Signa, but too late. "My boy Nanni was stricken and in a day and a half I buried him. And in Florence the destruction moves one to compassion." *

For a few years there is silence, and then, in 1389, there is another epidemic, beginning this time in Prato itself. "Come to Florence," wrote Domenico di Cambio, "and I will teach you to keep well. We will follow the teaching of the doctor who says: 'Ere setting forth, eat a piece of toasted bread and drink half a glass of wine'; and in virtue of this prescription [4] he has himself already lived for seventy years." And Domenico added: "I would not you should stay so long picking up nails, that you lose the shoe!" *

Francesco, however, did not heed, and in the spring it was Niccolò who again begged him to hurry away. "I beseech you, delay not, for when the air begins to hold corruption, it proceeds and becomes heavier, in especial when the heat cometh, and it is most perilous towards August.[5] Wherefore with my whole heart I beseech you, fly before you or your household are stricken." He went on to explain that the bad air "generates evil humours in you, which appear not for a while, and then in the heat burst forth. . . ." *

---

[4] Domenico's simple prescription was widely believed in. "Light the fire," wrote Giovanni Morelli, "before you set forth and eat something, according to your stomach—a piece of bread or half a glass of malmsey." He also recommended as prophylactics, spices "such as cinnamon or saffron". . . "and refresh your pulse, temples and nose with strong vinegar." Early rising was recommended and great temperance with both wine and women, and the avoidance of pork, mushrooms, and fruit; and regular movements of the bowels, procured if necessary by an enema once a week. "And so you will purge your stomach, and the air's corruption will find naught whereto it can hang."

[5] So, too, Morelli: "In winter you may see tokens in the countryside or on our borders . . . and in February you begin to hear of it inside the city . . . and it waxes all through July and then begins to touch decent folk."

8. PLAGUE AND PENITENCE

Still, however, Francesco delayed, and in July Domenico wrote that he, for his part, had done what he could. "I have commended you to Our Lady of the Assumption, vowing, if she guards you from this pestilence, I will place before Her a waxen man [6] in your likeness." *

Again the plague died away, leaving the Datini household untouched, but four years later, in 1393, another epidemic broke out. Francesco warned his wife that he would not be able to get her a new slave, because the plague was raging in Roumania, "and those who come, die on board. It would be bringing the plague into our own homes." In 1395 it had got to Valencia; Francesco's agents wrote of a severe outbreak there. "It will come here, too," he grimly foretold, "and will dispel the tribulations of many folk who are grumbling now; and many will find rest, who are weary of the labours of this evil world." *

By 1398 it had reached northern Italy, and now Monna Margherita, too, took alarm. "Francesco, I shall never cease telling you, and you know I have done so for more than a year (though in vain), that anyone who wishes to flee, to any purpose, should flee now."

By the following summer panic spread through Tuscany again; town-dwellers moved out to the country, and country-dwellers back to town. One friend who had taken his whole family to Arezzo urged Francesco to join him there, but now Margherita —who had in the meantime moved to Florence—was in favour of remaining at home.

> My reason is [she wrote to her husband] this pestilence
> must be nursed speedily, and there are but one or two rem-
> edies of any avail. . . . And I would have immediate succour,
> both for body and soul. . . . For this disease is like unto the

[6] The making of these waxen images, carved and painted with the greatest skill, was one of the most flourishing minor Florentine arts, and the founder of the most famous *bottega* specializing in them, Benintendi Fallimagine, was a contemporary of Datini's. Cf. Piattoli, *Un mercante del trecento e gli artisti del tempo suo*, pp. 55–6.

Judgement in the Gospels, whereof we know not whether it will come upon us by day or by night.*

Mazzei, too, still had some faith in doctors' prescriptions. "The doctors praise *theriaca* daily, for fifteen days, and pills of aloe, myrrh and saffron, once every eight days." But, above all, he counselled resignation. "Let us comfort ourselves with the thought of God and of a good death, and let us pray." *

And indeed prayers were on every lip—protestations of contrition and vows of amendment. Rich men like Francesco felt peculiarly uneasy, for did not every preacher tell them that the greatest burden of guilt was theirs? Nor did even the most hardened deny it.

I have sinned in my life as much as a man can sin [Francesco wrote to his wife, after hearing a Lenten sermon] for I have ruled myself ill and have not known how to moderate my desires . . . and I pay the penalty gladly. But I would I could be like Job, who gave thanks to God for every affliction that came upon him, for that I cannot yet do.

This letter was written when the air was heavy with warnings and calls to penance; and Francesco, too, turned his thoughts from the immediate danger to his health and his purse, to anxiety about his latter end. "I fear me greatly that it will not be good," he added, "and I think of little else." And, a year later: "I should like to live awhile longer, to do a little good—for of harm I have done a great deal." *

Certainly every sermon that Francesco heard, whether in church or from the lips of Ser Lapo, must have increased his uneasiness. Anger and covetousness were the two sins against which every preacher thundered; and Francesco well knew that they were his own besetting sins. The whole house, we are told, resounded with his cries when he was quarrelling with his wife or scolding his servants—and even with the mild-spoken, reasonable Ser Lapo he would sometimes "begin to shout." "Leave vengeance

8. PLAGUE AND PENITENCE

to Messer Domeneddio, who will find a better one than we can," *
Monna Margherita had implored; but he had not heeded her.
For souls such as his—*"l'anime di color cui vinse l'ira"* [7]—the
fifth circle of Hell was waiting, the grey marsh beside the Styx,
in which naked and angry men perpetually came to blows and
tore each other to pieces with their teeth. Or might he not be
sent instead to an even more terrible torment—that of the fiery
desert of the seventh circle, where the usurers—the men who had
offended *"la divina bontade"* [8]—spent their eternity beside the
blasphemers and the sodomites, licked by flickering flames and
wearing about their necks a little money-bag? That such a fate
did not seem, to a man of the *trecento*, a mere poet's vision, but
a terrifying reality, can hardly be doubted by anyone who sees
(as Francesco must often have done, for similar frescoes were
being painted in most Tuscan churches at the time) Traini's
painting of the Last Judgement in Pisa, where monstrous demons
are carrying off the souls of the damned to eternal torment, while
a stern angel with a sword summons the just and the unjust to
render their last account. Among the rich merchants and the
usurers in their fine robes who drew back in fear, did Francesco
see or imagine his own portrait?

Sermons and popular tales, too, brought him to the same warning. In the pious literature of the *trecento* no subject was more
popular than that of the rich usurer's or merchant's deathbed.
There was the tale of the money-lender who was denied Christian
burial because he was so proud of his ill-gotten gains that "when
he was eating, he kept upon the table a golden cart with golden
oxen and ploughmen . . . and he made his servants rattle upon
the table purses containing 14 thousand golden ducats; and he
would say that one of these was Jesus Christ and one the Virgin
Mary, and the others the twelve Apostles." Another story described the deathbed of a usurer who, as he lay dying, saw "a

---

[7] "The souls of those whom anger overcame"—*Inferno*, VII, 116.

[8] "The divine goodness." Dante wrote: *"Usura offende la divina bontade."*
Inferno, XI, 96.

fiend with a sharp-pointed hat" (for a conical hat was a mark of infamy, worn only by the owners of gambling-houses) "who leaped upon his bed and then threw himself face downward upon him, caught him by the throat and strangled him." There was the tale of the wandering ghost of a usurer who appeared to his son—"a black smoke, as it were the shadow of a man"—to tell him that he had been condemned to eternal torment. And in yet another story the usurer was carried off to Hell by "an innumerable multitude of men, black as negroes of Ethiopia, dark and terrible beyond all human imagining . . . biting and smiting and rending and tearing." [9] So often, indeed, did preachers harp upon this theme that Sacchetti describes an occasion when a member of a very poor congregation at last cried out in protest: "But here there is none that has a single groat to lend!"—whereupon the preacher passed on to a more appropriate text, "Blessed be the poor." [1]

It is perhaps odd that under these circumstances Francesco should have been an assiduous sermon-goer; but so he was—perhaps partly in a faint hope that this, at least, would be counted in his favour, partly to please his wife and Mazzei, and partly because this pastime, if a duty, was also often a pleasure. Books, even for the educated, were few and dear; but sermons were frequent and often extremely entertaining. The Mendicant Orders had started the custom of preaching not only in churches but in the open squares, and of appealing not only to the learned but to common folk. Their sermons were held in the early mornings or at dusk, so that busy craftsmen and shop-keepers could attend them before going to their work, and housewives before setting to the day's task; and they adorned their exhortations with stories and "ensamples" taken from real life, with travellers' tales and rumours of strange portents; they even sometimes provided the women with household remedies and prescriptions.

These were the sermons that Francesco attended—in spite of

[9] Fra Filippo degli Agazzari, *Assempri.*
[1] Sacchetti, *Novelle,* C.

slight misgivings about the saintliness of the preachers. He himself has reported, in a letter, a conversation with one of these wandering friars. "I asked him: 'Wherefore will you not demean yourselves like Christ's Apostles, who were ready to die to preach the truth? Wherefore preach you not to those Florentines of yours touching the sins of the city, in especial the murders that take place every day?' And the friar answered me, laughing, that it was because there are now more confessors than martyrs." *

If we wish to know what these preachers said, we have only to read the sermons of the greatest of them, San Bernardino da Siena. Though a fine classical scholar, he never made a show of his learning. He wished his hearers to go away "contented and illuminated, not confused"; he delighted in the lively phrase, the concrete, familiar image. If he had to describe a vain man, he called him "*tutto pieno di chicchirichi*" ("full of cock-a-doodle-doo"); he would make his congregation laugh by imitating the croaking of a frog. "Know you how the frog talks? He says *qua-qua-qua*." No device was left unused to hold the attention of his hearers. If a woman's eye was wandering, he interrupted the sermon to call out to her: "Lo! I see a woman there who, if she were watching me, would not be looking where she is. Pay heed to me, I say!" Once a tired housewife dropped asleep while he was talking of the pit into which Lucifer fell. "You sleepy woman, there! Look to it, that you fall not into the same pit!" And on one occasion, when the attention of the whole congregation seemed to be flagging, the preacher drew out a letter: "Hark to this letter, which I received this morning." His hearers leaned forward eagerly. "Lo, you heed an unread letter, more than the word of God!"

To attend such sermons was indeed "as good as a play." And though not all preachers were as entertaining as San Bernardino, many were as forceful. In 1399, when the menace of the plague had arisen again, a remarkable man was drawing great crowds to his sermons in Santa Liberata and Santa Maria Novella: a Dominican preacher called Fra Giovanni Dominici. This monk's eloquence had been achieved by sheer strength of will, for in his childhood—according to his own account—he had been tongue-tied and had stammered so badly that when his mother first took him to a monastery the monks only laughed at him, saying that all he could hope for was to become the community's jester. But by sheer fervour and persistence he had entirely overcome his handicap, and had become one of the most admired preachers of his time. "He has only one fault," wrote Mazzei, "that he speaks too quickly, and preaches a furious sermon—but one precious to the ears of the devout, who know that they must die."

This was the man whom, on Ser Lapo's advice, Francesco now went to hear.

> I tell you [the notary wrote] there has never been such a sermon. Assuredly God's friends will rise up again, and will bring to an end this slothful life of both clergy and laymen. . . . You will think you hear one of the disciples of St. Francis, and will be born again. We were all in tears, marvelling at the clear truths he laid before us.*

The tenets which Fra Giovanni preached were not entirely orthodox—and perhaps that is why they so greatly pleased Ser Lapo, whose championship of the poor and humble was gradually leading him away from all the great men of this world, whether they wore a Prior's gown or a Cardinal's hat.

> He [Fra Giovanni] draws unto himself [wrote Francesco a year or two later] all men who would lead a good life; but those who will not hear God's words will not draw nigh, and calumniate him, as the Jews calumniated our Lord.*

The truth was that, when Francesco first heard Fra Giovanni preach, the monk had come to Florence under sentence of exile. He had been turned out of Venice and was in ill-odour with the Church for having encouraged the rise of a new penitential movement, whose followers—called, from the white robes they wore, I Bianchi—were already wandering from city to city across the whole of northern Italy, scourging themselves as they went, and imploring "peace and mercy." Only prayers such as theirs, cried Fra Giovanni, the prayers of the poor and humble, could avert the terrible calamities that God had sent to destroy the corruption and wickedness in high places. Only by penance and self-abasement could men again hope to come close to God.

Such penitential movements were, of course, nothing new. They were a social phenomenon quite as much as a religious one, and had already sprung up several times in various parts of Italy —born of the universal longing to obtain, through expiation, at least a semblance of peace and order in this world and a condonation of sins in the next. The penitents wandered in great companies from city to city, scourging themselves mercilessly in penance for their sins, praying before all holy sanctuaries and shrines, singing hymns, and preaching the Gospel of "a holy Communism" and a perfect freedom of the spirit. Most of these *flagellanti*, whose tenets reflected a mixture of the doctrines of holy poverty of the *fraticelli* and of the Messianic prophecies of Fra Gioacchino da Fiore, were humble men: landless peasants, homeless craftsmen, small shop-keepers or landowners ruined by oppressive taxes—all men who had nothing more to lose and whose diatribes were therefore directed against everyone in authority. Their impassioned supplications, their resonant hymns in the vulgar tongue, their apocalyptic prophecies of a classless brotherhood of the spirit endeared them wherever they went to the poor and discontented—and also aroused the alarm of both secular and clerical rulers. The rich merchants, whose interests both at home and abroad could not dispense with the support of the strong arm of the Church, treated them as lawless bandits and closed their city gates; the prelates stigmatized them as heretics, banished them from the lands of the Church, and threatened them with excommunication and exile. Yet so great was the general need and expectation, so obstinate the faith of humble folk, that such movements sprang up again and again. The first had taken place in the year of Francesco's birth—1335—when a

357

Dominican, Fra Venturino of Bergamo, had led a great company of *flagellanti* across the whole of Italy to Rome. They, too—dressed in long white tunics, with sky-blue cloaks, and wearing as their emblem the dove of the Holy Ghost—had cried out for mercy and peace and prophesied the coming of "a kingdom of the spirit." "Nor was there anyone so austere and old, but that he scourged himself gladly." [2] But both Church and State were swift to arm against them. Bulls were issued against false prophets; cities closed their gates; and in the end Fra Venturino and some of his followers were tried for heresy in Avignon.

Then, with the Black Death, a renewed wave of spiritual unrest swept over Europe. New groups of flagellants appeared in various parts of Germany and spread southward, preaching a return to evangelical simplicity and poverty, and everywhere undermining the power and authority of the Church. In Florence, during the interdiction of 1373, groups of penitents who declared that, although cast out by the Church, they still "saw God in their hearts" met every evening in the Florentine churches to sing hymns, and walked in procession, scourging themselves through the streets. "There were even boys of ten among them," wrote a contemporary chronicler, "and certainly more than 5,000 flagellants, and 20,000 or more following the processions, and many noble and rich young men were moved to conversion and made their conventicle in Fiesole and gave alms and fasted and prayed and slept on straw upon the ground. . . ." [3]

In vain did priests of more austere and orthodox tenets dryly point out that there were shorter and simpler ways of obtaining God's pardon than by donning a pilgrim's robe. Penitents, they remarked, instead of roaming across the country in lawless bands, would do better to take a shorter, less sensational journey across the street to their own church, and there obtain absolution from their parish priest! [4] But still the pilgrim's quest held, in the

[2] Fra Salimbene da Parma, *Cronaca.*
[3] *"Diario di Anonimo fiorentino"* in *Documenti di storia italiana,* vol. VI.
[4] Fra Giordano da Rivalto, *Prediche,* ed. Moreni, II, p. 50. So great was Fra Giordano's disapproval of these unruly fanatics that in Pisa he founded

popular imagination, the place that centuries of tradition had assigned to it—for could not all pilgrims be identified with the first great earthly Pilgrim, who had sought not His own salvation, but that of all humanity? How deeply the symbolism of this quest was imprinted upon the imagination of the *trecento* may be seen in a description of the pilgrim's garb by Datini's contemporary Franco Sacchetti.

> The first thing the pilgrim doeth on setting forth, is to don a pilgrim's robe and gird on his pouch, and place therein a needle and thread and coins of silver and gold; the needle and thread are to mend his raiment when it is torn, and the money to spend. He bears a staff to pass across the streams and to defend himself from dogs, and to lean upon; and he dons a very sober hat—and these are the things he bears with him.
>
> Thus did Christ wear a pilgrim's robe, clothing His divinity with humanity.
>
> He girded on a pouch and put thread in it: this was charity, which sews and binds; the needle was His penance; the silver coin, grace; and the golden coin, glory.
>
> He bore a staff, that is the wood of the Cross, resting upon it when He was crucified; and with it He defended Himself from dogs. . . .
>
> And the sober hat was the Crown of Thorns.[5]

It is not surprising that when, in 1399, the Black Death had already broken out again in Roumania and Spain and was spreading to northern Italy, yet another penitential movement should have arisen—and that it, too, should have begun among the poor. In a field of northern Italy—so the legend ran—Christ Himself appeared to a starving peasant, and miraculously filled his sack

---

a fraternity, the *Società di San Salvatore*, to counteract their influence and to advocate other, more sober ways of obtaining forgiveness.

[5] Sacchetti, *Sermoni Evangelici, Lettere Varie e Scritti Inediti. Sermone* XLVIII.

with bread, revealing to him that it was not the rich and the powerful, but the humble who would bring back peace to the world. "For since neither prelates nor wise men will bestir themselves, the Divine Mercy has elected to show its power through coarse working-men." [6] From northern Italy the movement spread swiftly to Tuscany and Umbria, and once again great companies of penitents were to be seen, praying at holy sanctuaries and shrines, scourging themselves mercilessly in penance for their sins. They, too, like their predecessors, marched through the cities and villages singing hymns and exhorting the people to follow their example.

Their white robes and cowls covered them from head to foot, with only a narrow slit for their eyes; they wore a cord about their waists, their feet were bare, their backs and chests adorned by a red cross. They carried lighted candles, and each company walked behind a great Crucifix, singing litanies and crying out for mercy and for peace.

> *Misericordia, eterno Dio,*
> *Pace, pace, Signor pio,*
> *Non guardare il nostro errore.*
> *Misericordia andiam gridando*
> *Misericordia non sia in bando*
> *Misericordia Iddio pregando*
> *Misericordia al peccatore.*[7]

Yet even as they cried for mercy the pestilence was spreading all around them; and fear is a great leveller. This time the penitents included not only the poor and disaffected and genuine religious fanatics, but every quaking burgher who hoped, through a belated penitence, to avert calamity from his home. And among them was Francesco di Marco—not alone, but, as befitted his posi-

[6] Giovanni Sercambi, *Le Croniche*, vol. II, p. 34.
[7] "Mercy, eternal God—peace, peace, O gentle Lord—look not upon our errors. Mercy we call upon—mercy be not denied—for mercy we implore—unto the sinner, mercy"—"The Hymn of the *Bianchi*," quoted by Giovanni Sercambi, *Le Croniche*.

Pilgrims
BY ANDREA DA FIRENZE

Tombstone of Francesco di Marco Datini
BY NICCOLÒ LAMBERTI

tion, at the head of a little group of twelve men: his brother-in-law, Niccolò dell'Ammannato, his two Florentine partners, Stoldo di Lorenzo and Domenico di Cambio, and eight of his *fattori*— "in all twelve men, who came with me to obtain the Pardon of the pilgrimage; and I paid for what was needful to eat and drink for each of them, as will hereafter be set down in this book."

It is fortunate for us that Francesco, as well as keeping a detailed record of his accounts in his private note-book, should also have left a description of the occasion.* This is much more pedestrian in tone than the stories of most pilgrims, and all the more informative. The Tuscan pilgrimages, it appears, were extremely domestic. The pilgrims—though they vowed never to sleep "within stone walls" or to take off their robes—seem never to have suffered any real discomfort. They never went more than fifty miles from home, nor were they absent for more than nine days; and though during this time they did not eat meat, they certainly did not stint themselves of eggs and fish, fruit and vegetables. It is difficult not to receive the impression of a gigantic nine-day picnic, only occasionally punctuated by sermons or prayers. But here is Francesco's account:

> Remembrance that on this eighteenth day of August, 1399 . . . I, Francesco di Marco, through the inspiration of God and His Mother, Our Lady, resolved to go on a pilgrimage, clothed entirely in white linen and barefoot, as was the custom then for many people of the city and territory of Florence, and also of the surrounding region. For at that time all men, or at least the greater number of Christians, were moved to go on pilgrimage throughout the world, for the love of God, clothed from head to foot in white linen. . . .
>
> And on that day I set forth with my company from my house in Piazza de'Tornaquinci, early in the morning, and we went to Santa Maria Novella, all barefoot, and there devoutly partook of the Communion of the Body of Our

Lord Jesus Christ: then devoutly we went out of Porta San Gallo, where we found the Crucifix of the Quarter of Santa Maria Novella and that of the Quarter of Santa Croce . . . all barefoot, and scourging ourselves with a rod and accusing ourselves to Our Lord Jesus Christ of our sins, devoutly and with good will, as all Christians should. . . .

The whole company—which numbered more than 30,000—walked in procession through the city "three by three, each with a lighted candle," and took the road along the Arno to Pieve a Ripoli.

And there we said a Mass for the Bishop of Fiesole, who was our father and guide and chief leader. And when the Mass was said, we all scattered in the road or the fields, to eat bread and cheese and fruit, and such-like things. For during the nine days that the pilgrimage lasted, none of us might eat any meat, nor take off his white clothes, nor lie in a bed.

And that we might have what was needful, I took with us two of my horses and the mule; and on these we placed two small saddle-chests, containing boxes of all kinds of comfits, and a great many small torches and candles, and cheeses of all kinds, and fresh bread and biscuits, and round cakes, sweet and unsweetened, and other things besides that appertain to a man's life; so that the two horses were fully laden with our victuals; and beside these, I took a great sack of warm raiment, to have at hand by day and night. And the mule I took in case one of us, through sickness or any other cause, could not walk; so that, whether on foot or on horseback, any man who met with an accident should yet, with God's help, be able to complete the holy journey, with a good and devout heart.

The pilgrims' route was by San Donato, San Giovanni, and Montevarchi (sleeping out for three nights on the way) to Arezzo, where they heard Mass "on a meadow within the city, and also a sermon," and slept in the Franciscan monastery. Then they returned by Laterina, Castelfranco, and Pontassieve, where they arrived on a Friday night "and received great honours, and were given many fish."

Then, in God's name, we returned in the evening to Florence, and each of us to his own house; but we went not to bed nor doffed our white garments until the Crucifix arrived in Fiesole, and a solemn Mass was said in the square by the Bishop of Fiesole, and he preached to us, and blessed us all. And then each man returned to his own house, and the journey and pilgrimage were ended. God make it profitable to our souls, if it be His will. Amen.

The first task of the *Bianchi*, wherever they went, was to "make peace"—i.e., to bring about a reconciliation between men whom a long-standing feud had estranged. And when the reconciliation was effected, and both parties had embraced each other with a kiss of peace, they often presented the peace-makers with some gift as a token of gratitude. Sometimes, too, the mere sight of the great Crucifix at the head of the procession would work miracles among the crowd: the lame would begin to walk, and the blind to see—and they, too, would offer to the *Bianchi* some tangible sign of their gratitude.

Yet still the plague approached. It had already broken out, men said, in Venice and Genoa; it was moving southward. And now it was the people of the smaller Tuscan cities who set forth on pilgrimage: little groups of frightened country folk, two or three hundred strong, from every hamlet, with a Crucifix at their head —kneeling at every wayside shrine to pray for mercy. In September—on the occasion of the annual festival of the *Madonna della Cintola*—it was Prato's turn, and here a large company assembled. "So that God may grant us this grace"— this time the account is given by Domenico di Cambio, who went with them—"we closed the shops for nine days, and all the city and territory went in procession." Francesco joined this pilgrim-

age, too, "with some of the men from his firm . . . thirty thousand in all, both men and women. And those who walked in
procession round the town were forty thousand; but they went
back to their homes for dinner."

The good Domenico boasted that, of all the companies of the
Bianchi, it was the one from Prato which had been the most
successful as peace-makers and which had received, in return, the
greatest number of gifts:

> They bore a most devout Crucifix before them; and it is
> said that they brought about so many reconciliations that the
> gifts given to them—a sword from one man, and a knife or a
> shoe from another—were so many, that the two mules could
> not carry them. And the Crucifix healed the lame and gave
> sight to the blind, and showed many miracles, and those who
> received this grace, gave in gift a gown or a cloak or towels
> or napkins—so many that eight men could barely carry them
> on four stretchers. . . . May God make all this profitable,
> and remove the plague from us! *

In September the *Bianchi*—ten thousand strong—set out from
Orvieto to Rome; they were joined by other companies, until at
the opening of the Jubilee of 1400—according to an eye-witness,
Giovanni Sercambi of Lucca—the Holy City contained as many
as 120,000 pilgrims. And the tale was told—again reported by
the credulous Domenico—that though at first the Pope had meant
to close the doors of Rome to them, "God sent certain signals
and the Pope took fright, and dressed himself in white with all
the Cardinals—and they, too, walked in procession."

Throughout Advent Fra Giovanni was preaching in Florence,
and men said that never had his sermons been so eloquent. "He
speaks in such a fashion of the Holy Nativity," wrote Ser Lapo,
"that he draws the living soul out of your body, and all men
follow him." * He preached again during the following Lent,
and Margherita, who had gone to Florence for the Lenten ser-

mons a few days ahead of her husband, wrote to beg him not to delay his coming.

> You will do well [she wrote] to hasten as much as you can, for never has this friar preached finer sermons than now; you may scoff at any others. It weighs heavily upon me, that you should have missed these few days, for God wot when there will be another like unto him.*

It was the words of this preacher, coming at a moment when his heart was already open to receive them, that at last brought Francesco to take a decisive step. For several years his conscience —sharpened by Ser Lapo's constant reminders—had been urging him to leave his whole fortune to the poor, and, indeed, his intention was already known by his friends, but he had never been able to decide on the best manner of carrying it out. Some years before, he had asked the advice of a monk of the Vallombrosan order, the Prior of the Abbey of San Fabiano, who proffered two suggestions. The first was that Francesco should buy some land and a monastery on a hill called *la Sacca* near Prato, endow it, and give it to any religious order he liked— provided it was not a feminine one. "For above all, according to my mind, do not ever make a congregation of females; methinks it is not a good devotion."

The second suggestion—which Francesco apparently accepted, since he caused the Prior to draw up the draft of a will incorporating it—was that he should leave the bulk of his fortune to be administered by the clergy of Prato, who would "secretly seek out, by means of monks and priests of good reputation, and of men of good conscience, any poverty that there may be" and use Francesco's legacy "to marry girls, succour the sick, or in other works of mercy."

But this plan was not one which Mazzei approved. The indignation which it aroused in him reveals very plainly the attitude of many devout but anti-clerical laymen.

Lo! [Ser Lapo wrote in a long, indignant letter] here is a man who possesses such a treasure that it might be a flame and a living stream to bear him up to eternal life! A man to whom God has lent time for more than thirty years, wherein to order the manner of his death and the bestowal of his fortune—and now he finds himself with a Will in which his heir is the holy Bishop of Pistoia!

The adjective is, of course, ironic—and must be understood in the light of the long and painful history, during the latter centuries of the Middle Ages, of the Church's mismanagement and rapacity. "Ravenous wolves in shepherd's clothing" [8]—that had been Dante's view of the spiritual pastors of his time, and certainly the last hundred years had brought nothing to alter men's opinions. Over and over again, large fortunes left to the poor by pious or guilt-ridden testators had been stolen by unscrupulous administrators, squandered in paying off an improvident bishop's debts, or had dwindled away out of sheer mismanagement. Moreover, in Prato in particular, men had reason to remember a long dispute between the Bishop of Pistoia and the Commune over the management of two charitable institutions, the *Ospedale della Misericordia* and the *Ospedale del Dolce*, "with great scandal to the people." All this Francesco knew as well as Ser Lapo, but for another two years he let his will stand—and then Mazzei protested again. "Oft have I had it in mind to say to you, if you add not some words to the Will you have made, the Bishop of Pistoia is like to get your whole fortune—and will squander it to free himself from debt, and in horses and banquets. . . ."

He suggested that Francesco should add a codicil to his will, stating that the poor people to whom he bequeathed his fortune should be nominated by the Commune of Prato or its consuls, or such men in Prato or Florence as he would appoint. . . . "Now consider this; the thought should please you. And make no mock

[8] *"In veste di pastor lupi rapaci"*—*Paradiso*, XXVIII, 55.

of the faith and the love your friends feel for you; and I am one of them, though of little use." *

It was not, however, until Francesco came under Padre Dominici's influence that he at last made up his mind. On Mazzei's advice, he went to talk to the friar one evening in the Lent of 1400 after his sermon. "And with God's grace," Mazzei wrote, "you will carry out his will in deeds, wholly or in part—and will then live at ease, whatsoever blows or storms may come. For then your roots will be in a good soil—noble tree as you are." *

What Fra Giovanni's counsels were, it is easy to surmise. Like many members of the Mendicant orders, he had no undue love for the high clergy, and, moreover, he showed a dry scepticism as to the disinterestedness of the motives of any man, whether clerk or layman. To a lady of his flock who was about to draw up her will he gave the following advice:

> If devotion should incline you to use these possessions for God's glory and Christ's poor, bethink you well as to who shall be the executor of these bequests—since well we know that money is much loved by both great and small, clerks and laymen, rich and poor, monks and prelates, for *pecuniæ obediant omnia.* . . . With such bequests the rich feed themselves, please their friends, clothe their servants and marry off their maids or bastards.[9]

With such warnings ringing in his ears, Francesco must have been glad to have Ser Lapo at hand, to make use of every precaution devised by the law. And indeed the new will which the notary drew up for him in the summer of 1400, with the plague at the door, was extremely explicit. It made clear (as was stated even more explicitly in another later will drawn up just before Francesco's death) that the administration of his fortune was to be left, not in the hands of the Church, but in those of his executors and some other friends appointed by him, and that the

[9] Beato Giovanni Dominici, op. cit., p. 128.

foundation was to be "in no respect under the authority of the Church or of officials or prelates or any other member of the clergy." Moreover, the document specified that "no altar or oratory or chapel" should ever be set up within the walls of the house, "by means of which the *Casa del Ceppo* might be considered a place belonging to the clergy [*luogo ecclesiastico*] and evilly disposed men might come in and occupy it, saying it was a benefice; all of which is against the testator's intentions." To this foundation he left not only the income from all his possessions and business enterprises, but also his own house, "for the love of God, so as to give back to His Poor what has been received from Him, as His gracious gift." [1]

It is hardly possible to express one's intentions more plainly, and Ser Lapo Mazzei, after all his efforts to bring his friend to this point, must have been well content. How seriously he took his own duties, as well as Francesco's, is shown in the letter he wrote to his friend on the day before the will was signed.

> Pray go tomorrow morn to hear Mass with devotion and to commend yourself to Him, who has no other intent but His boundless goodness, that He may strengthen you to devote your heart and fortune to His glory after your death, and in such a manner that God's Poor, whom you have had so much in mind, may have the greatest benefit and comfort, and that all your care and toil may not have been in vain. . . . I have already offered up this prayer; and tomorrow, by God's grace, will do my part, since you have chosen me to help you. And you, trust in God without fear. Tears keep me from writing more: God sees them! *

So Francesco at last set his conscience at rest—and not too soon, for already the plague was raging through the city. Everyone who had the means to leave, and somewhere to go, was running

---

[1] The wording is that of Francesco's later will, drawn up shortly before his death, which in these respects was the same as the earlier one. Mazzei, II, p. 290.

away; and Francesco—no less provident in this than in all his other worldly affairs—had already sent one of his factors ahead to secure a house in Bologna. On June 27, 1400—the very day on which he signed his will—he set himself and Margherita on their sure-footed mules, and Ginevra and one of the servants' children in paniers on another mule, and thus—followed by his *fattori* Stoldo di Lorenzo and Guido di Sandro, by several servants, and by his doctor's son, Bandino Banduccio—he rode away from Florence across the Apennines.

CHAPTER NINE

THE LAST YEARS

*"E l'unta quercia del suo banco in Ceppo
Ritornò, per i Poveri di Cristo."* [1]
—D' Annunzio, *Le Città del Silenzio*

WHEN Francesco di Marco fled from the plague to Bologna he was already a man of sixty-five. He had ten more years to live, but the time of his greatest activity was over.

His fourteen months in Bologna were not happy. He had taken a house of his own, at a rent of 200 *lire di bolognini*, and he seems to have lived in considerable comfort: he sent for his own oil and wine from Il Palco and Filetto, and distributed some of it to his friends; he gave them some excellent dinners.* He already possessed some old friends in Bologna, and he made some more, mostly belonging to a group of Florentine Guelphs exiled from their own city who were now plotting their return with their friends at home. But none of these was a close friend, like Ser Lapo, and Francesco was not the great man in Bologna that he had been in Prato and Florence.

Moreover, the news that followed him was all bad. His escape

---

[1] "He turned his polished counter back again
Into a hollow log, for Christ's own Poor."

370

from Tuscany had barely been in time: hardly had he left when Prato, Pistoia, Lucca, and Florence were all stricken at once; and to fly to the country became useless, for the Black Death was raging there, too. "No man is left," wrote a chronicler of Pistoia, "in the castles and farms; people fall down dead upon their feet; some die in one day, and some in two. Houses and shops are barred; only the dead and the sick remain, but find none to help them." [2]

"Yesterday," wrote Mazzei on July 6, "201 people died, without hospitals, priests, monks or monasteries, and even without grave-diggers." He added that a group of Florentines of all classes, "a fine and devout company," had founded an association to meet each day at the Loggia del Bigallo, and go from house to house, bearing food and comfort to the stricken. "If you are disposed to send them help," Ser Lapo added, "I will encourage you." *

Francesco sent a hundred florins, and also gave orders to Niccolò dell'Ammannato—who, in spite of all his earlier fears, had remained behind—to distribute white wine to the sick. It went very quickly.

> Your white wine has come to an end [wrote Niccolò in August], for many sick people sent for it, and it was refused to none. I sell it drop by drop, and two barrels of red wine are still full, and there is one that has been begun; and every sick man who asks for it, receives some, and thus we shall continue, as long as a drop is left.*

On July 11 another penitential procession of the *Bianchi* marched through Pistoia, bearing holy relics and crying out for mercy. But the next day, according to a local chronicler, "was worse than ever. Christ help us." In Florence, according to one account, a third of the population succumbed; in Pistoia, half; in Lucca, more than 150 persons a day. One after another, Datini's friends were carried off: in Prato, both his partners in the wool

[2] Ser Luca Dominici, *Cronaca* (1399–1400), p. 232.

371

trade—Niccolò di Piero and Francesco Bellandi—and also his notary, Ser Schiatta di Michele, whose death involved him in several tedious law-suits; in Pisa, Falduccio di Lombardo and Manno d'Albizzo; in Genoa, Andrea di Bonanno; while in Florence his trusted *fattore*, Barzalone, was also on the point of death. "His wife," Ser Lapo wrote, "who is very ill herself, is looking after him . . . and that is sweet, in death as in life. When I left him he was weeping, and for a long time my own eyes were not dry." Francesco's banking-partner, too, Bartolomeo Cambioni, who had followed him to Bologna to escape from the plague, was overtaken by the disease there, and died in a few days, leaving his children in Francesco's charge.*

Mazzei's descriptions of the desolation of Florence are as vivid and as grim as any page in the *Decameron*. "The shops scarce open their doors; the judges have left their bench; the Priors' Palace is empty; no man is seen in the courts. The dead are not mourned, and the only comfort is by the Cross."

Moreover, the disease had already spread over the rest of Tuscany and beyond. "They say here that Arezzo and Volterra, Colle, San Gimignano, Bologna, Venice, Genoa, and every other city both near and far are smitten by the scourge." So far, Ser Lapo added, his own family had escaped. "But every day I await a great chastisement from God."

It came very swiftly.

> I have seen two of my children [he wrote] (the oldest and the middle one) die in my arms, in a few hours. God knows how great my hopes were for the eldest, who was already my companion, and a father, with me, to the others. And how well he had got on in Ardingo's firm! . . . and God knows that, for many years, he never failed to say his daily prayers, at morn and even on his knees in his room, so that often I pitied him, in the cold or heat. And God knows, and saw, his demeanour when he died: what counsels he gave, and how he said he was called to judgement, and was

372

ready to obey. . . . And in the same hour Antonia was sick to death, and in the same bed with her the second boy, who died beside her. Imagine how my heart broke, as I heard the little ones weeping, and their mother not strong, and hearkened to the words of the eldest. Think of it; three dead! . . .

Francesco, take courage and trust in God and fear not; for if you put your hopes in Him, he will not fail you. Comfort your wife and she you; and loosen your spirit a little from these worldly possessions, and hold to God, and rest against His pillar, and you will be comforted. . . .

By God, write not to Prato to collect money from your debtors. I was grieved, for your honour's sake, when I heard of it a few days ago. There is a time to chastise, and one to forgive.

Commend me to Monna Margherita. I commend my family to you, if I, too, must leave this mockery of life; for indeed it is a mockery, and there is little diversity between life and death. Christ aid you, and turn His intentions to our good.*

Ser Lapo had other disquieting news, besides. The Florentine Priors were attempting to refill the city's empty coffers with a series of new loans—which fell, as was to be expected, most heavily upon the absent. But what disquieted Francesco most was a report that he was now in ill-odour with the government at home. In an irascible moment he had exclaimed that he intended to stay on in Bologna for at least a year, in case the plague flared up again, for he felt sure that God's wrath would again chastise "the most evil folk in the world—that is, the folk of Florence, Prato, Pistoia, and Pisa!" This unfortunate remark had been promptly repeated to the Florentine *Signori*. Not only did it not increase Francesco's popularity, but it confirmed the suspicion that he had a share in a plot which some of the exiled Florentines in Bologna had been fomenting from a distance, in the hope of getting home again.*

But, indeed, Francesco's prudence kept him from taking part in such matters; in Bologna, as in Florence, he kept strictly aloof from politics, and he even, for this reason, refused to use his influence in favour of Fra Giovanni Dominici, whose sermons were still bringing comfort to the plague-stricken Florentines. "He has converted," wrote Niccolò dell'Ammannato, "so many men and women in Florence that no evil deed has been done here for a long time and all, both men and women, live in good will and talk with each other in peace." * Fra Giovanni now wished to give another course of sermons in Bologna, but—since his subversive opinions had closed the doors of many churches to him—he wrote first to ask for the permission of the Prior of the Dominican Convent there, and besought Francesco, too, to support his request. But this the merchant was afraid to do. "It is needful," he wrote, "for me to beware of doing or saying anything that could expose me to calumny." So Fra Giovanni continued to preach in Florence, with the plague raging round him, and Francesco salved his conscience by sending him a butt of his best wine and as much oil, bread, and money as he required. "Of these things I shall let you have no lack. . . . And I beseech you, pray God for me, for Our Lord will hearken to you and not to me, who am a thief and an ungrateful traitor. And therefore I beseech you, be my advocate." *

For a while Francesco, uncertain of the welcome he would receive if he went back to Florence, played with the idea of moving to Venice: but now Ser Lapo took alarm, and implored him to come home instead. "For a Florentine you were, in your mother's womb." It was not true, he wrote, that the Florentine Priors were suspicious of Francesco—or if indeed they were, the best way to change their minds would be to come home again and promise to leave his whole fortune to the poor of Florence. "And as, until now, you have been honoured by every citizen, so you may hope to be again." *

At last Francesco made up his mind to go back, but the journey was a further obstacle, owing to the perils of the roads. First Ser Lapo suggested that he should use the simple stratagem of pretending to travel by one route and then taking another—the one, for instance, by Barberino di Mugello, "which is little travelled—and tell not even your wife of your intention." Then he proposed that Francesco should ride with some Florentine envoys who had just gone to Bologna, or with ambassadors returning from Bologna to Florence. But in the end it was settled that Francesco should take the main road across the Futa Pass, being met at Pianoro (nine miles from Bologna) by ten Florentine foot-soldiers, with a safe-conduct from the *Signoria*. And so, in September 1401, Francesco and all his family returned to Tuscany.

Most of the last nine years of Datini's life were spent at home in Prato, and Monna Margherita, at last, was almost always with him, so that few letters were exchanged between them. These few show that Margherita persevered in imploring her husband to take warning from the lessons of the plague, to throw off his business worries and his irascibility over trifles, and to turn to thoughts of God. "We have heard that the nag is dead," she wrote, a few days after their return to Tuscany, "and I care little about it, save that you are troubled. For methinks you and I have cause enough to offer praise to God, that He let us all come home in safety. . . . God has granted me so great a boon, I know not how to complain about a nag."

She implored her husband, too, to spend these last years peacefully in Prato—beside her, in his own house. All was in order, she wrote, "and you can live here in a way that will rejoice you." Surely the time had come at last for him to settle down in peace —and to desist from his eternal grumbling!

I bear quietly the misadventures that occur every day, and they cause me little vexation, save for what they give to you. . . . Let me remind you: to my mind, only two things are needful: the first, to do what is pleasing to God, and the second, to spend the little time that is left you so that you

375

may give back to God what He, in His goodness, has lent you.*

Ser Lapo had much to say in the same vein. "I only pray you," he wrote, "in the name of all our love and friendship, to be joyful, come what may, and then you will know God better."

In another letter he implored Francesco to do one thing for his sake—to rise a little earlier every morning and go to Mass— "and, having heard it, stay long enough to say five *Our Fathers*, without moving your lips; but in your heart, call upon God to help you. . . . And you will be home again by the hour whereat the others set forth—and then you can write as much as you please!" And at the end of the letter he added: "I fear me you remember not, save when I bring it to your mind, how the past years have flown by as a breath of wind, and even so will the few years that are yet to come, both for you and for me." *

Once such remarks would have fallen on deaf ears, but now the death of so many of his friends had shaken Francesco; he began to wonder whether perhaps his wife and friend were right. His letters at this time to one of his partners in Spain—Cristofano di Bartolo—whom he wished to persuade to come home, seem almost an echo of the advice he himself had received.

> You take no account of time [he wrote] and remember not that you must die. . . . You count on your fingers and say: "In so much time I shall have made so much, and shall have so much time left, and when I am rich indeed, I shall go back to Florence and take a wife." . . . But you remember not our five men, who died in this same year: Falduccio and Manno, Niccolò di Piero, Andrea di Bonanno, Bartolomeo Cambioni and a hundred others. . . . I do otherwise: I give more thought to how matters will go after my death, than to those of this world.

It was more than two years, he wrote, since Cristofano had decided to come home, but now he went on delaying. "Methinks you have found some good flesh that pleases you, and love drives you so hard, you have forgotten death." Cristofano, he said, might come to any of the branches in Italy that he chose—"Genoa, which becomes more pleasant to live in every day . . . or Pisa which you know well, and I well like . . . or Florence, which is a fine and great city. And in these three cities one can make more money than any wandering traveller: for you know these cities are renowned throughout the world." For his own part, he added, he had decided to withdraw all his money from Spain and to bring it home.

> God's Poor will be more certain of getting what is theirs, if it be in Genoa or Pisa, than in Catalonia. . . . I must do only two more things in this sad world: set my matters in order with all men, that all things are clear between us, as they should be—and then die, and in the time I am still alive, do a little good.*

In the end these good intentions, like so many others in the past, came to nothing. Cristofano did not come home, and Francesco did not withdraw from his Spanish companies. On the contrary, four years later Ser Lapo was congratulating him on the safe arrival in Venice of two of his ships from Catalonia, "which have brought ashore twenty thousand florins." He did not perhaps spend quite such long hours at his desk, and sometimes, as his doctors required, he allowed himself an hour's exercise and a little more sleep: he took the waters of Porretta for his gravel. But his restless activity still had to find some vent: he set to building again—not chapels or monasteries, as Ser Lapo would have wished, but houses for his labourers. And, above all, he took an ever increasing pleasure in entertaining guests in his fine house in Prato. "You were always desirous of paying honour to great lords," one of his friends had said many years before, and this taste, apparently, only grew on him with advancing years.

> Pray see [he wrote to the son of his notary] if you have a book which Ser Schiatta possessed, wherein were written

377

many letter-headings to the highest temporal and spiritual lords, such as Emperors, Popes, Cardinals, Ambassadors and so forth. . . . And Abbesses and Nuns, down to advocates, doctors and any other noble citizen who holds office.

This book he required, he wrote, "so that when I must address a letter to one of these, I may not have to take thought." * His correspondents included, in addition to Fra Giovanni Dominici and the Blessed Chiara Gambacorti, several cardinals—in particular His Eminence of Bologna, Baldassarre Cossa, who later became Pope John XXIII—and Venetian and Genoese patricians such as Polo Giuntini, Simone Doria, and the Contarini—and the list of his guests is equally impressive. In the past he had entertained Francesco Gonzaga, the Seigneur of Mantua, Matteo d'Humières, Charles VI's ambassador to Florence, and Leonardo Dandolo, the Doge's son, and now in 1409 he received Cardinal d'Ailly, who came for the christening of Ginevra's first child. When Florentine ambassadors were sent to Bologna or Venice, it was in Francesco's house that they halted on the way; whenever, twice a year, a new *Podestà* was sent to Prato, it was in *casa Datini* that he dined; and it was Francesco who offered hospitality to any distinguished guest who came to gaze upon the precious relic in the Cathedral, the Virgin's girdle. But what preparations each of these visits entailed, what fussing and fuming! At such a time Ser Lapo refrained from setting foot in the house, "for when you have guests, I well know what a turmoil you are in." *

If by any chance Francesco was away—as occurred at the time of the visit of Messer Filippo Corsini, on his way to Genoa as an envoy of the Republic—full instructions were sent to Margherita. She was to prepare the double-bedded room on the ground floor and to light a fire and drape the bench with fine stuffs, and put the whole house in order. And she was to buy a box of comfits—half of sugar-coated *confetti* and half of *pinocchiato*. Moreover, the next day Francesco sent to her, to help her preparations, a mule laden with sweets, ten herrings, and two big saucepans. "And you must give thanks to Messer Filippo Corsini for the help and good advice he gave me in my case, and tell him he may dispose of me and all I have, according to his pleasure."

A little later on it was Guido del Palagio, one of the *gonfalonieri* of Florence, who came to stay. "I know not who will come with him, so I cannot tell you," wrote Francesco to Margherita, but added that she must hasten to make up the best bed, and another for the servants in the warehouse, and clean the loggia, and send for two extra servants, and have ready "three or four pairs of good capons." *

When a foreign guest was expected, even more elaborate preparations were required. They are fully described in some letters about the visit of Matteo d'Humières, Charles VI's ambassador to Florence, who was sent to Francesco by his agent in Venice, Zanobi di Taddeo Gaddi. This distinguished guest was coming to Prato to see the city's treasure, the *Madonna della Cintola*, and for this purpose he required a special permit from the *Signoria* of Florence. The whole house was set upside down to prepare for him—and Francesco sent a message to Zanobi that the guest could not possibly come at a single day's notice.

"Say to him, Zanobi: 'Francesco wishes to do honour to this man, for his sake and for yours, but Prato is not a *castello* wherein what is needful can be procured so speedily!' And then tell me how long the Ambassador will stay, that I may do him honour. . . ."

A later letter describes the complete spring-cleaning which then took place:

> I must clear out the whole loggia, which is full of wood and tables from the warehouse and barrels and benches and scrap iron and barley and wheat and gorse and millet. And furthermore I must order all the papers that lie on the tables in the rooms, and I would order them in such a fashion that, when I need a paper, I need not scrabble through them all.

... And furthermore the plates and bowls have been scalded, which will be needed for the table: and I must have bread baked, and cannot do it ere Monday; and I must buy some red and white wine. . . . And this is not a place where you can say: "Go to the market, and find all you need!" for there is a scarcity of all. . . .*

Small wonder that Margherita's quick temper would sometimes flare up, and she would tell her husband that he was turning her into an inn-keeper's wife! Moreover, she also resented his instructions to make herself agreeable to the wives of his new grand friends. "You have so bound me to this *Podestà's* wife," she wrote, "she will never take a step out of her *palazzo*, save I go with her. And you well know how I feel touching that matter!" *

We may suspect, however, that Margherita, too, derived some satisfaction from the presence of the most distinguished guest of all, who stayed with Francesco in the last year of the merchant's life: Louis II of Anjou, who styled himself "King of Sicily and Jerusalem, Prince of Capua, and Duke of Apulia." This prince based these claims on the fact that his father, Louis I, the brother of Charles Quint, had been adopted by Joanna, Queen of Naples, who, being childless, intended to make him her heir. But Charles of Durazzo, the rightful heir, gathered an army together, entered Naples, took the Queen prisoner, and put her to death, while Louis—in spite of being recognized by Clement VII and solemnly crowned in Avignon—failed in every attempt to avenge her and to regain his kingdom. His son's fate was scarcely more fortunate. A first attempt to land in Naples, in 1390, had ended in failure, and now he was hoping for the somewhat precarious support of Pope Alexander V, who, having just been elected Pope at the recent Council of Pisa, had recognized his rights in return for a promise of military aid. The meeting between the two men—each counting on the other to support his claims—was to take place in Prato, and Louis, who declared he also wished to take this opportunity of venerating the Virgin's girdle, was to be Francesco's guest. This was an honour indeed. Francesco promptly turned out of his own house, leaving it, with his good food and wine, entirely at his royal guest's disposal —but deplored that he was not able to do him still greater honour. His agitation was so great as to exasperate all his friends. "Were I to be beheaded for it," wrote Luca del Sera, "I must speak my mind. I see Louis demeans himself as is his wont, and has caused you to make ready twice for him and then wrote not even a word, but sent a message. . . . I tell you, all this smacks of naught but simony and tyranny! . . . You stand in no need either of him or of the Cardinal—even if the one were Pope [3] and the other Emperor." *

Ser Lapo, too, in a gentler tone, rebuked his friend's love of ostentation.

> We hear you are vexed, deeming you did not all you might for so great a lord, but this I beseech you to banish from your mind. I trow he thinks the better of you, and deems you a more solid and wiser man, than had he seen you do too much, as light men do. Remember the 30 florins spent on his dinner, and the 500 lent him! And he showed you his mind, in his sweet and friendly leave-taking.*

Louis proceeded to Rome at the head of Pope Alexander's troops and succeeded in turning out the Neapolitan soldiers who, on behalf of the other claimant to the throne of Naples, young King Ladislaus, already occupied the papal city. He then returned to Provence to gather reinforcements before proceeding to Naples, but in the following spring he was back in Pisa again —this time with the approval of the new Pope, John XXIII— and Francesco, in spite of his age and infirmities, proposed to go and do him homage there. But now Luca del Sera protested again.

[3] Luca, as an old-fashioned Guelph, did not recognize the claims of either Pope Alexander or Louis of Anjou.

You said you would live in peace and eschew worldly fame, as befits your great age, and pay honour only to those who come to your own house. But I now see, either because of worldly vanity or some other men's counsels, you have changed your intent and would go to Pisa to see the King. . . . I could tell you of the backbiting and harm this may bring upon you—but you are assured that, since God has protected you until now, he will do so for ever!

He advised Francesco to send his son-in-law, Lionardo, to Pisa in his stead, to make his excuses and take the King a present of "comfits, wax and malmsey," and, above all, he warned him that if this friendship continued, "it will not be without great cost. For in the end, howsoever rich he may be, he will ever need money, and you will be besought for it—and then, if you will not render him the service, you will lose his favour, and if you render it, you will come to harm." *

Thus Luca, summing up the perpetual dilemma of merchants who put their trust in princes, and apparently Francesco thought over the advice, for, after all, he did not go to Pisa. But a few days later he was again entertaining Louis in Prato. This time the King stayed no less than eighteen days, and was joined by the great Hungarian condottiero *"Pippo Spano,"* [4] with a great following of lords, barons, and other notabilities. In the course of this visit Louis bought 12 rods of scarlet cloth of Prato—and, before leaving, he presented Francesco with the gift which, of all others, was most likely to delight him: a royal charter granting him, in return for his hospitality, the right to add to his arms the royal lily of France, "gold, on an azure ground." [5] But not, it

[4] Of Tuscan origin, his real name was Filippo Scolari (*ispàn* = count). He fought in the service of King Sigismund of Luxemburg and had been sent to Italy to treat with the new Pope.

[5] The charter specified that it was granted to the King's "dear and devoted friend, Francesco di Marco, for the generosity which on various occasions he has bestowed on us, receiving us in his house in all love and honour . . . that he and his descendants may feel they have received, to their perpetual honour and glory, an especial and illustrious token of our Royal gratitude." Mazzei, *Proemio*, pp. cxxviii–cxxix.

would appear, without a return. "According to Andrea de'Pazzi," wrote Luca del Sera indignantly, "the King bestowed on you the lilies in your arms, but it has cost you, beside the money you spent on him, a loan of 1,000 florins. God knows how this grieves me, if it be true." *

This was Francesco's last worldly satisfaction. On July 22 Louis of Anjou rode away from Prato; on the 31st Francesco— who for a long time had been troubled with gravel and kidney trouble—was so ill that he called Ser Lapo to his bedside, and— in the presence of two notaries, five Francescan friars, and two of his *fattori*—drew up the final version of his will. His death came a fortnight later, on August 16, 1410.

Popular sayings with regard to death abound in the literature of the *trecento*. One was "*Chi più ha, più lassa, e con maggior dolore passa.*" [6] Another:

> *Lascia quel che non puoi portare,*
> *Porta quel che non puoi lasciare.*[7]

To these Ser Lapo, in writing to Francesco, added his own comment: "This whole life of ours is but a race towards death." Unceasingly, during the last two years of Francesco's life, he reminded him that his days were now numbered, and that it would indeed be shameful, "since God has granted us so much time," to leave the completion of his will until the last hour, "with all the doctors around you." "Your writing," he relentlessly pointed out, "clearly shows that the tree has begun to fall; the boughs are already shaking, and it is vain to prop it up. Let us plant it now in a soil wherein it will never perish." *

Fra Giovanni, too, sent similar counsels. "Pray take thought for your soul, as you do for your body—and make haste to set

[6] "The man who has most, leaves most behind, and his passage is fraught with the greatest grief."

[7] "Leave what you cannot take [riches],
Take what you cannot leave" [sins].

all your worldly affairs in order, that you may give the whole of this short time to God entirely." *

Yet still Francesco—though he knew he had already passed far beyond what was then considered the normal human span—did not really believe that the end was near. "He thinks," wrote Ser Lapo, "he has had a warrant of long life from God." Most men, before their last hour has come, have already shaken off some of the dust of their worldly cares. But Francesco, even on his deathbed, could not take in that his masterful will was now powerless: he resigned himself to death as little as he had to life. "Of his death," wrote Ser Lapo to Cristofano di Bartolo in Spain, "I will tell you little, for it would take a whole quire: his sufferings and his sayings, and his passing, which was in my arms. For it seemed to him very strange that he should have to die, and that his prayers should be of no avail." *

The terms of his final will did not differ greatly from the one he had drawn up ten years before during the Black Death, except that, whereas the first document had left half his property to the Foundling Hospital of Florence, this one gave the whole residue to his own foundation in Prato, to which he gave the name of *"Casa del Ceppo dei poveri di Francesco di Marco."* ⁸

His bequest to the foundation comprised not only his own house, "with the garden and the house opposite, and every room, loggia and adornment . . . for the perpetual use of the Poor of Jesus Christ"—but all his other houses and farms, and (after the payment of a few minor bequests) his share in all his companies, which were to be wound up within five years of his death. As in his previous will, he laid down that the foundation was to be a private one, "and in no way controlled by the Church or by any ecclesiastic." *

⁸ See Part II, chap. IV, p. 241. The administration of the *Casa Pia de'Ceppi* in Prato is now in the hands of a council of five members appointed by the Commune, and of four *buonomini* (one from each quarter of the city), who distribute the income of the foundation to the poor of Prato—in particular to widows, orphans, and poor students—to an amount of about 700,000 *lire* a year.

His executors were four—his wife, Monna Margherita; his partner, Luca del Sera; his son-in-law, Lionardo di Giunta; and his trusted *fattore* in Prato, Barzalone di Spedalieri—and they, together with four *"buonomini"* appointed by the Commune of Prato and their respective descendants, were to administer the foundation. One of the four executors, Barzalone, had followed his master's example in drawing up a will leaving all his possessions to the *Ceppo;* and a similar will had been drawn up by Lapa, the widow of his partner Niccolò di Piero.* Apparently, however, the four men portrayed by Filippo Lippi as kneeling with Francesco at the Virgin's feet, in the panel reproduced in the frontispiece of this book, are not, as would have been customary, his fellow donors, but merely the four *buonomini* (elders) in office in 1453, when the panel was completed and paid for.[9]

The minor legacies are few. To his wife—*sua donna diletta*—his bequest was a small one: 100 gold florins a year, so long as she remained "a widow and chaste," as well as "a suitable house" during her lifetime and the use of a plot of land, "two furnished beds" (i.e., with curtains and bedding) for herself and her maid, any household goods she needed, and both her own and Francesco's clothes, "so that she may give some in charity, for the good of our souls."

To his daughter, Ginevra, he left 1,000 florins—to revert to the *Ceppo* after her death—and dowries for her daughters.

His gifts to churches and monasteries included one of 1,000 florins to the Hospital of S. Maria Nuova of Florence, to build a new Foundling Hospital (which indeed was begun soon after and became the *Spedale degli Innocenti*)[1] and another of 500

---

[9] The relevant documents, from the *Archivio dei Ceppi*, Prato (*Libro di entrate e uscite*, 1452, and *Libro debiti e crediti E*, May 28, 1453), are printed by E. Strutt, *Fra Filippo Lippi*, London, 1901, pp. 180, 189. The panel had been ordered for a tabernacle over the well of the *Ceppo*, and Fra Filippo received 84 florins in payment. The four *buonomini* were Ser Andrea di Giovanni Bertelli, Filippo di Francesco Malassei, Pietro di Messer Guelfo Pugliesi, and Jacopo degli Albizi.

[1] Archivio Spedale degli Innocenti, Florence. "Register of Wills and Donations" (1411–1576), p. 22.

florins to the Monastery of the Romiti of Florence, besides 300 florins for 12 silver lamps in the Cappella del Sacro Cingolo in the Cathedral, "to burn perpetually in honour of Our Lady." In the margin of this paragraph of the will Ser Lapo wrote the single word "*Brunus*"—for his son Bruno was already apprenticed to the goldsmith's trade and later on made the exquisite bronze gates—worthy to be compared with Ghiberti's—of this same chapel. Francesco left a cloak to his confessor, and five *lire* to every church in Prato, for Masses for his soul.

The pleasantest bequests are those to his dependents or servants. They include a house and an income for life to Monna Domenica, the widow of his servant, Saccente, "so that she may lack none of the things without which one cannot live in comfort," and 100 florins as a dowry to each of the daughters of his kinsman Chiarito di Matteo, "a poor and foolish man." He also left 500 florins to Guido di Sandro da Firenzuola, "whom he has brought up almost from childhood," and similar legacies of 500 florins each to his *fattori* in Avignon, Tieri di Benci and Tommaso di Giovanni, as well as a dowry of 500 gold florins to each of the daughters of Luca del Sera.

He freed all his slaves, "in whatever part of the world they may be, restoring to them their original freedom."

He released from their debts to him "Betto, the trumpeter of Prato, a very poor person," and all master masons, carpenters, blacksmiths, and carriers, or other persons who had worked for him. And he requested his executors "to be kind to Francesco's poor friends, who are well known to them."

He left 1,000 gold florins to his executors, to repair any omissions. "For Francesco the testator, being much oppressed by gravel and inflamed urine and also feverish, has assuredly forgotten many things."

Finally, there is a cryptic legacy of 1,500 florins, "about which my executors are well-informed," to be distributed by them after taking counsel "for the good of Francesco's soul" with "doctors of theology and canon law." This bequest must have been intended (as was often the custom) for the restitution of profits made unjustly or by usury, but to which Francesco did not wish to refer more specifically.

Monna Margherita survived him by several years, living mostly in Florence with Ginevra and her husband. The only portrait of her, in the refectory of S. Niccolò in Prato, shows her as a small figure in the robes of a Dominican tertiary in the foreground of a fresco of St. Dominic dining with his monks. She drew up her will in 1423, died soon after in Florence, and was buried in S. Maria Novella.

Ser Lapo, though fifteen years younger than his friend, survived him by only two years. After Francesco's death he asked Cristofano di Bartolo in Barcelona, with whom his son Piero was working, whether he would consider forming a new company in Spain with Piero—but advised him to remain there only a few years longer and then come home. "For verily I deem the man who is neither rich nor poor to have as joyful a life as a rich man, and indeed more joyful. . . ." * This conclusion had been reached by every man who knew Datini well.

Fra Giovanni Dominici gradually toned down his belligerent sermons, made peace with his spiritual masters, and was rewarded, to Ser Lapo's regret, with a Cardinal's hat. His *Regola della cura del governo familiare* remains a book of considerable wisdom and charm—in particular, the passages dealing with the education of children.

All Francesco's other friends, partners, and servants slip back into the obscurity from which only their connection with the rich merchant had drawn them.

In his will Francesco had written that he wished to be buried in San Francesco, the church which he had so generously adorned and endowed. He himself had bought the marble two years before his death, and had ordered the carving from the same Fiesolean stone-mason, Goro, who had done so much work in his house. But Goro died before Francesco, and afterwards the order was handed on to a well-known sculptor, Niccolò

Lamberti. Luca del Sera, who saw to the matter, ordered a slab of the same marble for his own tomb in S. Maria Novella—"for," he wrote, "I should like to lie under a stone similar to that of the man who was fond of me." Francesco's tomb was placed at the foot of the High Altar, and round his recumbent figure the citizens of Prato may still read the worn inscription: "Here lies the body of the prudent and honourable man Francesco di Marco Datini of Prato, citizen and prosperous merchant of Florence, who died on August 16, 1410. May his soul rest in peace."

Francesco had written that his funeral was to be conducted "only with such preparations and adornments as are decent and usual," instructing his executors to pay more heed to his soul's welfare "than to what is mere vanity." The city council, however, when they saw that his end was near, summoned an especial meeting to decide whether or no he was to be granted a funeral at the Commune's expense—and though the majority voted that this should be awarded him, in view of his services to the city, there were twenty members who, prompted by some old grievance or envy, voted against it. "If he rendered some service to Prato," they said, "it was only because he stood to profit by it." In the end, however, the majority won, and a great public funeral took place, which the whole of Prato attended; the church was hung with 52 banners, and over 790 florins were spent in mourning-garments. The council decreed that every year, on the date of Francesco's death, his eulogy should be preached in the Cathedral—a custom which continued for many years—and the administrators of the *Ceppo* set aside the sum of 278 florins to decorate the walls of his house with sixteen frescoes telling the story of his life. We know that the work was carried out—not without much haggling—by six Florentine painters, and was paid by the yard, the area covered being 2,200 square *braccia*.

Singularly few, however, of the works of art commemorating Francesco have survived. The tombstone in San Francesco, on which the passage of many feet has long since worn away his features; Filippo Lippi's portrait, which has become somewhat faded after standing for several centuries in the court of the *Casa del Ceppo;* a forbidding portrait by Allori, painted over a hundred years later for the council room in the Palazzo Pretorio—these alone remain. Of the works painted in his lifetime, mementoes of his piety and pride, the frescoes in San Francesco have all disappeared; the altar-pieces with their *fondi d'oro* and the great Crucifix in the nave of San Francesco have been taken down. Thus the poor painters with whom Datini haggled over every single groat have been avenged.

As to the frescoes on the walls of his house, hardly a trace of them is left. The administrators of the *Ceppo* paid for their execution but not for their restoration. After five and a half centuries of rain and wind, the gilt has fallen off, the colours have faded, the plaster has crumbled. Even the outlines have become so faint that one can barely trace, here and there, the outline of a portly merchant's robe or a beggar's outstretched hand. In a few years even these will have disappeared: the last flakes of plaster will have fallen into the street below.

Yet, even so, Francesco Datini's memory has remained more alive than that of some greater men. The grasping, wilful man who even in his last hours "thought it a very strange thing that he should have to die" has succeeded—by the preservation of his papers and the gift of his fortune—in avoiding total oblivion. Economists and historians remember him with gratitude, and so, to this day, do some of the poor of his native city, to whom what is left of his fortune is distributed every year. Still, on the day of his death, a Mass is said for him, at the city's expense, in the Cathedral of Prato; still, in the Cappella del Sacro Cingolo, his silver lamps burn before the Virgin's shrine; and still the passer-by may read the inscription carved over his doorway: "The *Ceppo* of Francesco di Marco, Merchant of Christ's Poor."

APPENDIX A

NOTE ON TUSCAN MONEY, WEIGHTS,
AND MEASURES

MEDIEVAL coins, weights, and measures are practically untranslatable into modern terms, owing to the extent to which they varied in different times and places. In nearly all countries of medieval western Europe the monetary system was based upon the following ratio, established by Charlemagne—which is still the basis of the English monetary system: £1 = s. 20 = d. 240. £ stands for *libra, lira* (pound), s. for *soldi, sols* (shillings), and d. for *denari, deniers* (pence). But not only were there many states with varying standards, but many states simultaneously used coins of different weights and alloys. The ratio between gold, silver, and the base metal used for the petty *denari* varied according to the fluctuations in value on the market of precious stones, and thus independent systems of credit were built up, based on each coin. One system was attached to the *denaro picciolo* (petty denier), another to the *grosso* (silver groat), and yet another to the gold coin—the florin in Florence or ducat in Venice.

The following information relates only to Florence in Datini's time. For more general information, the reader is referred to the introductory note to R. S. Lopez and I. W. Raymond, *Medieval Trade in the Mediterranean World*, and to R. de Roover, *Money, Banking and Credit in Medieval Bruges*.

The Florentine gold *fiorino*, engraved with the figure of St. John the Baptist and the lily of Florence, was first coined in 1252 and remained in use until the middle of the fifteenth century. Its coinage (and that of the Venetian ducat, soon after) was a great event in international trade, since until then no other coin but the Byzantine *hyperper* had had a stable value and had been internationally accepted. The florin contained 3.53 grammes of fine gold (i.e., about 54 grains, as compared to the first English gold florin, in 1343, which contained 108 grains). Consequently—at the present official valuation of $35.00 an ounce—it was worth nearly $4.00. 1 gold florin = 29 *soldi a fiorino* = 348 *denari a fiorino*.

Money of account in Datini's books

1 *lira a fiorino* = 20 *soldi a fiorino* = 240 *denari a fiorino*; 1 *lira di piccioli* = 20 *soldi di piccioli* = 240 *denari piccioli*. (All these were

imaginary, except the *denari piccioli*, which were real coins, silver pennies.)

Silver coins in use in Datini's time

1 *denaro di piccioli* = ½ of a *soldo* (money of account). 1 *quattrino* = 4 *denari*; 1 *grosso* (silver groat) = about ½₄ of a gold florin. (The English groat, coined in 1351, was worth only a little more than a penny, but with the gradual debasement of the penny it came to be worth fourpence.)

It would be very unwise to make any precise estimate, however, of the purchasing value of these coins. Undoubtedly in Datini's time it was very much greater than today—perhaps as much as twenty or twenty-five times greater. But this figure can only be conjectural, on the basis of salaries and other prices of the time.

It would be equally unwise to hazard generalizations about medieval weights and measures. Even such measures as the *palmo* (hand's breadth) or *braccio* (arm) based on a part of the human body, or the *canna* (rod) based on a familiar object, varied greatly in different times and places, and there is almost no limit to the variety of such containers as the "sack" or "cart." The following weights and measures are, as closely as possible, those in use in Florence in Datini's time.

Cloth Measures

Braccio, arm's length (about ⅔ of an English yard). This measure varied in different cities. In Florence it was 58 cm. = about 23 in.

Canna, ell, rod = 3-4 *braccia* = about 2½ yards.

Palmo, hand's breadth = about ⅛–⅙ of a Florentine *canna*. (Fine silken stuff, silk and gold thread and fringe were sometimes also sold by the ounce.)

Wine Measures

Metadella = ½ of a *fiasco*.
Fiasco = ½₀ of a *barile* (about 4 pints).
Barile = 20 *fiaschi* (about 10 gallons).
Cogno = 10 *barili* (455 litres, about 100 gallons).
Botte = 1 Florentine *cogno*.

Oil Measures

Orcio, oil barrel or jar weighing 85 lbs. and containing 32 *metadelle*.
Metadella = about ½₂ of an *orcio*.

APPENDIX A

Dry Measures

Staio (Florentine) = about 1 Winchester bushel. (The Venetian *staio* was 3 times as much.)

Moggio (Florentine) = 24 bushels.

Land Measures

Staioro, the extent of land required to produce 1 *staio* of wheat.

Weights

Ongia or *oncia* = about 1 ounce.

Carato, carat (for gold, silver, pearls). 144 carats = 1 ounce.

Chiovo, clove (for wool). About 6–7 lbs. = 50–60 cloves = 1 sack.

Libbra, pound. *Libbra grossa* (heavy pound) and *libbra sottile* (light pound). In Venice 100 heavy lbs. = 158 light lbs.

APPENDIX B

(See illustration facing page 104)

1 cloth of silk embossed in velvet, the ground vermilion embossed in green, with flowers in relief, pale blue and white with gold brocade, one branch drawn here . . . [drawing in margin].

1 cloth of silk embossed in velvet, the ground blue embossed in blue, with crimson and white flowers in relief and stems in fine gold brocade, of which there are five in the width of the cloth.

1 cloth of silk embossed in velvet, the ground blue embossed in green, with embroidery of gold crowns, and a fine gold cord drawn across it—drawn here.

1 cloth of silk embossed in velvet, the ground green embossed in vermilion, with fine embroideries of two fine gold crowns, joined by a fine gold cord—drawn here (five also of these).

1 cloth of silk embossed in velvet, the ground scarlet embossed in green and embroidery in fine gold—and four of these to the width.

3 cloths of silk embossed in velvet, the ground scarlet without embroidery, embossed in two greens, of which one is almost yellow and the other partly spotted, partly striped and partly with leaves.

2 cloths of silk embossed in velvet, the ground green and worked like damask, of vermilion silk embossed in green with little embroidered red, blue and white flowers.

1 cloth of figured velvet in scales of four colours—blue, green, white and crimson—as is drawn opposite, with 8 scales to the width.

1 cloth of green embossed silk, embossed in green on a green ground, with embossed stems in crimson and white, and there are many of these stems.

4 cloths of oriental silk, two *braccia* wide . . . two on a green ground, the other [incomprehensible].

8 cloths of striped taffeta, of which 4 on a red ground and 4 on a blue, and the stripes are two finger-breadths wide, with one finger-breadth between each stripe—half of silver and half of silk in four cloths, and in the other four, of gold and silk—and the silk is of several colours, almost like this.

And the cloths of all the above silks and velvets are of 39–40 *braccia*.

393

BIBLIOGRAPHY & SOURCES

I. UNPUBLISHED DOCUMENTS

A. THE ARCHIVIO DATINI

The documents on which this book is based are contained in the Archivio Datini in Prato. All quotations from them are unpublished, except when a published source is stated. They consist of:

(1) Some 150,000 letters, both on private and on business matters. These are classified under the headings of Datini's eight principal branches—in Avignon, Prato, Pisa, Florence, Genoa, Valencia, Barcelona, and Majorca—and contain the letters exchanged not only between these branches, but with every other city where he had correspondents or agents. In addition there are two sections, entitled *Carteggio familiare e privato* (Files Nos. 1086–1109) and *Carteggio privato a diversi* (Nos. 1110–1114), given up to his private correspondence.

(2) Over 500 account-books and ledgers (see part I, chap. v, and part II, chap. vi).

(3) About 300 deeds of partnership. Only a few of these, of course, refer to Datini's own companies, most of them belonging to other companies in some way connected with his.

(4) About 400 insurance policies, or memorandums regarding them, in some of which Datini's companies are the under-writers, in others the insurers.

(5) Several thousand miscellaneous business documents: bills of lading, letters of advice, contracts, bills of exchange, letters of credit, cheques.

The completeness of this collection is due to Datini's strict orders to all his partners and underlings that none of his papers should be destroyed. He began to collect his papers in 1364, but some of those in Avignon must have been lost after his departure from Provence, for the greater part of those which have survived date from 1382 to 1410.

The first man to find the papers, in 1870, was an Archdeacon of Prato, Don Martino Benelli, a man of taste and scholarship, who at once began—with the help of Don Livio Livi—to set them in order. In 1887 the letters from Ser Lapo Mazzei were edited and published by Cesare Guasti, and towards the beginning of this century the papers were rearranged by Professor Giovanni Livi in approximately their present order. His monograph *Dall'Archivio di Francesco Datini, mercante pratese* (1910) contains 20 more unpublished letters by various hands and 7 holographs.

B. THE ARCHIVIO DI STATO IN FLORENCE

(1) *Diplomatico, Ceppo di Prato*. Numerous powers of attorney made out by Datini between 1397 and 1408 to his partners Cristofano di Bartolo, Simone d'Andrea, Luca del Sera in Spain and Majorca, and to Stoldo di Lorenzo in Pisa, as well as several deeds of purchase of land.

(2) *Notarile, A. Cosiminiano.* Further deeds of purchase and sale and powers of attorney, mostly drawn up by Ser Lapo Mazzei, and a codicil to Datini's will, dated September 8, 1406.

(3) *Prestanze* 1999 and 2161.

C. PUBLIC RECORD OFFICE, LONDON

Information about the Italian wool and cloth merchants in London who were Datini's correspondents, and about their exports to Italy, in the Exchequer L.T.R. Customs and Subsidy Accounts, London and Thames Ports to Gravesend and Southampton, Wool Subsidy, and Wool Subsidy and Petty Custom (1382–1410).

II. PUBLISHED

A. DATINI AND HIS TRADE

BENSA, E., *Francesco di Marco da Prato*, Milan, 1928. In the notes this book, after its first mention, is throughout referred to as "Bensa, op. cit."

This is the only full biography, but gives much more prominence to Datini's trading-activities than to his life. The private papers have been little drawn upon, while whole chapters deal with the structure of the companies, transport, insurance, bills of exchange and cheques, and accountancy. The appendix contains a large selection of business documents.

Other monographs by Professor Bensa based on material from these Archives:

Il contratto di assicurazione nel Medio Evo, Genoa, 1884.

Di alcune importanti notizie attinenti alla storia del commercio che emergono dai documenti dell'Archivio Datini, Genoa, 1923.

Le forme primitive della polizza di carico, Genoa, 1925.

"Margherita Datini" in *Archivio Storico Pratese*, May 1926.

Other portraits of Datini appear in:

GUASTI, C., *Lettere di un notaro ad un mercante del secolo XIV*, Florence, 1880 (referred to throughout as "Mazzei"). This contains, as well as Ser Lapo Mazzei's letters to Datini and his wife, numerous other letters from the Archivio Datini, and the full text of Datini's will.

LIVI, G., *Dall'Archivio di Francesco Datini, mercante pratese*, Florence, 1910.

MELIS, F., *"L'Archivio di un mercante e banchiere trecentesco, Francesco di Marco Datini da Prato"* in *Moneta e Credito*, 1954.

SAPORI, A., *"Economia e morale alla fine del trecento"* in *Studi di Storia economica medievale*, Florence, 1940, and "Ser Lapo Mazzei" in *Archivio Storico Pratese*, 1950.

DEL LUNGO, I., *"Francesco di Marco Datini mercante e benefattore"* in *Conferenze fiorentine*, Milan, 1901.

A detailed study of Datini's activities in the cloth trade is given in:

MELIS, F., *"La formazione dei costi nella industria laniera alla fine del trecento"* in *Economia e Storia*, Nos. 1–2, 1954.

Short monographs or articles in periodicals based on material in the Archivio Datini:

BIBLIOGRAPHY & SOURCES

BRUN, R., *"Quelques italiens d'Avignon au XIVème siècle: 1° Les Archives de Datini è Prato, 2° Naddino da Prato, médecin de la cour pontificale"* in *Mélanges d'archéologie et d'histoire,* publiés par l'École française de Rome, 1923.

——, *"Notes sur le commerce florentin à Paris à la fin du XIVème siècle"* in *Cooperazione intellettuale,* VI.

——, *"A Fourteenth-Century Merchant of Italy: Francesco Datini of Prato"* in *Journal of Economic and Business History,* 1930.

——, *"Notes sur le commerce des objets d'art en France et principalement à Avignon à la fin du XIVème siècle"* and *"Notes sur le commerce des armes à Avignon au XIVème siècle"* in *Bibliothèque de l'École des chartes,* 1934 and 1951.

CORSANI, G., *I fondaci e i banchi di un mercante pratese del trecento,* Prato, 1922.

NICASTRO, S., *L'Archivio di Francesco Datini in Prato,* Rocca S. Casciano, 1914. (Incomplete and sometimes inaccurate.)

PIATTOLI, L., *"La legge fiorentina sull'assicurazione nel Medio Evo"* in *Archivio Storico Italiano,* s.VII, 1932.

——, *"L'assicurazione di schiavi imbarcati su navi ed i rischi di morte nel Medio Evo"* in *Rivista del Diritto Commerciale e del Diritto Generale delle obbligazioni,* 1934.

PIATTOLI, R., *"In una casa borghese del secolo XIV"* in *Archivio Storico Pratese,* 1927.

——, *"Gli Agli a Prato e cinque lettere di Agnolo di Lotto"* in *Archivio Storico Pratese,* 1927.

——, *"Codicillo al testamento di Marco Datini"* in *Archivio Storico Pratese,* 1927.

——, *"L'origine dei fondaci datiniani di Pisa e Genova"* in *Archivio Storico Pratese,* 1927–30.

——, *Un mercante del trecento e gli artisti del tempo suo,* Florence, 1930.

——, *"Il problema portuale di Firenze"* in *Rivista storica degli Archivi toscani,* 1930, Fasc. 3.

——, *"Un inventario di oreficeria del trecento"* in *Rivista d'Arte,* January–June 1931.

——, *"Lettere di Piero Benintendi mercante del trecento"* in *Atti della Società Ligure di Storia Patria,* vol. I, 1932.

——, *"Il Pela, Agnolo Gaddi e Giovanni d'Ambrogio alle prese con la giustizia (1392–3)"* in *Rivista d'Arte,* July–September 1932.

——, *"Due lettere inedite di Francesco Datini da Prato a Giovanni Dominici"* in *Memorie Domenicane,* Florence, 1934.

ROOVER, R. DE, *"Appunti sulla storia della cambiale e del contratto di cambio"* in *Studi in onore di Gino Luzzatto,* 1949.

——, *L'évolution de la lettre de change au XIV–XVII siècles,* Paris, 1953.

Professor de Roover also quotes much information from the Archivio Datini and reproduces some letters, cheques, and bills of exchange in *Money, Banking and Credit in Medieval Bruges,* and F. Edler de Roover quotes numerous phrases from these papers in illustration of her *Glossary of Medieval Terms of Business,* Cambridge (Mass.), 1934.

Extracts from letters referring to the slave trade are printed by R. Livi, *La Schiavitù domestica nei tempi di mezzo e nei moderni,* Padua, 1928.

BIBLIOGRAPHY & SOURCES

The deeds of partnership of one of Datini's companies, one of his bills of exchange and orders of payment, some memorandums concerning some insurance policies under-written by his Pisan company, and a letter to him from Piero Benintendi are printed—translated into English—by R. X. Lopez and I. W. Raymond, *Medieval Trade in the Mediterranean World*, London, 1955.

B. HISTORY AND TOPOGRAPHY OF PRATO

CAGGESE, R., *Un Comune libero alle porte di Firenze: Prato*, Florence, 1905.
Consigli del Comune di Prato (1252–85), ed. R. Piattoli, 1940.
"*Dante e Prato*," scritti vari in *Archivio Storico Pratese*, Suppl. I, 1922.
GIANI, G., "*La Fonte Procula*" in *Archivio Storico Pratese*, December 1926.
MINIATI, G., *Narrazione e disegno della terra di Prato*, 1597.
NICASTRO, S., *Sulla Storia di Prato dalle origini alla metà del secolo XIX*, Prato, 1916.
NUTI, R., *La topografia di Prato nel Medio Evo*, Prato, 1937.
REPETTI, *Dizionario geografico-fisico-storico della Toscana*, vol. IV, Florence, 1843–6.

C. THE WOOL TRADE

Statuti dell'Arte della Lana di Prato (secolo XIV–XVIII), ed. R. Piattoli, Florence, 1937.
Statuti dell'Arte della Lana di Firenze (1317–19), ed. A. M. Agnoletti, Florence, 1940.
BISORI, G., *Origini e sviluppo dell'industria laniera pratese*, Florence, 1951.
BRUZZI, E., *L'Arte della Lana in Prato*, Prato, 1920.
CARUS-WILSON, E. M., "The Woollen Industry" in *The Cambridge Economic History of Europe*, vol. II, Cambridge, 1952.
——, *Medieval Merchant Venturers*, London, 1954.
GIANI, G., "*Per la Storia dell'Arte della Lana in Prato*" in *Archivio Storico Pratese*, July 1952.
LUZZATTO, G., "*Lana*" in *Enciclopedia Treccani*, Rome, 1935.
PIATTOLI, R., "*Documenti per la Storia dell'Arte della Lana di Prato*" in *Archivio Storico Pratese*, 1952.
POWER, E., *The Wool Trade in English Medieval History*, London, 1941.
——, "The Wool Trade in the Fifteenth Century" in *Studies in English Trade in the Fifteenth Century*, ed. E. Power and M. M. Postan, London, 1933.
ZANONI, L., *Gli Umiliati nei loro rapporti con l'eresia e l'industria della lana*, Milan, 1911.

D. ITALIAN SOCIAL HISTORY IN THE FOURTEENTH AND FIFTEENTH CENTURIES

I. Contemporary Chronicles, Memoirs, Letters, Sermons, and Novels

ALBERTI, L. B., *Della Famiglia* (the three first books), ed. F. C. Pellegrini, Florence, 1948.
ANONIMO FIORENTINO (Diario di) in *Documenti di Storia Italiana*, ed. by R. Deputazione di Storia Patria per la Provincia Toscana, vol. VI, Florence, 1867.

397

BIBLIOGRAPHY & SOURCES

Boccaccio, Giovanni, *Il Decamerone*, ed. A. Bartoli in *Classici Italiani*, Milan, 1929.

Una curiosa raccolta di segreti e di pratiche superstiziose fatta da un popolano fiorentino del secolo XIV, ed. G. Giannini, Città di Castello, 1898.

Della Casa, Giovanni, *Se s'abbia da prender moglie*, ed. U. Paoli, Florence, 1944.

Dominici, Giovanni [Beato], *Regola del governo di cura familiare*, Florence, 1927.

Dominici, Luca, *Cronaca della venuta dei Bianchi e della Moría (1399-1400)*, published by "Società Pistoiese di Storia Patria," 1933.

Fra Filippo degli Agazzari, *Assempri*, Siena, 1922.

Fra Giordano da Rivalto, "*Prediche inedite*" in *Collezione opere inedite e rare dei primi tre secoli della lingua*, Bologna, 1867.

Fra Jacopo Passavanti, *Lo Specchio della Vera Penitenza*, Florence, 1926.

Francesco da Barberino, *Reggimento e costume di donna*, Bologna, 1875.

Macinghi Strozzi, A., *Lettere ai figlioli*, ed. Guasti, Florence, 1877.

Marchionne di Coppo Stefani, *Cronaca fiorentina*, ed. N. Rodolico, vol. XL, part I, "*Rerum italicarum scriptores*," Città di Castello, 1903.

Morelli, G., "*Cronica (1493)*," appendix to R. Malespini, *Storia fiorentina*, Florence, 1718.

Naddo di Montecatini, "*Cronica (1374-98)*" in *Delizie degli Eruditi Toscani*, vol. XVIII, Florence, 1784.

Odorigo di Credi, "*Ricordanze (1405-25)*" in *Archivio Storico Italiano*, vol. IV, 1916.

Paolo di Messer Pace da Certaldo, *Il libro di buoni costumi*, ed. A. Schiaffini, Florence, 1945.

Pitti, Bonaccorso, *Cronica (1412-29)*, ed. A. Bacchi della Lega, Bologna, 1905.

Sacchetti, Franco, *Novelle*, Florence, 1938.

——, *Sermoni evangelici, lettere varie e scritti inediti*, Florence, 1857.

San Bernardino, *Le Prediche Volgari*, ed. L. Banchi, Siena, 1880.

——, *Le Prediche Volgari* and *Le Prediche Volgari inedite*, ed. P. Dionisio Pacetti, Siena, 1935.

Sercambi, Giovanni, *Le Croniche*, ed. S. Bongi, Rome, 1892.

Velluti, Donato, *La Cronica Domestica (1367-70)*, ed. I. del Lungo and G. Volpi, Florence, 1914.

Villani, Giovanni and Matteo, *Cronaca*, ed. F. Gherardi Dragomanni, Florence, 1864.

II. *Tuscan Social History*

Biagi, G., *Fiorenza, fior che sempre rinnovella*, Florence, 1924.

——, *Men and Manners of Old Florence*, London, 1909.

Cambridge Medieval History, vol. VII, chaps. II and xxv, Cambridge, 1952.

Chiappelli, A., "*Due responsi astrologici dell'anno 1382*" in *Bollettino Storico Pistoiese*, December 1922.

Chiappelli, L., "*La donna pistoiese del buon tempo antico*" in *Bollettino Storico Pistoiese*, 1913.

D'Ancona, P., *Le vesti della donna fiorentina nel secolo XIV*, Perugia, 1905.

Davidsohn, R., *Firenze ai tempi di Dante*, Italian translation, Florence, 1929.

——, *Forschungen zur Geschichte von Florenz*, 4 vols., Berlin, 1896-1908.

FALLETTI FOSSATI, C., *Costumi senesi della seconda metà del secolo XIV*, Siena, 1882.

FRATI, L., *La vita privata a Bologna nel Secolo XIII*, Bologna, 1900.

GUERRINI, O., *La tavola e la cucina nei secoli XIV e XV*, Florence, 1884.

HAUSER, A., *The Social History of Art*, London, 1951.

HEYWOOD, W., *A Study of Medieval Siena* (Fra Filippo degli Agazzari), Siena, 1901.

The Legacy of the Middle Ages, ed. C. G. Crump and E. F. Jacob, Oxford, 1926.

Libro di cucina del secolo XIV, ed. L. Frati, Leghorn, 1899.

LIVI, R., *La schiavitù domestica nei tempi di mezzo e nei moderni*, Padua, 1928.

MAZZI, C., "*La mensa dei Priori di Firenze nel secolo XIV*" in *Archivio Storico Italiano*, serie V, vol. XX, 1897.

——, *La Camicia*, Florence, 1915.

MEISS, M., *Painting in Florence and Siena after the Black Death*, Princeton University Press, 1951.

MORPURGO, G., *57 ricette da un libro di cucina del buon secolo della lingua*, Bologna, 1890.

NICCOLINI DI CAMUGLIANO, G., *The Chronicles of a Florentine Family*, London, 1933.

NOVATI, F., *Freschi e Minii del Dugento*, Milan, 1908.

ORIGO, I., "The Domestic Enemy: Eastern Slaves in Tuscany in the Fourteenth and Fifteenth Centuries" in *Speculum*, vol. XXXIX, July 1955, pp. 321–66.

POLIDORI CALAMANDREI, E., *Le vesti della donna fiorentina nel quattrocento*, Florence, 1924.

RODOLICO, N., *La democrazia fiorentina nel suo tramonto* (1378–82), Bologna, 1905.

——, *Il popolo minuto, note di storia fiorentina* (1343–78), Bologna, 1899.

——, *Storia degli Italiani*, Florence, 1954.

SALVEMINI, G., *Magnati e popolani in Firenze dal 1280 al 1295*, Florence, 1899.

SCHIAPARELLI, A., *La casa fiorentina e i suoi arredi nei secoli XIV e XV*, Florence, 1908.

TAMASSIA, N., *La famiglia italiana nei secoli XV e XVI*, Milan, 1910.

La vita italiana nel Rinascimento (Lectures in Florence given in 1892), Milan, 1906.

ZAMBRINI, F., *Il libro della cucina del secolo XIV*, Bologna, 1863.

ZDEKAUER, L., *La vita privata dei Senesi nel Dugento*, Siena, 1897.

——, *La vita pubblica dei Senesi nel Dugento*, Siena, 1897.

E. MEDITERRANEAN TRADE

Cambridge Economic History of Europe, vol. II, Cambridge, 1952.

CHIAUDANO, M., "*I Rothschild del Dugento: la Gran Tavola di Orlando Bonsignori*" in *Bollettino Senese di Storia Patria*, n.s. VI, 1935.

CIASCA, R., *L'Arte dei Medici e Speziali nella storia e nel commercio fiorentino dal secolo XII al XV*, Florence, 1927.

"*Consigli sulla mercatura di un anonimo trecentista*," ed. G. Corti in *Archivio Storico Italiano*, CX, Disp. I, 1952.

Della decima e delle altre gravezze imposte dal Comune di Firenze, della moneta e della mercatura dei fiorentini fino al secolo XVII, ed. G. F. Pagnini, 4 vols., Lisbon-Lucca, 1765-6 (vol. II contains Pegolotti, vol. IV Giovanni da Uzzano's *La pratica della mercatura*).

DOREN, A., *Storia economica d'Italia nel Medio Evo*, translated by G. Luzzatto, Padua, 1937.

EDLER, F., *Glossary of Medieval Terms of Business*, publ. by The Medieval Academy of America, Cambridge (Mass.), 1934.

FANFANI, A., *Saggi di Storia Economica Italiana*, Milan, 1936.

——, *Un mercante del trecento*, Milan, 1937.

HEYD, W., *Histoire du Commerce du Levant au Moyen Age*, 2 vols., Leipzig, 1885.

LUZZATTO, G., *Storia Economica dell'Età Moderna e Contemporanea*, Padua, 1950.

——, *Storia del Commercio*, Florence, 1915.

——, "*Piccoli e grandi mercanti nelle città d'Italia del Rinascimento*" in *Studi in onore di G. Prato*, Turin, 1930.

PEGOLOTTI, F., *La pratica della mercatura*, ed. A. Evans, publ. by The Medieval Academy of America, Cambridge (Mass.), 1936.

RENOUARD, Y., *Les relations des Papes d'Avignon et des compagnies commerciales et bancaires de 1316 à 1378*, Paris, 1941.

ROOVER, R. DE, *Money, Banking and Credit in Medieval Bruges*, Cambridge (Mass.), 1948.

——, "*Il trattato di Fra Santi Rucellai sul cambio, il monte comune e il monte delle doti*" in *Archivio Storico Italiano*, 1953.

SAPORI, A., *Studi di storia economica medievale*, Florence, 1946. (The various essays in this volume are referred to by their individual titles, followed by "in *Studi*, etc.")

——, *Il mercante italiano nel Medio Evo*, Milan, 1941.

——, *La crisi delle compagnie mercantili dei Bardi e dei Peruzzi*, Florence, 1926.

——, *Una compagnia di Calimala nei primi del trecento*, Florence, 1932.

——, *Mercatores*, Milan, 1941.

NOTES
(DATINI ARCHIVES)

(References to "Mazzei" are to letters from the Datini Archives published in C. Guasti, LETTERE DI UN NOTARO AD UN MERCANTE DEL SECOLO XIV. *All letters quoted are from Mazzei to Francesco, unless another correspondent is mentioned.)*

PART I, CHAPTER 1: *The Years in Avignon*

P. 5 l. 24 File 1117. Monna Piera to Francesco, Aug. 28, 1376, and Aug. 29, 1373.

P. 10 l. 17 File 1093. Maestro Naddino Bovattieri to Francesco, Jan. 21, 1378.

P. 12 l. 13 File 1112. To Stoldo di Lorenzo, Feb. 10, 1378.

P. 12 l. 15 *Memoriale* 52, p. 216, vi.

P. 12 l. 19 File 1112. To Stoldo di Lorenzo, Feb. 12, 1382.

P. 13 l. 13 *Memoriale* 58, p. 78.

P. 13 l. 34 File 1110. *A vari in Valencia,* March 22, 1398.

P. 14 l. 24 File 1115. Francesco to Niccolaio di Bonaccorso, June 4, 1389.

P. 15 l. 17 File 1112. To Stoldo di Lorenzo, Feb. 10, 1378.

P. 16 l. 1 File 1168. Contract between Bonaccorso di Vanni of Prato and Geri di Andrea of Pistoia "in the craft of money-changing and of trading in silver-ware and gold-ware and in jewels and precious stones and all auxiliary things," May 5, 1355.

P. 16 l. 22 File 1112. To Stoldo di Lorenzo, Feb. 12, 1382, and Feb. 5, 1380.

P. 18 l. 2 *Carteggio Avignon-Prato,* May 3, 1384.

P. 18 l. 7 *Carteggio di Firenze,* 1387.

P. 18 l. 10 *Carteggio di Barcelona,* Nov. 15, 1394. Quoted by Brun.

P. 18 l. 26 *Carteggio di Firenze,* Aug. 30, 1396.

P. 19 l. 2 *Mandate e ricevute di balle,* 123, p. 49.

P. 19 l. 25 *Ragione di Avignone, Memoriale* 52, July 10, 1373.

P. 20 l. 14 March 27, 1387. This letter is printed (in English) in Lopez and Raymond: *Medieval Trade in the Mediterranean World,* pp. 114–15.

P. 20 l. 28 Mazzei, Letter CCCXVI (undated).

P. 22 l. 23 File 1117. Francesco to Monna Piera di Pratese, Jan. 21 and March 22, 1372.

P. 22 l. 28 File 1117. Niccolozzo di Ser Naldo to Francesco, Sept. 18, 1372.

P. 23 l. 3 File 1116. *Ricordanze di Avignone* (probably 1373).

P. 23 l. 9 File 1117. Francesco to Monna Piera, March 28, 1373.

P. 23 l. 18 Ibid. Niccolozzo di Ser Naldo to Francesco. Feb. 14, 1374.

P. 24 l. 24 Ibid. Francesco to Monna Piera, Feb. 5, 1375.

P. 24 l. 29 Ibid. Monna Piera to Francesco, Jan. 29, 1376.

P. 25 l. 8 Ibid. Niccolozzo to Francesco, Sept. 20, 1375.

P. 25 l. 26 Ibid. Monna Piera to Francesco; March 6, 1376.

P. 26 l. 10 Ibid. Niccolozzo to Francesco, Aug. 16, 1375, and March 1376.

P. 26 l. 24 Ibid. Francesco to Monna Piera, Aug. 28, 1376.

P. 27 l. 22 File 1110. Francesco to Cristofano di Bartolo, undated but written in 1401 or 1402.

P. 28 l. 17 File 1117. Francesco to Monna Piera, Sept. 7, 1376.

P. 29 l. 7 Ibid. Niccolozzo to Francesco, Nov. 6, 1379, Oct. 12, 1380, and June 20, 1381.

P. 29 l. 25 File 1103. Niccolò dell'Ammannato to Francesco, Dec. 10, 1382, and Feb. 28, 1382.

P. 29 l. 32 File 1112. Francesco to Stoldo di Lorenzo, Oct. 16, 1380.

P. 32 l. 6 File 1112. To Stoldo di Lorenzo, Oct. 11, 1381.

P. 32 l. 15 File 552 Andrea di Maestro Ambrogio in Florence to Aglio degli Agli in Pisa, June 26, 1378. Quoted in Piattoli, "*L'origine dei fondaci datiniani di Pisa e Genova*" in *Arch. St. Pratese*, 1927–30.

P. 32 l. 25 File 1112. To Stoldo di Lorenzo, March 23, 1381.

P. 33 l. 2 Dec. 31, 1382. This deed of partnership is also printed in full in Bensa, op. cit., Doc. III.

P. 33 l. 19 File 1166. *Ricordanze dei fondachi di Firenze e di Prato.*

P. 34 l. 11 File 540. *Carteggio Prato-Pisa.* Monte d'Andrea in Prato to Francesco di Marco in Pisa, Jan. 29, Jan. 31, and Feb. 1384.

PART I, CHAPTER 2: *Prato and the Cloth Trade*

P. 39 l. 20 File 236. List of Francesco's possessions in Prato, April 30, 1407. These *ordi* were fairly large—some being of 4 or 5 *staiora*, and one of as much as 11 *staiora*.

P. 42 l. 19 Mazzei, *Proemio*. This challenge was sent in 1387.

P. 48 l. 10 File 1102. Maestro Lorenzo Sassoli to Francesco.

P. 48 l. 29 Mazzei, *Proemio*, XLIII.

P. 49 l. 8 File 1909. Niccolò di Giunta to Francesco, Oct. 6, 1390.

P. 49 l. 23 Mazzei, *Proemio*, p. xiv.

P. 49 l. 30 File 1182. Unaddressed letter, dated July 7, 1359.

P. 50 l. 9 Mazzei, *Proemio*, XLI.

P. 50 l. 31 File D 705. Dec. 26. 1393.

P. 51 l. 12 Ledger 277; this was the book of the "dyers and tanners."

P. 51 l. 29 File 1101. Piero di Giunta to Francesco, Feb. 11, 1373.

P. 52 l. 3 Ledger 277.

P. 52 l. 26 File 1099. Niccolò di Giunta to Francesco, 1385, June 12 and Aug. 27, 1388, and Feb. 23, 1396.

P. 53 l. 28 File 301. List of wools imported by Francesco di Marco, Aug. 30, 1384.

P. 54 l. 5 File 1099. Niccolò di Giunta to Francesco, April 25, 1385.

P. 54 l. 23 Ibid. Niccolò di Giunta to Simone d'Andrea Bellandi, Nov. 30, 1396.

P. 56 l. 13 File 664. Giovanni Orlandini and Neri Vettori & Co. in London to Francesco di Marco & Co. in Florence, April 15, 1401, and July 2, 1403.

P. 56 l. 24 Ibid. Francesco Tornabuoni & Domenico Caccini & Co. to Francesco di Marco in Florence, May 10, 1404.

P. 56 l. 29 Ibid. Alamanno and Antonio Mannini in London to Francesco di Marco & Co. in Florence, Jan. 4, 1392. A later letter from another firm refers to "the good and fine fair of *Boriforte*" (Burford?) where the wool that year was "very fine and white, better than we had expected." 120 sacks were promptly bought up by "our men [i.e., Florentines] and the rest by the drapers of Bristol and London." The same buyers were going on to a fair at Northleach (*Norleccio*) and at the *"Badia alla Venante"* (?). File 664. Domenico Caccini & Piero Cambrini in London to Francesco di Marco & Co. in Florence, June 21, 1403.

P. 57 l. 7 File 734, p. 359.

P. 57 l. 18 File 257, p. 52.

P. 58 l. 11 File 220. *Memoriale A. Banco di Prato.* Bill for 317 florins 8 *soldi* for one large bale of Essex cloth, March 22, 1402. File 528. Matteo Dini of Bruges from London to Francesco di Marco & Co. in Pisa, Feb. 27, 1397, and File 1059, Alberto degli Alberti in Bruges to Francesco di Marco & Co. in Majorca, May 22, 1396.

P. 59 l. 20 File 664. Alamanno and Francesco in London to Francesco di Marco & Co. in Florence, Aug. 6, 1392.

P. 63 l. 15 Nos. 257, 303, and 306; No. 267, "the workmen's book" (beaters, carders, combers, and warpers); No. 272, "the spinners' book"; No. 276, "the weavers' book"; No. 280, "the book of the dyers, tanners, washers, carders, menders, tenterers, and fullers"; and Nos. 257, 305, and 296.

P. 63 l. 29 File 565, pp. 140, 149, 152.

PART I, CHAPTER 3: *Trade at Home and Abroad*

P. 68 l. 19 File 1112. Francesco to Luca del Sera, 1397.

P. 70 l. 5 File 552. Andrea di Maestro Ambrogio in Florence to his partner Lotto degli Agli in Pisa, Oct. 20, 1378.

P. 71 l. 7 File 1092. Domenico di Cambio to Francesco, Aug. 10, 1391.

P. 71 l. 11 File 1114. Lorenzo di Matteo to Francesco, Jan. 29, 1393.

P. 71 l. 16 File 856. Giovanni Orlandini & Co. in Bruges to Datini's branch in Barcelona, June 17, 1408.

P. 71 l. 21 File 1060. Diamante and Altobianco degli Alberti in Bruges to Datini's branch in Majorca, May 21, 1410.

P. 73 l. 9 File 678. Francesco Tornabuoni & Co. in Bruges to Francesco di Marco & Co. in Florence, May 28, 1404.

P. 73 l. 12 File 854. *Carteggio Bruges-Barcelona*, March 11, 1400.

P. 73 l. 16 File 653. *Carteggio Genova-Firenze* (undated).

P. 74 l. 12 File 853. *Carteggio Bruges-Barcelona*, Oct. 4, 1399.

P. 74 l. 22 *Carteggio Paris-Majorca.* Deo Ambrogi to Cristofano di Bartolo, Aug. 16, 1395. Printed by Livi, *Dall'Archivio di Francesco Datini*, p. 7.

P. 75 l. 23 File 1092. Domenico di Cambio to Francesco, March 21, 1389.

P. 79 l. 21 File 1092. Domenico di Cambio to Francesco, Jan. 22, 1392.

P. 82 l. 13 This document is dated 1383 and is therefore about 60 years earlier than the similar one quoted by Uzzano. A further list quotes the tolls paid by goods on their entry into Florence. File 1174. Published by Piattoli, op. cit., Doc. I.

P. 82 l. 33 Mazzei, Jan. 23, 1406.

P. 83 l. 12 File 1113. Agnolo degli Agli to Francesco, March 14, 1392.

P. 84 l. 22 File 1092. Domenico di Cambio to Francesco, Jan. 7, 1391.

P. 85 l. 17 File 1114. From "Galvano mercante," March 7, 1390. Piattoli, op. cit., Doc. V.

P. 85 l. 29 Ibid., Jan. 23, 1392.

P. 87 l. 12 File 727. *Libro di Mercanzia.* Genova, 1395–1400.

P. 87 l. 22 *Valute in Barzelona a dì 15 settembre 1385.* Bensa, op. cit., Doc.

CXXXV, and File 893. *Carteggio Malaga-Barcelona*, Dec. 17, 1402.

P. 88 l. 20 File 653. *Carteggio Genova-Firenze*, Dec. 11, 1390 and File 714, *Carteggio Venezia-Firenze*, July 28, 1403.

P. 88 l. 23 File 524. *Carteggio Livorno-Pisa*, April 10, 1392, and File 531, Jan. 16, 1400.

P. 89 l. 3 File D 885. *Carteggio Ibiza-Barcelona*, April 15, 1404.

P. 89 l. 22 File 705. Andrea di Bonanno in Valencia to Francesco, Aug. 18, 1390, and *Carteggio Valencia-Firenze*, Nov. 30, 1390.

P. 91 l. 23 File 1142. *Valute di merci e cariche di navi*. "Bill of lading of the ship of Nicholoso Usodimare, which comes from Roumania," May 21, 1396, and "List of goods received from the ship of Ser Giovanni Obizo of Venice," Sept. 1, 1400. *Carteggio Siracusa-Majorca*, March 2, 1400.

P. 92 l. 8 File 994. *Carteggio Ibiza-Valencia*, Sept. 20, 1400. *Carteggio Valencia-Ibiza, and vice versa*, Aug. 2, 1400.

P. 92 l. 24 File 889. *Carteggio Majorca-Barcelona*, June 12, 1409, and File 181, *Carteggio Barcelona-Avignon*, undated.

P. 92 l. 33 File 1159. *Assicurazioni*, No. 257. Cf. Piattoli, *L'Assicurazione di schiavi imbarcati su navi e i rischi di morte nel medioevo*.

P. 93 l. 14 File 994. *Carteggio Valencia-Ibiza*, Dec. 3, 1400 and Jan. 27, 1401.

P. 93 l. 22 File 778. *Carteggio Majorca-Genova*, July 11, 1392.

P. 94 l. 14 File 1115. *Carteggio misto*. Draft of a letter in Datini's hand to Niccolaio di Bonaccorso in Avignon. June 1, 1389.

PART I, CHAPTER 4: *The Trading-Companies and Their Members*

P. 97 l. 12 File 1110. Francesco to Cristofano di Bartolo, undated.

P. 97 l. 21 File 1092. Domenico di Cambio to Francesco, Jan. 16, 1391.

P. 97 l. 23 File 1112. Francesco to Stoldo di Lorenzo, Jan. 14, 1394.

P. 98 l. 7 Ibid., Francesco to Luca del Sera, May 28, 1397.

P. 98 l. 23 File 1087. *Carteggio familiare e privato*, Jan. 5, 1399. The address is missing, but the handwriting is Francesco's.

P. 98 l. 29 File 1114. *A vari in Valencia*, March 22, 1399.

P. 100 l. 5 File 1092. Domenico di Cambio to Francesco, Aug. 9, 1391.

P. 100 l. 12 File 801. *Carteggio Firenze-Pisa*, Jan. 4, 1402.

P. 100 l. 20 Mazzei, June 7, 1401.

P. 100 l. 29 File 1112. Francesco to Stoldo di Lorenzo, Feb. 5, 1380.

P. 100 l. 35 File 1110. Francesco to Cristofano di Bartolo, Feb. 27, 1401.

P. 102 l. 29 File 1110. Francesco to Cristofano di Bartolo, Feb. 27, 1402.

P. 103 l. 2 File D 698. *Carteggio Prato-Firenze*. Francesco to Stoldo di Lorenzo, Jan. 14, 1394.

P. 105 l. 20 File 1112. Francesco to Luca del Sera, Jan. 25, 1399.

P. 107 l. 8 File 1092. Domenico di Cambio to Francesco, Jan. 23, 1389.

P. 107 l. 17 *Iscritta della compagnia di Francesco e Domenico*, 1405, winding up, after 18 years, the affairs of this company. Bensa, op. cit., Doc. X. Here, too, Francesco was the senior partner, having supplied 3,400 florins, while Domenico gave 600 and his services.

P. 108 l. 16 File 1112. Francesco to Stoldo di Lorenzo, March 23, 1382.

P. 108 l. 26 Ibid., Sept. 18, 1381.

P. 109 l. 7 Ibid., Feb. 26, 1399.

P. 110 l. 24 Mazzei, May 18, 1401.

P. 110 l. 30 Ibid. To Cristofano di Bartolo, March 3, 1405.

NOTES

P. 112 l. 3 File 1112. Francesco to Stoldo di Lorenzo, Oct. 31, 1390.
P. 112 l. 16 File 1115. Agnolo degli Agli to Francesco, March 14, 1392.
P. 112 l. 33 File 1089. Francesco to Margherita, Nov. 10, 1380, and Oct. 25, 1397.
P. 113 l. 17 Mazzei. To Simone d'Andrea, Jan. 14, 1404.
P. 113 l. 27 File 501. *Carteggio Firenze-Pisa.* Undated and with no address.
P. 114 l. 18 File 1092. Domenico di Cambio to Francesco, March 21, 1390.
P. 116 l. 15 File 1112. Francesco to Cristofano di Bartolo.
P. 116 l. 19 File 1112. Francesco to Luca del Sera, May 26, 1397.
P. 116 l. 27 File 1114. *A vari in Valencia,* Oct. 24, 1408.
P. 116 l. 34 File D 1062. Francesco to Cristofano di Bartolo, March 20, 1398.
P. 117 l. 6 Mazzei. To Simone d'Andrea, March 3, 1406.
P. 117 l. 13 File 1111. Francesco to Cristofano di Bartolo, undated.
P. 117 l. 28 File 1111. Francesco to Simone d'Andrea, May 6, 1391.
P. 118 l. 25 From a letter written by Francesco to the tax-exactors of Florence. Mazzei, *Proemio,* p. xxx. The original has disappeared.
P. 118 l. 29 Mazzei, II, p. 42, n. 2.
P. 119 l. 29 File 1111. Francesco to Simone d'Andrea, March 9 and April 20, 1399, and March 3 and Oct. 8, 1403. After Simone's death, in 1403, Cristofano di Bartolo was transferred to take his place in Barcelona.
P. 122 l. 19 *Copia de'chapitoli sopra fatti de'Taliani, deliberati per lo molt'alto senyor de Aragona e per lo suo consiglio,* Dec. 25, 1402. Livi, *Dall'Archivio di Francesco Datini,* pp. 52-3.
P. 122 l. 34 File D 705, Luca del Sera to Francesco, Jan. 30, 1394.
P. 123 l. 15 File 994. *Carteggio Ibiza-Valencia,* undated.
P. 124 l. 11 File 994. *Carteggio Valencia-Ibiza.*
P. 125 l. 6 Mazzei. To Simone d'Andrea, April 16, 1401.
P. 125 l. 10 File D 1062. Francesco to Cristofano di Bartolo, March 20, 1398.
P. 125 l. 12 File 1111. Francesco to Simone d'Andrea, Jan. 26, 1401.
P. 126 l. 15 File 1110. Francesco to Cristofano di Bartolo, undated.
P. 126 l. 22 File 1115. Biagio d'Arezzo in Barcelona to Checco Naldini in Florence, Jan. 26, 1407.
P. 127 l. 16 Mazzei, to Simone d'Andrea, April 27, 1403, and Jan. 15, 1404.
P. 128 l. 6 Mazzei, II. Letter CCCXLVII, undated.
P. 129 l. 21 File D 1062. Francesco to Cristofano di Bartolo, March 20, 1398.
P. 130 l. 21 File 1089. Francesco to Margherita, Feb. 17, 1394.
P. 130 l. 25 File 994. *Carteggio Valencia-Ibiza,* Dec. 3, 1400.
P. 131 l. 22 Mazzei. To Francesco, undated, and to Cristofano di Bartolo, April 30, 1400.
P. 132 l. 7 File 994. *Carteggio Ibiza-Valencia,* Oct. 26, 1400.
P. 134 l. 7 File 994. *Carteggio Ibiza-Valencia,* Sept. 20 and 23, 1400.
P 134 l. 20 *Carteggio di Pisa.* From Matteo Benini of Arles, June 17, 1393. Cf. Brun, *Quelques Italiens d'Avignon au XIV siècle.*
P. 134 l. 29 *Carteggio di Majorca,* July 13, 1404. Livi, *La schiavitù domestica,* p. 301.
P. 135 l. 8 Ibid., dated only 1404.

PART I, CHAPTER 5: *Money*
P. 137 l. 4 File 1089. Francesco to Margherita, April 5, 1395.
P. 138 l. 27 Ibid. Francesco to Margherita, 1393.

P. 138 l. 33 File 721. *Carteggio Venezia-Bologna.* Bindo Piaciti & Co. to Francesco, April 23, 1401.

P. 139 l. 7 File 771. *Carteggio Firenze-Genova,* May 24, 1398. See Bensa, *Il contratto di assicurazione nel medioevo,* and F. Edler, "Early Examples of Maritime Insurance," in *Journal of Economic History,* V (1945).

P. 139 l. 14 File 1089. Francesco to Margherita, 1393.

P. 141 l. 2 File 1089. Francesco to Margherita, May 1394.

P. 141 l. 10 File 1092. Domenico di Cambio to Francesco, Feb. 11, 1390.

P. 142 l. 2 File 1112. Francesco to Stoldo di Lorenzo, Jan. 19, 1394.

P. 142 l. 8 File 1089. Francesco to Margherita, Feb. 22, 1394.

P. 142 l. 26 File 1112. Francesco to Stoldo di Lorenzo, Jan. 31, 1394.

P. 142 l. 32 File 1089. Francesco to Margherita, April 29, 1394.

P. 143 l. 14 Mazzei, March 2, 1394.

P. 143 l. 20 File 1109. Margherita to Ser Lapo Mazzei, April 13, 1394.

P. 143 l. 24 File 1089. Francesco to Margherita, May 7, 1394.

P. 144 l. 13 File 1089. Francesco to Margherita, May 12, 1394.

P. 144 l. 24 From the draft of a letter in Francesco's writing, on the back of a list of insurance policies. *Assicurazioni marittime.* Undated.

P. 145 l. 9 File 1093. Giuliano di Giovanni to Francesco, July 30, 1396.

P. 146 l. 13 File 1089. Francesco to Margherita, May 12, 1394.

P. 147 l. 2 File 1110. Francesco to Cristofano di Bartolo, Feb. 27, 1401.

P. 147 l. 24 Mazzei, May 5 and July 8, 1401.

P. 148 l. 6 Ibid., Aug. 25, 1401.

P. 148 l. 16 File 1111. *A vari in Valencia,* March 22, 1399.

P. 148 l. 24 File 1112. Francesco to Luca del Sera, Jan. 25, 1399.

P. 150 l. 17 File 1145. *Cambiali.*

P. 151 l. 4 File 1092. Domenico di Cambio to Francesco, March 12, 1390.

P. 151 l. 23 File 853. *Carteggio Bruges-Barcelona* and File 1146. Quoted in De Roover, op. cit., pp. 65 and 74.

P. 152 l. 12 The bank's seven ledgers are among the papers of the *Fondaco di Prato,* in a section entitled *"Libri del banco di Prato."* They are the following:

   1) No 219, *Quaderno di cassa segn. A* (1398–9)
   2) No 220, *Memoriale segn. A* (1398–1400)
   3) No 221, *Entrata e Uscita segn. A* (1398–1400)
   4) No 222, *Quaderno di lettere del banco segn. A* (1398–1403)
   5) No 223, *Libro grande segn. A.* (1398–1403)
   6) No 224, *Quaderno di cassa segn. B* (1400)
   7) No 225, *Quaderno di suggello segn. B* (1400)

P. 152 l. 28 File 1111. *Carteggio Prato-Barcelona,* Aug. 7, 1409.

P. 152 l. 32 File 223.

P. 153 l. 19 File 1092. Domenico di Cambio to Francesco, Aug. 30, 1398.

P. 154 l. 17 Mazzei, Jan. 29 and Feb. 4, 1397.

P. 158 l. 6 Mazzei. To Simone d'Andrea Bellandi, Jan. 15, 1404.

P. 158 l. 18 File D 705. Luca del Sera to Francesco, Jan. 30, 1394.

P. 159 l. 4 File 1111. Francesco to Simone d'Andrea, June 26, 1400, July 27, 1402, and Feb. 1, 1406.

P. 159 l. 18 File 1092. Fra Giovanni Dominici to Francesco. Jan. 29, 1401.

P. 159 l. 24 Ibid. Domenico di Cambio to Francesco, Dec. 11, 1390, and May 11, 1389.

P. 159 l. 35 Mazzei, Jan. 24, 1386.
P. 161 l. 18 File 1111. Francesco to Stoldo di Lorenzo, Feb. 8, 1399, and March 18, 1391.

PART II, CHAPTER 1: *Husband and Wife*

P. 166 l. 1 File 1117. Monna Piera to Francesco, Aug. 25, 1380.
P. 166 l. 7 Ibid. Niccolozzo di Ser Naldo to Francesco, June 20, 1381.
P. 166 l. 22 File 1103. Niccolò dell'Ammannato Tecchini to Francesco, July 2, 1381, Jan. 26, 1382, Feb. 28, 1382, and Aug. 19, 1381.
P. 167 l. 5 File 1093. Maestro Naddino Bovattieri to Francesco, Feb. 11 and Aug. 15, 1395.
P. 167 l. 20 File 1103. Francesca Tecchini to Margherita, Sept. 7, 1393.
P. 167 l. 31 Ibid. Niccolò dell'Ammannato to Francesco, April 23, 1395.
P. 169 l. 29 File 1089. Francesco to Margherita, Feb. 23, 1385.
P. 170 l. 13 Ibid. Margherita to Francesco, Feb. 27, 1385, and Jan. 20, 1386.
P. 171 l. 3 Ibid. Francesco to Margherita, Jan. 22, 1386.
P. 172 l. 10 Ibid. Margherita to Francesco, Jan. 23 and Jan. 28, 1386.
P. 172 l. 26 File 1101. Monna Lapa to Margherita, April 9, 1385.
P. 173 l. 2 File 1092. Domenico di Cambio to Francesco, Jan. 16, 1389.
P. 173 l. 9 File 1103. Niccolò dell'Ammannato to Margherita, Sept. 21, 1387.
P. 174 l. 5 File 1089. Margherita to Francesco, April 5, 1386, and Aug. 29, 1389.
P. 174 l. 10 Ibid. Francesco to Margherita, Aug. 29, 1389.
P. 174 l. 23 File 1103. Niccolò dell'Ammannato to Francesco, Jan. 30, 1385.
P. 175 l. 11 *Quadernacci e Memoriali di Francesco di Marco proprii. Quadernaccio A* (1386-8), pp. 14 and 23.
P. 175 l. 24 File 1099. Niccolò di Piero di Giunta to Francesco, Feb. 2, 1388.
P. 175 l. 31 *Quadernaccio A.*
P. 176 l. 15 File 1099. Niccolò di Piero to Francesco, Sept. 28 and 30, 1390.
P. 177 l. 26 *Quadernaccio A.*
P. 180 l. 20 File 1089. Francesco to Margherita, April 8, 1394, March 15, 1397, April 11, 1398, May 23, 1397, July 19, 1398, and May 23, 1397.
P. 181 l. 22 Ibid. Margherita to Francesco, Dec. 5, 1398, Nov. [19], 1397, and Nov. 25, 1397.
P. 182 l. 5 Ibid. Francesco to Margherita, Aug. 22, 1398.
P. 182 l. 32 Ibid. Margherita to Francesco, Aug. 22, 1398.
P. 183 l. 8 Ibid. Francesco to Margherita, May 7, 1394.
P. 184 l. 27 Mazzei, July 18, 1394, Sept. 15 and 23, 1394, June 9, 1395, June 20, 1395, Jan. 9, 1396, Feb. 4, 1399, June 7, 1401, and Feb. 21-6, 1401.
P. 185 l. 1 Ibid. Letter XLVI, undated.
P. 185 l. 18 File 1089. Francesco to Margherita, July 20, 1395, and June 4, 1395.
P. 187 l. 9 Ibid. Margherita to Francesco, July 21, 1395, April 5, 1397, April 7, 1397, Dec. 3, 1398, May 7, 1399, and May 3, 1399.

PART II, CHAPTER 2: *"La Famiglia"*

P. 190 l. 29 Mazzei, II, p. 277.
P. 191 l. 22 File 1114. Monna Dianora Bandini to Francesco and Margherita, March 28, 1387.
P. 191 l. 35 File 1090. Bartolomeo Bandini to Monna Margherita, Jan. 24, 1399.

P. 192 l. 11 File 1089. Margherita to Francesco, May 3, 1399.

P. 192 l. 16 This letter has neither signature nor address, but is plainly a copy of Margherita's letter to her brother.

P. 193 l. 3 File 1090. Bartolomeo Bandini to Monna Margherita. Undated, but the reference to the Holy Year places it in 1399.

P. 139 l. 9 Ibid., March 9, 1408.

P. 193 l. 12 *Quadernaccio A*, p. 151.

P. 194 l. 4 File 1103. Niccolò dell'Ammannato Tecchini to Francesco, Feb. 28, 1381.

P. 194 l. 28 Ibid., July 2, 1381.

P. 195 l. 5 File 1089. Margherita to Bartolomeo Bandini. This is a draft, among Margherita's letters to her husband.

P. 195 l. 15 Ibid., Margherita to Francesco, Feb. 17, 1393.

P. 195 l. 33 File 1103. Niccolò dell'Ammannato to Francesco, April 10 and June 18, 1401.

P. 196 l. 32 File 1101. Niccolò di Piero di Giunta to Francesco, Oct. 3, 1388.

P. 197 l. 2 Ibid. Simona di Piero di Giunta to Margherita, Jan. 11, 1394, and Dec. 21, 1395.

P. 197 l. 14 Ibid. Niccolò di Piero to Francesco, Lent 1385.

P. 197 l. 28 File 1101. Niccolò di Piero to Francesco, Lent 1385.

P. 198 l. 2 Ibid. Simona di Piero to Margherita, Aug. 2, 1390.

P. 198 l. 10 File 1109. Piero di Stenni di Montelupo to Francesco, Aug. 8, 1395.

P. 198 l. 21 File 1089. Margherita to Francesco, Dec. 1, 1398, and Jan. 20, 1402?

P. 199 l. 33 *Quadernaccio A*, p. 5.

P. 200 l. 31 File 1100. Niccolò di Piero to Francesco, Feb. 14, 1399.

P. 201 l. 11 File 1091. Niccolò Compagni to Francesco, Nov. 24, 1406.

P. 202 l. 5 Mazzei. To Ginevra, April 23, 1407.

P. 202 l. 19 *Quadernaccio B*, p. 261. "And for each of the above matters, a contract has been drawn up by the hand of Ser Lapo Mazzei."

P. 203 l. 11 File 603. *Memoriale B*, pp. 163 and 172.

P. 203 l. 16 File 599. *Libro bianco B*, Nov. 30, 1407. One of the cook's duties was to report to the Commune the list of the dishes he had prepared and the number of guests.

P. 204 l. 14 Mazzei, II, p. 217, n. 1.

P. 205 l. 3 File 599. *Libro bianco B*, Dec. 8, 1400, "for a dinner at home in Prato when Ginevra came back from Lionardo's house."

P. 205 l. 14 Mazzei, *Proemio*, p. xliv.

P. 205 l. 17 File 1115. *Carteggio misto, Copie e minute di lettere.* Francesco to Margherita, July 8, 1385.

P. 205 l. 23 *Quadernaccio A*, pp. 159, 203, and 204.

P. 205 l. 29 Mazzei, *Proemio*, p. xlv.

P. 206 l. 8 File 1113. Francesco to Andrea di Bonanno, May 12, 1393.

P. 206 l. 12 Ibid. Francesco to Andrea di Bonanno, Aug. 26, 1393.

P. 206 l. 17 File 341. *Carteggio Genova-Prato*, Dec. 20, 1393.

P. 206 l. 21 File 212. *Spese di casa*, 1394-8.

P. 206 l. 24 File 599. *Libro bianco B*, pp. 120, 160, 163, 272, and 289.

P. 207 l. 1 File 603. *Memoriale B*, p. 193.

P. 207 l. 20 File 1089. Francesco to Margherita, Feb. 23, 1384.

P. 207 l. 26 File 1101. Niccolò di Giunta to Francesco, Lent 1385.

P. 207 l. 30 File 1089. Margherita to Francesco, Aug. 23, 1389.
P. 209 l. 12 File 346. Stefano Guazzalotti to Francesco, Oct. 2, 1392, Dec. 13, 1392, and Jan. 9, 1393.
P. 210 l. 28 File 1089. Francesco to Margherita, April 15, 1386.
P. 211 l. 11 File 355. *Carteggio Firenze-Prato*, Nov. 6, 1396.
P. 212 l. 15 File 1089. Francesco to Margherita, April 15, 1395.
P. 213 l. 8 File 1113. Lotto degli Agli to Francesco, Feb. 22, 1391.
P. 213 l. 19 File 599. *Libro bianco B.*
P. 213 l. 28 *Quadernaccio A*, p. 189.
P. 214 l. 10 File 1089. Margherita to Francesco, Dec. 1, 1398.
P. 214 l. 15 Ibid. Francesco to Margherita, Aug. 4, 1385.
P. 216 l. 22 Ibid. Margherita to Francesco, April 5, 1397, and Aug. 19, 1398.

PART II, CHAPTER 3: *The Family Friend*

P. 217 l. 15 File 1109. Andrea Bellandi to Francesco, March 14, 1372. This letter appears to have been known to neither Guasti nor Bensa, since neither of them refers to any early connection between Datini and Mazzei.
P. 218 l. 18 Mazzei, Nov. 6, 1400.
P. 221 l. 27 Mazzei, Letter CCCII, undated, and April 14, 1409.
P. 223 l. 2 Ibid., Dec. 6, 1392, Dec. 15 and 18, 1397, and Feb. 4, 1398.
P. 223 l. 25 Ibid., April 10, 1394.
P. 224 l. 31 Ibid., March 18, 1394, June 8, 1395, and March 20 and Aug. 31, 1401.
P. 225 l. 2 File 1080. Margherita to Ser Lapo Mazzei, April 10, 1394.
P. 225 l. 9 Mazzei, Aug. 31, 1401.
P. 225 l. 15 File 1089. Francesco to Margherita, March 16, 1395.
P. 225 l. 20 Mazzei, Sept. 1392.
P. 226 l. 7 Ibid., Letters CCCLXXV, CCCLXXVI, and CCCLXXVII.
P. 226 l. 13 Ibid., Dec. 11, 1392.
P. 226 l. 25 Ibid., Aug. 4, 1396.
P. 227 l. 13 Ibid., Oct. 11, 1390, and Jan. 29, 1397.
P. 227 l. 19 File 1089. Margherita to Ser Lapo Mazzei, April 8, 1396.
P. 228 l. 4 Mazzei, April 10, 1394, and April 8 and Dec. 4, 1396.
P. 228 l. 13 File 1089. Francesco to Margherita, undated.
P. 228 l. 24 File 1092. Domenico di Cambio to Francesco, undated.
P. 229 l. 5 File 1089. Margherita to Ser Lapo Mazzei, Jan. 17, 1395.
P. 230 l. 8 Mazzei, Dec. 2, 1400.
P. 230 l. 32 Ibid., Jan. 9, 1395, Feb. 21, 1400, and Feb. 21, 1409.
P. 231 l. 32 Ibid., Aug. 21, 1394, Sept. 28, 1398, March 15, 1397, Oct. 30, 1399, and Feb. 4, 1408.
P. 232 l. 8 Ibid., Letter CLXXIV, undated.
P. 232 l. 15 Ibid., Feb. 4, 1398.
P. 233 l. 19 Ibid., Jan. 26, 1392, and Dec. 6, 1409.
P. 235 l. 3 Ibid., Letter LXXI, undated, April 29, 1395, Dec. 30, 1397, Feb. 4, 1398, and summer 1398. This last letter, unpublished by Guasti, is in Livi, *Dall'Archivio di Francesco Datini*, pp. 37–8.
P. 235 l. 34 Ibid., April 16 and Nov. 13, 1395, April 8, 1396, Feb. 2, 1400, and March 29, 1401.
P. 236 l. 20 Ibid., Jan. 9 and Sept. 12, 1395, and May 25 and 27, 1401.
P. 237 l. 14 Ibid., June 24, 1391.

P. 237 l. 26 Ibid., May 13, 1392, and Aug. 10, 1407.
P. 238 l. 28 Ibid., Letter CCLVI, undated. Jan. 27, 1395, and Jan. 29, 1400, to Margherita.
P. 239 l. 21 Ibid., undated but probably 1407.
P. 240 l. 9 Mazzei, *Proemio*, p. cxl, n. 4.

Part II, Chapter 4: *The House*

P. 242 l. 9 Mazzei, Aug. 20, 1391.
P. 242 l. 24 File 1092. Domenico di Cambio to Francesco, Aug. 11 and Dec. 21, 1389.
P. 243 l. 27 File 1117. Niccolozzo di Ser Naldo to Francesco, Jan. 12, 1375, Nov. 6, 1379, and Aug. 12, 1380.
P. 244 l. 14 File 335. *Carteggio Firenze-Prato.* Niccolò and Ludovico del Bono to Francesco, June 3 and 8, 1383.
P. 244 l. 20 File 1111. Francesco to Simone d'Andrea, March 31, 1386.
P. 244 l. 25 File 1101. Piero di Giunta to Francesco, Feb. 8, June 4, and Sept. 16, 1388.
P. 244 l. 31 File 236. List of Datini's real estate in Prato, April 7, 1407.
P. 245 l. 3 File 1111. June 5, 1392. This letter is only signed "Piero."
P. 245 l. 8 File 236. List of Datini's real estate in Prato, April 7, 1407.
P. 245 l. 16 Mazzei, II, p. 412. Bill of Arrigo di Niccolò *dipintore*, sent in after Francesco's death, 1410.
P. 246 l. 4 *Libro giallo A* (1380–90), Mazzei, II, p. 387.
P. 248 l. 4 File 1092. Domenico di Cambio to Francesco, June 20, 1390.
P. 249 l. 20 File 236. Inventory dated July 10, 1397. All the information about Datini's furniture and linen is derived from two inventories of his house in Prato, dated Oct. 23, 1394, and July 16, 1397, and one of his house in Florence, dated 1400. (See also *Carte del Fondaco di Prato*, 215, K, II, 2.)
P. 252 l. 17 Mazzei, Aug. 20, 1391.
P. 258 l. 17 File 1092. Domenico di Cambio to Francesco, Nov. 27, 1390.
P. 259 l. 9 Mazzei, II, 408. Niccolò Gerini to Francesco, March 24, 1395.
P. 259 l. 18 *Libro giallo A* (1380–90).
P. 259 l. 32 File 1112. Agnolo di Jacopo to Luca del Sera, June 29, 1399.
P. 260 l. 1 File 1111. *Lettere di Goro e Nencio lastraiuoli,* Nov. 17, 1388.
P. 261 l. 4 Agnolo Gaddi to Francesco, Oct. 20, 1383. Livi, *Dall'Archivio di Francesco Datini,* p. 19.
P. 261 l. 8 *Quadernaccio A,* p. 799.
P. 262 l. 3 *Ricordanze* (1387–90), Dec. 1390. A master carpenter received only half a florin a day.
P. 262 l. 12 File 212. *Spese di casa,* May 5, 1396.
P. 262 l. 22 Francesco to Domenico di Cambio, 1392. Livi, op. cit., p. 17.
P. 263 l. 2 Mazzei, II, p. 399. Niccolò Gerini to Francesco, April 18, 1393.
P. 263 l. 11 Ibid., Mazzei to Francesco, March 8, 1392.

Part II, Chapter 5: *The Farm*

P. 264 l. 6 File 236. An inventory of Datini's real estate, dated April 30, 1407.
P. 266 l. 22 Mazzei, Jan. 9, 1396.
P. 267 l. 16 Ibid., Jan. 13, 1406.
P. 268 l. 6 Ibid., Oct. 29, 1407.
P. 269 l. 22 Inventory, p. 3 r.

NOTES

P. 271 l. 16 File 1112. Francesco to Stoldo di Lorenzo, Nov. 8, 1398.

P. 272 l. 4 Mazzei, Oct. 29, 1407.

P. 272 l. 12 Mazzei, I, p. 382, n.2. *Ricordanze*.

P. 273 l. 17 File 1103, Niccolò dell'Ammannato to Francesco, June 19, 1394.

P. 273 l. 30 Mazzei, Nov. 18, 1393, and Dec. 15, 1395.

P. 274 l. 6 Ibid., Jan. 24, 1396.

P. 274 l. 14 File 1092. Domenico di Cambio to Francesco, Jan. 19, 1389, and Oct. 20, 1395. "Were you as solicitous of your soul," he added, "as of building, you would soon become a saint."

P. 274 l. 18 File 1112. Francesco to Stoldo di Lorenzo, June 1, 1396.

P. 274 l. 26 File 1089. Margherita to Francesco, March 18, 1396.

P. 278 l. 4 File 1089. Francesco to Margherita, March 19, 20, 23, 26, and 27, 1397.

P. 279 l. 8 Mazzei, May 2 and Aug. 10, 1407.

PART II, CHAPTER 6: *The Private Account-Books*

P. 280 l. 13 These books are:

File 212. *Quadernaccio A di Ricordanze di Francesco di Marco proprio*, 1383–8.

File 212. *Spese di casa*, 1394–8.

File F VII, 16. *Quadernaccio di Francesco proprio*, 1399–1403.

File F VII, 18. *Quadernaccio B di Francesco di Marco proprio*, 1404–8.

File 599. *Libro Bianco segnato B.*

File 603. *Fondaco di Firenze, Memoriale B.*

File 1116 and File 236 M VI, 20. *Ricordanze.*

File 351. *Memoriale di spese varie, tenuto da Monte d'Andrea* (1383–9).

File 618. *Quaderno di balle segnato B.*

Quadernaccio A di Francesco di Marco proprio (1401–4) (no reference number).

P. 281 l. 29 File 212. *Spese di casa*, Nov. 10, 1397.

P. 281 l. 34 File 1113. To Andrea di Bonanno, June 29, 1393.

P. 282 l. 14 File 1092. Domenico di Cambio to Francesco, Feb. 16, 1390, and June 14, 1390.

P. 282 l. 19 File 212. *Spese di casa*, Feb. 19, 1395.

P. 282 l. 25 File 1089. Margherita to Francesco, March 31, 1387.

P. 283 l. 3 File 599. *Libro Bianco B* and *Quaderno di Bologna*, 1400.

P. 283 l. 7 Ibid. *Libro Bianco B.*

P. 283 l. 13 Ibid. *Libro Bianco B*, and File 603. *Memoriale B. Bill of Antonio di Maso, sarto*, 1399–1407.

P. 283 l. 21 File 212. *Spese di casa*, and File 599. *Libro Bianco B.*

P. 283 l. 22 File 236. Inventory of Datini's lands, April 30, 1407.

P. 283 l. 24 File M V, 15. *Quadernaccio A di Ricordanze di Francesco di Marco proprio* (1386–8), pp. 203–4.

P. 284 l. 19 Mazzei, June 7, 1401, and Letter CDXXXIV, undated, and File 212. *Spese di casa.*

P. 284 l. 24 File 599. *Libro Bianco B.*

P. 285 l. 3 File 1112. Letters dictated by Francesco to Luca del Sera, Feb. 6, 1395, July 1, 1396, and Nov. 1396.

P. 285 l. 9 File 599. *Libro Bianco B*, pp. 391 v. and 408 v. (1407 and 1408).

P. 285 l. 19 File 1082. Domenico di Cambio to Francesco, April 2, 1389.

P. 286 l. 2 File 215. *Carte del Fondaco di Prato.* Inventory of the house in

Prato, 1394. File 236. Inventory of the house in Prato, 1397, and of the house in Florence, 1400.

P. 287 l. 8 File 1086. Francesco di Marco to Nanni di Luca, *fattorino*, Nov. 13, 1396, and File 603. *Fondaco di Firenze, Memoriale B*. Bill of Francesco & Gherardo Davizi & Co., London, Aug. 3, 1408.

P. 287 l. 27 File 1092. Domenico di Cambio to Francesco, June 19, 1390.

P. 289 l. 32 Ibid. Domenico di Cambio to Francesco.

P. 292 l. 10 File 1113. N. 2116. Francesco di Marco in Prato to Andrea di Bonanno in Genoa, April 14, 1392.

P. 294 l. 16 File 1089. Margherita to Francesco, April 14, 1398.

P. 295 l. 3 File 1092. Domenico di Cambio to Francesco, June 24, 1390.

P. 296 l. 5 File 1089. Margherita to Francesco, Jan. 18, 1398.

P. 296 l. 17 File 603. *Fondaco di Firenze, Memoriale B*, p. 187. Bill of the tailor Antonio di Maso, 1399–1407.

P. 297 l. 12 Ibid., p. 174, and File 599. *Libro Bianco B*, pp. 330, 345, 383, and 398.

P. 298 l. 10 File 599. *Libro Bianco B*. All these ornaments came from a Florentine goldsmith in Por S. Maria, Domenico di Deo.

P. 299 l. 26 File 599. *Libro Bianco B*. Another account-book mentions some scarlet cloth bought at 6½ florins the canna, and rosato at 6 florins the canna.

P. 300 l. 12 File 698, *Carteggio Prato-Firenze*. Francesco to Stoldo di Lorenzo, July 29, 1393.

P. 302 l. 8 *Fondaco di Firenze, Libro Bianco B*, 599, 1406.

P. 303 l. 3 File 1089. Margherita to Francesco, Aug. 20, 1398.

P. 303 l. 17 File 1103. Francesca Tecchini to Margherita, Sept. 7, 1393.

P. 304 l. 7 File 236. Inventory in Prato, July 16, 1397.

P. 304 l. 29 Ibid. Inventory in Florence, 1400.

P. 305 l. 20 Mazzei to Monna Margherita, Nov. 13, 1395. The book cost 5 florins.

P. 306 l. 5 *Quadernaccio A*, pp. 69 v., 129 r., and 177 v.

P. 306 l. 17 *Quadernaccio di Francesco proprio*, and *Libro Bianco B*.

P. 306 l. 20 File 1116. *Ricordanze*.

P. 307 l. 4 File F VII, 18. *Quadernaccio B*, p. 213.

P. 307 l. 15 File 1092. Dec. 31, 1406, and Mazzei, II, p. 335.

P. 308 l. 25 Mazzei, Aug. 21, 1405.

P. 309 l. 2 File 1089. Francesco to Margherita, Feb. 23, 1385.

P. 309 l. 12 File 599. *Libro Bianco B*, and File 212. *Spese di casa*, Jan. 15, 1399.

P. 309 l. 18 File 1092. Beato Giovanni Dominici to Francesco, May 22, 1403.

P. 310 l. 12 File 212. *Spese di casa*, File F VII, 18. *Quadernaccio B*, and File 1087. Francesco to Guido di Sandro, Sept. 12, 1399.

P. 310 l. 21 Mazzei, Jan. 6, 1409.

P. 311 l. 15 Ibid., Nov. 16, 1390, Jan. 6, 1408, Oct. 12, 1395, and April 8, 1396.

P. 313 l. 15 File 1091. Jacopo da Montepulciano to Francesco. The letter is addressed to "The honourable Francesco di Marco, his chief friend and benefactor . . . from Le Stinche." This letter is also printed in Mazzei, II, pp. 344–6.

P. 313 l. 30 Ibid., undated. Jacopo da Montepulciano to Margherita.

P. 314 l. 1 File F VII, 18. *Quadernaccio B*, Jan. 1, 1405.

P. 314 l. 8 File 1091. Jacopo da Montepulciano to Francesco, Sept. 8, 1407.

NOTES

Part II, Chapter 7: *Food, Drink, and Physic*

P. 316 l. 3 File 1092. Domenico di Cambio to Francesco, Sept. 14, 1392.

P. 316 l. 13 Ibid., Jan. 16, 1390.

P. 316 l. 16 Ibid. Domenico di Cambio to Francesco, Nov. 16, 1399.

P. 316 l. 32 Mazzei, Letter CCCIV, undated.

P. 317 l. 13 File 1086. *Carteggio familiare e privato.* "To Barba of Maestro Francesco, in the house of Francesco di Marco in Prato," Sept. 13, 1389.

P. 317 l. 25 File 1092. Francesco to Margherita, undated.

P. 318 l. 24 File 1102. Maestro Lorenzo Sassoli to Francesco, May 1404.

P. 319 l. 13 File 1086. Francesco to Nanni di Luca *fattorino*, Aug. 29, 1396.

P. 319 l. 20 Ibid. Francesco to Stefano Guazzalotti, Aug. 10, 1398.

P. 319 l. 30 File 1089. Francesco to Margherita, April 12, 1398.

P. 320 l. 18 Ibid. Francesco to Margherita, April 9, 1396.

P. 320 l. 24 Ibid. Francesco to Nanni di Luca, Aug. 9, 1396.

P. 321 l. 5 Ibid. Margherita to Francesco, April 8, 1399.

P. 321 l. 17 Mazzei, Letter CCCIII, undated.

P. 321 l. 29 File 1102. Maestro Lorenzo Sassoli to Francesco, May 1404. Printed in Mazzei, pp. 370–4.

P. 322 l. 16 File 1089. Francesco to Margherita, April 1, 1397.

P. 323 l. 18 File 1089. Francesco to Margherita, undated.

P. 323 l. 27 File 1086. Francesco to a servant, March 9, 1396.

P. 327 l. 4 File 603. *Fondaco di Firenze, Memoriale B*, pp. 96 and 119. Bills of Filippo di Lapo & Co., *speziali*, 1406. Legacies were sometimes left to hospitals for the specific purpose of buying sugar for the sick.

P. 328 l. 3 File 1102. Maestro Lorenzo Sassoli to Francesco.

P. 328 l. 21 File 1093. Giovanni di Banduccio da Prato to Margherita.

P. 328 l. 27 File 1092. Domenico di Cambio to Francesco, July 31, 1390.

P. 329 l. 21 File 1102. Maestro Lorenzo Sassoli to Francesco, May 1404 and June 25, 1404.

P. 330 l. 22 Mazzei, Sept. 1392, Sept. 2, 1401, and Aug. 27, 1392. And the letter, after all that good wine, is signed "Your Lapo, on Sunday night, very sleepy."

P. 331 l. 25 Mazzei, Sept. 27, 1395, Sept. 22, 1401, and April 25, 1394.

P. 332 l. 10 File 1087. Francesco to Guido di Sandro, Oct. 1, 1399.

P. 332 l. 17 File 1100. Niccolò di Piero to Francesco, Nov. 10, 1399.

P. 332 l. 28 *Quaderni di Bologna*.

P. 332 l. 34 Mazzei, Oct. 2, 1400.

P. 335 l. 9 File 1092. Domenico di Cambio to Francesco, June 20, 1390.

P. 335 l. 29 Mazzei, *Proemio*, p. cxx.

P. 336 l. 13 Mazzei, II, p. 355. Niccolò Falcucci to Francesco di Marco, undated. This doctor was a famous consultant in Florence.

P. 336 l. 15 File 212. *Spese di casa.*

P. 336 l. 22 File 599, *Libro bianco B* and *Quadernaccio B*, p. 51.

P. 336 l. 27 File 1102. Maestro Lorenzo Sassoli to Francesco, June 2, 1404.

P. 337 l. 2 File D 699. Francesco to Guido di Messer Tommaso del Palagio, May 8, 1396.

P. 338 l. 11 File 1092. Domenico di Cambio to Francesco, Dec. 24 and June 26, 1390.

P. 339 l. 6 File 1103. Niccolò dell'Ammannato to Francesco, Nov. 7, 1388.

P. 339 l. 18 Mazzei, II, p. 355–6. Niccolò Falcucci to Francesco, undated.

P. 340 l. 25 File 1102. Maestro Lorenzo Sassoli to Francesco, Feb. 8, 1400, and Jan. 1, 1401.

P. 341 l. 9 Ibid. Maestro Lorenzo Sassoli to Francesco, Nov. 15, 1401, June 8, 1402, Aug. 30, 1402, and June 2, 1404.

P. 344 l. 7 Ibid., Nov. 24, 1402, Nov. 6, 1404, Aug. 27, 1407, Sept. 22, 1404, and May 1404.

P. 344 l. 29 File 1186. Francesco to Maestro Giovanni di Banduco (*sic*), July 24, 1387.

P. 345 l. 21 Mazzei, July 10 and 17, 1408.

P. 346 l. 24 Ibid., May 18, 1401, and March 3, 1400.

PART II, CHAPTER 8: *Plague and Penitence*

P. 350 l. 7 File 1103. Niccolò dell'Ammannato to Francesco, May 23, June 6, June 22, July 31, and Sept. 23, 1383. This epidemic is described by Marchionne di Coppo Stefani in his *Cronaca*.

P. 350 l. 16 File 1092. Domenico di Cambio to Francesco, Nov. 18, 1389.

P. 350 l. 25 File 1103. Niccolò dell'Ammannato to Francesco, May 30, 1390.

P. 351 l. 5 File 1092. Domenico di Cambio to Francesco, July 5, 1390.

P. 351 l. 15 File 1089. Francesco to Margherita, Feb. 17, 1394, and July 2, 1395.

P. 352 l. 2 Ibid., Margherita to Francesco, Nov. 10, 1398.

P. 352 l. 7 Mazzei, Letter CLXXXVIII, undated.

P. 352 l. 25 File 1089. Francesco to Margherita, July 20, 1395, and March 19, 1396.

P. 353 l. 1 Ibid., Margherita to Francesco, March 19, 1396.

P. 355 l. 8 File 1086. Unaddressed, but in Francesco's hand, Dec. 18, 1395.

P. 356 l. 18 Mazzei, Letter CLXXXIV, undated, and Letter CLXXVII, undated.

P. 356 l. 27 File 1110. Francesco to Cristofano di Bartolo, undated.

P. 361 l. 9 *Quadernaccio A. di Francesco di Marco proprio.*

P. 364 l. 18 File D 388. Domenico di Cambio to Francesco, Sept. 27, 1399.

P. 364 l. 32 Mazzei, April 8, 1400.

P. 365 l. 7 File 1089. Margherita to Francesco, April 8, 1400.

P. 367 l. 2 Mazzei, Nov. 17, 1395, and Nov. 25, 1398. Prato was in the diocese of the Bishop of Pistoia.

P. 367 l. 9 Ibid., Letter CLXXVIII, undated.

P. 368 l. 28 Mazzei, June 10, 1400. There must, however, have been some further slight delay, for the will was not actually signed until June 27.

PART II, CHAPTER 9: *The Last Years*

P. 370 l. 10 File 234. *Quaderno di Bologna*, pp. 2, 31, 41, and 50.

P. 371 l. 16 Mazzei, July 6, 1400.

P. 371 l. 26 File 1103. Niccolò dell'Ammannato to Francesco, Aug. 17, 1400.

P. 372 l. 12 Mazzei, Aug. 22, 23, and 24, 1400.

P. 373 l. 18 Ibid., July 21, 31, and Aug. 6, 1400.

P. 373 l. 33 File 1115. Francesco to Fra Giovanni Dominici, Nov. 18, 1400. Cf. Piattoli, *Memorie Dominicane*, March—April 1934.

P. 374 l. 8 File 1109. Niccolò dell'Ammannato to Francesco, March 29, 1402.

P. 374 l. 22 File 1115. Francesco to Fra Giovanni Dominici, Nov. 1, 1400, and Feb. 1, 1401.

NOTES

P. 374 l. 32 Mazzei, May 27, Aug. 4 and 25, 1401.

P. 376 l. 8 File 1089. Margherita to Francesco, Sept. 24, 1401.

P. 376 l. 15 Mazzei, Feb. 2, 1400, and May 27, 1401.

P. 377 l. 16 File 1110. Francesco to Cristofano di Bartolo in Majorca, Feb. 27, 1401.

P. 378 l. 6 File 1088. Francesco to Ser Bastiano di Ser Schiatta, Dec. 22, 1400.

P. 378 l. 26 Mazzei, Sept. 2, 1406.

P. 379 l. 11 File 1089. Francesco to Margherita, March 5, 1394, and Feb. 5, 1396.

P. 380 l. 6 File 1112. Francesco to Stoldo di Lorenzo, May 5, 1397.

P. 380 l. 14 File 1089. Margherita to Francesco, May 9, 1397.

P. 381 l. 13 File D 340. Luca del Sera to Francesco, July 9, 1409.

P. 381 l. 22 Mazzei, Nov. 10, 1409.

P. 382 l. 16 File D 340. Luca del Sera to Francesco, May 14, 1410.

P. 383 l. 5 Ibid. Luca del Sera to Francesco, July 21, 1410.

P. 383 l. 27 Mazzei, Nov. 10, 1409, and Letter CCCXXXI, undated.

P. 384 l. 2 File 1092. Fra Giovanni Dominici to Francesco, Jan. 29, 1401.

P. 384 l. 15 Mazzei. To Cristofano di Bartolo in Barcelona, Aug. 24, 1410.

P. 384 l. 30 Francesco's will and its three codicils are printed in Mazzei, II, pp. 273–310.

P. 385 l. 9 File 1110. Francesco to Cristofano di Bartolo, undated.

P. 387 l. 18 Mazzei. To Cristofano di Bartolo, Aug. 24, 1400.

INDEX

i

INDEX

iii

Iris Origo was born in England in 1902, the child of an Anglo-Irish mother and an American father. Privately educated in Florence, she has since devoted herself to the development of La Foce, her Tuscan farming estate, and to her writing. Her work in biography includes *Leopardi: A Study in Solitude* (1935, Rev. Ed. 1954), *The Last Attachment* (1949), a study of Byron's love affair with Teresa Guiccioli, and *A Need to Testify: Portraits of Lauro de Bosis, Ruth Draper, Gaetano Salvemini, Ignazio Silone* (1984). During World War II she served in the Italian Red Cross. In 1943 and 1944 she and her husband, the Marchese Antonio Origo, converted La Foce into a refuge for children from the bombed cities of northern Italy and escaped Allied prisoners of war; her book *War in Val d'Orcia: 1943–1944* (U.K. 1947, U.S. 1984) is the moving record of this troubled period. The Marchesa Origo is a Fellow of the Royal Society of Literature in England. She lives in her country house in Tuscany and in Rome.

A NOTE ON THE TYPE

The text of this book was set on the Linotype in a face called Janson, a recutting made direct from type cast from matrices made about 1700. Anton Janson, a Dutchman who worked at Leipzig in this period, and for whom the modern version of the type was named, is now thought not to have been responsible for its design, which is, however, probably of Dutch origin, although the matrices have been in Germany for many years. The type is an excellent example of the influential and sturdy Dutch types that prevailed in England prior to the development by William Caslon of his own designs, which he evolved from these Dutch faces. The Dutch, in their turn, had been influenced by Garamond in France. The general tone of Janson, however, is darker than Garamond and has a sturdiness and substance quite different from its predecessors.